LITERATURE STUDY
IN THE HIGH SCHOOLS

PREFACE

To bring onto today's whirling scene of educational change a book on as broad a subject as literature study in the high schools requires a certain brashness; the subject so obviously presents a wide range of problems. This third edition is dedicated to the same general proposition as that of the first two editions: that literature should occupy the place of centrality in secondary school English in order to maintain a humanistic orientation in the curriculum. I do not mean to imply that composition, oral and written, language study, and the nonprint media are not valuable components of the curriculum and may not also be "humanistic." I simply want to reassert my belief that literature should occupy the place of greatest prominence, and restate what I consider are the major rewards to the student of literature.

Part of this brashness results from my attempt to make this text serve as a one-volume handbook for teachers and prospective teachers in courses in English or literature instruction for adolescents. I have tried to consider the relationship of literature in the secondary school to new trends and problems, but I am aware that some highly important matters need more intensive, specialized treatment than I have been able to give. Literature for culturally deprived students, for example, or literature and the nonprint media are subjects that deserve volumes of their own.

Part One, new in this edition, presents an analysis of the position of literature in the secondary English curriculum, and is meant as a general lead-in to the specifics discussed later in the book. I hope that the opening chapters will lead to intensive investigation of the various topics briefly outlined. Part Two is a combination of new material and material from the previous two editions. Gladys Veidemanis has revised her chapter on teaching drama. In Part Three, I have consolidated material on literature for adolescents, added to it, and updated the sample bibliographies. I retain my conviction that literature written specifically for adolescents has an important function in the literature program of the school and in the literary education of young people.

It would not be possible to acknowledge each and all of the individuals who have commented on the earlier editions and made suggestions for this one. The discussion, constructive criticism, and encouragement involved in the preparation of this book since the original edition appeared in 1959 have enriched my life personally and professionally.

D.L.B.

Tallahassee, Florida
December 1969

CONTENTS

part one
THE LITERATURE CURRICULUM IN THE JUNIOR AND SENIOR HIGH SCHOOL: BASIC CONSIDERATIONS

1
Why Teach Literature?

The answer to the question "why teach literature?" which is asked in this first chapter has not changed for the author since his preparation of the first edition; and most teachers and prospective teachers can give the ready answer, because love of literature was probably the major reason they chose the career of teaching English. But a number of things have changed in the school situation, including student attitudes, since publication of the revised edition. Movements to define the content and structure of English and to establish bases for sequences, to find more effective ways of bringing students and teachers together, and to create new materials for study have swept the country in the past few years. One of the objectives of the present edition is to relate the study of literature in the secondary school to changing conditions and to promote the humane orientation of the English curriculum.

To open a book with such a purpose on a negative note may seem unfortunate. But there is a reality which teachers of literature must face. At the time this edition was completed, it was obvious that the literature program of most high schools lacked relevance and virility for many students. Except perhaps for some girls in the upper and middle class, students tended to view the literature course as a garden not populated with real toads. Evidence of the relevance gap for many young people was found in the kind of paraliterature program that students had established for themselves outside of school, a program in which shockers such as *Last Exit to Brooklyn, In Cold Blood,* and *Giovanni's Room* carried more impact than the books studied in the classroom; in which motion pictures such as *The Graduate* and *Guess Who's Coming to Dinner?* were major happenings; in which *Eye* magazine claimed a wide following; in which Simon and Garfunkel were more important than Wordsworth and Frost. These specifics will be replaced by the time this edition appears in print, but the relevance gap may even have widened. A first approach to the problem is that teachers individually must identify basic rewards of literature study for their students, rewards in which each teacher can truly believe. Traditionally, the profession seems loath to be specific and hardnosed about the objectives of literature study.

The English-teaching community seems to have passed through three general prevailing attitudes toward the study of literature in the past three decades. In the late 1930s and early 1940s, as the country emerged from an economic depression and entered World War II, teachers of literature displayed a marked inferiority complex, covertly admitting that literature was not, after all, very important in the school program. Practicality and immediacy dominated high school curricula. Literature did not contribute much to the aims of secondary education as then identified. Writers of textbooks on education assigned to literature a vague place in the esthetic development of the student, or viewed it as a kind of recreational dessert capping the solid nutriment of the really important components of the curriculum. Literature study as such disappeared in many junior high schools, and in some senior high schools. "Core" programs or "common learnings" became widespread, and in the resulting "bloc," literature appeared only when ingenious teachers could drag it into units on "Modern Transportation" or "Home and Family Problems."

The era of the inferiority complex was succeeded by an era characterized by a lofty, rather precious attitude toward the values of literary study. Literature, many teachers felt, offered a moral guide to life. There was a preoccupation with theme and idea. Slogans were legion. "Literature as Equipment for Living" was a phrase used by the eminent critic and scholar Kenneth Burke. The author of the present book wrote an article entitled "Literature and the Heightened Mind." The slogans were titillating, but the sour fact was that in many classrooms literature study was not equipping students for living nor heightening their minds.

A period of reaction naturally followed, representing a delayed response in the high schools to the influence of the "New Criticism."

Now literature was made a discipline and there was much emphasis on "close reading" of individual works. The function of literature was to be true to itself—whatever that meant to individual teachers. To be specific about the rewards of literature was to be somehow unsophisticated. The distinguished Commission on Literature of the National Council of Teachers of English had great difficulty agreeing on a statement of the purposes of literary study. Fear of "going outside the text" frequently resulted in overconcern with technique and often students groaned under the process of meticulously picking selections apart.

The profession at present seems to be in a period of synthesis and rapprochement in which the favorite word attached to literature study is "engagement." Reporting on the Anglo-American Conference on the Teaching of English held at Dartmouth College in September 1966, Herbert J. Muller wrote that a favorite theme at the conference was: "The immediate object of the teacher should be to get the child actively 'involved' or 'engaged'. . . . In simpler terms, the teacher should make or keep literature alive, as it naturally is for little children." [1] Obviously, there is concern with getting students involved, intellectually and emotionally, with a work on its own terms so that a full literary experience will ensue.[2] Although most teachers feel the obligation to help students learn to deal with selections in sophisticated terms—allowing the final rewards to be the student's private business—there is a feeling that there should be some sureness in the teacher's mind as to what the ultimate rewards might be. These ultimate rewards, to this writer's mind, are discussed in the rest of this chapter.

LITERATURE AS LIBERATION

Literature is liberating in the sense that it helps to free us from the inherent shackles fastened upon us by our society. Crucial in the

[1] *The Uses of English* (New York: Holt, Rinehart and Winston, 1967), 79.
[2] Two important publications relating to students' involvement with literature appeared as this manuscript was in preparation: The revised edition of Louise Rosenblatt's *Literature As Exploration* (New York: Noble, 1968), and *Response to Literature,* edited by James R. Squire (Champaign, Ill.: NCTE, 1968), one of the Dartmouth Seminar monographs.

quest for identity, as opposed to a deadening relating to the crowd, is the ability to shake off, when necessary, the emotional censors of society. One can accomplish this in the literary experience and therein lies the great enduring value of literature. Northrop Frye says something similar when he distinguishes among three levels of the mind which also represent three levels on which words are used: (1) The level of ordinary experience and necessary public self-expression. (2) The level on which language is used in the practical world to convey knowledge and information, the level on which language is used, that is, in organized bodies of knowledge and doctrine—philosophy, history, religion, and so on. (3) The level of the imagination represented by the use of language in literature. These uses of language represent, to Frye, the dual categories of living, "what you have to do and what you want to do—in other words, necessity and freedom." The imaginative use of language, he says, allows a person to construct a "vision or model in your mind of what you want to construct." [3]

It is a mistake therefore to view involvement in a literary selection as merely a momentary escape from reality. Experience with literature enables the reader to build a level of imaginative living which is real in itself, lying somewhere between dead-level literalness and hallucination. Even in so-called escape reading, for example, one comes to terms with experience while escaping from it at the same time. There is particular significance, for instance, in the adolescent boy's zest for stories of physical adventure—whether they are laid in the northern forest, in the Old West, at sea, or on the battlefield. All these settings represent freedom from the complexities of social machinery. Men survive here through individual strength and resourcefulness. Through projection into these stories, the young reader tests himself vicariously, as he must inevitably do in reality. A major ingredient in growing up is the haunting trepidation about one's adequacy to play an adult role, to handle adult problems and experience. A lifetime is a long time to wait to find out what life is like. Thomas Bailey Aldrich notes at one point in *The Story of a Bad Boy* that "I certainly would have committed suicide if I could have done so without killing myself." And Tom Sawyer, at a low point in his romance with Becky, rues the fact that he can't die *temporarily.*

[3] *The Educated Imagination* (Bloomington: Indiana University Press, 1964), pp. 17–21.

If I could only know what it is *like* to be in crucial situations, the young person agonizes, before I get into such situations! G. Robert Carlsen focuses on this problem when he says that young people "come to a semi-integrated picture of themselves in many kinds of roles that it is possible for a human being to play. . . . He (the adolescent) wants to know what it would feel like to be a murderer, even though he is not planning to be one. He wants to know what it feels like to give one's life to religion, to be corrupt in politics." [4] In a real sense, he can find out through literature. One reason why imaginative literature is so important in the quest for the "I," for identity, is that it serves as pre-experience on the imaginative level. Thus the thirteen-year-old girl may enjoy reading a novel about a seventeen-year-old girl's first serious love affair more than would an actual seventeen-year-old. And the teen-aged boy's interest in war stories does not necessarily indicate a morbid zest for blood and violence but affords him a vicarious tryout in the most crucial of all human situations—facing death.

It seems appropriate to note here that there is, in general, a need for greater permissiveness and flexibility in school libraries and classrooms. Teachers and librarians are sometimes too concerned with the quality of books made available to students. By all means young people should be introduced to works of high literary quality, but it is important to realize, too, that there is a vital developmental dimension in enthusiasm for reading.[5] Studies show that adults who are enthusiastic readers of mature works almost invariably went through an undiscriminating, voracious state in their own reading during which they devoured tons of frequently trashy and juvenile pages of the vintage, for example, of the Bobbsey Twins, Nancy Drew, Tom Swift, or the Joseph Altsheler books.

It has become clear that many of the restrictions on the kinds of books and other reading materials to be placed in libraries and classrooms have crippling effects on reading interest. Sometimes there is an invidious, and often unconscious, censorship imposed on reading at the very points where restrictions of the right to read should be resisted most vigorously. This censorship is inflicted by teachers who in-

[4] "Behind Reading Interests," *English Journal*, XLIII (January 1954), 10.
[5] Daniel Fader's *Hooked on Books* (Berkeley: University of California Press, 1966) furnishes an object lesson.

sist that students should read only "great" books, that is, literary masterpieces; and by school librarians who will not stock certain kinds of books nor permit some books to be in general circulation. One must, however, be sympathetically aware of the complexities surrounding such policies. But frequently adults underestimate the potential of young people to cope with the powerful emotions engendered by what they read.

The general point being made is that literature is a liberating force. For young people, especially, it liberates first through helping to free them from the emotional and intellectual blockings that result from inadequate knowledge of human nature. A book, a story, a play, or a poem may help to ease what James Street called "just the damn hurt of youth, which I contend is not a happy time, but a rather terrifying time of doubts."

Growing up involves, fundamentally, a developing understanding of human nature; and a principal touchstone of maturity is the awareness of its complexity. Characters in good literature exemplify the complexity of human motivation. The mysteries of personality are explored in literature, beginning with the child's first exposure to it. Even the characters in nursery rhymes, for the most part, are people of fault as well as of virtue. Commentaries on the human species, its nobility and its foibles, come early in the experience of some children who may read in the elementary school years, books such as Kenneth Grahame's memorable *Wind in the Willows*.

It is no wonder that *Huckleberry Finn* has been translated into virtually every language known to man. For Huck represents universal adolescence as he discovers the complexity of his own motivations in his battle with his conscience about whether to turn Jim over to the authorities. His tortured conclusion, "All right, I'll go to hell!" echoes every adolescent's painful conviction regarding his own dark and lonely thoughts.

In literature the young person comes to grips with the most pervasive of all themes in human experience—the struggle between good and evil. In *Tom Sawyer,* Mark Twain was concerned both with this struggle and with the rendezvous with evil—the inevitable destiny of the person growing up. Tom's rendezvous is traumatic—the stabbing scene in the graveyard—as was Mark Twain's own, since he himself had witnessed a real stabbing near his home in Hannibal, Missouri, an event that gave him nightmares for many weeks. This rendezvous with evil is dramatized impressively, too, in contemporary novels for adolescents. For example, in Paul Annixter's *Swiftwater,* a boy fights and finally kills a wolverine he encounters on his father's trapline. The wolverine here symbolizes evil, and it waits inescapably along the boy's path of responsibility.

Awareness of the complexity of human personality is gained partly, too, through reflection on the factors in the greatest moments in the human drama, no matter what the individual's station in life. Courage, for example, is one of these factors. It is of great concern to the adolescent who realizes that he must plumb the depths of his own courage in coming to terms with himself, his environment, his fellows, his universe, his god. This inward reaching is exhibited by the hero of Armstrong Sperry's *Call It Courage,* who has to prove his courage to himself and others; by the protagonist who has to make his separate peace with life in John Knowles's *A Separate Peace;* by Anne Frank who, as revealed in her diary, had to accept a martyr's role she never wanted.

Young people are becoming aware, sometimes bewilderingly, of the clash of values among men. Literature, as a humanistic study, is necessarily concerned with human values. Underlying its study are such eternal questions as these: What is the good life? What do men do with their lives? What do men live by and for?

Selections of literature, from Chaucer's *Canterbury Tales* to James Michener's *The Bridges at Toko-Ri* and Archibald MacLeish's *J.B.,* dramatize what men live, and perhaps die, for. Biography plays an important part here. Careers as diverse as those of Albert Schweitzer, Jane Addams, Lord Nelson, Mary of Scotland, and Louis Armstrong illustrate what real people have made of life under varying conditions.

Literature reveals, too, the revolt of men against some of the prevailing values of their culture. With regard to revolt, traditionally associated with youth, the adolescent is in a paradoxical position. On the one hand, he is a rebel against adult authority and certain adult values; on the other, he is a slavish conformist within his own peer culture. In truth, the timeless conflict between conformity and individuality is a genuine concern. This conflict furnishes the theme for many selections of literature, past and present.

Another awareness, too, is important in the struggle to come to terms with experience. Major problems, whether of an individual or a society, lie in the reaches that stretch between man and man. Our comfort is prey to John Donne's seventeenth-century admonition, "No man is an island." Literature plays an important part in developing awareness of the commonness of the human drama. What an impact a work has when the reader finds in it a fellow sufferer, one who obviously knows "what it is like"!

Of course no one, least of all young people, seeks to be depressed. Yet a feeling for the tragic elements in experience provides a needed tempering of the spirit, an attuning to the "still, sad music of humanity" that Wordsworth heard, and it is all to the good for adolescents to feel, for example, the slash of the sleety New England wind in *Ethan Frome*. Tragedy, after all, makes suffering bearable by making it understandable, and understanding of tragedy should be an aim of the senior high school literature program. Students may often finish their reading of *Macbeth* without really understanding why it is a tragedy when good triumphs at the end. Certainly, an understanding can be developed of the difference between tragic and "sad" in the Hollywood connotation. Students can learn rather quickly that the "weepy" story is not necessarily the tragic one.

Another criterion of the mature mind is the ability to perceive significance and beauty in the humdrum. Overwhelmingly, the television and movie screens, the radio, and the popular magazines feature one limited kind of experience—the exotic, melodramatic aspects in which few people can share directly. Prose and poetry that treat of everyday sights and sounds and people, and through which everyday experience can be evaluated, are the leavener in all this. A novel such as James Street's *Goodbye, My Lady* can do for young adolescents what any good literature can do—illuminate beauty. And the adolescent is more likely to associate beauty with a dog and the natural sounds of the swamp than with, for example, a field of daffodils; but the beauty of the daffodils or a Grecian urn or a stand of birch trees or a brickyard by moonlight may later become real, through the chemistry of experience and verbal symbol.

The chemistry of experience and verbal symbol bears repeating, not for any lyrical value it may have, but because it is probably the key to the ultimate function of literature. Literature brings insights into human experience because of the properties of its subject matter. Certain other disciplines, however—psychology, sociology, ethics, for example—share some of these properties and also furnish certain insights. But the unique kind of knowledge to which literature leads— call this "felt knowledge"—arises from the particular functions of *language* in imaginative literature and the particular interplay of language and content.

It is the particular power of serious literature to produce lyric thinking that helps us, as Wallace Stevens phrased it, "not to fear to step barefoot into reality." Language, lyrically ordered, gives us the metaphors before which our most toxic fears dissolve. Each person, consciously or unconsciously, feels at his back "Time's wingèd chariot hurrying near." Fear of death is a human legacy. It is impossible for most people to think of death in any but a metaphorical way, religious or otherwise. Browning in the poem "Prospice" finds his metaphors: "the snows begin and the blasts denote I am nearing the place . . . the press of the night . . . the fog in my throat . . . the mist in my face." Tennyson chose other metaphors: "Sunset and evening star, and one clear call for me."

To identify metaphorically the fears that obsess one is to experience the power of tragedy "in which all man's knowledge, wisdom, joy, sorrow, triumph, despair—and even the awareness of death's inevitable hour—may come together in a pattern of rhythm, imagery, reason, and emotion." [6] Tragedy as represented in the total metaphor of a *Moby Dick* or a *King Lear,* for example, is the realistic conquering of evil, for evil is represented by the debilitating fears and temptations that beset one.

But one need not talk only about high tragedy in this connection. There are lesser fears and confusions against which the power of metaphoric language is a major defense. Thomas Wolfe, in his archetypal wanderings in the dead of the Brooklyn night or through the dream-laden streets of his boyhood town, concluded in the last words he wrote for publication: "I believe that we are lost here in America, but I believe we shall be found . . . A wind is rising and the rivers flow." [7] In the symbolism of rivers and winds, with their timelessness and inexorable movement, Wolfe expressed the stay of anguish so es-

---

[6] Albert Upton, *Design for Thinking* (Palo Alto: Stanford University Press, 1961), p. 219.

[7] *You Can't Go Home Again* (New York: Dell, 1960), pp. 669, 671.

sential in the separate peace everyone must negotiate. And Archibald MacLeish, knowing that he could not grasp, as Omar Khayyam put it, "this sorry scheme of things entire," wrote during the confusions and inchoate yearnings of his expatriate years, "America is West and the wind blowing. America is alone and the gulls calling."

It is sometimes through the ironic metaphor that one finds comfort as did Toulouse-Lautrec when he declared sourly that "Marriage is a dull meal with the dessert at the beginning," or as did the children in Harper Lee's *To Kill a Mockingbird* when they viewed their not-too-welcome aunt: "Like Mt. Everest, she was cold and she was there."

This relationship of imaginative language to the preoccupations that lie below the threshold of expression is a particularly important one to young people, for whom the emotional conflicts of adulthood are still amorphous. To look over the brink into the abysses of life and to return unafraid is the catharsis literature provides.

People often mourn the emphasis on the sordid, the unhappy, and the perverted which they find so frequently in present-day literature. But works which present in artistic language the sordid and distorted, the dark sides of experience, represent highly moral art to which students at appropriate levels of development should be led, not protected from. Attempts at blind protection or suppression, characteristic of some segments of the lay public and even of the literary profession, arise from ignorance, not morality. Many Americans, sophisticated in technology and informed on space science, are at the same time ignorant of the function of the literary or esthetic experience.

The serious literature of today is morally, rather frequently religiously, oriented. It is no vagary of literary history that the two predominant forces in contemporary American fiction, for example, are the southern writers and the northern Jewish writers. The Jews have a sense of mythology and a broad and saving conception of irony born of a tradition of suffering. Bernard Malamud's novel *The Assistant* has its share of the sordid—there is a rape scene, for example—but his major theme is the meaning, morally and spiritually, of being a Jew—to what extent are all men Jews? The southerners have their knowledge of the Bible and a sense of history plus a laid-on guilt complex stemming from the days of slavery. The overall theme of the late Carson McCullers, a major Southern writer whose works contain many grotesque elements, is that of love without reciprocation, and the late Flannery O'Connor's principal theme is redemption through suffering. The latter's purpose was to make people aware of evil and to reveal the nature of redemption.

Probably the ultimate power of liberation in literature is to lead — from the narrower limits of thinking and feeling—political ideology, sociological theory, sexual mores—to broader systems of belief, the identification of central myths in our culture.

The literary experience conjures up, in the words of C. C. Jung, the racial memories or emotional memories out of which we recognize the significance of archetypes and myths, those generalizations, latent within us, to which we can relate all the trivia of experience. This fact has given imaginative literature its staying power over the centuries, for we are at once the victims and the beneficiaries of the myths and archetypes of our tradition, and our dreams and aspirations are the products of these myths and archetypes. Each person needs before him a vision of human life, an archetype, that will give meaning and order to existence. It is through the reading of literature that many young people may frame their conceptions of the archetype, a vital part of the search for the "I." It is essentially the vision which literature may give that accords it a place in the curriculum equal in importance to that of mathematics or science.

SELECTED BIBLIOGRAPHY

Farmer, Paul, "Literature Goals: Myth or Reality?" *English Journal,* LVI (March 1967), 456–460.
   Suggests approaches which might make the goals of "delight" and "human understanding" more attainable and more self-evident to students.
Frye, Northrop, *The Educated Imagination* (Bloomington: Indiana University Press, 1964).
   A profound statement of the importance of literature to today's students.
———, "Criticism, Visible and Invisible," *College English,* XXVI (October 1964), 3–12.
   A serious argument for the position that we can never really "teach literature," but can only teach criticism, the reading of literature.
Hipple, Ted, "Through Literature to Freedom," *English Journal,* LV (February 1966), 189–191.

Argues for the use of literature to develop in students a broader sense of their own "humanness," especially with regard to racial issues.

Irmscher, William F., "An Apology for Literature," *English Journal*, LII (April 1963), 252–256.

Argues that the humanistic and liberal apologies are inadequate, that we can and should defend the teaching of literature for its contribution to other language skills, especially composition.

Knights, L. C., "The Place of English Literature in a Liberal Education," in Brian Jackson and Denys Thompson (Eds.), *English in Education* (London: Chatto & Windus, 1964), pp. 214–227.

Justifies literature study for its "skills" values, its value in educating the imagination, and for its relation to important aspects of civilization.

Miller, James E., "Literature in the Revitalized Curriculum," *NASSP Bulletin,* LI (April 1967), 25–38.

Argues for the centrality of literature in the English curriculum and for a more virile program.

Rosenblatt, Louise M., *Literature as Exploration,* rev. ed. (New York: Noble, 1968).

An important book on the totality of the literary experience.

Shoben, Edward Joseph, "Texts and Values: The Irrelevance of Literary Education," *Liberal Education,* LII (May 1967), 244–251.

Discusses the significant contribution of literature to the development of personality, emphasizing the distinction between "literary scholarship" and "direct literary experience."

Squire, James R. (Ed.), *Response to Literature* (Champaign, Ill.: NCTE, 1968).

A summary of the Dartmouth discussions on the subject with selected individual essays.

Stafford, William, *Friends to This Ground* (Champaign, Ill.: NCTE, 1967).

A statement by the Commission on Literature of the NCTE on objectives and issues in the teaching of literature.

Sutcliffe, Denham, "The Heart Needs a Language," *Teachers College Record,* LXV (January 1964), 318–323.

Briefly takes issue with the arguments against literature as an "impractical" subject, and develops an eloquent argument for literature as a "language of the heart."

White, Helen C., "New Perspectives on Teaching Literature," *College English,* XXIII (March 1962), 433–436.

A statement to English teachers of objectives in teaching literature which was subsequently reflected in many NDEA summer institutes.

Wilhelms, Fred T., "Using the Curriculum To Build Personal Strength," *NASSP Bulletin*, XLVIII (January 1964), 90–115.

The author uses literature to demonstrate how a subject may accentuate the individual and his "growth in power of personality" while maintaining "a deep and necessary commitment to knowledge."

2
The Shape of the Literature Curriculum

section I
THE STRUCTURE OF LITERATURE

The word "structure" has been a key word in education since the publication of Jerome Bruner's now famous book, *The Process of Education*.[1] Bruner's thesis is that there are certain key principles in every discipline which can furnish the basis for a "spiral" sequence. These key principles, Bruner says, can be taught and understood at all grade levels with the materials and examples becoming more mature as the pupil moves upward in school.

Curriculum planners in English have paid due homage to Bruner's theory, but views of the nature of structure in literature take various shadings, and judgments differ as to the practical usefulness of Bruner's theory in planning literature programs. Purported discussions of structure in literature frequently eventuate in discussions of the structure of individual selections rather than in consideration of the basic principles in the "discipline" of literature. Such discussions are helpful, generally, but arguments such as whether the overall structure of a work must be grasped before the component parts are considered, for example, are largely irrelevant in the planning of literature programs.

A succinct and inclusive discussion of varying approaches to the structure of literary selections is that by Walker, who lists nine points

[1] Cambridge: Harvard University Press, 1960.

16

of agreement among teachers who advocate these various approaches.[2]

1. The study of literature should include a careful analysis of the work itself to see what structural relationships exist.
2. The investigation of structure should be inductive. All advocates of structure proceed by discovering particular relationships to make later generalizations.
3. The structure of literature is what gives it unity or enables it to have a unifying effect.
4. Structure is the overall pattern of relationships that holds the parts together.
5. The study of structure involves the study of form and content.
6. The study of structure should begin with a view of the whole.
7. The study of structure facilitates understanding and interpretation of literature.
8. The understanding of structure broadens the base of literary appreciation by enabling the reader to appreciate literature not only for its appeal or meaning to them, but also for the craftsmanship involved in its creation.
9. The study of structure facilitates transfer of general principles pertinent to literature, composition, and the process of investigation. An understanding of the relationships found in a piece of literature should hasten the understanding of a similar work. An understanding of how writers combine parts to produce wholes should help students improve their own writing. The systematic process of investigation involved in the study of structure can be used in other studies.

Walker and Evans find particular advantages in one view of structure, namely, "that structure exists in the interaction between a reader and the work of literature, in the literary experience." [3] These authors go on to say that "The significance of this view of structure for the student is that it makes him a collaborator in the work of art and frees him from having to account for everything in the work. He need account only for what he attends to." [4]

---

[2] Jerry L. Walker, "The Structure of Literature," *English Journal,* LV (March 1966), 305–315.
[3] William H. Evans and Jerry L. Walker, *New Trends in the Teaching of English in Secondary Schools* (Chicago: Rand McNally, 1966), p. 42.
[4] Evans and Walker, p. 43.

One must, of course, accept the importance of the interrelationship of reader and selection, an interrelationship that often can be guessed at but never predicted with sureness for individual students. Yet such acceptance is not very useful in planning a sequence in literature. Teachers need to know what they are teaching in literature and what are the valid components of literature. Then they are in a position to decide how to make their teaching and the sequence in their school bear on these components.

As efforts to lay a basis for sequence in literature accelerate, through the Curriculum Study Centers funded by the U.S. Office of Education, among others, a skepticism has grown toward Bruner's theory as applied to literature. Frank Whitehead, the British educator, asks, "Can the concept of structure, however, be applied to the 'subject' of English in anything more than a loose metaphorical sense?" [5] Stoddard Malarkey, associated with the Curriculum Study Center at the University of Oregon, says: "Agreement as to what constitute the 'great and simple structuring ideas' of literature seems impossible of achievement." [6] Referring to Bruner's concept of a spiral curriculum, the authors of a pamphlet produced in the Oregon center say: "This is fine in theory, but how is it to be applied to a literary work in which no single aspect—imagery, form, structure, point of view—is an island unto itself in the totality of the esthetic effect?" [7]

The Oregon writers, in fact, avoid the term "structure" and proceed to say that the study of literature subdivides under "three main headings—subject, form, and point of view." These three aspects of literature are considered directly in grades 7–9 in the Oregon curriculum with more sophisticated aspects and implications left to the upper grades.

The work of the Oregon authors was of value to this writer in identifying the structure or subdivisions in literature which can serve as a basis for planning a sequence. Teaching literature must involve three aspects: substance, mode, and form.

In considering substance, the teacher will lead students to a percep-

---

[5] From an unpublished "working paper" written for the Anglo-American Conference on the Teaching of English, September 1966.

[6] "Sequence and Literature: Some Considerations," *English Journal*, LVI (March 1967), 395.

[7] *A Curriculum in English, Grades 7–12* (Eugene: Oregon Curriculum Center, University of Oregon), pp. 3–4.

tion of what the selection is really about, not only on the surface, but in terms of the themes and ideas that are developed or dramatized about human experience. All literature is concerned with four major relationships: man and deity; man and other men; man and the natural world; man and himself. A great variety of specific themes may be developed from these four relationships, but a balanced literature program will introduce works representing different periods and forms which deal with each of the four major relationships.

Mode refers to the general point of view on life experience which the selection represents. Since each work is by an individual, that individual's vantage point on life is often evident, though many selections cannot be classified neatly as to mode. The modal approach has been given especial vitality through the work of Northrop Frye who identifies four modes—romantic, comic, tragic, and ironic—and holds that the romantic and comic modes are more easily comprehended and therefore should be stressed in the early school years with later emphasis on the tragic and ironic modes.[8] The author, finding support from a number of other sources, adds a fifth mode—satiric. Frye, in his book, *Fables of Identity,*[9] identifies basic modes in terms of the human condition which they frame: the nature and predicament of the hero or protagonist. If the hero is superior in *degree* to other men and to his environment, we have the typical romance and its literary affiliates, the legend and folktale. If the protagonist is superior in degree to other men and is a leader but is not superior to his natural environment, we have the hero of most tragedy and epic. If the hero is superior neither to other men nor to his environment, we have the comic mode. If he is inferior in power or intelligence to ourselves so that we have a sense of looking down on a scene of frustration or absurdity, the protagonist belongs to the ironic mode. Frye also identifies the typical subordinate characters that go with these modes and links the modes with basic archetypal patterns related to solar movement. Romance and comedy are linked with birth, dawn, and spring, and with marriage, triumph, zenith, and summer; while tragedy and irony relate to death, sunset, autumn, and to dissolution, darkness, and winter.

Form, of course, refers to the various genres and sub-genres of lit-

---

[8] *Design for Learning* (Toronto: University of Toronto Press, 1962), p. 10.
[9] New York: Harcourt, 1963, p. 16.

erature as well as to certain elements of structure—point of view, setting, dialogue, and the like—and certain devices—metaphor and symbol, for instance—which are common to more than one genre.

section II
AN ILLUSTRATIVE SEQUENCE

A definition of the structure of literature, such as that just presented, should serve the practical purpose of providing a basis for sequence. It has been suggested earlier that not everything can be sequential and incremental in a literature program. There is still room for necessary opportunism on the part of individual teachers and for application of the threadbare slogan, "Take them where they are," regardless of the neat course of study that may exist. Yet it is necessary for school faculties to develop some kind of overall sequence. The specific nature of the sequence must depend on the view English faculties have of the structure of literature and on the characteristics of students in given schools.

The illustrative sequence that follows, based on the analysis of structure of literature in Section I of this chapter, was developed in part through the work of the Curriculum Study Center at the Florida State University * and in part through the writer's work with curriculum committees in Miami and Pensacola, Florida.

SEVENTH GRADE

Substance

Two thematic units designed to show how literature is concerned with the problems of everyday living:

1. "Man against Nature"—short selections showing facets of man's struggle with natural elements and his attempts to control the natural environment, culminating in study of the novel, *Third Man on the Mountain* by James R. Ullman. (Other approaches

* The work of the Center in junior high school English, which featured test programs in six Florida schools, was completed in June 1968.

to the novel are featured also. See "Mode" and "Form" below.)
2. "The Hero"—short selections in prose and poetry showing qualities of heroism in everyday life. Students should frame some tentative answers to the question, "What are the qualities of the present-day hero?" (This unit follows the one on myth, legend, and folklore.)

Mode

Concern with the romantic mode is incorporated in the study of *Third Man on the Mountain*. General characteristics of romantic literature provide the focus.

Form

1. Myth, legend, and folklore—the extensiveness of the unit depends on the background a class has developed in the elementary school.
2. Introduction to the major imaginative genres with certain emphases.
   a. Short story—attention to elementary symbolism in fiction.
   b. Poetry—narrative verse, especially ballads; simple lyrics about aspects of everyday life.
   c. Novel—consideration of the genre in connection with *Third Man on the Mountain*. An alternative, if teachers wish to form a separate unit around another novel, is study of *Shane* by Jack Schaefer.
   d. One-act play.

EIGHTH GRADE

Substance

Two thematic units designed to show how events become ideas or abstractions in literature.

1. "Courage"—use of the Scholastic Literature Unit, *Courage,* or a similar one designed to show illustrations of the various guises of courage in everday life. Short selections.
2. "The Frontier Spirit"—short selections illustrating qualities of life and character on the Western frontier. Some concern with how

historical events and backgrounds are used in imaginative literature.

Mode

Comic mode—centered around *The Matchmaker* by Thornton
Wilder. Use of some old silent comic films. Some emphasis on the
difference between "comic" and "funny."

Form

1. Novel—the idea of allegory illustrated by *The Pearl* by John Steinbeck or *Call of the Wild* by Jack London.
2. Short story—emphasis on characterization in fiction. Consideration of point of view.
3. Poetry—relatively simple lyric poems that express ideas or abstractions. Consideration of the "three voices of poetry."
4. Full-length comic drama—*The Matchmaker*.
5. TV drama—study of *Visit to a Small Planet* by Gore Vidal.

NINTH GRADE

Substance

Two thematic units emphasizing human conflicts:

1. "Individualism versus Conformity"—short selections, a key one of
   which is "Paul's Case" by Willa Cather.
2. "The Quest"—the central selection is Hemingway's *The Old Man
   and the Sea*. Introduction of the idea of archetype with the quest
   as example.

Mode

1. Satire—short selections with the unit culminating in either Orwell's
   Animal Farm or Leonard Wibberleys' *The Mouse that Roared*.
2. Introduction to tragedy—*Antigone* and, for more able classes,
   Romeo and Juliet.

Form

1. Novel—devices of the satiric novel.
2. Short story—further consideration of point of view. Protest in fiction.
3. Poetry—consideration of tone and attitude in poetry.
4. Drama—the verse play.

TENTH GRADE

Substance

Two thematic units featuring the protagonist's relationship with self.

1. "The Human Equation"—short selections dealing with human weakness such as "A Piece of String" by de Maupassant; "The Queen of Spades" by Pushkin; "Mr. Flood's Party" by E. A. Robinson.
2. "Wisdom through Ordeal"—autobiographical narratives, or excerpts from them, such as those by Heyerdahl, de Poncins, and so on. Some war selections.

Mode

Introduction to the ironic mode centered around *Face of a Hero* by Pierre Boulle.

Form

1. Short story—further concern with point of view and narrative techniques; the modern short story as "epiphany"; introduction to several short stories in translation from non–English-speaking countries.
2. Novel—the ironic novel.
3. Epic—some medieval epics, or excerpts, such as *El Cid, The Song of Roland,* and so on.
4. Poetry—symbol and metaphor; concern with free verse.

ELEVENTH GRADE

Substance

Four thematic units which attempt to get at what is American about American literature.

1. "The Frontier in Literature"—similar to an earlier unit in the eighth grade, but featuring more mature selections. A good sampling of American folklore and its consideration in term of traditional American values and the American "dream."
2. "The Puritan Tradition"—centered around *The Scarlet Letter* by Nathaniel Hawthorne and *The Crucible* by Arthur Miller. (To be omitted in classes of lesser ability.)
3. "The American Concern with Success"—a central selection is *Babbitt* by Sinclair Lewis.
4. "Initiation into Adulthood"—further concern with the idea of archetype. Central selections are *A Separate Peace* by John Knowles or *Member of the Wedding* (play) by Carson McCullers. (Possibly both with able classes.)

Mode

No new concepts.

Form

1. Short story—the function of setting and use of local color.
2. Novel, poetry, drama—further reinforcing of concepts introduced earlier.

TWELFTH GRADE

Substance

Three thematic units.

1. "The Modern Anti-Hero"—small-group consideration of several appropriate contemporary novels. Relation of the antihero to existential thinking.

2. "The Carpe Diem Theme"—some stress on the Cavalier Poets with comparison to more modern selections.
3. "The Search for Identity"—with more able groups, study of Conrad's *The Secret Sharer*. Short selections with less able groups. Further concern with the idea of archetype.

Mode

1. Shakespearean tragedy—*Macbeth* or *Othello*.
2. Cosmic irony—Hardy's *The Mayor of Casterbridge* (to be omitted in less able groups.)

Form

1. Short story—ambiguity as method in the short story.
2. Novel—the novel as allegory; use of symbol.
3. Poetry—the dramatic monologue; the sonnet; the nature of metaphysical poetry.
4. Drama—Shakespearean drama.
5. The novel as allegory (if *The Secret Sharer* is studied).

Any specific sequence in literature will not be feasible for all schools. It is not *the* sequence that is important, but rather *a* sequence. A literature program in the junior and senior high school is more than just six years of reading selections of literature; it should be six years of considering literature in some significant pattern. The sequence outlined in this chapter is an illustration of one attempt to fashion such a pattern.

SELECTED BIBLIOGRAPHY

Booth, Wayne C., *The Rhetoric of Fiction* (Chicago: The University of Chicago Press, 1961).
A brilliant analysis of the relationship of author to audience, examining most structural aspects of the novel in light of their rhetorical significance.
———, "The Use of Criticism in the Teaching of Literature," *College English*, XXVII (October 1965), 1–13.
Questioning Frye's premise of a unified structure of literature, Booth

suggests that teachers shift their attention from abstract structures to the students' reactions to the literature.

Cottrell, Beekman W. and Lois S. Josephs, "A Genuine Accumulation," *English Journal*, LIV (February 1965), 91–94.

An examination of the Carnegie Institute's Curriculum Center courses for Grades 11 and 12, illustrating the use of theme as a basis for sequential ordering of the program.

Dunning, Stephen, "Sequence and Literature: Some Teaching Facts," *The High School Journal*, XLVII (October 1963), 2–12.

Suggests six basic concerns based on the principle of students' and teachers' individual differences which must be considered in planning for sequence in the literature program.

Guth, Hans P., "Approaches to Literary Study," and "The Meaning of Literature," in *English Today and Tomorrow* (Englewood Cliffs, N.J.: Prentice-Hall, 1964), pp. 220–252.

Guth discusses the promise and many of the teaching problems raised by the structural approaches to literature.

Hillocks, George Jr., "Approaches to Meaning: A Basis for a Literature Curriculum," *English Journal*, LIII (September 1964), 413–421.

Outlines a literature program based on three basic but relatively accessible structural areas: man in his environment, levels of meaning, and genre.

Lansu, Helvi, "The Shape of Literature," *English Journal*, LIV (September 1965), 520–524.

Demonstrates approaches to teaching an understanding of literary structure on three levels: plot, theme, and tone.

Malarkey, Stoddard, "Sequence and Literature: Some Considerations," *English Journal*, LVI (March 1967), 395–401.

Miles, Josephine, "Reading Poems," *English Journal*, LII (March 1963), 157–164.

In her discussion of the "literal" and "metrical" aspects of poetry, Professor Miles illustrates an important use of the structural approaches to literature.

Ojala, William T., "Thematic Categories as an Approach to Sequence," *English Journal*, LII (March 1963), 178–185.

Outlines a curriculum for Grades 7–12 based on thematic units.

Scribner, Duane C., "Learning Hierarchies and Literary Sequence," *English Journal*, LVI (March 1967), 385–393.

Relates recent developments in learning theory to determination of sequence in the teaching of literature.

Walker, Jerry L., "The Structure of Literature," *English Journal,* LV (March 1966), 305–315.

An excellent brief summary of three dominating points of view on what constitutes the "structure of literature."

3
Approaches to Literature: Old and New

The title of this chapter may seem presumptuous since entire books have been written that could bear the same title, and a number of possible approaches to a work of literature will not be identified. But the chapter itself is meant only to touch briefly on certain approaches to a work of literature that may be appropriate in the high school classroom. No matter what definition of the structure of literature or what design for sequence a teacher may adopt, he comes inevitably to choices of approach and strategy in teaching individual selections. Each teacher may have his prejudices concerning approaches to works of literature, but it is obvious that students should be introduced to the variety of ways in which a selection of literature may be considered.

"Close reading" of individual selections has been considered in recent years as a new development. Hans P. Guth, for example, refers to "the close reading of the text itself" as one of four major movements affecting the teaching of English in the past few decades.[1] Intensive (one could say laborious) reading of texts is nothing new in the classroom. But the almost word-for-word reading of *Silas Marner* or *Macbeth* or some other canonized work that in the past (and in the present, to some extent) was featured in high school classrooms is not the close reading being discussed today. "Close reading" now most often refers to a formalistic or intrinsic approach promoted by what for a number of years has been called the New Criticism.

Though the intrinsic approach is valuable, there is some tendency

[1] *English Today and Tomorrow* (Englewood Cliffs, N.J.: Prentice-Hall, 1964), p. 18.

among teachers to view it as the only avenue to close reading of the text. This chapter identifies several approaches to a work, all of which may require close reading. (A later section deals with classroom procedures in leading discussion of individual selections no matter what the specific approach.) The first part is devoted to older, established approaches; the second part to newer ones.

TRADITIONAL APPROACHES

Moral Approach

The label "moral" as an approach to literature may make some teachers shudder as they recall the dogged search for "the moral" in literary selections that marked an earlier era. But "moral" taken in a broad sense—"humanistic" might be a synonym—is a most valuable and interesting approach with young people. In their book *Teaching Language and Literature,* Loban, Ryan, and Squire make an essential point: "Literature cannot be taught apart from the morality of humanity. . . . To view literature as a formula for moral action is to mistake its nature and miss its rewards. However, because it can enlarge our awareness of values and refine our discrimination among values, literature is a force of tremendous potential for education." [2]

It is difficult to keep a class, especially one composed of younger students, from veering away from the text in a discussion of values or human conduct which may be touched off by a selection of literature. The immature reader is inclined to judge human acts and motivations in actual life situations which he knows about rather than in the situation developed in the work. Yet the study and discussion of literature — furnishes the young student with one of his major opportunities for reflection on values. In works built around ethical or moral ideas or assumptions, the moral approach is obviously the path to what is central in the work, though matters of form need not be neglected.

Psychological Approach

Mention of a psychological approach to literature may cause some negative reactions, too, if one thinks of forced Freudian interpreta-

[2] New York: Harcourt, 1961, p. 602.

tions or dubious deductions about the personal lives of authors as a way of illuminating their works. But the psychological approach is of long standing, and one of the monuments of criticism is probably Ernest Jones' interpretation of Hamlet's dilemma in the light of the oedipus complex.[3]

Facts about an author's life may sometimes help to interpret his work, but much time has been wasted in having students learn insignificant personal facts about writers. Far more important is another dimension of the psychological approach, that in which motivations and actions of characters are analyzed. In modern literature, especially in fiction and drama, the psychological element is very strong whether one thinks of Proust, Mann, and Joyce or Salinger, Malamud, and Bellow, or writers of junior novels. The principal preoccupation of modern fiction is with the relationship of man and his inner self. The modern short story often represents an "epiphany," a label attached by Joyce to the story in which a character achieves some flash of insight after which he is never the same again. Careful reading is required if the student is to comprehend what really has happened to the character.

Directing students to analysis of the motivations and the mental and emotional states of characters need not mean turning the literature class into a psychology class if teachers make sure that the students work within the context of the text itself.

Sociopolitical Approach

High school students have as natural an affinity for the sociopolitical approach as they have for the moral, though literary scholars have fumed over making literature study into bastardized sociology, and one can think of the excesses of Marxist criticism. Yet literature may be an examination of group living, and it is not difficult to document Harry Levin's statement that ". . . the relations between literature and society are reciprocal. Literature is not only the effect of social causes; it is also the cause of social effects." [4] In modern literature, again, the sociological and geographical contexts are important. Saul Bellow cannot be read without regard for the large northern cities in

---

[3] "The Oedipus Complex as an Explanation of Hamlet's Mystery," *The American Journal of Psychology*, XXI (1910).

[4] "Literature as an Institution," *Accent* VI (Spring 1946), 164.

which most of his novels are set, and the small southern town is a vital element in the fiction of Carson McCullers, to cite two examples among major contemporary writers.

Literature with sociopolitical themes, especially satire, is appealing to older adolescents in whom social and moral idealism often tends to clash with a certain mood of cynicism. Social protest has been traditionally an important element in literature, and students need to be made aware of how imaginative literature can illuminate social and political problems.

Modal Approach

The definition of structure of literature presented in the preceding chapter makes clear the author's belief that a modal approach to selections of literature is a useful one in the secondary school. Clearly there are limitations to this approach, as most teachers of literature are aware. There are selections that do not fit one of the modal pigeon holes, and bootless arguments have taken place over whether Hemingway, for example, was or was not a romantic. But there is value in the student's perceiving that literature tends to cluster in modes which represent various interpretations of the human condition. An excellent foundation for the modal approach is furnished by Northrop Frye's celebrated work. Frye identifies four basic modes (romantic, comic, tragic, and ironic) in terms of the human condition as they frame it, in terms of the nature and predicament of the protagonist. A brief summary of Frye's theory was given in the preceding chapter. It seems legitimate to add a fifth mode, the satiric.

Mere classification of selections will defeat the aim of the modal approach, but well-directed analyses of selections as examples of basic modes may enrich literature study.

Mythic or Archetypal Approach

The mythic or archetypal approach, sometimes termed the anthropological or totemic approach, is much in the forefront in recent literary criticism, but little application of this approach has been made in the secondary school. "Myth" and "archetype" are not synonymous, and both terms are put to many uses as Willard Thorp points out in the opening chapter of the monograph, *The Teacher and American*

Literature.[5] Yet the two words may be combined appropriately in ti-
tling an approach in the high schools. The mythic approach has captured the imagination of young people as John Gerber testifies: "The
— mythical approach . . . is the one that most immediately engages the
student and causes him to see the literary work as an expression of
life. Nothing seems to excite our students so much about a poem or
novel as the discovery of a reformulation of a primitive myth. They
pounce upon it as a personal treasure that is inside them—as indeed it
is—as well as inside the poem or novel." [6] Gerber cautions, however,
that "The difficulty is holding the students under control. They are
willing to see the reenactment or the Fall of Man every time the
nonhero gets dead drunk and drops to the floor." [7]

There are probably four dimensions which the mythic approach
may assume in the high school. (1) Concern with specific mythic
figures such as Job in MacLeish's *J.B.* or Faust in John Hersey's *Too
Far To Walk*. (2) Identification of archetypal symbols such as certain animals—the lamb or the eagle, for instance—and certain
flowers—the red rose and the lily. (3) Identification of archetypal
themes such as the edenic or the fall, the quest, and initiation. (4)
Perception of the basic kinds of myths as Northrop Frye outlines
them in terms of the predicament of the hero: (a) Birth of the hero,
triumph over the powers of evil, with father and mother as subordinate characters. (b) Marriage and success of the hero; his entry into
paradise or perfect happiness; the bride and the companion are subordinate heroes. (c) Isolation of the hero and his death or downfall,
often violent death; traitors and sirens are subordinate characters. (d)
Defeat of the hero or leader and the triumph of the powers of darkness; often there are great physical calamities such as fires, floods, or
eruptions; ogres and witches are the subordinate characters.[8]

Probably the key to the value of the mythic approach is to be found
in Erich Fromm's statement that a myth is "a message from ourselves
to ourselves, a secret language which enables us to treat inner as if
outer event." [9]

5 Champaign, Ill.: NCTE, 1965.
6 John Gerber, "Literature—Our Untamable Discipline," *College English*,
XXVIII (February 1967), 357–358.
7 Gerber, p. 358.
8 Northrop Frye, *Fables of Identity* (New York: Harcourt, 1963), p. 16.
9 As summarized by W. Y. Tindall in *Forces in Modern British Literature*
(New York: Vintage Books, 1956), p. 311.

As suggested in the opening chapter, development of the archetypal approach may be a major breakthrough in literature in the high schools.

Formalistic or Intrinsic Approach

Form and structural elements in a work of literature will never be lost sight of no matter what the approach, for, as stated earlier, consideration of form keeps literature from becoming ethics, psychology, sociology, or something else. The major cautions are that teachers not do too much too early with form and structure and that consideration of form not become a high and dry concern.

A formalistic approach, under the direction of a competent teacher, will become a full-bodied thing in which concern with the generic characteristics of story, novel, poem, or play or with literary devices such as foreshadowing, symbolism, or metrical patterns will not prevent parallel concern with the historical and biographical context of the work nor with its ideas, meanings or effects. As Harold Osborne writes:

> The form of a poem, the prosodic structure, the rhythmic interplay, the characteristic idiom, are nothing any more when abstracted from the content of meaning; for language is not language but noise except in so far as it expresses meaning. So, too, the content without the form is an unreal abstraction without concrete existence, for when it is expressed in different language it is something different that is being expressed. The poem must be perceived as a whole to be perceived at all. There can be no conflict between form and content . . . for neither has existence without the other and abstraction is murder to both.[10]

NEWER APPROACHES

A certain restlessness with traditional ways of approaching literature is a part of the present scene in the teaching of English, and a brief review of several newer concepts concerning study of literature seems appropriate, although the author can claim only rudimentary acquaintance with each one.

[10] *Aesthetics and Criticism* (New York: Philosophical Library, 1955), p. 289.

Field Theory

It is inevitable that science would have an impact on the teaching of literature as it has had on practically everything else in the past few years. The field theory of the physical sciences as applicable to literature has gained momentum. William Holtz [11] and Edward Fagan [12] have written lucidly on the subject. The basic tenet of field theory as applied to literature is that a selection of literature or an integral part of it is perceived as an element of an organized whole. Holtz writes:

> Any given thing participates in many larger systems (fields) which always include the observer himself, and in which all elements interact in a complex, dynamic balance.[13]

And Fagan holds that a work of art occurs in the reader's mind only to the extent that a fusion or unity occurs between the ideas of the author and those of the reader.

These writers find in literature an analogy to the *particle* and *wave* which in physics are the ultimate units. The particle is a unit isolated from its context while a wave is a unit perceived within a continuum, merging with the adjacent units. Both particles and waves are parts of space or fields. Holtz points out that in a poem images may correspond to particles and lines to waves.

Holtz illustrates how field theory can be applied to the reading of *Tristram Shandy*. The work, Holtz maintains, is a problem of field or space apprehension where the field is that of Tristram's consciousness. The reader has to put discrete particles together as mental property of a self like himself. Similarly, Fagan illustrates application of field theory to George R. Stewart's *Storm,* in which, Fagan believes, the reader needs to see that the people in the work are symbols—and symbols as areas of meaning in motion correspond to waves— representing a composite man who "is fearless because he is confident, in his flexibility, that he can meet any emergency."

[11] "Field Theory and Literature," *Rhetoric: Theories for Application* (Champaign, Ill.: NCTE, 1967), pp. 52–65.

[12] *Field: A Process for Teaching Literature* (University Park: Pennsylvania State University Press, 1964).

[13] Holtz, "Field Theory and Literature," *Rhetoric: Theories for Application,* p. 54.

Cognitive Psychology

The interest in the work of Jerome Bruner and other cognitive psychologists has been noted earlier in discussion of structure and sequence of literature. Some applications of cognitive psychology are also pertinent to method in choosing and approaching individual works. The most direct application of which the writer is aware is that of Herbert Karl [14] who draws on the work of Jean Piaget. Karl shows how the "thought matrix" of Piaget—involving the processes of identity, inversion, reciprocity, and correlation—might form the basis for approaches to works of literature. The student often must form "identities" to understand a selection of literature. If, for example, someone named Bonnie is referred to in a poem, the reader must identify her as a person, a girl. Identity is the process necessary generally in getting the plain sense of the work—basic plots, meanings of terms, and so on.

Inversion, the second process, implies negation or elimination. "When a learner conceives a structural relationship in terms of inversion," Karl writes, "meaning is achieved by recognition of the effect of opposing elements." Inverse relationships underlie such literary matters as irony, satire, paradox, contrast, and others. The third process, reciprocity, connotes symmetry or analogy, and analogical relationships result from sets of details that are similar in some way. Obviously, reciprocity underlies such matters as metaphor, simile, personification, and allegory.

The fourth process, correlation, is that of structuring relationships between two separate contexts. Within a selection of literature, for instance, the student might need for purposes of interpretation to relate the title of a poem to an image within the poem. Or beyond the context of the selection itself a reader may need to correlate his own experience with that in the work if he is to enter imaginatively into the work. Finally, Karl says, the process of correlation is the basis for relating works of literature, or elements within them, to other media such as art or music.

[14] "An Approach to Literature through Cognitive Processes," *English Journal,* LVII (February 1968), 181–187.

Rhetorical Approach

Both the rhetorical approach and the linguistic approach discussed below are really variations on the intrinsic or formalistic approach. The recent revival of interest in rhetorical studies has brought attention to the possibilities of rhetoric as an approach to literature. In his preface to *The Rhetoric of Fiction*,[15] Wayne C. Booth makes the point that a selection of literature, as a work of art, must communicate itself if it is successful. Therefore, there is a rhetorical dimension, obvious or otherwise, in any selection. Booth's approach is to examine "the rhetorical resources available to the writer of epic, novel, or short story as he tries, consciously or unconsciously, to impose his fictional world upon the reader."

Specific lines of inquiry in the rhetorical approach can be illustrated from an essay by Sam Meyer.[16] Meyer is interested in exploring the relationships of the poet to his subject. Using the "Concord Hymn" as an example, he lists questions that might serve as basis for examination of the poem:

> Is concentration on the present paramount in the "Concord Hymn"? What is the speaker's attitude toward time?
> What seems to be the speaker's mode—dramatic, oratory, ritualistic? What is the rhetorical level—colloquial, formal, or something else?
> Does assigning the title "Concord Hymn" require the poet to have a perspective different from the one needed to project the *person* who speaks in the poem?
> Who seems to be the speaker's immediate audience? Is there a removed or fictive audience as well? Is the address to the spirit at the end really a "turning aside," in the literal meaning of the word *apostrophe*? [17]

Linguistic Approach

The attempt to relate linguistic analysis to literature is one part of the general burgeoning of ramifications of linguistics during recent years.

---

[15] Chicago: University of Chicago Press, 1961.

[16] "Teaching the Rhetorical Approach to the Poem," *Rhetoric: Theories for Application* (Champaign, Ill.: NCTE, 1967), pp. 82–89.

[17] "Teaching the Rhetorical Approach to the Poem," p. 89.

The aim of linguistic analysis of literature is descriptive and analytical, not evaluative, as Seymour Chatman points out.[18] Linguistic
analysis, of course, is concerned with the phonological and structural
aspects of a work of literature. In the essay alluded to above, Chatman says that the job of phonemic analysis in poetry is to furnish a
description of how esthetic effects are achieved from sources involving
patterns and clusters of phonemes, and that such effects are achieved
mainly through unusual frequency and unusual patterning of phonemes. Dell Hymes, for example, has made a phonological analysis
of a sampling of English sonnets.[19] Chatman has shown, too, how
linguistic analysis can serve oral interpretation of literature.[20]

W. Nelson Francis demonstrates the analysis of syntax in poetry,
using the first sonnet from "Alterwise by Owl-light" by Dylan
Thomas.[21] Francis states that the major contribution of syntactic
analysis is to resolve syntactic ambiguities in poetry, but he cautions
that such analysis will not "lead us to a lucid interpretation of the
poem. But it will supply the framework which such an explication, if
one is possible, must follow, and set the bounds beyond which it must
not venture." [22]

This very cursory review of newer approaches to literary study is
meant only to indicate trends and to provide bibliography for those
readers who may wish to pursue a specific approach in greater
depth.

The point implied throughout this chapter is that eclecticism is the
key to approaching literature for high school students. Some students
will become intrigued with a particular approach. But all students
should develop a repertoire of approaches if literature study is to
achieve its vital and rich potential. John Gerber makes the case for
eclecticism cogently:

[18] "Linguistics, Poetics, and Interpretation: The Phonemic Dimension,"
Quarterly Journal of Speech, LXIII (October 1957), 239–256.
[19] "Phonological Aspects of Style: Some English Sonnets," *Style in Language,*
Thomas Sebeok (Ed.) (Cambridge: Massachusetts Institute of Technology,
1960), pp. 109–131.
[20] "Linguistic Analysis: A Study of James Mason's Interpretation of 'The
Bishop Orders His Tomb,'" *The Oral Study of Literature* (New York: Random House, 1966), pp. 94–130.
[21] "Syntax and Literary Interpretation," *Applied English Linguistics,* Harold
B. Allen (Ed.) (New York: Appleton, 2nd ed., 1964), pp. 515–522.
[22] Allen, p. 518.

The kind of eclecticism I think I see ahead will require the most astute teaching. We have developed great facility in teaching those matters requiring detachment: we have been chary of those which demand the student's engagement. And well we might be. For in engaging the student's belief or disbelief we must steer between the Scylla of indoctrination and the Charybdis of an undiscriminating relativism. Yet this is the course we *must* steer if the literary work is to engage the student's whole mind. We must learn how to raise issues of belief as adroitly as we have learned how to raise issues of form and content. In the process we may come to feel that our discipline is less tamable than ever. But we must make the attempt if we would successfully exploit our subject matter and if we could meet the deep psychic needs of our students.[23]

SELECTED BIBLIOGRAPHY

Bodkin, Maud, *Archetypal Patterns in Poetry: Psychological Studies of Imagination* (London: Oxford University Press, 1963).
   One of the major references on archetypal criticism.
Booth, Wayne C., *The Rhetoric of Fiction* (Chicago: University of Chicago Press, 1961).
   The major work on the rhetorical approach to literature. Illustrates with much discussion of specific selections.
Daiches, David, *Critical Approaches to Literature* (Englewood Cliffs, N.J.: Prentice-Hall, 1956).
   A readable and useful standard reference.
Fagan, Edward R., *Field: A Process for Teaching Literature* (University Park: Pennsylvania State University Press, 1964).
   Defines the field approach, suggests its uses and applications, and advocates training teachers to use the approach.
Fraiber, Louis, *Psychoanalysis and American Literary Criticism* (Detroit: Wayne State University Press, 1960).
   A depth treatment of the influence of psychoanalysis on criticism.
Frye, Northrop, *Anatomy of Criticism: Four Essays* (Princeton, N.J.: Princeton University Press, 1957).
   This celebrated work contains these essays:
   (1) "Historical Criticism: Theory of Modes"
   (2) "Ethical Criticism: Theory of Symbols"
   (3) "Archetypal Criticism: Theory of Myths"
   (4) "Rhetorical Criticism: Theory of Genres"

[23] Allen, p. 358.

Gerber, John C., "Literature—Our Untamable Discipline," *College English,* XXVIII (February 1967), 351–358.
A thoughtful statement on how to involve students with literature most profitably.

Guerin, Wilfred L., and others, *A Handbook of Critical Approaches to Literature* (New York: Harper & Row, 1966).
A very useful discussion and illustration of a number of approaches to literature.

Holtz, William, "Field Theory and Literature," *Rhetoric: Theories for Application* (Champaign, Ill.: NCTE, 1967), pp. 52–65.
Succinct discussion of the basis of field theory as an approach to literature.

Hook, J. N., "Multiple Approach in Teaching Literature," *English Journal,* XXXVII (April 1948), 188–92.
Discusses the possibilities of six approaches—historical, sociopsychological, emotive, didactic, paraphrastic, analytical—in heightening interest in literature.

Karl, Herbert, "An Approach to Literature through Cognitive Processes," *English Journal,* LVII (February 1968), 181–187.
Discusses the use of cognitive process—including identity, inversion, reciprocity, and correlation—in studying literature.

Lucas, F. L., *Literature and Psychology* (Ann Arbor Paperbacks: The University of Michigan Press, 1962).
Divided into "The Interpretation of Literature" and "The Judgment of Literature"; presents various interpretations of works of literature along with corresponding case studies in psychology.

Ohmann, Richard, "Literature as Sentences," *College English,* XXVII (January 1966), 261–267.
Argues that "at the level of sentences, the distinction between form and content comes clear, and that the intuition of style has its formal equivalent."

Pike, Kenneth L., "Language—Where Science and Poetry Meet," *College English,* XXVI (January 1965), 283–293.
The author explains the application of tagmemic theory to the teaching of poetry.

Pingry, Lillian S., "Some Approaches to the Teaching of Literature in the High School," *Peabody Journal of Education,* XXXI (January 1954), 227–239.
Various approaches are cited along with illustrative selections, but always the approaches are derived from interest in the student and his development.

Richards, I. A., *Principles of Literary Criticism* (New York: Harcourt, 1926).

A landmark work, still helpful.

Scott, Wilbur, *Five Approaches of Literary Criticism* (New York: Crowell-Collier-Macmillan, 1962).

A collection of modern essays illustrating the moral, psychological, sociological, formalistic, and archetypal approaches to literature.

Sebeok, Thomas A. (Ed.), *Style in Language* (Cambridge: Massachusetts Institute of Technology, 1960).

A series of essays illustrating linguistic analyses of style.

4

The Relationship of Literature Study
to Composition and Language Study

The basic question—What is English?—that has been vexing the profession for years still has no one final answer. There is agreement, of course, that literature, language, and written and oral composition are the major components of the curriculum and that teaching should relate them when possible and desirable. But there is still lack of agreement on the nucleus or integrating center of the subject.

This author, for reasons stated or implied in chapter 1, believes that the nucleus of the English curriculum is literature. By this statement I mean simply that literature should occupy the position of greatest prominence in the curriculum. I do not imply that all other study should or can grow out of literature study. However, literature study can be related profitably to composition and language study at a number of points. The purpose of this chapter is to identify some of these points.

LITERATURE STUDY AND ORAL
AND WRITTEN COMPOSITION

Spoken language, surprisingly long neglected in English classrooms, is today for the first time getting serious attention by the profession. Most of this impetus comes from England. The following statement by Andrew Wilkinson represents the current mood:

> The spoken language in England has been shamefully neglected. There are many reasons for this. One, certainly, is that teachers and educa-

tionists have not considered it important. Of the oral skills, reading aloud (which few people are ever called upon to use) has had some attention in the classroom, usually for the wrong reasons. But the ability to put one word of one's own text to another of one's own in speech, to create rather than to repeat, a skill which everybody is exercising most of the time, has not been regarded as worthy of serious attention.[1]

The recognition of the need for greater attention to spoken language in general has accelerated attempts to integrate oral language activities with literature study. The two major types of such activities are oral reading of literature and dramatic exercises.

Oral reading of literature.   When Andrew Wilkinson, in the statement cited above, spoke of oral reading getting attention "usually for the wrong reasons," he probably was thinking of such practices as having students take turns reading aloud a selection of literature as a substitute for prepared teaching of the selection or of the word-by-word oral reading of Shakespeare or some other author the class has had difficulty reading silently. Despite such deadly procedures as these, reading aloud is an important concomitant of literature study. But if it is to be profitable, two rather obvious conditions must obtain: the reading should be prepared and it should have a valid purpose. Impromptu reading often results in the student stumbling through a selection to the agony of himself and his class, and is a sure antidote for enjoyment of literature. One can think of occasions when impromptu reading might be appropriate—citing passages to support points in discussion, for example—but any extended reading should be prepared in advance. It is not avuncular to say that this admonition applies as well to the teacher who is planning to read something for the first time.

Oral reading by the teacher is an important ingredient in the literature classroom. Some teachers spend too much time reading aloud, to the detriment of their students' developing individual silent reading abilities. But again and again, studies of the characteristics which make English teachers popular with students show that oral reading by the teacher is remembered with pleasure. The teacher who is a skilled oral

---

[1] National Association for the Teaching of English, *Some Aspects of Oracy,* II (Summer 1965), 3.

reader and interpreter of literature has a real advantage, and there is some tendency in teacher education to include, or at least encourage prospective teachers of English to get, some training in oral interpretation.

What is "a valid purpose," which was posited as the second condition necessary for effective use of oral reading of literature, may be variously interpreted by different teachers. It seems however that there are two major purposes: the esthetic one of providing another dimension of experience with literature and the practical one of helping students gain further comprehension and appreciation of selections.

As I have said already, it is important to give students the opportunity to hear skillful oral reading of prose and poetry. The reading need not come only from students and teachers since there are rich opportunities to hear professional readers and literary artists themselves on recordings. The National Council of Teachers of English and various commercial agencies have available a great array of recorded readings from which every English department should have a well-selected stock.

Discussion of literature accompanied by oral reading can often increase comprehension and enrich appreciation. For example, it is sometimes helpful for students to hear a recorded reading of a selection while they follow the printed text. This method may be especially beneficial to students of lesser ability.

Oral reading of whole selections or even of selected passages also will often increase students' awareness of the effect of literary devices. Certain poems, for instance, must be read aloud if some students are to sense the effect of particular types of rhyme or meter or understand such devices as onomatopoeia. The significance of the choice of certain patterns of syntax in prose may become clearer too when passages are read aloud.

Consideration of the contribution oral reading may make is an essential part of the planning of any lesson in literature.

Dramatic activities. Dramatic activities of various kinds long have been prominent in elementary schools but have had little place in English programs at the secondary level. Some educators, particularly in England, are now demanding that great emphasis be put on dramatic activities at all levels, both related and unrelated to literature that is studied. Several purposes are cited: to provide imaginative experience; to promote fluency and skill of expression; to provide therapy for the student; and to aid in personality development, comprehension, and preparation for literature that is to be read. Concerning these last two purposes, J. W. Patrick Creber writes:

> It must be clear that many novels offer situations that lend themselves to dramatic treatment, but it is worth noting that this is essentially a two-way process, for the acting out of such situations may be expected to modify and deepen the actors' comprehension of the novel whence they were taken. Furthermore the children's receptivity to a particular play may sometimes be notably improved by dramatic improvisation on some of the situations, themes, and characters it contains, before the play itself is read. It is possible also to act scenes that are not in the play, but which are taken for granted or referred to. Occasionally the understanding of the bias of the play may be helped by enacting a scene on the same lines as one actually in it, but concentrating upon the feelings of characters who achieve no such prominence in the original. Devices such as these are particularly helpful when working on plays where the language constitutes an initial barrier that is often never effectively overcome when the text is studied *in vacuo*.[2]

Another Englishman, Frank Whitehead, asserts that there is strong reason for "giving dramatic work a place of honour near the very centre of the curriculum" and he has treated dramatic activities in detail in his book, *The Disappearing Dais*.[3] Whitehead believes that the main value of dramatization of literature in the classroom is that it is a "fulfilling" experience, "a vital imaginative experience," and an "outlet for wish fulfillment." Whitehead believes, as Creber does, that mime is an essential activity in preparing for dramatization with speech, and dramatization to him is central to the study of literature. In his book, Whitehead gives many specific suggestions on the handling of dramatization in the classroom.

Closely paralleling the views of Whitehead are those of James Moffett. In his monograph, *Drama: What Is Happening,* Moffett argues that "drama and speech are central to a language curriculum, not peripheral," and he discusses several types of speech and dramatic activi-

---

[2] *Sense and Sensitivity* (University of London Press, 1965), p. 93.
[3] London: Chatto & Windus, 1966.

ties, two of which are closely related to study of literature—dramatic improvisation and performing of scripts.[4]

In dramatic improvisation, students create and act out an original drama based on a selection of literature or a part of it. Moffett assigns various values to this activity, but its specific contributions to literature study he expresses as follows:

> Before a child can enjoy drama in script form—play reading—he can do so by creating the imitative actions of which scripts are a blueprint. Later, his power to bring a script alive in his mind is constantly recharged by his continued experience in inventing dramas. For narrative, improvisation renders a special service: it translates *what happened* back to *what is happening*. . . . For older students, converting narrative to drama demonstrates the relationship of the two: plays specify what narrative summarizes, and narrative, unlike drama, is told by someone addressing us.
>
> And, finally, improvisation can be used as an entree into a literary work soon to be read: the teacher abstracts key situations—say, Cassius' efforts to persuade Brutus to join the conspiracy—and assigns this as a situation to improvise before students read the work, so that when they do read it they already have an understanding of what is happening and of how differently the characters *might* have behaved. This kind of prelude also involves students more with the text.[5]

Performing of scripts, Moffett says, may involve dramatizing short plays written either by the students themselves or by professionals. As indicated in the passage above, he shares the view of Creber and Whitehead that dramatizing is a necessary prelude to reading plays silently.

Writing about Literature

Much of the writing program, though not necessarily all of it, can grow out of the study of literature. There seem to be three basic kinds of writing related to literature study: (1) Noncritical writing for which ideas or literary elements in a selection serve as springboards; (2) Interpretative and critical writing; (3) Imitative writing.

---

[4] Champaign, Ill.: NCTE, 1967.
[5] Moffett, pp. 27–28.

Ideas or literary elements as springboards.   Writing that stems from ideas or meanings in a work is common in English classrooms; writing triggered by literary elements much less so. The following is a fairly typical example of writing activity of the first type, devised by the author for a tenth-grade class:

> This unit is entitled "Conflict in Allegiances." The kind of conflict symbolized in *Antigone* is a universal human problem. Perhaps this problem of conflict of allegiances is an especially crucial one for young people. For example, a high school student often may be caught in a situation in which his friends put pressure on him to do one thing, and his parents, to do another. Write a paper in which you identify some of the kinds of conflicts of allegiances in which high school students may become involved. Give examples of specific conflicts. You need not write about yourself, but rather write about high school students generally.

In this type of writing literature serves as motivation and furnishes preparation. Writing and literature can be brought together in a more reciprocal relationship when writing activities are designed to clarify or reinforce understanding of literary structure and technique. The difference between this kind of writing and critical and interpretative writing may not be apparent immediately, but the following example of a writing activity designed by the author may show that there is a difference:

> (After a reading of Pierre Boulle's *Face of a Hero*)
> Irony is evident, as we have noted, in *Face of a Hero* from the title through the final scene. There are various uses of the term "irony," but in literature irony, in general, involves a discrepancy between surface reality and actual reality in what is said or in what happens. Irony, humorous or otherwise, is very common, of course, in everyday experience.There are many stock situations in popular movies, television programs, and comic strips, for example, based on humorous irony. Johnny's father wonders why Johnny suddenly is treating him with elaborate consideration. Johnny replies that he has decided his father is "a great old pop." But Johnny and the reader know that Johnny is about to get a bad report card. Or Maisie, the glamorous blonde, meets her rival and treats her with dripping sweetness, but we know that she has the urge to kill. Write a brief paper in which you describe a scene or event

or relate an incident which was ironic. The paper may be humorous or serious, and what you write may be based on your actual experience or may be imagined.

An interesting and different way of developing this basic relationship between literature and writing is illustrated by Rev. William J. O'Malley, S. J.[6] In teaching poetry, for example, Father O'Malley has students read a poem like Masters' "Levy Silver" in which there are the lines: "Why did I sell you plated silver? . . . The question at stake is why did you buy?" Then he asks the students to write "brief, concrete pictures of the faces and clothes and actions of a couple buying imitation jewelry in a pawn shop."

Father O'Malley's premise for his techniques is that "Writing exercises should be geared to elicit student reduplication of the elements of the poem." He illustrates his method, also, with traditional devices of poetry. He gives students statements or phrases with blanks where key words or groups of words are to be filled in. Some examples follow. (The italicized words are those filled in by the students.)

Simile: "The old man's eyes looked like *freshly opened oysters.*"
Personification: "Poverty is a *child with a runny nose.*"
Onomatopeia: "the *whump* of motar shells."

Interpretation and criticism. Interpretation and criticism of literature continues to be, as in the past, the most frequent type of writing about literature in English classes. Such writing can take many forms but the overall objective of any particular form used in the high school is to deepen student understanding and appreciation of literature.

The major criterion, to the author, for student assignments in interpretative and critical writing is that they be addressed to specific points about a work. Overall commentary on a selection often is of little value to the student in sharpening his perception. Among the most appropriate *foci* for critical and interpretative writing in the high school are these: analysis of actions of characters; discussion of the ways character is developed in a work; interpretation of specific passages, events, or symbols; comparison of works on specific points; dis-

[6] "Literary Craftsmanship: The Integration of Literature and Composition," *English Journal*, LII (April 1963), 247–252.

cussion of the ways theme is developed in a work; criticism of specific techniques; support or refutation of given generalizations about a work. Edgar V. Roberts' book, *Writing Themes about Literature,* treats and illustrates fifteen kinds of interpretative and critical writing.[7] Though designed for college freshmen, the book is a useful resource for high school teachers.

Imitative writing. A stock-in-trade of the English class earlier in the century, imitative writing apparently is the object of a minor revival today. The specific values of imitative writing long have been debated. The basic argument for it has been based on analogies: for example, one will watch a bowling contest with greater enjoyment and understanding if he has tried his hand at bowling. Yet it is difficult to establish objective evidence in this area; consequently there is no basis for believing that imitative writing contributes to greater ability in reading literature.

Aside from its possible contribution to literature study, imitative writing may have inherent values, of course, in providing another kind of imaginative experience and in injecting variety into the classroom. Certainly students should be given a chance to try their hands at imaginative forms from fable to *haiku,* though rarely should students be assigned imaginative writing that is to be graded by the teacher.

Imitating stylistic and syntactic models apparently is the major direction of imitative writing today. Such exercises usually connect writing and factual or nonfictional prose with which this chapter has not been concerned. Imitation of these models has more to do with skill in writing than with literature study. However, James F. McCampbell illustrates a broader use of imitating models. He has students read a descriptive passage from Kipling, for example. They analyze the patterns of the passage, then invent their own substance to fit the patterns. Maintaining that "The structural conventions of our language are a key to understanding literature as well as improving composition,[8] McCampbell urges inductive analysis of the models by the entire class, then small-group writing, and finally individual writing.

[7] Englewood Cliffs, N.J.: Prentice-Hall, 1964.
[8] "Using Models for Improving Composition," *English Journal,* LV (September 1966), 772–776.

LITERATURE AND LANGUAGE STUDY

Broadening of language study has been a key trend in the secondary English curriculum in recent years. More excitement, in fact, has been generated by the "new linguistics" than by any other aspect of English study. Until the last few years language study in the junior and senior high school English curriculum meant traditional grammar, "correction" of usage, vocabulary development and use of the dictionary, and mechanics of language. This range may still exist in some school programs, but in many others the language program is now concerned with such additional aspects as nature of language, semantics, phonology, dialects, lexicography, history of the language, and transformational grammar.

The general explosion of activity and knowledge in linguistics has quickened interest in linguistic analysis of literature, as noted in the preceding chapter. Some scholars, including James McCampbell, maintain that understanding of language structure furthers comprehension of literature, and no one would deny the probability of such a general relationship. However, no specific evidence yet exists as to how study of language structure can aid comprehension in reading. Literature is language used in certain ways and in certain forms, so in the basic sense, study of literature *is* study of language. Recognizing this, the staff of the Curriculum Study Center in English at the University of Minnesota has built a secondary English curriculum on certain basic concepts about language which are illustrated and reinforced at each of the grades. Literature becomes a part of the study of these concepts.

Whether or not one agrees that such an approach will allow literature study to assume its full dimensions, one can agree that literature can become involved in any aspect of language study from history of the language to phonology. How to develop approaches that will exploit relationships for the benefit of both language study and literature study is frontier work that needs doing.

One such relationship with mutual rewards for language and literature study is in the field of dialects where students can study the use of dialects in literature. Illustrating possible activities in this connection is the following from *Discovering American Dialects* by Roger W. Shuy:

1. Compare a dialogue sequence in *The Yearling* or *Hie to the Hunters* with one in *The Catcher in the Rye* or *It's All Right, Cat!* Note the differences between back country and urban spoken language. Are the vocabulary differences related to different times, different needs, and different environments?

2. Discover some of the influences of Norwegian or American English by reading John Van Druten's play, *I Remember Mama*. You may do the same thing with Ole Rolvaag's *Giants in the Earth* and *Peder Victorious* as well as Martha Ostenso's *The Mad Carews*. Look up the Norwegianisms in a Norwegian-English dictionary.

3. Make a list of Pennsylvania Dutch words and phrases (especially in word order) found in Elsie Singmaster's short story "The Belsnickel" and in Patterson Greene's play *Papa Is All*.

4. Note the Nebraska vocabulary found in the novels of Willa Cather (*O Pioneers!* and *My Antónia*, for example). On the basis of the word lists given in chapter 2 would you call Nebraska a Northern or Midland dialect area?

5. Observe the influences of Yiddish on American English in the short stories of Arthur Kober ("That Man Is Here Again" and "Bella, Bella Kissed a Fella," for example) and in the novels of Leo Rosten (*The Education of Hyman Kaplan*), Bernard Malamud (*The Natural*), and Saul Bellow (*Seize the Day; Herzog*).

6. Collect examples of Chicago Irishisms in the novels of Finley P. Dunne (*Mr. Dooley Says* and other "Mr. Dooley" novels) and James T. Farrell (*Studs Lonigan*).

7. Note east Tennessee vocabulary and syntax in the novels of Mary Murfree (*In the Tennessee Mountains* and *The Prophet of the Great Smoky Mountains*) and in the collections of short stories by Mildred Haun (*That Hawk's Done Gone*).

8. Observe the different dialects found in Mark Twain's *Huckleberry Finn*. Do Huck and Jim speak a prestige dialect? Does the fact that Twain realistically describes the speech of Negro slaves affect his argument against slavery and racial discrimination?

9. Note the grammatical structure and vocabulary of Quaker speech as you observe it in the short stories of Jessamyn West ("The Battle of Finney's Ford") and Mabel Hunt ("Little Girl with Seven Names"). Pay particular attention to the second person personal pronouns and third person singular present tense verb forms. In Albert C. Baugh's *A History of the English Language*,

look up the history of these forms, noting especially the influence of George Fox and the Quaker movement.

10. Examine Irene Hunt's short story "Across Five Aprils" for its use of eye-dialect. Assuming that the author wants us to note the maturity of Jethro and the simple-minded weakness of Eb, how does her use of eye-dialect contribute to this purpose? Note especially the words fer (for), git (get), comfert (comfort), jest (just), fergit (forget), yore (your), stummick (stomach), ner (nor), kin (can). Who uses them? Who does not? Should an author have only the "bad guys" use dialect? [9]

Underlying what has been said in this chapter is the author's fear that the rather wide acceptance of a "tricomponent" curriculum in English of language, literature, and composition may lead to compartmentalization of these components and a resultant dehumanization of the curriculum in which language study smacks of the scientific and composition seems solely skill oriented. All of the components can represent humanistic study in themselves, but when they are related at appropriate points the sum is greater than the study of each part in isolation can produce.

THE MASS MEDIA IN THE ENGLISH CLASS *

One of the most obvious principles of teaching is that the clearer the presentation of a lesson or an idea, the more it will be remembered by students. The obligation to be clear, to ask unambiguous questions, to delineate the limits of a particular subject, to lead students through an orderly series of lessons, is clearly an obligation which is accepted unquestioningly by any teacher worthy of the name. It is also an obligation accepted by school administrators, who spend a great deal of time and effort in designing student schedules so that the school day will be—from the students' point of view—highly organized, full of precise injunctions about where the student should be and when he should be there. To do otherwise would be to invite chaos. Yet it is precisely this constant striving for order and pattern and sequence which brings the *school* (considered as an environment) into direct

* Written by Daniel A. Lindley, Jr., Yale University.
[9] Champaign, Ill.: NCTE, 1967, pp. 61–62.

and sometimes irreconcilable conflict with the *world*. Insofar as the world itself is ambiguous and puzzling, the clarity of the school world seems unrealistic and over-simple. The school is, in fact, in conflict with what Marshall McLuhan has called the "electric age," and the student, who has been exposed from infancy to the "cool" and involving medium of television, is quite likely to be put off by the "hot" and linear patterns of school. The terms "hot" and "cool" are used here in the way McLuhan uses them, and will be discussed further below.

This conflict between the world of school and the world as experienced by the student is a central problem for the teacher who wishes to teach the mass media. For if we assume, with McLuhan, that the student is already more involved with television and his own music than he is with what is going on in the English class, then the teacher, by bringing these media into the classroom, appears to be doing so merely to capitalize on the student's involvement; in other words, the teacher runs the risk of appearing to try to "con" the student into being interested in English-in-general. Furthermore, the teacher's way of understanding and analyzing media may be far removed from the student's way of understanding the same items. For example, it is easy to imagine a poetry lesson based on George Harrison's lyrics to the Beatles' song, "Within You, Without You"—the theme of which is surely similar to that of "The Love Song of J. Alfred Prufrock" or Emily Dickinson's "I Cannot Live With You," or even—stretching the point a little—"Richard Cory." And having gotten to "Richard Cory," the teacher could bring in Simon and Garfunkel's version of that poem, and so on. But this method, which appears so logical and appealing, may appear to the student as essentially phony, an attempt on the part of the teacher to buy his attention and his loyalty. And this problem must be overcome in teaching the mass media. For what the student finds in "Within You, Without You" may have nothing to do with the associations the teacher finds in it. In general, the teacher's problem is not to "relate" the mass media to the existing curriculum in English, because that would merely aggravate an already existing conflict between the world and the school.

The solution to this problem is to involve students in the actual production of materials which use the technologies of the media. This means the making of films, videotapes, speech essays, and taped "expansions" of poems, news stories, and the like.

Most teachers—perhaps especially English teachers—are naturally somewhat intimidated by the prospect of having to master various machines, such as movie cameras or tape recorders. But in many schools, the advent of the electronically amplified guitar and the re-recorded lyric has brought with it a legion of technologically sophisticated students who would be delighted to run the machines needed.

Let us consider first the making of a film. What follows is an account of an actual project undertaken by a teacher who had never before made a film. The project was undertaken with the basic objective of teaching the concepts of unity, coherence and purpose in writing, and the idea was to use the making of a film to demonstrate what these principles actually mean in a concrete situation: after all, a film must have these qualities for the same reasons that apply to a piece of writing. Another idea, that of point of view, is also implicit in the production of a film.

The first step was to look at several short films, mostly with the idea of learning together some elementary principles of camera use. During this phase of work, several books were a considerable help with terminology. The effects of fades, dissolves, and various kinds of cuts became increasingly obvious when attention was paid to them. The motion of the camera (in panning and dollying) turned out to have profound effects on how the viewer came to understand what was going on. Students began to notice many details of filming which they had taken for granted. For example, in the film *Shane,* students saw that if an actor is supposed to be walking (or riding) from the farm to the town, he must always be photographed from the same side, so that he will move in the same direction throughout the sequence. They noticed also that a person moving from left to right on the screen seems to be going *toward* something, while a person moving from right to left seems to be *going away*.

The next step was the making of an actual film. The football coach kindly loaned the 16-millimeter camera used to make game movies. Economics dictated that the film be short—film and processing are expensive items. The students, working in small committees, came up with several plots. Some were too elaborate and had to be rejected. The one finally agreed upon by the class (the teacher scrupulously stayed out of the decision-making process) was a simple enough story: a teacher becomes so carried away with his irrelevant lesson that he does not notice that his students are sneaking out of his class —all but one, who stays because he has fallen asleep. After a number of scenes showing the teacher teaching (frantic and oblivious) and the students sneaking out, the movie ends with a close-up of the sleeping student. Although the whole film is only four minutes long, there are eighteen different scenes in it. A tape recording of a honky-tonk piano is used as backgroud music, which underlines the silent film style in which the picture was made.

A project such as this one has several desirable outcomes. In the first place, the necessity for careful planning and script writing becomes apparent. Many students who are "reluctant writers" will write a great deal of material for such a project when they understand that the success of the finished product really does depend on the care with which it is planned. But just as important is the fact that students see that they are involved with basic issues in communication: the film must make sense to *anyone* who may see it. It cannot have a private meaning for one particular group of students, or for just one teacher, as most student writing does. Communicating to an unknown audience is a rigorous discipline by comparison.

All the above remarks about film apply with equal force to the making of videotapes by students. There is, however, a trap for the unwary teacher in this medium. Videotape, unlike film, makes it possible to see results immediately. But if mistakes are made, there is no expense involved in re-shooting, as there is with film. The comparative ease with which videotapes may be made is all too likely to tempt teachers to make videotapes of what are really stage productions: students acting out scenes from plays, and the like. This is in no sense a use of the *medium,* which should be treated in the same way that film is, with the same considerations of camera use, scene continuity, and so on. In addition and especially if a portable camera is available— students can put together news and feature programs involving people and events in the school and the community. Here again, intelligent choices must be made: what is important to show and why? how much time should each segment of the show receive? Once again, the old issues of unity, coherence, and emphasis reappear in this use of the medium. Note however—and the point cannot be made too strongly—that it would be a gross error for the teacher to call attention to these issues *as such,* for that would be to behave as a teacher is expected to behave: that is, he would be making serious intellectual efforts designed to take all the fun out. The concepts will inevitably assert themselves in the planning and the execution phases just described. If the teacher hangs official labels on these principles, the time to do it is when the product—tape or film—is finished.

It is true that both film and videotape imply a certain amount of technical skill on *someone's* part. On the other hand, the speech essay involves nothing more intricate than a tape recorder and a record player. Basically, in this exercise an extended statement of a single idea is recorded (usually a statement made "off the cuff" by some reasonably articulate person); the original tape is edited, and relevant material is added to give it more coherence and force. Tapes of radio or television broadcasts may be altered and augmented in the same way. The simplest technique for this exercise is to use a stereophonic tape recorder, putting the speech on one track and the added material on the other. An example of the effectiveness of this technique is provided by Simon and Garfunkel's *The Seven O'Clock News*. This recording consists of short news items on topical events such as: "Richard Speck, accused slayer of eight student nurses . . . Nixon predicts the Vietnam war could last five more years . . ." and similar fragments—*and,* playing simultaneously, a sentimental rendering of *Silent Night* in the background. The bitterly ironic contrast is obvious but extremely powerful. It is this sort of juxtaposition which is central to the technique of the speech essay. And again, the material to be added, and the editing of the original speech, are matters which students must decide in the process of planning and executing such a production. By way of a demonstration it is helpful to have prepared in advance an example of the speech essay. The script of a portion of one such essay is provided here merely as a suggestive example. (Note: if a stereophonic tape recorder is not available, similar effects may be obtained by reading the speech part of the material into a microphone while records or other material is added simultaneously—by other people speaking at the same time, for example. Note also that, if a record player is used, it is possible to vary its volume appropriately as the speech segment proceeds. The more the speech elements are obscured —within limits—by other sounds, the more involved the audience will be in attempting to understand what is happeninng. Intense audience involvement is an essential principle of all mass media, and we will return to it in the general discussion which closes this chapter.) Here is a transcript of a portion of a speech essay:

Narrator's Voice

Tallahassee Democrat, Florida's Capital Newspaper
Sunday Morning, May 26, 1968 — Twenty Cents
Partly cloudy—rain
High 88 low 70

A Poor Vigil Held at Capitol
They came bearing signs. They sat in a one-hour silent vigil on the steps of the Capitol. They prayed together and departed. Florida State University Graduate School of Social Welfare showed up in force. A graduate student said, "We support the proposals for bettering the plight of the poor overwhelmingly . . ."
Pompidou Suspends Right of Assembly
Paris' Latin Quarter was calm last night after three days of rioting . . . Students linked arms and helped police . . .
You can't see or touch integrity . . . but it's one of our most valuable assets . . . that's why we're proud to carry Kuppenheimer suits. Come in and see why. Alford Brothers, 212 South Monroe.

New FSU Phase Seen . . . (AP) A student leader says that the protest movement at FSU has entered a new phase with demonstrators more discouraged than they were and wary of a stall by the administration. The president of the 15,200-member student body said that the committee focused the issues involved when it recommended that the FSU president be insulated from student publications.
Bob is twenty years old . . . a Junior at Florida State University, majoring in English. He will leave for Florence shortly to spend a year abroad. I asked him over the other night . . . to talk about education.

Bob's Voice:

So much of college is removed from life in the outside world, outside the community of scholars . . . one thing I would do would make it necessary—I would have a three-hour course in ghetto studies, poor-people studies, right here in Tallahassee. On three sides of the campus you've got ghettoes. So many of the kids go all the way through college and don't know what's there. Anyone who gets a four-year degree and doesn't know what's across the street. Just what kind of people are there? I think it's an aspect you don't get on campus. // * The whole

* Double slashes indicate places where tape has been edited.

idea of this course is that you're not going to read your damn sociological studies. You're not going to read statistics. You're not going to read graphs. You're not going to talk to a PhD sitting in Classroom Building "A" talking about black people. You're gonna be talking *to* black people—who don't understand the complexity of their problems, they just know they have them. // Let's do the same thing with people in Appalachia. // You see, all we're getting is a view of what the upper 10 percent think. All we know is what the PhD's think. // We sit in front of a textbook and when we're through we get a sheet of paper that says we have a degree. // I think we need more firsthand information and less secondhand information. // To get on to another question that puzzles a lot of people today, and that is, what the hell is going on with young people, what do they think, what do they want? What are they doing, what are they trying to do? Well, first of all, it's not a homogeneous group, but I think the majority of them is increasingly questioning the values that have been handed to us, spoon-fed to us for so many years, and all of a sudden we find that they don't hold up; they just don't hold up, they just don't work // they don't hold up // they don't hold up, they just don't work // they don't hold up, they just don't work //

We don't have a set of values, of dictums, that we can rely on, to show us the way //

> Beatles—"It's Getting Better All the Time" brought up in volume as the following proceeds:

We're moving so fast now, and I think that education has to change, to keep up with it; we have to take a more total approach //

Narrator's Voice:

McLuhan talks about the "information overload."
He says, "the young student today grows up in an electrically configured world. It is a world not of wheels but of circuits, not of fragments but of integral patterns. The student today lives mythically and in depth . . ." //

> Beatles—"It's Getting Better All the Time"

Bob's Voice:

// Things move so fast we can't keep up with them. And now education has to change. It has to be—the leader of the change, it has to be on the vanguard. I think the textbook is fading because I think we have other media that are taking over. Simon and Garfunkel are college graduates; they are spokesmen, they are, as accurately as anyone, reflecting what is happening. By the same token, we've got a hell of a lot of conservative //

Narrator's Voice (quoting McLuhan):
Technologies begin to perform the functions of art, in making us aware of the psychic and social consequences of technology. Art as antienvironment becomes more than ever a means of training perception and judgment. Art offered as a consumer commodity rather than as a means of training perception is as ludicrous and snobbish as always. //

Narrator's Voice (quoting newspaper):
Remember your graduate with the most significant gift of all:
Magnavox Solid State Stereo // 1968 Zenith Color TV. We'll take a trade to make you an even better deal // A Mercury outboard is designed to catch fish, not weeds // 1968 Zenith Color TV // Magnavox // Play it cool with an ARA Auto air conditioner // (*Bob's Voice:*) If all of a sudden they know that they can prevent hookworm / Financing available, Capitol Lincoln-Mercury // *Bob's Voice:* . . . that's something. What . . . the hell is going on with young people. The majority of them are increasingly questioning the values that have been handed to us . . . they don't hold up. They just don't work. // They don't hold up. They just don't work. //

Simon and Garfunkel's *Sound of Silence:* volume brought slowly up then volume is dropped until the tape runs on in silence.

It can readily be seen that the basis for the foregoing speech essay is to be found in the remarks of "Bob," the college student, and that the thesis of his remarks provides the theme for the essay as a whole. There are, however, other possible starting points besides informal speech. One particularly promising technique is that of the "expansion" of a poem. In this use of the medium of tape, a poem (preferably as read by the poet) is used as the starting point for associations which are added to the poem as it proceeds. For example, in "The Love Song of J. Alfred Prufrock" there is this line, "There will be time to murder and create." In making a tape of the poem, the reading was interrupted at that line, and the voice of Chief Justice Earl Warren reading the oath of office to President Kennedy was added. The effect is both poignant and startling. Another line in the poem, "They will say/How his hair is growing thin," is recorded just as the poet reads it, but the lyrics of the Beatles' "When I'm Sixty-Four" can be heard in the background. Again, after the line "I have measured out my life with coffee spoons," the words "coffee spoons" are made to echo in the following lines. The final product is certainly more than a simple recording of a reading of the poem. Rather, it represents the poem and some possible associations by a sensitive reader.

There are two hazards in working with poetry in this way. The first is that the technique puts a premium on random, rather than on disciplined, associations with the poem. In other words, there is some possibility that students may get the idea that they are quite free to find anything they can think of in any poem under consideration, because anything may seem to "fit" with the poem as the tape is being made. The teacher, on the other hand, may quite reasonably object to this treatment of the poem as a source for any and all associations, however wild. A poem, after all, is not a Rorschach inkblot, and there is discipline and orderly method involved in working through to the meaning of a good poem. The need for discipline indeed is in conflict with the freewheeling spontaneity which should be operating when students are thinking up material to add to the recording of the "straight" poem. The anxiety on the part of the teacher that the poem itself may disappear under a cacophony of speeches and songs is entirely understandable; and for this reason the making of such tapes is probably best done as a means of entry into the study of poetry, not as the entire study. To use this technique in this way is entirely appropriate, not only because it produces all sorts of excitement and curiosity, but—more importantly—because it demonstrates that the teacher recognizes that any person reading a good poem for the first time *ought* to think of all sorts of things, *some* of which may turn out to be irrelevant, but *many* of which will continue to enrich the poem for any reader. Much of the teaching of poetry carried on since the development of the "new criticism" has represented an overrational search for *the* meaning of the poem, with a consequent denial of what the student may be developing as *his* meaning of it. The tapes recognize and reward whatever associations students may bring to a poem. Thus the students feel more free to get into the poem, and the teacher learns something about the students' ways of thinking. After all, the tape is made from what the students bring to the poem.

What the students bring.   Throughout this section on the media, the emphasis has been on student production and student creativity. Thus these exercises in the media have not been plans to teach *about* them (except in incidental ways) but rather to involve students in the media themselves. The distinction is a crucial one because, as I pointed out at the beginning of this chapter, it is very important that work on those techniques which touch the lives of students so intimately in the "electric age" does *not* appear to them as just another part of the school routine. McLuhan says,

> The young student today grows up in an electrically configured world. It is a world not of wheels but of circuits, not of fragments but of integral patterns. The student today *lives* mythically and in depth. At school, however, he encounters a situation organized by means of classified information. The subjects are unrelated. They are visually conceived in terms of a blueprint. The student can find no possible means of involvement for himself, nor can he discover how the educational scene relates to the "mythic" world of electronically processed data and experience that he takes for granted. As one IBM executive puts it, "My children had lived several lifetimes compared to their grandparents when they began Grade One.[10]

Unless, in short, students are involved with the media, there is no way to teach anything about them. Students presumably know everything about the media except how it feels to create in them. So the teacher's task is simply one of providing that chance.

SELECTED BIBLIOGRAPHY

Barnes, Douglas (Ed.), *Drama in the Classroom* (Champaign, Ill.: NCTE, 1968).
  A summary of the discussions of the subject at the Dartmouth Seminar, including a drama syllabus for the secondary school.
Cannon, Garland, "Linguistics and Literature," *College English,* XXI (February 1960), 255–260.
  Considers possibilities for relating linguistics to the teaching of literature.
Cohen, B. Bernard, *Writing about Literature* (Glenview, Ill.: Scott, Foresman, 1963).

[10] Marshall McLuhan, *Understanding Media: The Extension of Man* (New York: McGraw-Hill, 1964), p. 9.

Reviews various principles of writing and analysis and focuses on the practical problems encountered in writing about literature.

Creber, J. W. Patrick, *Sense and Sensitivity* (London: University of London Press, 1965), pp. 85–108.
A discussion of the values of dramatic activity and its relation to the teaching of literature.

Evertts, Eldonna L., "Composition through Literature," *Instructor,* LXXV (March 1966), 105.
Praises the teaching units from the Nebraska Curriculum Center which stress the teaching of composition through literature.

Farrell, Edmund J., *English, Education, and the Electronic Revolution* (Champaign, Ill.: NCTE, 1967).
A comprehensive discussion of the implications for the classroom of the electronic age, with a chapter on the specific place of various media in the English classroom and an extensive bibliography.

Judy, Stephen, "Style and the Teaching of Literature and Composition," *English Journal,* LVI (February 1967), 281–285.
Argues that teaching style as "effects" or connotations created by language and manipulated by writers, the teacher helps the student to understand style in literature and supplies him with more concrete advice and instruction in writing.

Marckwardt, Albert H., "Linguistics and the Study of Literature," *Linguistics and the Teaching of English* (Bloomington: Indiana University Press, 1966), pp. 100–121.
Holds that linguists offer ordered, systematic procedures dealing with the language of literature.

McCampbell, James F., "Using Models for Improving Composition," *English Journal,* LV (September 1966), 772–776.
Describes a plan for teaching composition through imitation of models.

Media and Methods. Published monthly, September through May. Publishing office: 134 North 13th Street, Philadelphia, Pa. 19107.
A highly useful periodical with helpful articles on a wide range of topics relating to the media and the classroom.

Moffett, James, *Drama: What Is Happening?* (Champaign, Ill.: NCTE, 1967).
A plea for greater stress on oral language and discussion of the nature and function of dramatic activities in the classroom.

O'Malley, William J., S.J., "Literary Craftsmanship: The Integration of Literature and Composition," *English Journal,* LII (April 1963), 247–252.
Specific description of how literature and writing can be related.

Postman, Neil and Charles Weingartner, "Linguistics and Reading," in *Linguistics: A Revolution in Teaching* (New York: Delacorte Press, 1966), pp. 176–196.

Treats the two kinds of problems involved in reading: "cracking the code" and analyzing and evaluating the language. Attention is given to different responses to passages, according to the meaning of meaning.

Roberts, Edgar V., *Writing Themes about Literature* (Englewood Cliffs, N.J.: Prentice-Hall, 1964).

Identifies and illustrates a number of types of writing about literature.

Tacey, W. C., "Cooperative Activities for English and Speech Teachers," *Education*, LXXX (April 1960), 463–467.

Suggests plans for unifying the study of literature and speech.

Vanderlain, Aldona S., "Dramatic Approach in Teaching Literature," *Baltimore Bulletin of Education*, XXVII (March 1960), 28–30.

Suggests dramatizing literature as a way of interpreting it. *Treasure Island* is the example.

Whitehead, Frank, *The Disappearing Dais* (London: Chatto & Windus, 1966), pp. 122–151.

Goes into detail on how to organize and conduct dramatic activities in the classroom.

part two
TEACHING PROBLEMS

The student's involvement in the literature program in the junior and senior high school may take various forms. He will discuss selections of literature in the total class and in small groups. He will read individually. He will write about what he reads and he will participate in oral activities based on what he reads. He will be introduced to various approaches to a work of literature, and he will be involved in units of study organized in various ways. But underlying all his activities is the need to learn to read the several genres of literature as maturely as his potential will permit.

Alan C. Purves and Victoria Rippere, from an analysis of students' written responses to literature, have identified four basic categories of response: *Engagement-involvement*—". . . the various ways by which the writer indicates his surrender to the literary work, by which he informs his reader of the ways in which he has experienced the work or its various aspects." *Perception*—the reader's perception of structure, technique and craftsmanship, the "ways in which a person looks at the work as an object distinct from himself." *Interpretation* —the reader's attempts to find meaning, to generalize, to draw inferences, to relate a work to the universe. *Evaluation*—the reader's judgments of the goodness or badness of the work.[1]

This classification of responses is useful as a paradigm for the teaching of reading skills. The teacher cannot teach responses, but he can

[1] *Elements of Writing about a Literary Work,* Research Report No. 9 (Champaign, Ill.: NCTE, 1968).

help his students develop skills that will enable them to become sophisticated in each of the four dimensions of response. The net result should be a continually deepening experience with literature. The power of imaginative entry into a work of literature is the basis for engagement or involvement. Again, the teacher cannot teach imaginative entry but he can promote it and help set the stage for it; and he can help students to overcome the obstacles to imaginative entry that the various genres may present. Underlying the power of perception is the understanding of conventions and devices and the ability to relate them to the whole of a work of literature. Of course, interpretation and judgment of the artistic and personal significance of a work of literature will depend on everything the student has learned about reading and on his ability to relate his own experience to the work.

The following four chapters, though not organized identically, are all concerned with the ways in which students can be helped to develop and refine the skills and understandings identified above.

5
Fiction in the Literature Program

The decline of fiction since World War II has been noted by many observers in the literary world. In contemporary publishing, nonfiction titles far outnumber those of fiction, and magazines devote much less space to fiction than they did some years ago. But if the post-World War II era may be a golden age of nonfiction, fiction nevertheless is far from moribund. The novel flourishes today and may be the characteristic form of our time as, for example. the epic and verse drama were in certain earlier periods.

In fact, it is quite possible that there has been no real "decline" in the popularity of fiction, only less reason on the part of the general public to seek fictionalized experience in printed form. Television is now the chief medium for popular fiction, satisfying mass taste better than does the printed page. The popular magazine story has lost its patrons to the television screen. For the high school teacher, television can be a stimulant as well as a depressant in teaching literature. Television provides a handy, interesting (to most students) avenue through which to approach the world of fictionalized experience, offering examples and comparisons on which understanding can be built and discrimination heightened, not only in televiewing but in reading fiction. It comes as something of a revelation to the adolescent that fiction, that is, stories, are all around him in everyday life—in television, radio, motion pictures, newspapers, conversation, and juke-box ballads—not just entombed in his anthology or in books in the library. A discussion beamed to this revelation is a good way to introduce a unit on fiction for younger students.

Because of this prevalence of fictionalized experience and because the pupil enters the junior high school with some natural interest in stories, fiction probably will be the keystone of the literature program in the secondary school, although students should certainly have broad experiences with the several literary genres. It is in the high school that many adolescents, naturally inclined to action and concerned with happenings, should realize, paraphrasing the philosopher Santayana, that one of the chief functions of literature is to turn events into ideas. It is only then that the student will be able to derive, in his own experience, the real rewards of literature discussed in the opening chapter of this book. Sterile teaching and poor choice of selections are the surest ways of guaranteeing that students will remain at the television level of fiction. And this curtailed development is unfortunate, because the highest rewards of fiction come from that written by the serious artist and read by the serious reader. Through studying how to read fiction, in constant interplay with wide experiences in reading the novel and short story, many students will develop the ability to read serious fiction well.

TEACHING THE SKILLS OF READING FICTION

The short story and the novel, like other forms of literature, pose special problems for the reader. Although there has been, in the past thirty years, a vast number of publications about the skills involved in reading—and although reading-skill programs are now features of many high school textbook-anthologies—there is a paucity of specific suggestions for the teachers to follow in helping students develop skill in reading fiction or other literary forms. There appear to be two major explanations for this lack of detailed instruction. First, skill in reading fiction simply may involve the application of those much-discussed skills in vocabulary, "word-attack," [1] and comprehension. Second, the process by which the mature reader reads a significant novel or story may defy analysis, making it impossible to enumerate

---

[1] "Word-attack" refers to the methods a student uses in trying to handle a word unknown to him which he meets in his reading. It may be of three kinds: phonetic analysis, structural analysis (as of prefixes, suffixes, roots), and guessing from context clues.

the specific skills involved. Attempting the full description of such a process would be as impossible, perhaps, as delineating the process by which a music lover "got that way."

The relation of skill in reading literature to the broader objective of appreciation is a knotty problem that cannot be examined in any detail here. Obviously, critical skill in reading fiction—knowledge of criteria for judging value and ability to apply these criteria—does not guarantee that the reader will enjoy a book or a story, or be moved by it. A technically masterful novel or story may leave even some highly intelligent readers "cold." Undoubtedly certain factors enter in—type of personality, point of view of the selection, the total context in which the selection is experienced, and a host of others. Many writers have attempted to define "appreciation" in literature or to identify the factors in appreciation. For example, Robert C. Pooley writes: "Appreciation, then, I shall define as the emotional responses which arise from basic recognition, enhanced by apprehension of the means by which they are aroused." [2] James R. Squire, in a study of adolescents' responses to four selected short stories, identifies several factors that commonly obstruct mature response: (1) *Failure to grasp the meaning.* Obviously readers must comprehend the narration in stories. Squire found that there were three common difficulties in grasping the "essential intention" of the author: (a) Failure to understand key words; (b) Failure to grasp the implications of details; (c) Incorrect inferences. This difficulty frequently took the form of failure to keep details suspended in memory and to relate them to later details in the story. (2) *Reliance on stock responses.* Some students tend to rely on stereotyped patterns of thinking as they interpret situations in literature. Squire identified five general stereotypes in ninth graders' responses to the four stories ("All the Years of Her Life" by Morley Callaghan; "Prelude" by Lucille Vaughan Payne; "Reverdy" by Jessamyn West; and "The Man in the Shadow" by Richard Child): (a) Adolescents are not responsible for their own actions; (b) A boy or girl in trouble does not have a very healthy home life; (c) Wealth and happiness are incompatible; (d) When adults and adolescents are in conflict, the adults are almost always wrong; (e) Punishment for adolescent wrongdoing accomplishes little and should be avoided. (3)

[2] "Measuring the Appreciation of Literature," *English Journal*, XXIV (October 1935), 628.

Happiness binding. Some students "continually assume, infer, and hope for the best. They are 'happiness bound' both in their demand for fairy tale solutions and in their frequent unwillingness to face the realities of unpleasant interpretation." (4) *Critical predispositions.* Some readers bring to fiction critical yardsticks which they attempt to apply to any story—whether it is "true to life" or includes "good description," for example. (5) *Irrelevant associations.* Random associations from memories of personal experience tend, in some students, to get in the way of a unified view of the work. (6) *The search for certainty.* Some readers insist on clarity and definiteness in interpretation even when a story gives no definite basic for a single interpretation.[3] Squire's findings make clear that the junior or senior high school teacher of literature needs to identify the skills important in reading fiction and to provide direction and practice in those skills. It is vital, first, that the student be made aware of the things that are important to think about when one reads fiction. Then, naturally, the student must be given much practice—criticized practice—in applying these processes of thought to fiction appropriate to his level of experience, since the constant relation of one's experience to the printed page is essential in any true comprehension. These processes of thought, which lead to skill in reading fiction, seem to divide into two general categories: those necessary to comprehend form and therefore to determine the significance of a short story or novel, and those necessary to apprehend a variety of implied meanings inherent in fiction.

Reading To Comprehend Form

Because the novel or the short story is a particular way of reconstructing experience, the special way in which the author has used the form may be important for the meaning or significance of the selection. Many students (and adults, for that matter) read only for "the story," for the literal sequence of events. They tend to read all stories in the same way, and if the given story does not jibe with their way of thinking about what a story should be, as Squire's findings show, they are likely to complain that they "don't get it." Yet the same student who

[3] *The Responses of Adolescents While Reading Four Short Stories.* Research Report No. 2 (Champaign, Ill.: NCTE, 1964), pp. 37–49.

is impatient with form as a factor in understanding the selection may be the boy who would never be content with knowing only the amount of yardage gained on an around-end play in a football game; he would want to know how the play was executed and from what formation it was run, for this awareness would add to his enjoyment. Or the impatient student may be a girl who is sophisticated in music—at least in the form popular at the moment. She would never be satisfied merely to recognize the melody; she also would be a keen critic of the artistry of the musicians and arranger. Analogies such as these, presented in class, may help students to see the importance of form in literature—at the least, they may break down some antagonisms.

High school students are frequently baffled by certain modern fiction of the highly symbolic or elliptical variety. For example, this author has been most unsuccessful in teaching a favorite short story, Hemingway's "The Killers," to senior high school classes. Merely following the events of the story, the students come out blank and virtually snarling with frustration. On the surface the story seems stupid (a favorite word in the adolescent's vocabulary of literary criticism). Two sinister-appearing men turn up in a diner in a small town. They carry on a rather pointless conversation with the counterman in the diner. Finally they produce guns, holding the countermen and the cook prisoner, waiting apparently to kill one Ole Andreson, who usually eats at the diner. Ole doesn't come and the men give up and go away. Nick Adams, one of the waiters at the diner, goes to warn Ole, who seems resigned to his fate. The baffled young waiter goes back to the diner, where he exclaims to his partner. "It's too damned awful." The partner's reply is the last line of the story: "Well, you better not think about it."

Furiously, the students want to know why the men are out to kill Ole Andreson. And they want to know how the story *ends*—does Ole get killed or doesn't he? The impasse results from their failure to take into account the role played by the form of the story in expressing its meaning—a failure certainly excusable in the average adolescent, though not in the able student. The mature reader realizes, perhaps from a previous reading of Hemingway, that the author is pointing to the pervasiveness of evil in the world, and it does not matter at all, for instance, whether or not Ole Andreson actually gets killed nor why the men want to kill him. The psychological plot of the story involves Nick Adam's traumatic rendezvous with evil, and in terms of that plot the end is just right. Such understanding comes, of course, from sustained experience in reading fiction under the guidance of a skilled teacher.

Studying Plot

What is the starting point in developing the overall skill of organizing a selection of fiction in terms of its form and content? In the junior high school the students can learn the various purposes that fiction may have: simply to entertain through a funny, exciting, or unusual story; to present some serious idea about life; to satirize or burlesque something; to create some kind of effect or impression; to portray or dramatize an emotion; to present an insight into a person's character. In the senior high school the student should learn the way in which traditions of romanticism, realism, and naturalism have affected fiction, and he should have some experiences with historical, sociological, and psychological fiction. More specific ways of dealing with these matters are suggested in the following sections.

Since students enter the junior high school naturally interested in "the story" in a piece of fiction, work with plot and its role in the art of fiction may be stressed in the early years, although in classroom work the various elements of fiction should never be isolated one from another. Students will need practice with various methods of plot construction. As the writer has stated elsewhere:

> Most will have little trouble with the plot which presents a straight chronological sequence of events, but they will need training in following the story which starts with a problem, regresses in time to tell how it arose, and moves forward in time to tell how it was solved; or the one which starts at the end, goes back to the beginning, and runs on to meet the starting point, the end of the person's life. In their early acquaintance with plots of this type, it may help students to draw jagged time lines to show the chronology of the story. In the novel, particularly the long nineteenth-century novels, students have the problem of following several plots involving various groups of characters through hundreds of pages. Simple charts showing the various plot strands and the characters involved may help, although the need for too many charts and dia-

grams may indicate that the novel is too difficult for the level of ability of the readers.[4]

The study of plot will involve students in important discrimination ⭠ in reading fiction. The mature reader rejects improbability and too much coincidence in what he reads, recognizing the fact that in good fiction, as in the experience it reconstructs, there is a basis of cause and effect in the happenings. A good study question for students is: "Was there any preparation for this happening, any reason for it in what has gone before, or did this happen purely by chance or coincidence?" The literary matter of "foreshadowing" is the point. After reading a "surprise-ending" story, such as those by O. Henry, students may enjoy looking back over the story to see whether the writer purposely led them astray in order to trick them at the end, or whether the surprise ending could grow logically out of the story.

Judging Character

Teachers are fond of asking students to "characterize" so and so after reading a selection. This task, too, will be difficult for the student who has not learned to work with a variety of clues. Discussion of ways to use such clues might be introduced by asking, "How do we arrive at our judgments of people in real life?" Students will usually answer this question with such responses as: "By the way they act." "By what they do." "By what other people say about them." "By the way they talk." "By the way they dress." "By the kinds of things they like to do." Then the teacher can point out that in fiction one arrives at estimation of character through the same kinds of clues, perhaps listing for the class "The nine basic methods of revealing a character," as ⭠ identified by J. N. Hook:

1. Telling what kind of person he is.
2. Describing the person, his clothing, and his environment.
3. Showing his actions.
4. Letting him talk.
5. Relating his thoughts.
6. Showing how other people talk to him.

[4] "Developing Competence in Reading," in Angela M. Broening (Ed.), *The English Language Arts in the Secondary School* (New York: Appleton-Century, 1956), p. 185.

7. Showing what other people say about him.
8. Showing how other people react because of him.
9. Showing how he reacts to others.[5]

It is important for the teacher to point out the close relationship of characters and events in mature fiction. That is, a character is often revealed by his reactions in the crisis that provides a climax for a story. And in artistic fiction certain traits of certain characters lead to events. It is a mark of immature, formula fiction that this close relationship of characters and events is lacking, as, for example, when characters do highly improbable and unpredictable things merely for the sake of the plot.

Using Clues to Setting

Often the setting in fiction is obvious. Yet occasionally, especially in maturely written short stories, the reader has to infer the time or place, and it may be most important that he do this. Simple stories of the Far North, the desert, and the tropics, for example, in which there are obvious clues to setting, will provide training for junior high school pupils in making this type of inference. This training will make it easier for them to handle more subtle clues later, when it may be important for them to understand that a story about a pepper-eating contest is taking place in Mexico, or a certain Christmas story is set in Wales. Consideration of the geographical setting is important, too, in the local-color stories of American literature. Occasionally, the inference of time from clues is also important. Certain excellent but "dated" stories of the World War II period would be bewildering to the student who had not determined the setting in time. Or a story such as Faulkner's "Race at Morning" would lose its impact if the reader did not determine from rather scanty clues that it took place many years ago.

Reading for Implied Meanings

A readiness to draw inferences, to read between the lines, is essential to successful reading beyond the literal story level. A typical response

[5] *The Teaching of High School English* (New York: Ronald, 1965), pp. 174–75.

of adolescents to a teacher's or a classmate's interpretation is an astonished "Where'd you get that out of it?" To the highly trained but inexperienced teacher in literature, it sometimes seems inconceivable that a student does not recognize an elementary matter of symbolism. Yet to many youngsters beginning junior high school English, the whole matter of symbolism in literature is foreign, and it never occurs to them to look beneath the surface of happenings for implied ideas. They are often loud in their protest against the writer who doesn't "come right out and say what he means." The process of learning to think with literary material develops gradually through the junior and senior high school years—but it can develop.

Using Details To Determine or Illuminate Theme

Not all fiction is concerned with any definite theme—to cite an extreme example, the stories of Poe. However, it is important that students develop the ability to handle theme in mature fiction. Certainly there is no pat outline of devices by which this ability could be developed since the factors involved in dealing with an author's theme are so complicated. Yet, after students have an understanding of what theme in fiction is, they can be made aware of the way in which understanding the use of details can aid them to perceive it. Often there will be statements of the theme by the author or by his characters. This is the case, for instance, in James Michener's novel of the Korean war, *The Bridges at Toko-Ri,* in which the theme—why American men had to fight and die in a strange, little-known country—is rather clearly stated near the end of the book. This statement of theme was overlooked by the girl who complained that she did not like the book because "it had such a sad ending." In view of the theme, there could be no other ending!

In order to deal with theme, and the general significance of a selection, high school students need to learn to judge details in terms of the author's attitude toward his material. These attitudes lie on a continuum between symbolism and naturalism. Of course, the problem of interpreting symbolism underlies the entire study of literature and is as important to the reading of fiction as to the reading of poetry or any other form of literature. To the symbolist, such as James Joyce or D. H. Lawrence, details are likely to be unimportant, or even meaningless, at the literal level, and this makes reading their work extremely difficult. Only a few high school students will be able to comprehend Joyce or Lawrence, for example, but a general acquaintance with symbolism and a habit of looking below the surface of details can begin in the junior high school. Seventh-graders may discuss the significance of the blue willow plate in Doris Gates's *Blue Willow,* and eighth- or ninth-graders may consider the symbolic value of the black coffee in James Street's *Goodbye, My Lady.* Naturalistic writing, in which the author presents a stark cross section, or "slice," of life, may be as baffling to adolescents as the highly symbolistic. It helps them to know the purpose of naturalistic writing. In the senior high school, students should learn something of the continuum of authors' attitudes toward their material. Preparation for reading the major writers of fiction includes placing them on this continuum.

An author's central meaning or theme in a piece of fiction may be dependent upon such devices as irony, satire, and allegory. In addition to explaining these devices, the teacher needs to provide practice in reading selections in which they are used, selections appropriate to the students' level of awareness. If there is careful preparation, the junior high school is not too early for introduction of these matters.

APPROACHES TO THE NOVEL

At all grades in the junior and senior high school, the novel has been important in the literature program, but because of the amount of time that must be invested in study of the novel, teachers have encountered some particular difficulties, both practical and philosophical. The practical problems center on the availability of material for class use. Library facilities vary widely from school to school. Some teachers have one copy per student of several novels and multiple copies of many others at their disposal, whereas some teachers are virtually restricted to the selections in the anthology—and sometimes there is a shortage of anthologies! Editors and publishers have been loath to include full-length novels in anthologies because so much space is required and because no matter what novel is included, many teachers often are dissatisfied with the choice. Only in the books for the ninth and the tenth grades have full-length novels commonly been included. However, a great boon has come to the teacher—the phenomenon of paperbound books. Use of paperbacks in the classroom and their inclusion in school and public libraries have become commonplace in the last decade.

Other problems in teaching the novel are philosophical ones. For a long time there has been among teachers a rather widespread suspicion of selections that are popular and that students find easy to read. Teachers have insisted upon choosing for common reading novels that really give them something to teach. However, the commendable zeal ← to provide challenging experiences has resulted frequently in the choice of novels that are appropriate only for the upper third or fourth of the class, and only frustrating to the rest. It is probable, for example, that *Silas Marner* and *A Tale of Two Cities* are more appropriate for the twelfth grade, if they are to be taught, than to the tenth, where they—*Silas Marner,* at least—are practically canonized items. However, many teachers have ignored the nature of a student's growth toward maturity in reading fiction. This gradual type of growth makes it necessary for a girl to learn to read, say, *Seventeenth Summer* well before she can read *Wuthering Heights* well. To some extent a rather widespread burden of contempt for the "juvenile" and the contemporary has crippled teaching of the novel.

A major philosophical problem in teaching the novel, or any other ← form of literature, for that matter, involves the teacher's view of his point of departure—does he consider more important the novel itself, or the experience in reading it he wants the students to have? To those teachers who accept a certain novel, or group of novels, as their point of departure, their problem becomes one of getting the selection "across" to students, of making it meaningful and, if possible, interesting. Articles in the *English Journal* and other professional magazines have shown the ingenuity and resourcefulness that teachers have mustered to meet this problem. Commitment to this point of departure in literature has resulted in production of "simplified classics," abridged or rewritten versions of famous selections. Though these books may have some uses in the general reading program, the disadvantages of using them outweigh the advantages. It is questionable, for one thing, ← whether a really fine piece of literature can be simplified or even abridged without creating something entirely different. There is a danger that many students may get the idea that they are really experiencing *Les Misérables,* for instance, when they read a simplified edition. (There are even comic-book versions of this and other masterpieces!) Some students who might ultimately read a selection in the original may be discouraged from doing so through the early reading of the simplified version. It seems legitimate to reason that if students are not prepared to read a certain selection in its original form, they should read another selection that, though of lesser merit or complexity, preserves its unity and integrity as a work of art.

Many other teachers, especially in recent years, have maintained that the point of departure should not be any one novel or group of novels but rather the kind of intellectual and emotional experience that students should have. For these teachers the problem is to determine what experiences a certain class of students should have, and then to find the novels most likely to provide those experiences.

No doubt this basic cleavage concerning point of departure in the literature program will continue to exist among teachers and others concerned with the reading and literary experiences of young people. Yet the research and experimentation of the past several decades lend support to the viewpoint that the point of departure in teaching the novel should be determination by the teacher of the type of experience he desires his students to have, and then selection of the novels most likely to induce that experience. Considering the entire literary tradition, it is difficult to defend the position that any two or three novels are the *sina qua non* of the literary education during adolescence. It is quite obvious that, no matter what may be a teacher's opinion of a particular novel and no matter what position the book has held in literary history, it will be rewarding to a student only in terms of *his* reactions to it and of the value *he* perceives in his experience of reading it. It is unfortunately apparent that the majority of high school graduates look back on their tenth-grade experience with *Silas Marner,* for example, as relatively unpleasant, though the novel has a secure reputation in the literary tradition. As noted in the opening chapter of this book, a greater permissiveness must characterize choice of selections for classroom use. Canonized selections may need to be thrown out, with works such as Golding's *Lord of the Flies* and Baldwin's *Go Tell It on the Mountain* replacing *Silas Marner* and *Great Expectations.*

Novels for Reading in Common

Regardless of many differences of opinion, there seems to be one
unanimous point of agreement among teachers of literature: there
should be *some* reading in common. Exactly what that common reading should be at each grade and how much of it there should be may
be controversial, but the value of occasional experiences in having
a class all reading the same novel at the same time is universally ac-
knowledged. At least one novel should be read in common in each
grade, seven through twelve, although, as this author frequently has
stated, there is no pat formula to prescribe which selections should be
read in a particular class. Probably each novel chosen for reading in
common should meet three general criteria:

1. Any novel chosen should furnish a profitable experience for a
   typical class, heterogeneous in its intellectual and esthetic potential. It should provide appropriate opportunities for the able without being either completely incomprehensible or unrewarding to
   those at the lower ranges of ability.
2. The work chosen should pose reading problems and demands that
   are, in large part, common to many other novels. That is, the
   unique or greatly experimental work might legitimately be ruled
   out for total class study. Among commonly taught novels, *Huckleberry Finn* is such a book. To be sure, many students should read
   Huckleberry Finn, but the work is so much in a class by itself
   that it may lack real value for in-common study. Of particular
   value is the book that has a concrete, literal line of progression
   and at the same time a possible continual allegorical or symbolic
   progression, for example, *The Old Man and the Sea, The Secret
   Sharer,* and *The Pearl.*
3. The novel must have some natural affinity with youth, with adolescence. There is, of course, no sure way by which this amorphous
   quality of "affinity" can be judged, but it seems important that
   teachers consider it with as much insight as they can muster. For
   adolescents, however bright intellectually or mature socially and
   physically, are different, in general, from adults. There are certain
   themes, attitudes, mind-sets that are naturally more acceptable or

comprehensible than others to young people. A work must be appraised carefully in terms of the resources of a given class for entering imaginatively into it and responding to it.

In order to give some practical help to teachers in choosing novels for common reading at the various grade levels, the author surveyed articles on the teaching of the novel appearing in the *English Journal,* recent syllabuses and courses of study, and a number of reading lists published by the National Council of Teachers of English, the American Library Association, and other organizations. He also talked personally and corresponded with teachers from various parts of the country. The following list of suggested novels for reading in common is the result. Several somewhat obvious things should be pointed out about the list. First, there is nothing "objective" about the placement of the selections in the various grades; this placement was determined both in terms of common practice across the country and in terms of the writer's opinions about appropriateness. For example, *Great Expectations* appears in the twelfth-grade list, although a cut version that appears in a widely used anthology is commonly taught in the ninth grade. On the other hand, *Old Yeller* could be read before the ninth grade by many students. Second, it is obvious that some of the selections would be useful only for certain groups—*Shane* for students of lesser ability and *The Dead* for highly able readers, for example. One of the real problems of selecting novels for reading in common by seventh- and eighth-graders is that boys and girls at those levels have such markedly different interests. Therefore, in the main, the selections for those grades have been suggested because of their appeal for both boys and girls.

In the list that follows, those books available in paperback edition when this volume went to press are marked with an asterisk.[6]

Seventh Grade

Buck, Pearl, **The Big Wave.* A typhoon destroys a Japanese village.
Knight, Eric, **Lassie Come-Home.* The original story of the famous
    fictional collie.

---

[6] Teachers should check in the most recent edition of *Paperbound Books in Print* (New York: Bowker).

Shotwell, Louise, *Roosevelt Grady*. Story of family life among migrant Negro workers.

Sperry, Armstrong, *Call It Courage*. A South Sea island boy proves his courage in a lonely ordeal.

Ullman, James Ramsey, *Third Man on the Mountain*. A boy conquers a great mountain on which his father met death.

Eighth Grade

L'Engle, Madeleine, *A Wrinkle in Time*. A fantasy of travel through time, with a strong ethical theme.

London, Jack, *Call of the Wild*. One of the great dog-and-man stories.

Steinbeck, John, *The Pearl*. Short allegory of the curse of a great pearl.

Stevenson, Robert, *Treasure Island*.

Street, James, *Goodbye, My Lady*. A boy and an unusual dog in the Mississippi swamp country.

Wojciechowska, Maia, *Shadow of a Bull*. The son of a great Spanish bullfighter feels impelled to follow in his father's footsteps at the same time that he feels he is not suited to be a bullfighter.

Ninth Grade

Barrett, William E., *The Lilies of the Field*. Unusual story of a young Negro who helps a group of German refugee nuns build a chapel.

Forbes, Esther, *Johnny Tremain*. A young silversmith's part in the turbulent pre-Revolutionary War days in Boston.

Gipson, Fred, *Old Yeller*. Family life and an incorrigible yellow dog in pioneer days in Texas.

Neville, Emily, *It's Like This, Cat*. Episodic story of a year in the life of a New York City boy and his pet cat.

Richter, Conrad, *Light in the Forest*. A white boy is returned to his parents' civilization after years of captivity by the Indians.

Schaefer, Jack, *Shane*. A quality western.

Wibberley, Leonard, *The Mouse that Roared*. A lighthearted satire of the tiny Grand Duchy of Fenwick's "war" on the United States.

Tenth Grade

Annixter, Paul, *Swiftwater*. A Maine woods boy, his ambitions, his family, and the girl in his life.

Boulle, Pierre, *Face of a Hero*. An ironic story of a prosecuting attorney who sends an innocent man to his death.

Hemingway, Ernest, *The Old Man and the Sea*.

Hilton, James, *Lost Horizon*.

Wilder, Thornton, *The Bridge of San Luis Rey*. The patterns of the lives of five people who are killed when a Peruvian bridge collapses.

Eleventh Grade

Baldwin, James, *Go Tell It on the Mountain*. Hard-hitting novel about Harlem Negroes who try to find meaning in religion.

Borland, Hal, *When the Legends Die*. A Ute Indian boy becomes a successful broncobuster in the white man's world, but returns to his people.

Clark, Walter Van Tilburg, *The Ox-Bow Incident*. Psychological story of the lynching of innocent men in early Nevada.

Crane, Stephen, *Red Badge of Courage*.

Faulkner, William, *The Bear*.

Hawthorne, Nathaniel, *The Scarlet Letter*.

Knowles, John, *A Separate Peace*. An outstanding prep school story with an "initiation" theme.

Lewis, Sinclair, *Babbitt*. An attack on the philistinism and hypocrisy of middle-class business culture in the 1920s.

McCullers, Carson, *The Heart Is a Lonely Hunter*. Strangely assorted personalities come together in a Southern town.

Melville, Herman, *Billy Budd*.

Wharton, Edith, *Ethan Frome*.

Twelfth Grade

Boulle, Pierre, *The Bridge Over the River Kwai*. An ironic tale of World War II soldiers and their Japanese captors.

Bronte, Emily, *Wuthering Heights*.

Conrad, Joseph, *Heart of Darkness* and *The Secret Sharer*.

Dickens, Charles, *Great Expectations* and *A Tale of Two Cities*.

Golding, William, *Lord of the Flies*. A group of boys, marooned on an island, regress to savagery.

Hardy, Thomas, *The Mayor of Casterbridge* and *The Return of the Native*.

Joyce, James, *The Dead*.

Paton, Alan, *Cry, the Beloved Country*. Lyrical novel of race relations in South Africa.

Intensive Study of the Novel

The student's ability to read fiction will develop gradually through the junior and senior high school years. But his experiences in intensive class study of the novel are crucial because these experiences—and there is time for but few of them—will be the milestones toward perceptive reading of the mature novel.

Three kinds of abilities need attention in intensive study of the novel:

Those needed for imaginative entry into the novel

Those needed for perception of meaning or central purpose in the novel

Those needed for perception of artistic unity and significance

Imaginative Entry

Imaginative entry or empathy is the first essential, otherwise the reader is barred from an esthetic experience; he is not *reading* literature. Unless he can enter imaginatively into the work, he cannot determine for himself the meaning or purpose, though he may take someone else's word for it. And if he has not experienced literature deeply enough to perceive its meaning or purpose, he has no business judging its artistic unity or significance. It is our common failing that we demand judgment of literature by students before they know what the literary experience is, and we have the sterile tradition of class periods in which students criticize the plot, the style, the imagery, the characterization before they know how any of these relate to meaning or central effect.

We know, of course, that some students are more imaginative than others, more ready to suspend disbelief. But regardless of quickness of imagination or inherent flair for the nonliteral, all students are capable of imaginative entry into vicarious experience merely because they *are* human and because they have had many experiences. The problem is to relate the experience recreated in the work to their own experience, and the answer lies in the identification of correlative experience. Just as the novelist expresses emotion indirectly through his work, so the reader must cull up experiences in the *general* field of emotion represented, for only occasionally can the reader's actual experience closely match that reproduced in the work. Our student reads a novel in which a man is killed, and he must empathize with the killer. He has not ever killed anyone—we hope—but perhaps he has seen someone killed. Or perhaps he has killed an animal or seen someone else do so. The reader of *Huckleberry Finn* has not traveled down the Mississippi on a raft with a runaway slave and tussled with his conscience over knowledge of law versus feeling of personal loyalty, but he probably has been in some situation which involved a conflict between his relations with an individual and his relations with society or a group. The reader of *The Old Man and The Sea* has not spent a day and night upon the ocean fighting and finally subduing a giant marlin, vainly fighting off sharks, bringing to shore, in complete exhaustion, only a great skeleton, but perhaps he *has* realized the hollowness of a victory or carried on a lonely struggle that no one has understood.

But the student must learn to *use* his experience, to examine it constantly for its relevance to the work of literature. This is not easy for, by and large, in his early years he has read in the escape tradition. Reading of literature, from the fairy tales forward, has represented escape from his experience. In general, he has learned to approach literature as something divorced from his own life, and therein, in fact, has been its appeal. His experience with television further fortifies his approach. The happenings in the horse opera or space opera or blood-and-thunder piece are related only to an unreal world to which he likes to escape occasionally. Escape is, of course a legitimate function of literature, but a minor one.

The secret of the success of juvenile fiction, the junior novel, is that it often is read literally, requiring only literal identification, with no search for correlative experience. Perhaps this is as it should be in early adolescence. Mary or Joe reads a novel about a school like theirs, a family much like their own, people like those they know, problems similar to those they are encountering. The work then has true meaning since they can find themselves in it so easily.

Abstract identification or entry, through the avenue of correlative experience, is quite another matter, but it is not beyond most high school students. What is the teacher's role? Perhaps we cannot really *teach* imaginative entry but certainly we can *promote* it. We can help, first, by selecting for study those novels which offer a legitimate chance for the student to use his experiences as the touchstone for imaginative entry; second, by helping him to think about his experiences in connection with those recreated in the work.

There is one question teachers must live with: what basis does the student have for entering into the emotional experience of this novel through plumbing of correlative experience? Most seventeen-year-olds could not be expected to identify with Jake Barnes in his frustration over the impossibility of consummating his love for Brett in *The Sun Also Rises*. Nor can most adolescents understand why the attractive and wealthy Tom and Daisy Buchanan always seem so tired and bored in *The Great Gatsby*. But even the younger student can identify with Bucky Calloway, who in Annixter's *Swiftwater* meets the dreaded wolverine on his father's trap line, because most high school students already have had to face evil in obvious form and make decisions about it. And though *A Tale of Two Cities* presents a number of difficulties, its Sidney Carton is a natural for adolescent identification. His final grand sacrifice is the stuff of adolescent dreams. Identification with Sidney Carton induces pseudo emotions, central in the esthetic experience. These pseudo emotions are not less powerful than "real" emotions, but they are more satisfying, as Aristotle said so long ago. The essential problem is to propel students from the launching pad of literal identification into the rewarding process of abstract identification. The teacher must make students aware that their experiences to date are the key to imaginative entry into a novel of whatever time, place, problem, or situation.

Thomas Hardy once wrote that the "writer's problem is how to strike the balance between the uncommon and the ordinary so as on the one hand to give interest, on the other to give reality." The student's problem is parallel: how to immerse himself in the experience of the work and yet retain his esthetic distance so as to organize the work for the perception of meaning or purpose. The word "easy" (a most slippery term when used in connection with literature) can best be applied to those novels in which very little organization for perception of meaning is required—the traditional romance, for example, in which the experience represented in the novel is exempt from the conditions that we know are usually found in reality. *The Prisoner of Zenda* is a good example.

Perception of Meaning

The second emphasis therefore should be on helping the student build those skills by which to perceive meaning or purpose in a novel, on acquainting him with the devices involved in the constant interplay of form and content. It is possible here to cite only a few examples of things students must learn if they are to perceive meaning in a novel.

In general what is required might be called the method of hypothesis in reading a novel. That is, from the very first, the reader constantly has to hypothesize about what happens, what is said, what objects or scenes are introduced. The reading becomes a matter of continually positing and testing hypotheses. Some of these hypotheses will receive sufficient test in a few pages; others, not until the book is finished and the reader has reflected on it. For example, the hypothesis that Zeena's feigning of illness is used as a weapon to control Ethan Frome cannot be finally accepted or rejected until the end of the book. This is not to suggest that any two readers necessarily will come to the same conclusions or even raise the same hypotheses, but it is the process that is important. Student interpretations will be judged, then, mainly in terms of the process the student has used in arriving at his interpretation.

It is easy and natural for the immature reader to flow along with the plot of the story, going from episode to episode, without any real consideration of the value or use of the individual episode. Such a reading makes *The Red Badge of Courage,* for example, a rather flat tale of a farm boy at war. Episodes or scenes may be used for various purposes—to reveal character, to heighten effects, to provide meaning through allegory or satire, simply to satisfy the reader's curiosity about what happened to someone or what happened as aftermath to some event. The reader, then, must be willing to hypothesize about each scene. For example, the scene from *Swiftwater* in which a boy fights and kills a wolverine, is generally symbolic of the meeting with evil and of the coming to terms with it. This is a key scene in developing the theme of a boy's growing up. In *Huckleberry Finn,* to take a far different example, individual scenes assume key importance. For instance, the scene in which Colonel Sherburn shoots Boggs and then faces down and disperses the mob that follows him to his house has broad meaning of itself in Mark Twain's view of the world. This meaning can be interpreted without reference to other things in the novel.

But, of course, individual scenes or episodes usually cannot be interpreted without reference to all the rest of the work, and the student must be willing to hypothesize not only about immediate meanings but also about the possibility of total allegorical or symbolic framework in a novel. Such hypothesis seems necessary for a sophisticated reading of *The Old Man and the Sea* or Walter Van Tilburg Clark's *The Ox-Bow Incident,* to cite two novels rather commonly taught in high school, although students might profitably read these books at lesser levels of perception.

Interpretation of symbolism especially requires use of the method of hypothesis. Yet at the mention of the word "symbolism" cautions may flicker across teachers' minds since occasionally the bright and well-meaning student "gets hot" on symbolism and mires himself in a bog of symbols. However, the reader of *The Great Gatsby* who, early in the book does not set up hypotheses concerning the use and meaning of the valley of ashes, the great dumping ground outside New York City, or of the billboard with the eyes of T. J. Eckleburg, cannot accomplish a full reading. The same is true of Conrad's *Heart of Darkness.* Here the ivory is a basic symbol. It accounts for the ruin of Kurtz and it symbolizes what may account for the ruin of mankind. Much is lost if the reader does not perceive this meaning. It may be well in this instance to direct students' reading by telling them in advance that ivory is the basic symbol. Where they go from there will be up to them.

Hypothesis is important, too, in considering point of view. How much the narrator can be expected to know is a crucial question for the student to keep in mind if he is to read discriminately. But, more important, meaning in the novel may be definitely tied up with the nature of the narrator. Why did Mark Twain force himself to see the world through the eyes of Huck Finn, Stephen Crane through the eyes of Henry Flemming, Scott Fitzgerald through the eyes of Nick Carraway, Herman Melville through the eyes of Ishmael? Though final answers may differ, unless these questions are asked, the student is not on the track of important meaning.

A not insignificant function of hypothesis may be that it is often a student's means of avoiding boredom and keeping his interest alive through dull parts of otherwise rewarding books. The author has always found it necessary to warn students about the openings of *The Secret Sharer* and *Heart of Darkness:* it takes patience to become engaged with a Conrad novel. It takes patience, too, to wade through the middle of *A Tale of Two Cities* in order to discover what it has to do with the end. In this context, the method of hypothesis may improve the student's morale if not his interpretation!

Perception of Artistic Unity and Significance

It is the rare high school teacher of literature who has not been confronted many times with the time-honored questions, "Why is this supposed to be so good?" or "What's so great about this?" These questions may only reflect the student's rebellion at being told, implicitly or explicitly, that he should appreciate this selection because it is great literature. Or, more hopefully, the questions may signal a genuine quest for insight into the literary experience. Whatever the genesis of the questions, satisfying answers to them can come only as the individual is able to perceive the artistic unity and, beyond that, the artistic significance of the novel.

I mentioned earlier the possibility of falling into the fallacy of forcing students to judge a work of art before they have made sufficient progress in the skills leading to imaginative entry and perception of meaning or purpose. The experience of too many students in studying a selection of literature is limited to reading of the piece followed by discussion in which the selection is criticized or dissected. Is it true to life?—whatever that may mean. Were the characters real? Was the plot improbable? Was the author skillful in description? These are germane questions for the classroom, but until the student has become aware of the central meaning or purpose of the work—this awareness in turn dependent upon imaginative entry—he is in no position to answer such questions sincerely.

For example, what about this much-used phrase, "true to life"? It is important to make students understand that it is verisimilitude, the appearance of truth or reality, that we are talking about, not reality itself. Literature is not life, and verisimilitude in a selection has to be judged not only by the reader's experience with life, but by life as presented in the work. Is the coincidence that brings Stephen Kumalo and Jarvis together toward the end of *Cry, The Beloved Country* contrived, if we consider all that has gone before? What about the reality of characters? It is all to the good that we have worked hard to make students aware of stereotypes of character. Yet it seems important, too, at the level of judging artistic unity and significance, to make a distinction between stereotypes and archetypes. Archetypes are a part of our mythology. Representing a type of man the archetype may be greatly individual as is Joe, who, in *Great Expectations,* is a representative of the poetic approach to life. The stereotyped character, on the other hand, lacks individuality and is based not on racial experience but on oversimplification and half-truth.

The student who is to judge the artistic unity of a work of literature must be able to recognize any discordancies: the irrelevant details and descriptions that clutter bad fiction; the forced rhymes and stale metaphors with which bad poetry is studded. The perfectly unified selection is like the equation in mathematics—everything in balance, nothing unessential. The result is a truth that is truer than real life itself.

Beyond consideration of the unity of a work of literature lies judgment of significance. Laurence Perrine poses as the ultimate test of significance in literature: "How many and how diverse are the materials which are unified in the work?" When the student reaches a level at which he can deal with this question, he will be able to assign a proper niche to the story of plot, no matter how ingenious, and he will be beyond asking, "Why can't we read this just to enjoy the story?"

THE SHORT STORY IN THE LITERATURE PROGRAM

Junior and senior high school English teachers universally find the short story a most successful form of literature with adolescents. Stories are eminently "teachable" partly because they are inherently appealing. Everyone from three to threescore years likes a story, whether in printed or visual form. Also, the magazine, the television screen, and the school anthology make the short story the most available form of literature. Furthermore, the form is especially suited for reading in common. Simply in terms of time investment, the story far above (or below) the level of individual students does not carry the same amount of penalty that the novel or drama or epic poem does; reading the short story gives the poorer reader a sense of accomplishment impossible for him to have from reading these longer forms. Most short stories can be read and discussed within one class period, and using a group of stories gives the teacher a chance to cover a great deal of ground in teaching the skills of reading fiction.

Despite the ease with which it can be used in the classroom, however, the short story should not be overstressed at the expense of the novel, for it lacks the power of the novel. Although it has been pointed out that the short story is to literature what the microscope is to science,[7] giving us otherwise impossible glimpses of experience, it cannot give the same opportunity for identification, for insight into human motivation that the novel affords. The short story's scope is "moral revelation"; the novel's, "moral evolution." [8]

Though the short story has been a major literary form since early in the nineteenth century, the last three decades have brought wide variety and experimentation in the genre, and high school students need definite training if they are to deal intelligently with many serious stories. It may be profitable to discuss with them, and illustrate by specific stories, the four "amalgamations" discussed by Mark Schorer: story method, character portrayal, attitude toward material, and style.[9]

The "older" story is narrative in method, like the older novel, proceeding, by and large, in chronological sequence with a tightly knit plot leading to a definite climax, denouement, and conclusion. In the modern period the short story has often been dramatic rather than narrative in technique, presenting a single scene, often featuring a seemingly abrupt ending, as if the curtain fell while the characters were still in full action. The contrast between a Hawthorne tale and a *New Yorker* story shows the evolution in story method. In character

---

[7] Ray B. West, "The Modern Short Story and the Highest Forms of Art," *English Journal,* XLVI (December 1957), 531–539.

[8] Mark Schorer, *The Story: A Critical Anthology* (Englewood Cliffs, N.J.: Prentice-Hall, 1950), p. 433.

[9] Schorer, p. 431.

portrayal the range is from the highly subjective to the highly objective. Short-story writers of the nineteenth century, particularly, furnished much direct background material about the characters, whereas in the modern story, as has been pointed out earlier, the author often forces the reader to infer the background from scanty clues to character. Dickens and Hemingway might illustrate the contrast of these extremes in character portrayal.

The author's attitude toward his material, ranging from naturalistic to symbolistic, has been discussed earlier in this chapter. The fourth "amalgamation" which Schorer identifies is that in style, from "low" to "high." Hemingway, again, illustrates clearly the "low" style. That is, his stories are written in the language his characters speak. Part of Hemingway's effectiveness lies in his ability to reproduce the speech patterns and idioms of the kinds of people he writes about. O. Henry, perhaps, is a good example of the "high" style. Though he may write about a New York City tramp, as he does in "The Cop and the Anthem," the speech patterns and vocabulary are still O. Henry's.

Classroom Illustrations

Because units on short stories and aids to teaching individual stories are widely available to teachers in the many anthologies on the market, a detailed discussion of classroom approaches to the short story seems unnecessary here. However, a few techniques that have proved effective in actual teaching situations are suggested below.

Study of magazine fiction.   Although the amount of space given to fiction in magazines has been decreasing in favor of the nonfiction article, still, because of the wide distribution of magazines in the United States, the short story is virtually at everyone's fingertips:

> More short stories are bought and read today than any other form of literature. In fact, when historians write about the twentieth century they may well decide that the short story is the typical and representative literary form of this age, just as the drama has been the great literary form in some periods and the poem in others.[10]

Study of magazines, valuable in itself in high school classes, can be tied in profitably with the study of short stories as students build crite-

[10] Wilbur Schramm, *Great Short Stories* (New York: Harcourt, Brace & World, 1950), p. 2.

ria for themselves by which to distinguish poor, mediocre, and superior fiction. A senior high school class might be divided into three groups, each group to study the fiction in a certain class of magazines. Group I might consider such periodicals as the *New Yorker,* the *Atlantic Monthly,* and *Harper's,* and possibly even some of the literary magazines. Group II could study such middle-grade "slicks" as *McCall's* and *Redbook,* while Group III would consider low-grade "slicks" and even the pulps. Each group would work out a descriptive "profile" of the fiction appearing in its group of magazines, with generalizations concerning plot, characters, theme, and style. Each group could then make a report to the class, and the profiles would be compared. General differences in the fiction in the various groups of magazines will become apparent, although students should be given to understand, naturally, that occasionally a truly outstanding story appears in *McCall's,* for example, while a bad story may turn up even in one of the literary magazines.

This device helps students at least to see the differences between commercial-formula and serious fiction. The reports by the groups of students probably will bring out points of difference such as those listed below, which were established by the writer's own analysis of large numbers of short stories from magazines generally considered to be "high quality" or "low quality."

1. The "low quality" stories not only have very definite plot structure but rely on several stereotyped plot patterns. Plots deal more frequently with romantic love, crime, and violent adventure than with any other subjects.

   Stories from "quality" magazines tend to have looser plots and much greater variety of subject matter.

2. Stories from "low quality" sources tend to resolve problems very conclusively and definitely. Endings are satisfyingly final. (Of course, marriage is the usual ending for the love story.)

   The stories from more literary sources frequently present no definite solutions to problems. (To the immature reader, endings often seem abrupt and mystifying.)

3. Coincidence and improbability often characterize the stories from "low quality" sources, though they are usually cast in a realistic framework.

4. Physical action is paramount in the "low quality" stories. The stories from "quality" sources often rely on psychological action.
5. The "low quality" stories rely on character stereotypes.

Plot summary device. The author has found that the material reproduced below is useful in promoting discussion and in illustrating important points of difference between the mature and the immature short story. The material may be used, too, as an evaluating device at the end of a unit on short stories. Each item below summarizes a story up to a certain point; then three possible completing summaries are given. The student rates these three in order. The ranking of the completing summaries in each item was agreed upon unanimously by twenty college and high school teachers of English. This ranking is given in parentheses after each summary ("best" is 1; "poorest," 3).

PLOT SUMMARY EXERCISE [11]

Directions to students. After each Roman numeral below is a summary of a short story. The summary of the story stops at a certain point. Then three summaries—lettered A, B, C—are given of how the story could be developed from that point. Decide which of these three versions would be the best development of the story—that is, which most probably would give the best quality story. Then decide which would be second best and which poorest. Rank the summaries by putting a number before each letter—1 for best, and so on. Be ready to defend your choices.

I. At Midwestern University, fraternity and sorority initiation week for freshman pledges was coming to an end. Jerry Barnes was thankful that this was his last evening of initiation. He had been doing zany stunts all week. Now he had been assigned his last stunt. He was to go to the streetcar stop, stop the streetcar as if he wanted to get on, and then put his foot on the step, tie his shoe, and thank the streetcar operator for the use of the car. So Jerry, following instructions, stopped the first streetcar. He calmly put his shoe on the step and began to tie it, but the irate operator, accustomed to college pranks, saw what Jerry was doing and kicked his foot.

[11] Teachers have permission from the publisher to reproduce the following exercise for use in individual schools.

A. Jerry sprawled backward into the street. As he scrambled to his feet, he realized that a pretty girl who had just gotten off the car was laughing. She asked if he was being initiated. He explained as they started down the street, and he told her the worst one was having to go in and ask silly questions of old "Frozen Face" McDougal, history professor. He told her what a pill "Frozen Face" was. She accepted his invitation to have a coke, and after they sat down in the drugstore, he asked her what her name was. "Helen McDougal," she answered, smiling. " 'Old Frozen Face' is my dad!" Jerry, completely embarrassed, apologized heartily. The girl laughed gaily and invited Jerry to her house "to see how Dad really is." Jerry found that Professor McDougal was very human, and he left that evening having made a date for Saturday with Helen. (2)

B. Jerry sprawled backward into the street. Hearing someone laugh, he looked up to see a pretty girl on the curb. "Are you being initiated?" she asked. Jerry told her about the initiation and they walked down the street together. He told her of all the stunts he had had to do, and she accepted his invitation to have a coke. After the coke, she invited him to her sorority house. When they reached the house, she said, "I'm afraid you'll have to go now. We're having a meeting. I'm sorry, but you'll understand. I'm being initiated, too, and I had to pick up a boy and get him to walk home with me!" (1)

C. Jerry lost his balance, slipped, and fell, his legs going under under the car, which had already started. He lost consciousness as the wheels passed over him. As Jerry recovered in the hospital, something happened to his thinking. When he finally left the hospital with an artificial leg, he knew what his purpose was. He returned to school and started a one-man campaign against the initiation week. He was determined to save others from being victims of silly and dangerous stunts. At first, he made himself very unpopular. A fraternity group threatened him. But gradually he turned sentiment to his side. Finally, through his efforts, the university outlawed the initiation week, and at a convocation, Jerry was commended personally by the president of the university. (3)

II. Old Mr. Farnsworth, millionaire, wasn't given too long to live. He had no particular illness, the doctors said, but his mind was slipping badly. The old man had no important reason for living longer. He had a million dollars with nothing in particular to spend it for. His wife had divorced him many years before. His niece and her husband, with whom Mr. Farnsworth lived, were engrossed with their own concerns. They were instructed not to let the old man out of the house alone. But one stormy night, Mr. Farnsworth was taken with the desire to go out. About midnight he managed to slip out of the house. An hour later he was hopelessly lost and half frozen in the swirling snow. A youngish woman, probably a waitress on her way home, encountered the old man groping along the deserted street. He was unable to tell her where he lived, so the woman took him to her little apartment. She installed him near a warm radiator and made coffee.

A. Meanwhile, Mr. Farnsworth's absence had been detected and the distraught niece and her husband had the police start a thorough search. Early the next morning the old man was found walking happily along a street some distance away. He told the amazed officers a strange story about a young woman who had taken him in and given him coffee. He had stolen away after she had gone to sleep in a chair. He couldn't remember where she lived now, but he insisted that his niece advertise for the woman and offer a $10,000 reward. A few months later when the old man died, the reward was still unclaimed as his disgusted niece had told her friends it would be. (1)

B. In a few minutes the old man went to sleep. Unable to find any identification in the clothes he wore, the puzzled young woman made him comfortable on the couch and dropped to sleep herself in a big chair. In the morning the old man's mind was clear. He was humbly grateful and gave the young woman his niece's telephone number. While they waited for the niece's husband to come, the young woman made breakfast and they talked. She told him about her job at the restaurant. When the old man was safely home again, he sent for his lawyer with more animation than he had shown in months. Within two days, Mr. Farnsworth had bought an attractive restaurant and installed the young woman as manager. With great enthusiasm, he went to the restaurant often and watched from a private little booth. The doctors changed their predictions. (2)

C. After talking happily for a few minutes, Mr. Farnsworth dropped to sleep. The puzzled young woman went through his pockets for identification. She found his wallet and a little diary the old man was fond of writing in. As she looked through the diary, she grew pale and trembled, and she began to shake with sobs. Now she knew who her father was, whom her mother had always refused to discuss! Here he was, in her apartment, and he was a millionaire! She put back the diary and wallet and made the old man comfortable on the couch. As she regarded him, she thought bitterly of her own life, her job in the disreputable cafe. She did not sleep. In the morning the old man's mind was clear. He was very grateful and began to thank the young woman. In tears, she told him who she was. The old man became very angry at what he thought was a trick by an unscrupulous woman. He stamped out, throwing a little money on a table as he went. He told the woman it would have been more if it had not been for her shabby trick. (3)

III. Victims of bad train connections, James F. Webster and his two business associates, Hal Russell and Winston Crane, found themselves faced with a five-hour stopover in the little town of Hutchins, sixty miles away from their home city. This loss of time was a great irritation to James F. Webster who had never lost any time in his life. It was his ability to make every minute count that had made him president of the company at thirty-six. He hadn't even taken time to marry any of the attractive young women who had come into his life. The three men decided to take a hotel room and clean up. There was only one room left vacant at the town's one hotel, not a very good room, but they took it, resignedly. Mr. Webster took a bottle of expensive liquor from his suitcase and suggested a drink. There was no room service, so Mr. Crane volunteered to go for some soda. The other two sprawled in chairs. Mr. Russell reached down and picked up a crumpled piece of paper lying on the floor. He smoothed it out and examined it lazily. Then with a smile he handed it to Mr. Webster. On the paper was scrawled "Cash on hand . . . 17.60." Then there was a column:

Jimmy's doctor bill	163.50
Back rent	52.00
Owe Thompson	15.00
Grocery	17.00
Need	246.00

Then there followed some aimless doodling. Then the notation, "Try to borrow from Mr. Hadkins."

A. Mr. Webster looked at the paper with boredom and tossed it on the table as Mr. Crane arrived with the soda. As they sipped their drinks, Mr. Webster grunted, "What a place to spend five hours!" He picked up the paper again and toyed with it idly. He noticed that the calculations had been made on the back of an envelope. On the other side was the address:

J. A. Manley
Hopkins Falls
Illinois

Mr. Webster, grinning, called the desk and asked to have a call put through to J. A. Manley in Hopkins Falls. When the call came through, Mr. Webster asked an amazed Mr. Manley if he had gotten the loan from Mr. Hadkins. When the answer was that he had not, Mr. Webster said, "Well, you will," and hung up. Handing Mr. Crane the paper, he took a coin from his pocket. "A little game of chance," he grinned. "Loser sends Mr. Manley the money he needs." Groaning, the others agreed. Mr. Webster was the loser. "First time I've lost on a coin in a long time," he complained as he reached for his checkbook. (2)

B. Mr. Webster read the note with boredom. He noticed that it was written on the back of an envelope. On the other side was the address:

J. A. Manley
Hopkins Falls
Illinois

He knew the town. It was a suburb of his home city. Suddenly he picked up the phone receiver and sent a telegram to J. A. Manley, Hopkins Falls, Illinois: "COME OFFICE J. F. WEBSTER ILLINOIS PRODUCTS CORP. TOMORROW STOP HAVE OFFER FOR YOU" The next day, a pretty but puzzled young woman was presented to Mr. Webster, who asked if she had gotten the loan from Mr. Hadkins. More amazed than ever, the woman said that she hadn't. Mr. Webster explained everything and offered her a position which the delighted young woman accepted. A few months later, the newspapers carried the news of Mr. James F. Webster's engagement to Miss Jane Manley. (3)

C. Mr. Webster read the paper. "Well, do you think the guy got the money from Mr. Hadkins?" he asked Mr. Russell with a smile.

"Naw," yawned Mr. Russell, "Mr. Hadkins probably told

him he was sorry, but times weren't good and he had expenses of his own."

"You're too pessimistic," Mr. Webster answered. "Hadkins probably gave him the money interest-free."

"Nuts," rejoined Mr. Russell. "The old skinflint probably has a mortgage on the house." Just then Mr. Crane came back. "We'll leave it up to Win to decide," Mr. Russell grinned. He handed the paper to Mr. Crane, who looked at it blankly and said, "I don't get it." The others laughed and Mr. Crane looked at the paper again. Then he said, "Oh, I see. It's added up wrong!"

Mr. Russell snatched the paper. "By Gad, it *is* added wrong!"

As the other two men roared with laughter, Mr. Crane said, "I still don't get it." (1)

IV. I had been seeing Sorenson at lunch for several weeks before our conversation got beyond the point of exchanging pleasantries. He and I usually sat next to each other at lunch. I eat at the Capitol Cafe, which is the kind of place that has a steady lunch clientele of clerks and bookkeepers like myself who have to live economically. We eat at large tables and everyone gets used to sitting at the same place each day. I had been interested in Sorenson from the beginning. He invariably ordered the cheapest thing on the menu. He never had a desert or a cigar. He always seemed quite preoccupied. Our conversation became more familiar at each lunch time. I found out what firm he worked for. One evening he invited me to his home for dinner, where I met his wife, a plain, quiet little woman. One hot day he told me his secret. For years he had been saving, skimping on every penny, to buy a little piece of land on which there was a supply of marble about which only he knew. Enough marble, he said with his cheeks flushed, to make him a small fortune. With shining eyes, he confided that in a few weeks he would have the necessary money. An insurance policy was to come due and it would enable him to buy the property. After that, we often talked about it. And as the day grew near when he would buy the property, I began to envy him and share his excitement. Through the years, I had often dreamed of a stroke of luck that would take me out of my humdrum existence.

A. One day, near the appointed time, he came to lunch, his face strained and grey. He told me that the property had gone up in price, and that he would lack $2000 of being able to pay the price. A loan was impossible; he had no security. He dared take no one into his confidence, he said. Suddenly a thought stabbed through my mind. I had a little over $3000 in savings. Hesitantly, I suggested that he accept me as a partner. He stared at me and then, as tears came to his eyes, he said, "Of course! I should have thought of you! But I had no idea. . . ." So I turned over the money to him and we signed the agreement. The next day I wanted to discuss some details with him, but he didn't appear at lunch, so I decided to go to his home that evening. He looked startled when he saw me. I noticed that he and his wife were packing. Suddenly I became suspicious. But he drew a pistol and forced me into a room which he locked. When I finally got free and reported to the police, I found that I was only one of a number of victims. The police had been looking for him for months. (2)

B. One day he didn't appear at lunch, nor the next. Curious, I called at the offices of his firm and inquired about him of a young man at a desk. "Oh, Old Marble is sick," the young man said.

" 'Old Marble'!"

"Yeah," the young man grinned. "Hasn't he ever told you about that marble that he's going to get rich on?"

"Well, yes, he has. . . ."

"I thought so," the young man laughed. "He's been telling that for twenty years. That insurance policy is always about to come due. He's told that so much he believes it himself. I think that's what keeps him going." (1)

C. A few days before Sorenson was to have his money, my firm sent me out of town on a business errand. I thought of him, envying him after I arrived home and he no longer appeared for lunch at the Capitol. I heard from him a month and a half later. He called one night, jubilant. He had allowed quarry operations to begin on his land; there was already a handsome profit. I couldn't help being chilly in my response. His success made me despair even more of my own lot. A year passed. One morning as I was reading the *Inquirer* hurriedly, some lines of print leaped out at me. ". . . week-end death toll was brought to twenty-four when F. J. Sorenson, president of Sorenson Marble Company, and his wife were killed when their car was struck by a train at. . . ." Two days later, a

lawyer called at my office. Sorenson had no relatives. In his
will I was the only beneficiary after his wife. I now owned
the controlling interest in the Sorenson Marble Company! In
later days I thought often of those lunches at the Capitol. I
named my summer mountain retreat "Sorenson Lodge." (3)

RELATED ACTIVITIES

Various assignments in writing and other activities may be developed
profitably from study of short stories. Susan Jacoby and Richard J.
LaVigne offer the following suggestions, for example, from experience
in their own classes in the John Read Middle School, West Redding,
Connecticut.

1. Pass out the story without the title. Ask the class to read the story
   and upon its conclusion write an appropriate title. This exercise
   is a good way to determine whether a student is aware of the impact and content of the story.
2. Give the students mimeographed copies of a suspense story minus
   the crucial ending. Ask them to write an appropriate ending. Here
   they must be able to carry out an author's style as well as infer his
   intent.
3. Phrase an old problem in modern terms. With Anton Chekhov's
   "The Bet," for example, you might make this assignment: Take
   the same situation (a wager), the same people (a greedy banker,
   an ambitious lawyer), the same title ("The Bet") and write a
   conversation between these two making a wager today. (The
   students might base their version of "The Bet" on such issues as:
   the space race, segregation, and Vietnam.)
4. Emphasize the various aspects of press reporting with a variety of
   assignments. A story of controversy might be editorialized while
   one of human interest might be written for the feature page. The
   story itself might be reviewed either from a present perspective or
   by past standards if it is not contemporary.
5. Some stories leave the reader with questions to ponder. Allow
   students to explore these situations through composition. What
   came out—the lady or the tiger? The lawyer in "The Bet" is seen
   fifteen years after his confinement. Where is he seen and why is
   he seen there?
6. Have the students rewrite an incident in a short story from

another viewpoint. In Truman Capote's "A Christmas Memory" we see everything through the child's eyes. How would things look through the eyes of the reader? of the elderly cousin?

7. Take a universal theme in a story and discuss the students' attitude toward it. If it is failure, success, or greed, for example, how do the students react to these things? Have them prepare a poem, a stream of consciousness essay, or dramatic dialogue illustrating their point of view.

8. If the element of suspense pervades the plot, assign a "How would you handle it if you were—an F.B.I. agent, Sherlock Holmes, James Bond, Perry Mason, Mike Hammer, and so on?"

9. Though characterization is not a strong point of the short story, many authors have done a superb job. How can one forget Fortunato, General Zaroff, or Professor Herbert? Students can be asked to write stream of consciousness essays about character (for example, Fortunato—thoughts of a man as he sits chained behind a brick wall approaching death).

10. (a) In schools where it is possible, and especially in the junior high school, make the short story a unit in the interrelated disciplines. With the aid of the music department, find suitable music for the background of short story dramatizations. Find the same themes appearing in literature in musical composition.

(b) In art have the students illustrate the story theme through photomontage. The following are some specific correlated art/ English projects we've developed for the stories listed:

1. "The Bet"—metal sculpture—to create a three-dimensional piece of work based on some human conflict.

2. "The Cask of Amontillado"—clay *en bas relief*—to explore the innate potential and deficiencies of a particular medium.

3. "To Build a Fire"—paper construction—to construct a model house for an extreme climate exploring the varied use of paper.

11. In some instances these short stories are available as movies. Read the story. Discuss ideas which would be pertinent to the production of a motion picture—impact, selectivity, color versus black and white, closeups, cinemascope, and so on. Then view the motion picture and compare the judgments of the class. This method also provides an adequate opportunity to explore the visual media available to see how literature can be adapted from the written form for sight and sound.

12. Often these stories are available on records. Read the story; then

play the recording. Cyril Ritchard reading "The Open Window" (Saki) or Basil Rathbone reading Poe might add some new light to the story. This is a very effective technique with the slow reader.[12]

TEACHING SUGGESTIONS
FOR SELECTED MODERN NOVELS

Shane by Jack Schaefer (eighth or ninth grade)

I. *The Novel*

   A. Outline the novel by arranging the following plot incidents in the order in which they occurred.

     1. Ledyard tries to overcharge for the cultivator.
     2. Shane fights Chris and breaks his arm.
     3. Fletcher and Wilson come to the ranch and threaten Joe.
     4. Shane and Joe fight Morgan and Curly.
     5. Shane knocks out Joe, straps on his gun, and goes to town.
     6. Fletcher returns with the gunslinger Stark Wilson.
     7. Shane meets Chris and walks off with cherry soda pop.
     8. Shane arrives at the Starrett ranch.
     9. Shane's gunfights with Stark Wilson and Fletcher.
     10. Bob discovers Shane's gun kept in his blanket.
     11. Chris comes back to the Starretts to take Shane's place.
     12. Shane and Joe cooperate in removing the stump.
     13. Shane shows Bob how to use a gun.

   B. Choose one of these as the turning point of the book. Be able to justify your statement. Is the turning point the same as the climax of this novel?

   C. Describe the following characters in two or three sentences each. What is the relationship of the characters to each other?

     1. Marian Starrett
     2. Joe Starrett
     3. Red Marlin
     4. Chris
     5. Stark Wilson
     6. Henry Fletcher

[12] From "The Super Short Story," *English Journal*, LVI (September 1967), 856–857. Used by permission of the authors and the National Council of Teachers of English.

D. What do you think Shane's past life had been? What was Shane running away from? Cite evidence in the book for your answer.

E. After reviewing the concept of a "symbol," consider Shane as a symbol. What does he represent? Do any of the other characters represent an idea or a human quality?

F. List several ways in which Shane changed the lives of the Starretts and the homesteaders in general.

G. What do you think happened to Shane after the end of the book?

II. *Collateral Work*

A. Describe in an essay how the novel might have been written from a point of view other than that of a young boy.

B. Compare the hero Shane with one of the following characters. You should tell how Shane is similar to and different from one of these heroes:
   1. Matt Dillon (or a similar TV hero)
   2. Robin Hood
   3. Davy Crockett

A Separate Peace by John Knowles (tenth or eleventh grade)

I. *The Novel*

A. Who is the main character or protagonist? Is this a study of Finny or of Gene?

B. Do we really get to know Gene? Is he left shadowy purposely? What is his motivation in pushing Finny off the tree? What mistake does he make about his relationship with Finny? Does he ever understand Finny?

C. Consider the "roundness" of other characters such as Leper and Brinker. What do they represent?

D. What is the significance of Leper's going to war? Discuss the meaning of the later meeting of Leper and Gene.

E. What is the theme of the book? What is the significance of the title? What "separate peace" is negotiated? What symbolic moment is tied to the theme? Cite passages that further the theme.

II. *Collateral Work*

A. Write an essay discussing the novel in relation to a theme of conflict between innocence and reality.

B. Any of the following is suitable for small-group reading and oral presentation in its relation to *A Separate Peace*:
   1. Joseph Conrad, *The Secret Sharer*.

2. Herman Melville, *Billy Budd.*
3. J. D. Salinger, *The Catcher in the Rye.*

C. Other related novels for group reading or for individual reading, with oral or written reports, include:
  1. Dorothy Baker, *Young Man with a Horn.*
  2. Henry Fielding, *Tom Jones.*
  3. Rumer Godden, *Greengage Summer.*
  4. James Joyce, *Portrait of the Artist as a Young Man.*
  5. Conrad Richter, *A Light in the Forest.*
  6. Betty Smith, *A Tree Grows in Brooklyn.*
  7. John Steinbeck, *East of Eden.*

The Old Man and the Sea by Ernest Hemingway (tenth or eleventh grade)

I. *The Novel*

A. Is this a tragic novel? In what sense is the novel tragic? Consider Aristotle's definition, for example.
B. Is this work a novel of affirmation? in what sense?
C. Is Santiago a hero? a tragic hero? an epic hero? In what ways is he an extraordinary man? Does he differ from other Hemingway heroes, or in what ways is he like them?
D. Is there allegory here? Is there a theme?
E. What is the significance of Santiago's experience to others?
F. What is the relationship between the boy and the old man?
G. What does the novel say about the relationship between man and nature?
H. Is there religious symbolism pervading the novel?
I. Discuss the possible meanings of the sharks, the skeleton of the great fish, the lions in Santiago's dream.
J. Find specific examples of the following aspects of Hemingway's unique style in the novel:
  1. Use of simple and compound sentences
  2. Naturalistic concern for authenticity of detail
  3. Sparse, objective, masculine tone and over-all style

II. *Collateral Work*

Write an essay in which you consider the novel in relation to the following: The honorable, honest man is scarred and battered by the forces of existence. He realizes the futility but struggles only to lose. In the struggle, however, is the only meaning of life, and in the struggle, man reveals his stature and dignity. Is Hemingway's final theme dealing with the dignity of man in the face of the adversity of life?

The Ox-Bow Incident by Walter Van Tilburg Clark (eleventh grade)

  I. *The Novel*

    A. Relate the time and place of the novel to the conflict with the character or characters. Would the theme of the book be meaningless if the time or the place were changed?

    B. What is the nature of the characters that brings them into conflict? Is there a main character or a protagonist? Are the characters representative of a minority group? What characters specifically represent groups and which characters are more representative of all man?

    C. Is the conflict with other men as individuals—as groups—or with intangible attitudes and institutions within the society?

    D. What is the outcome of the conflict? To what extent does the character control the outcome? To what extent does "fate" or destiny control the outcome?

    E. How does the author feel about man as indicated by this work?

    F. How does the author present the ideas? Does he give the situation without comment? Does he interpret the actions and situations of the character?

    G. Is the conflict in the novel a contemporary problem? Is the conflict also one that has always been present?

  II. *Collateral Work*

Accept the hypothesis that this novel is an allegory of humanity approaching the democratic life. In an essay choose three of the following characters and defend or reject them as representing the characteristics listed below.

    Art: Everyman.
    Gil: The good-natured, simple but emotional type.
    Farnley: Meanness and viciousness.
    Canby: Vested neutrality.
    Davies: The ineffectual, liberal, intellectual reformer.
    Osgood: The ineffectual representative of religion.
    Smith: The status-seeker.
    Gabe: The completely stupid follower.
    Mapes: Organized religion that has become corrupt.
    Tetley: The fascist.

The Bridge of San Luis Rey by Thorton Wilder (tenth or eleventh grade)

I. *The Novel*

    A. The setting is significant in that it is remote in time and place, thus indicating perhaps a romantic outlook. The idea of universality is implied so that the reader looks for meaning in terms of pervasive ideas rather than specific commentary on a certain period in history.

    B. The inner life and the outer life of the characters are narrated with objectivity. The author makes no didactic commentary.

    C. The concept of truth presented is that of an absolute or divine truth.

    D. The universe is viewed as having a plan or an ordering by a divine being. Each character, having reached a kind of climax in his life, had to die. Love is regarded not as an entity in itself but as a link—love links the living and the dead through memory. The love as a link is enough; it acts as a kind of end by being a means.

    E. Man is viewed as having relatively little free will and control of his destiny. The view is not pessimistic, however, but positive, since love is central in the order of the universe.

    F. Art and the imagination and the "poetic view of experience" enter into the characters of Uncle Pio, who has a need to create; Perichole, the actress; and to some extent into the literary letter writing of Dona Maria. Implied in the work are ideas on the function of the arts and the beauty of the imagination.

    G. Generally the novel discusses manifest forms of love—love that is not completed—but the existence of the love is enough. Thus, the idea of unfulfilled love as good in itself would place Wilder generally in the romantic mode.

II. *Collateral Work*

    A. Speculate on what would have been the fate of a character had the bridge fallen. Remain faithful to the character as portrayed in the novel.

    B. Discuss the symbolism of the bridge in these terms:

        1. Its calamity brought forth a revelation of love among men. These five accident victims are raised to a "universal" level through their means of proving this love in Juniper's investigation.

2. The bridge not only brings together suffering humanity but closes the gap between this world and the next.

The Bridge over the River Kwai by Pierre Boulle (twelfth grade)

I. *The Novel*

A. Consider the novel in the tragic-ironic mode. Is Colonel Nicholson a tragic hero? Consider these four typical situations of the tragic hero in relation to Colonel Nicholson:
1. The hero's role is basically but not solely a guilty one.
2. While above the average man, the hero is not completely good and just.
3. The hero is destroyed through fate or external evil, but he is not overcome with this evil.
4. From one point of view the hero's action is guilty. From another point of view his action is innocent.

B. Consider the symbolism of the bridge. For each of the separate characters, the bridge takes on a personal meaning. The construction of the bridge may be in a larger sense considered as a means of artistic expression or as creativity. Relate each of the following statements about art to the individual perceptions of the bridge in the novel.
1. Art is an expression of the reality of the spirit.
2. Art is a social sharing of man's best experiences.
3. Art is the language of emotional attitude.
4. Art is the imaginative expression of a wish.
5. Art is a secondhand copy of reality.
6. Art is the play of the man.

C. Consider the novel in a unit dealing with war in literature.
1. Discuss the setting historically and geographically and its significance.
2. Discuss the effect of war on an individual character and/or a particular group.
3. Discuss the conflict or conflicts in the novel. Is there resolution?
4. Does man have a choice as to his fate in this novel? Can the characters change their destinies?
5. What seems to be the author's point of view toward the issue of war?
6. How is the story told? Who tells it? Is it told in chronological order, by flashback technique, or the like?
7. Discuss the author's use of symbolism and of figurative language.

8. Can you see any relation of the structure or form of the novel to its effectiveness in communicating the theme?

II. *Collateral Work*

Consider the novel's presentation of man in relationship to the universe. In an essay discuss one of the following concepts in connection with the novel.

A. "Men are continually in competition for honor and dignity"— Thomas Hobbes

B. "Man is wholly and throughout but patch and motley"—Michel de Montaigne

C. "Man in nature is the mean between nothing and everything"— Blaise Pascal

D. "All events are interdependent and necessary"—Benedict Spinoza

E. "Perceptions are according to the measure of the universe"— Francis Bacon

F. "Struggle is an indispensable accompaniment of progress"—Immanuel Kant

G. "Man functions as an harmoniously operating 'divine machine' in a 'best of all possible worlds' "—Wilhelm Leibnitz

H. "Things are good or evil only in reference to pleasure or pain" —John Locke

I. "A cause contains as much reality as its effect"—René Descartes

J. "Good is obtained by harmonizing ideals and natural objects"— Plato

Cry, the Beloved Country by Alan Paton (twelfth grade)

I. *The Novel*

In this particular novel there seem to be nine characters—two main characters and seven very important minor characters, who should be considered separately and individually. The following questions could be asked in general about each:

A. What kind of person is he or she?

B. Describe this person, in particular the clothing and the environment.

C. Briefly give his importance in the novel.

D. Show the interrelationship among these characters.

1. Stephen Kumalo

Is he kind or unkind, patient or short-tempered, generous or selfish? Back up your opinion with examples. Did you feel sympathetic toward him? Would you say he is the main character—why?

2. James Jarvis

   What do you learn about James Jarvis in Chapters 18 and 19? Does he know his son? What sort of man does he portray? What do you think he felt upon learning of his son's death? Is there a great change in his attitude? Could this man be typical of the white man in Africa?

3. Arthur Jarvis

   Did we meet or read of this character? Could he be considered a living character or one we meet through the eyes of other characters? Why was he important? What was his contribution?

4. Msimangu

   Would you say this character was interesting? What do you think he means when he says, "I am a weak and sinful man, but God put His hands on me, that is all"? Why was he kind to Kumalo? What does this show about his character?

5. Absalom

   How do we know this character? What do we learn about him from the interview at the prison? during the trial? before he dies? What does this character contribute to the novel?

6. Gertrude

   What is your opinion of this character? Did she really repent or not? When she left, did you believe that she was going to become a nun? Why or why not?

7. The young white man at the prison

   Why is this man important? Is he honestly helpful or does he want to keep from failing or having the sense of failure in this case? What is his attitude in general?

8. John Kumalo

   What sort of person is he? Why was he cruel to his brother? What was his general attitude? What happened in the last meeting between the two brothers? What was your opinion of this event?

9. Stephen's wife

   Though this character is mentioned in only two places, why should she be considered a very important minor character? What is Paton saying about her when he writes, "Then she sat down at his table, and put her head on it, and was silent, with the patient suffering of black women, with the suffering of oxen, with the suffering of any that are mute"? What more do we learn about her in Book III?

II. *Collateral Work*

A. Discuss the thread of fear that runs throughout the novel.

B. In an essay discuss the paradoxical statements that are made in the novel:

    1. In Chapter 6, Msimangu's statement: "I am not a man for segregation, but it is a pity that we are not apart."

    2. In Chapter 22, the paradox concerning the law, justice, and being just.

    3. When Jarvis, in Chapter 32, learns that there is to be no mercy, he says: "I do not understand these matters, but otherwise I understand completely."

Lord of the Flies by William Golding (twelfth grade)

I. *Preparation*

A. Discuss the possibility and plausibility that the events told in the story could actually occur in this nuclear age.

B. Instruct the students to read the novel so they can visualize the problem and the actions and decisions made to overcome it, evaluate these actions, and offer alternatives based on their own viewpoint and experience.

C. Define the British expressions that might present problems in reading and understanding the novel.

II. *The Novel*

Class discussion of the book, either chapter by chapter or on the basis of three identifiable areas of the book: the world of the game; the world of fear; and the world of reality or destruction and evil. The following are representative questions from the chapters:

A. Chapter 1

    1. How is the glamour of the situation and the island conveyed to the reader?

    2. What suggestions are there that this glamour may be an illusion?

    3. How successful is the beginning government likely to be, and why?

B. Chapter 2

    1. How secure are the rules of government and on what are they based?

    2. Why do the characters feel that the other side of the island is unfriendly?

    3. Where does the blame for the child's death lie?

C. Chapter 3

    1. How would you describe the nature of the conflict between Jack and Ralph?

    2. What is the nature of Simon's experience and feeling?

D. Chapter 4

    Can degrees of seriousness and danger be distinguished?

E. Chapter 5

    1. What are the expressed attitudes toward the "beast" and what attitudes to life as a whole do they imply?

    2. What does "man's essential illness" mean to Simon?

F. Chapter 6

    1. What is happening to the importance of the rescue?

    2. What does the sign from the adult world mean?

G. Chapter 7

    1. What is the difference in Ralph's view of themselves and of the sea? Why does it produce such strain?

    2. Why is the ritual dance in this chapter different from other ritual dances?

    3. What is the effect of schoolboy language at this point?

H. Chapter 8

    In what ways can we now see that this novel is more than a boy's adventure story?

I. Chapter 9

    What on the mountain is a sign of man's inhumanity to man?

J. Chapter 10

    Why do none of the children fully recognize what they have done and its significance?

K. Chapter 11

    1. What is the full symbolic meaning of the conch?

    2. What power and desire have finally been liberated in the children?

L. Chapter 12

    Is the conclusion just a trick to make a happy ending, or does it serve deeper purposes?

III. *Collateral Work*

    Relate one of the following statements to the novel. Accept or reject the statement, using specific illustrations from the novel as evidence for your conclusion.

A. A democratic society must be mutually organized for the survival of all the members.
B. Each member must contribute to the general welfare of all.
C. Leadership in a democratic organization entails a responsibility to all members.
D. The more capable members must assume the guidance and control of the less experienced or less capable members.
E. Cooperation in a democratic society must be maintained or chaos will result.

USEFUL COLLECTIONS OF SHORT STORIES

Animal Stories, Nell Murphy (Ed.) (New York: Dell, 1965).
Twenty-two stories, some for younger readers, some sophisticated.
Best Short Stories by Negro Writers, Langston Hughes (Ed.) (Boston: Little, Brown, 1967).
A distinguished collection of twentieth-century selections.
Beyond Belief, Richard J. Hurley (Ed.) (New York: Scholastic Book Services, 1966).
Eight science fiction tales.
Big Woods (New York: Random House, 1955).
The hunting stories of William Faulkner. Contains "The Bear," "The Old People," "A Bear Hunt," "Race at Morning." Excellent for use in the eleventh and twelfth grades.
Hit Parade of Sports Stories, Dick Friendlich (Ed.) (New York: Scholastic Book Services, 1966).
Varied sports are represented, with both female and male protagonists.
The Hunting Horn, Paul Annixter (Ed.) (New York: Hill & Wang, 1957).
A fine collection of dog stories.
Out West, Jack Schaefer (Ed.) (Boston: Houghton Mifflin, 1955).
An unusual and varied collection of quality western stories, edited by the author of *Shane.*
Pioneers West, Don Ward (Ed.) (New York: Dell, 1966).
Fourteen frontier stories, mostly by name writers.
Point of Departure, Robert S. Gold (Ed.) (New York: Dell, 1967).
Nineteen stories of "youth and discovery" by modern name writers.

Stories, Frank G. Jennings and Charles J. Calitri (Eds.) (New York: Harcourt, Brace & World, 1957).
A splendid collection, highly varied in form, theme, and difficulty, with a good teacher's edition.

Stories for the Dead of Night, Don Congdon (Ed.) (New York: Dell, 1957).
A collection of horror suspense by modern writers.

Stories for Youth, A. H. Lass and Arnold Horowitz (Eds.) (New York: McGraw-Hill, 1950).
The stress is on human values—one of the best anthologies for teenagers.

The Story: A Critical Anthology, Mark Schorer (Ed.) (Englewood Cliffs, N.J.: Prentice-Hall, 1950).
A resource for the teacher. Furnishes insight into the art of the short story and contains some directly teachable material.

Tales Out of School, M. Jerry Weiss (Ed.) (New York: Dell, 1967).
Humorous school stories.

Tomorrow the Stars, Robert Heinlein (Ed.) (New York: Doubleday, 1952).
Fourteen good science fiction stories.

Treasury of Great Ghost Stories, Ira Peck (Ed.) (New York: Popular Library, 1965).
Classic stories of dark fantasy.

Twenty Grand, Ernestine Taggard (Ed.) (New York: Bantam Books, 1962).
A group of stories with great range in subtlety and variety. Several involve teenagers.

Young Love, Marvin E. Karp (Ed.) (New York: Popular Library, 1965).
Ten stories of first experiences with love, featuring John Updike, Eudora Welty, Jessamyn West, and others.

Youth, Youth, Youth, A. B. Tibbets (Ed.) (New York: Franklin Watts, 1955).
A brilliant collection of stories dealing with the problems of adolescence.

6
Teaching Poetry

Most teachers of high school English seem to agree that the study of poetry should occupy an important place in the English curriculum. At least, English teachers spend long, and often unrewarding, hours at the task of "covering" with their students the poems included in the anthologies to which so many teachers are bound. Whether this practice stems from the training and convictions of the English teacher or simply from the whims of the anthology publishers, the instinct that places special emphasis on the study of poetry is very sound.

It is a truism that there is poetry inherent in the human spirit. But, as the teacher of adolescents knows, it profits little to tell this to students. In poetry, perhaps more than in any other phase of the teaching of literature, lie the shoals of frustration, especially for the young or inexperienced teacher. Love of literature, and especially of poetry, is the characteristic bond among all teachers of English. But poetry is not popular with the majority of adolescents or of adults. In this fact of the culture lurks disillusionment for the teacher. Sam, the young college undergraduate preparing to teach English, probably has an unbounded enthusiasm for poetry. Perhaps he even strolls under the campus elms with a thin volume of verse. But then he reaches his senior year and, as a student teacher, meets his adolescent charges. Perhaps he will teach ninth graders who, redolent from the gym class the preceding hour, are not in any mood to "dig" his starry-eyed approach to all that poetry stuff. So, if Sam is truly devoted to teaching, he recovers, learns the facts of life and adolescent culture, and adjusts thereto. If not, he may get out of secondary school teaching, or stay in it and become more and more bitter toward his students and more and more unhappy within himself.

There *is* poetry in everyone; deep down beneath, where everyone really lives, lies poetry. For poetry represents one way of ordering experience and thereby of making it manageable. It may be interesting to adolescent boys to compare a poem with a formula or an equation in mathematics. Both represent a great compressing of experience into a small set of symbols. Both (if the mathematics is correct and the poem good) have nothing extraneous. Both are important ways of communicating experience. As a way of communicating and managing experience, poetry in one form or another is pervasive in modern living. One has only to look at television for a half hour to note the importance of jingles and various types of word play in advertising. And all around us are mottoes and slogans, helping to remind us who we are and what we are and supposedly helping to keep us oriented to whatever values we hold. Of course, as the semanticists remind us, there is the danger that our slogans may lead us to form tight categories—those of overgeneralization, of confusing words with the things they stand for. Yet mottoes and slogans are one form of poetry. So are proverbs, which, according to some anthropologists, started with primitive, nomadic peoples and represented a rudimentary system of laws when there were no statute books.

Poetry is not, however, only a means of communication; it has an esthetic function as well, and in this sense it reaches everyone, though not necessarily through the poems most often taught in high school and college courses in literature. There is a fundamental human need for rhythm which poetry serves, even though for some people the rhythm may be at the level of the barroom phonograph. In fact the current hits can be very useful in teaching poetry. Their use of the refrain and other devices of balladry, for example, can be compared to that in the old ballads found in almost any literature anthology.

For most people, the nursery rhyme is the first formal contact with poetry. And it is an important contact indeed. It is the rare child who does not like nursery rhymes. The child is very responsive, in general, to the esthetic possibilities of language. He likes to chant words even when he has no idea what they mean.

The seeming decline of the natural zest for poetry is the phenomenon that leaves many a secondary school teacher gloomy. What is the explanation for this decline? Probably, the answer lies partly in the nature of human growth. Poetry is emotional, and as one grows older, the emotions retreat further and further below the surface. Adolescence is particularly a time of inhibition.

But the explanation may lie partly, too, in the traditions of teaching and in the procedures used by many teachers. Two traditions in the teaching of literature, and especially of poetry, are relevant: the "academic" tradition and the "sentimental" tradition. The academic tradition implants the idea that poetry is a discipline, a rigorous vehicle for developing the mind, sharpening the powers of abstraction, and enlarging the vocabulary. Poetry can induce these accomplishments, but an emphasis on this tradition in the high school often results in painful dissection of poetry, in scansion of lines, analysis of rhyme schemes, and drill on figures of speech. Often there is compulsory memorizing and laborious, monotonous paraphrasing. Again, these elements may be important at times; certainly there are skills of reading poetry to be developed. Yet an overemphasis on poetry as discipline has undoubtedly been a factor in developing distaste for it.

On the other hand, the sentimental tradition features the sighing, rhapsodic approach, the idea that poetry is a precious form of experience reserved for the esoteric few. In this approach, normal adolescent boys may be expected to trip through the daffodils with Wordsworth when they should be reading Kipling's "Danny Deever" or Karl Shapiro's "Auto Wreck." Emoting *through* poetry is one thing; emoting *about* it, another.

How finally *do* we justify the claims we have made for the importance of poetry? Why, after all, do we say that poetry, particularly the intensive reading of poetry, should have an important place in the English program? John A. Myers, Jr., in the revised edition of this book, gave at least three reasons.[1] First of all, poetry can provide intense enjoyment, can add a rich dimension of delight in the language that is our heritage, can make us more responsive to the verbal world in which we do so much of our living. And because of this increased verbal awareness, students can find much more in and take much more from all their other reading, all their other experiences with language.

---

[1] Part of the material which John A. Myers, Jr. wrote on the teaching of poetry for the revised edition has been incorporated, with his permission, in this chapter.

Second, the close reading of poetry provides us with a kind of verbal or semantic safeguard and censor. It makes us more discriminating in our own use of language and more exacting in the standards of verbal honesty and precision we demand from others. It makes us less willing to tolerate language that is cheap and slovenly and fraudulent, less likely to fall victims to those who would manipulate us to their own ends, be they the political or merely the commercial persuaders. It is poetry, after all, that keeps the language alive and vital, that saves it from the ravages of time and hard use.

Finally, poetry extends the territory of our perceptions, enlarges and deepens and refines our emotional sensibilities, our capacity to feel—and by so doing makes us more sensitive, more responsive, more sympathetic human beings. This, indeed, may be its most important contribution to our lives. For it may well be that the crucial danger of our times is the terrible separation of thought and *feeling,* and the attendant atrophy of the imagination. Archibald MacLeish reminds us powerfully of this last and greatest contribution of poetry:

> Great poems are instruments of knowledge—a knowledge carried alive into the heart by passion . . . knowledge without feeling is not knowledge and can lead to public irresponsibility and indifference, and conceivably to ruin. . . . We are deluged with facts, but we have lost, or are losing, our human ability to feel them. . . . Slavery begins when men give up the human need to know *with the whole heart.* . . . The real defense of freedom is imagination, that *feeling* life of the mind which actually knows because it involves itself in its knowing, puts itself in the place where its thought goes, walks in the body of the little Negro girl who feels the spittle dribbling on her cheek. . . . The man who knows with his heart knows himself to be a man, feels as himself, cannot be silenced.[2]

CHOOSING POEMS

Junior and senior high school teachers and librarians are all painfully aware of the objections which students raise to poetry. Elizabeth Rose's summary of some of the complaints of junior high school pupils is still an apt one:

[2] "The Poet and The Press," *Atlantic,* CCIII (March 1959), 44–46, and elsewhere.

When the teacher has disproved the idea that all poets are strange-look-
ing, weak creatures, he has another misconception to straighten out
with the young: that poetry is written about sissy things, about sentimental love, pink and blue skies, and hosts of yellow daffodils, or about
death and the serious realities of life, about sad, unhappy, far-off things
and places long ago. Youth needs to be shown that all poetry is not sentimental or whimsical, moralistic or rhetorical.[3]

A first principle, therefore, in teaching poetry in either the junior or
senior high school is that selections must be chosen which show the
wide variety and virility of poetry and which are linked to student
concerns.

To choose poems that will show the true range of poetry and its
connection with everyday life, the teacher may have to go outside the
ordinary classroom anthology, which tends to include traditional poems
—many of which may not be appropriate for a given class at a given
time. The copy machine will be an important asset here; so will the
school librarian if she is willing to stock a variety of poetry anthologies. By working together, the teacher and the librarian can assemble
at least an adequate collection for use in the classroom. (See the suggested list at the end of the chapter.)

In introducing students to the range of poetry and its connection
with everyday experience, teachers will find the following categories of
poems rewarding:

Animals and the Outdoors—"Catalogue" by Rosalie Moore; "Crows"
by David McCord; "Seal" by William Jay Smith; "Giraffes," by
Sy Kahn.

Machines and Technology—"Buick" by Karl Shapiro; "Steam
Shovel" by Charles Malam; "Transcontinent" by Donald Hall;
"Crossing" by Philip Booth; "Southbound on the Freeway" by
May Swenson; "Fifteen" by William Stafford.

Sports—"The Base Stealer" by Robert Francis; "Foul Shot" by Edwin Hoey; "The Pheasant" by Robert P. Tristram Coffin.

Unusual Slants on Everyday Experience—"The Term" by William
Carlos Williams; "Gamesters All" by DuBose Heyward; "Reflec-
tions Dental" by Phyllis McGinley; "On a Squirrel Crossing the
Road in Autumn, in New England," by Richard Eberhart.

[3] "Teaching Poetry in the Junior High School," *English Journal,* XLVI (December 1957), 541.

Humor—The verse of Richard Armour, Phyllis McGinley, Ogden Nash.

By the time students reach senior high school, they should be growing aware of the variety of poetry, both in form and content. One might start an interesting discussion by asking a class what poetry is usually about. The answers probably will be stock ones mainly: poetry is about nature, love, death, "deep things." Then the teacher may add that poetry can be about dumping garbage and prove it with the following poem, "From This the Strength," by Fred Lape: [4]

The fog had made a twilight on the water.
The shore rocks rose, ugly and aged teeth
Of earth, discoloured at their bases where
The tide had ebbed. Upon their tops the gulls
Stood silently facing the hidden sea.

Two boys with garbage came to the land's edge.
The gulls rose in the mist, circling the boys,
Crying about their heads, gliding down air.
The boys leaned out and slung their load of waste
Over the rocks. Shrieking the gulls swept down.

Their bodies wove together by the cliff.
The strongest found the food. The others swung
In circles waiting turn, or poised on water,
Beating their wings like butterflies, or clinging
To the wet rocks, let the slow roll of surf
Surge under lifted wings. One gull flew out
With red meat in his bill. The fog received
Him in its arms; only the white tail shone,
A comet curving down the sphere of mist.
Two gulls settled upon the cliff again.
They stretched and shook their wings, and folded them
Feather by feather to their sides, like old
Housewives storing their linen into drawers.

The boys went back. The gulls had cleaned the waste
And one by one soared off into the fog.
The ugly was consumed, gone to the bone,
The sinew, feather, wing, to the sure grace
Of flight, the strength to beat against the air
And take the strong wide currents of the sky.

[4] Reprinted by permission of Fred Lape.

After reading the poem and discussing its content, the teacher should point out that this is an example of blank verse.

Or one might introduce a class to Wilfred Owen's "Dulce et Decorum Est" with its "ugly" lines:

If in some smothering dreams, you too could pace
Behind the wagon that we flung him in,
And watch the white eyes writhing in his face,
His hanging face, like a devil's sick of sin;
If you could hear, at every jolt, the blood
Come gargling from the froth-corrupted lungs,
Bitter as the cud
Of vile, incurable sores on innocent tongues,
My friend, you would not tell with such high zest
To children ardent for some desperate glory,
The old Lie: Dulce et decorum est
Pro patria mori.[5]

It may come as a healthy surprise to both boys and girls that such "unattractive" subject matter as the physical effects on soldiers of a gas attack in World War I can be the legitimate material for a poem. More important will be their realization (if it is clarified by the teacher) that when they respond with pleasure to such lines, they are responding to something infinitely more subtle and complex than the subject matter. What they are responding to, of course, is the *language* of the poem and the way in which the poet has *ordered* the various resources of language so as to give us a pleasing *esthetic* whole. The teacher can show that by his art the poet has resolved individually ugly items in the poem into an *experience of the poem* that is anything but ugly, an experience that gives not only pleasure but a kind of knowledge.

By skillful reading and then by careful questioning, the teacher can make the student aware that his response to the poem was both emotional and intellectual. Emotionally the student will have responded, albeit unconsciously, to such sound effects as the combination of alliteration and assonance in "watch the white eyes writhing" and "devil's sick of sin." Nor does the teacher have to use these technical terms to

[5] Wilfred Owen, "Dulce et Decorum Est," *Collected Poems.* Copyright Chatto & Windus, Ltd., 1946, © 1963. Reprinted by permission of New Directions Publishing Corporation and Chatto & Windus, London.

point out the onomatopoetic effect of such words as "gargling" and "froth-corrupted."

Intellectually, as well as emotionally, the student can be made to respond to the "drama" of these lines, to the bitter irony with which the speaker regards Horace's "old Lie"—"It is sweet and becoming to die for one's country," an irony that is emphasized by the rhyming of *glory* and *mori, zest* and *est.* It can be pointed out that even the most innocent tongues, deceived by dreams of glory, can be corrupted in war and that both *innocent* and *corrupted* have double meanings here. The teacher might ask if there is a connection between the "devil" simile and the idea of "froth-*corrupted* lungs." Students love word play, and they can easily be made to understand that the poet has dramatized—through his imagery, his sound effects, his tonal irony—how really *desperate* such glory can become.

Finally, young students can learn from this poem (there are three other stanzas) that it is the legitimate business of poets to use descriptive details, sometimes with no direct commentary on these details, to convey a deeply felt *attitude* toward some institution such as war.

CLASSROOM ACTIVITIES

The principal reason for including this rather vaguely and briefly titled subsection is to allow the author to make the point that enjoyment as well as understanding is an objective of teaching poetry to adolescents. Overseriousness about poetry and monotony of approach are two major pitfalls. The teacher with a great love of poetry and a feeling of mission, which it is hoped all teachers have, easily can become overserious. Monotony of approach is a particular by-product of the recent emphasis on "close reading." Reading of individual poems followed by explication is a valuable procedure, but when it drags on period after period, it can become deadly.

J. N. Hook succinctly puts the case for enjoyment:

> The solution [to helping students enjoy poetry] seems to lie in doing many things with poetry—not just one thing again and again. . . . Teachers and class can (1) read aloud, (2) dramatize, (3) present choral readings of, (4) sing, (5) discuss, (6) compare, (7) write about, (8) emulate or imitate, (9) illustrate with words, (10) illustrate with

pictures, (11) listen to recordings of, (12) laugh about, (13) memorize (voluntarily), (14) collect favorite poems or passages, and (15) with modern poetry, serve as co-creator.[6]

Poetry sometimes may have its closest connection with important aspects of adolescent experience, its greatest impact in the search for the "I," when it is read without being discussed or "worked with" in any way. Every person, and especially the adolescent, remains, to an extent, a bundle of inchoate thoughts, of poignant but formless feelings which lie far below the surface. Self-revelation is furthered when we find words to express these feelings and thereby give them form.

Adolescents are basically very serious people, much given to broad and vague semiconcepts which they are struggling to bring over the threshold of intellectualization. Some poems, which they may be loath to discuss, serve them well in this effort—poems, for example, of doubt and pessimism, such as those of A. E. Housman, the less sentimental poems of love, and poems of protest. One tenth-grade teacher organized a successful poetry unit around the theme "Private Moods."

It would be very easy to become wishy-washy in applying the obvious principle of having fun with poetry. The "Isn't this fun approach!" in teaching is highly suspect among adolescents. However, poetry study certainly can be a means for having fun occasionally. First, there is humorous poetry. Arthur Guiterman's "Pershing at the Front," for example, is almost sure to draw a laugh. The verse of Ogden Nash, W. S. Gilbert, Richard Armour, Phyllis McGinley, and Franklin P. Adams, among others, appeals to various senses of humor. With younger students, limericks might be a starting point in humorous verse.

Choral and group reading is another avenue toward students' pleasure in studying poetry. The teacher need not worry about turning out the kind of polished performance that might be wanted for an assembly or PTA program. The more experimental the attempts at choral reading in the regular classroom are, the better. Poems by Kipling, Poe, Service, James Weldon Johnson, and many others are appropriate for choral experimentation. Students should be encouraged to work out and suggest groupings to achieve certain effects. A simple

[6] *The Teaching of High School English,* 3rd ed. (New York: Ronald, 1965), p. 200.

arrangement for choral reading of Poe's "The Bells" is a good starting point.

Parodies are often enjoyable for adolescents, too, and can serve as a leavener even in units on serious poetry. Of course, students may write original parodies on well-known poems, or they may enjoy reading or hearing read the parodies that successful poets themselves have written. In a twelfth-grade class which has been studying English literature, for example, the reading of Yeat's "Lake Isle of Innisfree" could be followed by Ogden Nash's delightful "Mr. Fortague's Disappointment."

TEACHING STUDENTS TO READ POETRY

Enjoyment and skill go together in reading poetry just as they do in most other activities. The more interested a student becomes, the more he develops skill in reading; and the more skillful he becomes, the more interested in reading he gets. Establishing positive attitudes and arousing interest come first in teaching poetry to adolescents. But the student's friendship with poetry is likely to be short-lived unless he develops some skills and understandings important to reading mature verse.

There are many entire volumes on how to read poetry, and it is not the purpose here to attempt any comprehensive analysis of all the possible factors that might enter into mature reading of verse. Rather, the purpose of this section is to identify some elementary skills and understandings which are of legitimate concern in any high school classroom.

Students need to be made aware, first of all, that there are different kinds of poems; that poems, like short stories or novels, may have different purposes; that the form and technique of the poem, as well as the content, are designed to accomplish that purpose; and that different kinds of poems have to be read in different ways. In a narrative poem, the reader must be able to follow the plot just as he must in reading fiction. A didactic poem must be read slowly and reflectively, and paraphrased, to get the meaning. On the other hand, the poem which seeks merely to create a word picture or sensory impression— Sandburg's "Fog," for instance—cannot be paraphrased. Essential to reading most poetry is the ability and willingness to let the imagination be completely free to make what it can of the lines. Students need to discover, through group reading and discussion, that it is often worthwhile to reread a poem a number of times.

The mere mechanics of poetry may cause difficulty to some students—especially in the junior high school—who have a tendency to read line by line, letting their voices fall on the right margin, whether or not there is any punctuation to mark a stop or pause. Naturally, this kind of reading, oral or silent, can make comprehension impossible. Students have to be taught to observe punctuation in poetry as in prose. Again, oral reading by the teacher and group reading by the class can help.

Inversion in word order, characteristic of poetry, poses another difficulty for many students who might read through the following lines with no idea of the subject-predicate relationship:

> Full many a gem of purest ray serene,
>> the dark unfathomed caves of ocean bear

Ellipsis, also common in poetry, is a related difficulty in lines such as:

> Stone walls do not a prison make,
> Nor iron bars a cage

These difficulties are especially prominent in poetry of earlier periods with which senior high school students must deal in their anthologies. It is not unusual for the student to reach twelfth grade without a good orientation to the peculiar syntactic devices of poetry. In short, a starting point is to teach the student that in reading poetry, as in reading anything, he must be clear on the syntax.

The author has found it helpful to introduce students to the basic "pattern" of much lyric poetry. Many lyric poems fall basically into three parts. The first part is an expression of the experience that triggered the poem; the second, an immediate reaction to the experience, possibly just the expression of a mood or image; the third, some kind of universal application of the experience or broader reflection on its meaning or effect. In Karl Shapiro's "Auto Wreck"—a fine selection for teaching in high school—we have first the image of the ambulance, pulsing red light, racing to the scene of the accident where the mangled bodies are put aboard; then we have the immediate reaction, the stunned feelings of those who witnessed the accident, their banal remarks; finally, we have the reflection, a wonderment at the senselessness of this kind of death. If someone were to count all the lyrics in the language, he might find more that do not fit this pattern than do, but enough do fit to make the approach helpful.

Most artistic poetry can be interpreted at various levels of meaning. Robert Frost's much-explicated little poem, "Stopping By Woods on a Snowy Evening," for example, can be interpreted quite legitimately on at least three levels. First, it may be a poem about a man who stops to enjoy the beauty of a snowfall in the woods at night, but who can't stay long because he must get home. Second, it may be a poem about a man whose need to hurry on from a scene of beauty reminds him of the general way of life, the need for allegiance to responsibility. Finally, it may be an expression of the death wish, with the dark woods symbolizing death. Students should be encouraged to start with the simplest interpretation they can support and to branch out from there. Frequently students, especially bright ones, feel that if they cannot come up with an esoteric, far-out interpretation they have not done well. Other students, awed in the presence of serious poetry, feel that there is one official interpretation of a poem which can be unlocked by those who somehow have been admitted into the mysterious inner circle.

ANALYSIS OF POETRY

Since poetry embodies certain formal characteristics that distinguish it from other forms of literature and that figure prominently in its discussion and analysis, sooner or later the student will have to become familiar with certain technical terms used to identify these characteristics. Just as the study of grammar, usage, and rhetoric provides the teacher and the student with a common vocabulary for discussing writing problems, so poetry has its own "grammar," which can help to expedite and sharpen any discussion of a poem. Much as we desire the student's experience of the poem to be a felt synthesis of all its elements, we cannot teach a poem without being able to converse intelligently about its separable parts: its diction, its imagery, its figures of speech, its controlling metaphors, its sound effects, its tone, its dramatic structure, its rhythmical movement, even its punctuation and its grammar. The terms used to identify and describe these elements and their functioning should be kept to the very barest minimum, at least until the tenth grade; but there is no reason why the average student, in the upper two or three grades, should not be able to recognize and use such concepts as connotation and denotation, imagery, metaphor, symbol, and allusion. On the other hand, much more important than being able to distinguish between metaphor, simile, metonymy, synecdoche, and personification is the understanding of the *principle* of metaphor in its broadest sense, which is the analogical or comparative principle fundamental to poetry. As one writer reminds us, metaphor in its largest sense "is not, as we were taught at school, a figure of speech. In language it is the means by which we extend our awareness of experience into new realms. Poetry is a part of this process of giving apparent order to the flux of experience." [7]

As the student matures and gains more experience with language analysis, he should be able to recognize and manipulate the more intellectual terms related to *tone* in poetry: irony, understatement, overstatement, paradox. He should gradually become acquainted with the terms by means of which we describe the *sounds* of poetry: alliteration, assonance, consonance, onomatopoeia, and rhyme schemes.

Most difficult and perhaps least important in the student's equipment for reading poetry is the whole area of prosody and the various line and stanza forms. There is nothing intrinsically difficult about learning and recognizing the five basic feet in English poetry (iambic, trochaic, anapestic, dactylic, and spondaic) and the names for the number of feet per line (tetrameter, pentameter, and so on), and there is no particular reason for avoiding these terms; but nothing is more futile than having the student indulge in scansion *for its own sake*. If advanced students can be taught to relate meter and metrical variation (along with various sound effects) to the *sense* of the poem, if they can learn to view these aspects functionally and see their contribution to the *total meaning* of the poem, there is no reason for the teacher to hold back on them. But this is a subtle business, difficult for even the most experienced English teachers, and more time has

[7] David Holbrook, *English for Maturity* (New York: Cambridge, 1961), p. 69.

probably been wasted in the classroom on prosody than on any other aspect of the teaching of poetry.

Poetry analysis can be an exciting and enormously profitable intellectual experience for young students, but the teacher must remember that analysis should always be followed by synthesis or there has been no real response to the *whole* poem, which is always greater than and different from the sum of its parts. The terminology of poetry can easily become abstract and meaningless for the student, and a teacher's preoccupation with it can leave a student feeling that poetry is nothing more than an elaborate and boring system of jargon.

If, however, there are many traps for the teacher to avoid in teaching poetry, there are a number of tried and proven paths by which he can safely lead the student into the poem. It is not within the scope of this chapter to describe in detail the process of poetic analysis. Besides, there are so many excellent critical anthologies available today in inexpensive editions, and so many exegeses of individual poems, that no English teacher need remain uninstructed in these techniques. But it may be helpful to list some questions which teachers can ask, and train their students to ask, about any poem. The order in which these questions are asked and the different emphasis that each is given will depend upon the individual poem.

Who is the *speaker* of the poem (for all poems have a speaker, who is either a projection of one of the "selves" of the poet or a character created by the poet for a particular occasion and purpose) and what can you tell about him from his diction and his tone of voice? Whom is the speaker *addressing* and what is the *occasion* for this particular utterance? What is the *setting* in time and place? What is the purpose of the poem? What is its *theme* or underlying idea or main concern? Can you paraphrase the poem? How does the poem's *diction* and *imagery* contribute to its *tone?* What examples of figurative language do you find in the poem and what do these contribute to the overall effect? Do they seem appropriate? Is there a *pattern* to the imagery? the figures of speech? What evidence is there of *progression* in the *structure* of the poem? Are all the steps in the "logic" of the poem provided? Does the poem contain any words that can be regarded as *symbols?* Can the whole poem be regarded as an allegory? If so, what is the allegorical meaning? Are there any *allusions* and why has the poet used them? Do you find examples of *understatement, overstatement, irony, paradox?* What is their function? What striking devices of sound and meter do you find? How is the sound "an echo to the sense"? Do you understand the *syntactical structure* of each of the poem's sentences?

Grouping Poems for Study

Most experienced teachers agree that sustained units of poetry are usually unsuccessful. Poetry is too rich and concentrated for large dosages at one time; normal reading of poetry by mature adults does not proceed ordinarily in a systematic, day-after-day pattern. Of course, class study cannot be organized to fit the vagaries of individual mood, but it seems wiser to intersperse poetry with the reading of other types of literature than to concentrate it in long units.

Nevertheless, it is valuable occasionally to group poems in some logical fashion. Many of the literature anthologies which are organized chronologically or by literary types may tend to obscure the natural grouping which can be made for class study. Simple themes or topics may often provide the unity for a one- or two-day unit of poetry. For example, the teacher may choose the following poems on death: Seeger's "I Have a Rendezvous with Death," Arnold's "The Last Word," Browning's "Prospice," Tennyson's "Crossing the Bar," Landor's "Finis," and Stevenson's "Requiem." Then he may ask the students to match the poems with the following statements:

I have a meeting by appointment with death. (Seeger)
Death is rest. (Stevenson)
Death is the final defeat. (Arnold)
Death is an embarking. (Tennyson)
Death is a looking forward. (Browning)
Death is the end. (Landor)

In thematic organization of literature, the teacher might frequently introduce poems to reinforce and clarify the themes studied through prose. In one anthology of short stories, a story is often followed by a poem which treats a similar theme; thus Willa Cather's "Paul's Case" is followed by Robinson's "Richard Cory," and Roald Dahl's "The Great Automatic Grammatisator" (in which a machine is built which writes fiction) is followed by Stephen Vincent Benet's "Nightmare Number Three."

With twelfth-grade classes, the author found successful a unit on love, in which poetry and a few prose selections were used. The teacher opened the unit by commenting that probably more poems had been written about love than about any other subject, and that these poems, spanning centuries, reflected certain attitudes toward love. A group of light or cynical poems was read first: Housman's "When I Was One and Twenty," Thomas Moore's "The Time I've Lost in Wooing," Edward Vere's "A Renunciation," Suckling's "The Constant Lover" and "Why So Pale and Wan?" Herrick's "To Virgins, To Make Much of Time." Then Thomas Hardy's humorous short story, "Tony Kytes, the Arch-Deceiver," was read. After this, the class made a collection of the lyrics of the hit tunes of the moment, and compared them with some of the poems they had already read. A certain amount of hilarity went with learning at this point.

Next, a group of short poems, more serious in tone, all addressed to a particular lover, was considered: Herrick's "To Althea Who May Command Him Anything," Jonson's "To Celia," Burns's "A Red, Red Rose," Wordsworth's "She Dwelt Among the Untrodden Ways," Byron's "She Walks in Beauty," Shelley's "The Desire of the Moth," Conrad Aiken's "Music I Heard With You," and Witter Bynner's "Voices." The unit concluded with the reading of several short stories dealing with love, and a one-act play, "The Will," by James Barrie.

"People in poetry" is a subject that furnishes a good entree with adolescents who, like adults, are fundamentally interested in people. Treatment of this subject might form the basis for a unit, or might be incorporated in a unit of biography. Whatever the approach, there are many good poems about people, character studies in verse, from Chaucer to the present. Roger Hyndman describes an approach in which Robinson's "Richard Cory" is the first poem studied in eleventh-grade American literature:

> To prepare my pupils for a reading of the poems, I tell them that we are about to meet an outstanding inhabitant of an imaginary town. On the board they see written *Tilbury Town* and beneath it is a list of such notable names as Richard Cory, Miniver Cheevy, Bewick Finzer, Reuben Bright, Aaron Stark, Annandale, Cliff Klingenhagen, Uncle Anan-

ias, Flammonde. (Copies of these poems are available in the classroom library.) Richard Cory and his follow citizens, I explain, are the creations of Edwin Arlington Robinson, a writer reared in a small Maine community.[8]

Theme, of course, is not the only basis for grouping poems, as Stephen Dunning points out in his excellent treatment:

> Clusters can be arranged in many ways; the grouping principle need be valid only for a particular purpose. . . . One handful of poems represents a particular poet; variations on a given theme or subject; poems alike (or dramatically dissimilar) in form make up other sets; poems may be grouped for study of similar metaphors, for their uses of irony, and for similar narrative techniques. Ideally, groups of poems should show a progression toward difficulty and from emphases that are readily understood to emphases that are substantially demanding.[9]

Not all students—indeed, only a few—will leave the English classroom as avid readers of poetry. But the realization by many, through their experiences while in the classroom, that poetry speaks out of the depths of human need gives an important dimension to the task of the teacher of literature.

SELECTED BIBLIOGRAPHY

Collections of Poetry

A Journey of Poems, Richard F. Niebling (Ed.) (New York: Dell, 1964).
A paperback collection of poems for young people by selected British and American poets.
Story Poems New and Old, William Cole (Ed.) (Cleveland: World, 1951).
A paperback narrative collection especially appropriate for younger adolescents.
Cavalcade of Poems, George Bennett and Paul Molloy (Ed.) (New York: Scholastic, 1967).
A paperback collection of poems selected by high school students and the editors. Groupings are highly appropriate to adolescent interests.

[8] "The First Poem," *English Journal,* XLVI (March 1957), 158.
[9] *Teaching Literature To Adolescents: Poetry* (Glenview, Ill.: Scott, Foresman, 1966), pp. 75–76.

Poems for Seasons and Celebrations, William Cole (Ed.) (Cleveland: World, 1961).
Poems for all the major holidays and seasons.
New Negro Poets: U.S.A., Langston Hughes (Ed.) (Bloomington: Indiana University Press, 1964).
Poetry written by young Negro poets on a wide range of themes.
Sprints and Distances, Lilian Morrison (Ed.) (New York: Crowell, 1965).
A valuable book of poetry about sports.
Imagination's Other Places, Helen Plotz (Ed.) (New York: Crowell, 1955).
An unusual collection of poetry related to the sciences and mathematics.
Poems for Pleasure, Herman Ward (Ed.) (New York: Hill & Wang, 1963).
Poems selected by the editor's senior high school classes.
Immortal Poems of the English Language, Oscar Williams (Ed.) (New York: Simon and Schuster).
A paperback anthology covering the whole range of British and American poetry.
Stories in Verse, Max T. Hohn (Ed.) (New York: Odyssey, 1961).
An excellent collection of narrative poetry, with reading directions for students.
Story Poems, Louis Untermeyer (Ed.) (New York: Pocket Books, 1961).
Narrative verse—serious, fantastic, and humorous.
The Magic Circle, Louis Untermeyer (Ed.) (New York: Harcourt, 1952).
For young readers—narrative and dramatic poems.
A Gift of Watermelon Pickle and Other Modern Verse, Stephen Dunning, Edward Leuders, and Hugh Smith (Eds.) (Glenview, Ill.: Scott Foresman, 1967).
A beautiful volume of contemporary poetry brilliantly geared to adolescent concerns.
Poems for Young Readers (Champaign, Ill.: NCTE, 1967).
Selections from their own writings by poets who attended the Houston Festival of Contemporary Poetry, 1966, with commentaries by the poets. An accompanying record of the readings of the poems by the poets available from the NCTE.

The Teaching and Reading of Poetry

Brooks, Cleanth, and Robert Penn Warren. *Understanding Poetry* (New York: Holt, Rinehart, and Winston, 1960).

Holbrook, David, *English for Maturity*. 2nd ed. (New York: Cambridge, 1967). Ch. 5.

Perrine, Laurence, *Sound and Sense: An Introduction to Poetry* (New York: Harcourt, 1963).

Dunning, Stephen, *Teaching Literature to Adolescents: Poetry* (Glenview, Ill.: Scott, Foresman, 1966).

College Entrance Examination Board, *12,000 Students and Their English Teachers,* "Poetry."

7
Drama in the Literature Program[*]

Despite the very notable increase in publication of plays in paperback or special anthologies, drama still must be regarded as the Cinderella of the secondary classroom, a kind of stepchild relegated to fourth position after short stories, novels, and poetry. True, probably more plays are being taught in American high schools today than in any preceding decades. Such standard Shakespearean choices as *The Merchant of Venice, Julius Caesar,* and *Macbeth* have been supplemented by *Our Town, The Miracle Worker, The Glass Menagerie,* and frequently *Oedipus Rex* and *Antigone.* O'Neill is also likely to be represented by an inoffensive one-act and a biographical sketch, while the widely anthologized *Pygmalion* and *Arms and the Man* guarantee a painless showing for Shaw. Some communities, such as Providence, Rhode Island; New Orleans; and Los Angeles, are especially fortunate to have specially established resident companies, created and supported by government agencies to produce high-caliber drama for high school students and to stimulate wide-spread interest and involvement in drama, music, and art. The fact remains, however, that for far too many teachers drama continues to constitute a kind of pleasant interlude between the seemingly more serious concerns of the curriculum, a pleasant diversion inserted to make the daily routine more palatable.

This situation is not surprising when we consider both the problems of the contemporary theater and the limited drama background of most classroom teachers. Modern drama is clearly in a period of tran-

* Written by Gladys Veidemanis, Oshkosh High School, Oshkosh, Wisc.

sition, struggling to define new forms and even its place in American life. And along with the other performing arts, the theater is in serious financial trouble. As attested by the continually dwindling output of new plays each year, the Broadway theater is steadily losing in the struggle against spiraling production costs, outmoded theater buildings, and off-Broadway competition. Further, the theater is failing to attract the kind of adventurous, tolerant audience it needs if it is to progress—a dedicated following willing to support new plays and playwrights, not just sure "hits" and name-star musicals. Unfortunately, as the Rockefeller Report on the Performing Arts so candidly asserts: "As a nation we have traditionally possessed no great thirst for music, dance, drama; if anything, we have inherited a suspicion that the practice of these arts is unmanly and superfluous and that support of them is of no vital importance to our national well-being." [1] For most Americans, "live drama" still means a junior or senior class play or possibly attendance at a community theater production once or twice a year.

How necessary it becomes then to reassert drama's rightful position in the curriculum and the English teacher's responsibility to develop in students interest in and support of quality drama in all its forms. What emphasis drama should be given can best be demonstrated by a discussion of why it should be taught, what should be taught, and how.

DRAMA—A MIRROR OF LIFE AND OURSELVES

Why teach drama? Perhaps the most important reason is to discover more about what it is to be a human being, for man, in all his complexity and conflicts, constitutes the central subject matter of drama. Drama not only mirrors the environment, but helps us to surmount it, to grow in sympathy, imagination, and understanding. The very root of the term "drama"—the Greek *dràu,* to act, to do—suggests its possibilities: it is perhaps our most effective and direct means for depicting and working out social conflicts, moral dilemmas, and personal problems without suffering the specific consequences of our actions.

[1] Rockefeller Brothers Fund, *The Performing Arts: Problems and Prospects* (New York: McGraw-Hill, 1965), p. 184.

The dramatist compels us to empathize with the play's protagonist, to feel his emotions, and to experience his conflicts, yet spares us the actual suffering or indignity his characters must endure. Through tragedy, we are enabled with little pain to learn what life could so painfully teach and are provided a vision of man's endurance and nobility to admire and emulate. Through comedy we can enjoy the purging of laughter, the revelation of "human beings for what they are in contrast to what they profess to be." [2] Well-wrought melodrama, fantasy, or farce can dispel our skepticism, enlarge our imaginations, and take us temporarily out of ourselves. It is not surprising, therefore, that drama has become a recognized tool for therapy. Psychiatrists, for example, frequently utilize psychodrama as an effective means of enabling patients to gain insight into their past experiences and to prepare them in advance for "roles" they will have to resume in normal life. Sociodramas have been found to perform a similar function for small groups, enabling participants to assume fictional identities while working out conflicts that face them in family and community living.

Drama, then, must be viewed as an essential humanizer, a spur to imagination, to insight, to reflection, and, hopefully, to self-knowledge. Appraising the importance of the dramatic arts, business executive Fletcher B. Coleman, speaking at the dedication of the dramatic arts building at Illinois Wesleyan University, so eloquently commented:

> Are the dramatic arts important? Do they serve the welfare of a free society? I think they do for these reasons.
> They hold up the mirror in which society can see itself. They give life, impact, form and substance to the printed word. They stimulate popular support for noble goals; they prick pomposity. They bring light and color and sound and movement to great ideas. They resurrect history and remind us of its lessons.
> The dramatic arts rephrase and refreshen a society's ideals and aspirations and remind it of its failure. They help man see himself in an infinite variety of contexts. They bring to life experiences and situations remote in time or distance—they let us share the cultures of other peoples and give us new insight into the many worlds in which we live.

[2] Louis Krononberger, "Some Prefatory Words on Comedy," in Marvin Felheim (Ed.), *Comedy: Plays, Theory, and Criticism* (New York: Harcourt, 1962), p. 195.

They can probe as no other medium can into man's mind, his societies, his institutions. . . .

Yes, we are in a race with Russia, but we are locked in a larger combat . . . This is man's unending war with himself, his higher nature against the base animal, his age-old wavering choice between the bright stars and the black abyss, between his visions and venality.

From Aristophanes and Sophocles to O'Neill and Williams, this is the battle to which the dramatic arts have always been committed.[3]

The dramatic arts are actually the most direct link we have between literature and life.

DRAMA REDEFINED FOR THE TWENTIETH CENTURY

What drama should we teach? To consider only those works performed on the legitimate stage as "drama" would be tantamount to turning our backs on the mass media revolution that has permanently altered the character of American life and education. But to consider only television and movies as the theater of today betrays an equally limited perspective. We need, therefore, a broadened definition of drama that encompasses its various contemporary manifestations—living theater, television, and motion pictures—and which recognizes each as fulfilling valuable and complementary functions. That these media compete for attention is surely true, but to assume that one form need eclipse another, as some critics insist, is to overlook the distinctive features of each. Their very differences suggest a starting point for the teacher of English, who could profitably utilize a comparative approach to convey to students the rich possibilities of each medium.

Class discussion might be opened, for example, with the problem of what happens to Wouk's *The Caine Mutiny* when transferred from the stage to the movie lot to the television studio. As Father John Culkin first noted, the emphasis in this work has been shifted in every medium in which it has been presented.[4] In the novel, Willy Keith, the immature sailor who advances to self-knowledge, is the indisputable hero. The U.S. Navy dominates the film version, very likely because

[3] As cited in *The Milwaukee Journal* (Nov. 5, 1962), p. 22.
[4] Father John M. Culkin, S.J., "Of Media Study and Male Alligators," speech presented at NCTE Convention, Miami, Florida, Nov. 24, 1962.

of its more elaborate sets and sweeping camera eye. In the stage production, Greenwald, the intellectual, emerges as the commanding figure, while in the televised cutting, Captain Queeg preempts attention. Other works could be similarly analyzed. What happens to a *Pygmalion* when transformed into *My Fair Lady,* or to an *Advise and Consent* that moves from the massive novel to the stage, then to film? Or to *Romeo and Juliet* updated as *West Side Story?* And what transmutations can be traced in the Arthurian legends as they have come down to us through Tennyson, T. H. White, and *Camelot,* on stage and screen? By means of such comparisons, teachers can very effectively lead students to discover that one medium need not replace or imitate another but rather enhance, complement, and extend it more fully and richly.

In widening our definition of drama to include television and film, we must also emphasize the need for attention to drama of all periods. Without in any way undermining the value and appropriateness of the Shakespearean perennials, we would have to argue that one-sided attention to a few plays from a single historical period does injustice to the tradition from which they arose and which they helped to perpetuate. Students need to experience not only Elizabethan tragedy, but also the comedy of manners, farce, melodrama, and fantasy, and to discern for themselves the recurring themes, dilemmas, and human needs reflected in drama of every age. They should have the opportunity to discover that an Antigone joins hands across the centuries with a John Proctor of *The Crucible,* choosing personal integrity and death rather than life with dishonor; that a Medea shares the agony of jealousy with a passionately tormented Othello; that a fervid Lavinia in O'Neill's *Mourning Becomes Electra* emulates the vindictiveness and persuasiveness of her Greek counterpart, if not her enduring nobility.

Most important, we can not afford to exclude from the classroom representative drama since World War II. Young people who have personally witnessed on their television screens such events as the murder of a President's assassin, rioters plunging through the streets of Watts and Detroit, and daily views of American soldiers in ugly combat in Vietnam are not likely to be shocked by the recurrent themes of cynicism, violence, and alienation in contemporary drama. It is to be hoped that the experience of such works as Ionesco's *The Bald Soprano,* Albee's *The Zoo Story,* Sartre's *No Exit,* even Tom Stoppard's

Rosencrantz and Guildenstern Are Dead can underscore the need for genuine communication and love in a world that seems otherwise illogical and meaningless. *The Diary of Anne Frank,* Bolt's *A Man for All Seasons,* and Duerrenmatt's *The Visit* portray not only the evil of which man is capable, but also the nobility and endurance of the human spirit in the face of oppression. We indeed owe our students the critical and enlightening view of their own world that contemporary drama can uniquely provide.

OBJECTIVES FOR DRAMA TEACHING

Having broadened the definition of drama and affirmed its values in the English program, we need to formulate specific objectives that can, in turn, determine the nature and amount of drama emphasis at a particular level. These objectives should of course be defined within the larger context of the overall goals for the course and should include emphasis on the development of the skills of thinking and communication for which the total English program assumes major responsibility. The following set of objectives suggests goals that could be reasonably attempted in a four-year high school drama program:

Develop pleasure and skill in reading and interpreting drama, and acquaint students with some significant dramatic works and lists of plays for future reading. On the whole, the difficulties entailed in reading plays have probably been overstressed. Most students genuinely enjoy reading plays; and while they have to learn to interpret stage directions and to visualize scenes for themselves, they are rewarded by getting a lot in a short time, by fewer vocabulary problems than often face them in novels or short stories, and by peaks of action in every act. We would have to agree with Maynard Mack that "drama is by far the easiest of all the literary forms to make exciting in the classroom . . . and it is also the most effective introduction to the pleasure of reading literature and the skills involved in enjoying it." [5] We would also have to agree that unless a person learns to enjoy *reading* plays, he will never discover most of the great dramatic works

[5] Maynard Mack, "Teaching Drama: *Julius Caesar,*" in Edward J. Gordon and Edward S. Noyes (Eds.), *Essays on the Teaching of English* (New York: Appleton-Century, 1960), p. 320.

of the past, which are so rarely performed in our theaters. For that matter, he will know very little about contemporary drama, since only "smash hits" stay on Broadway and most community theaters cautiously limit their production choices to a few well-known and proven works.

Acquaint students with the dramatic tradition, the role of drama in the history of man. Since drama is so integral a part of our literary and cultural heritage, the study of its rich and varied history is warranted for its own sake as well as for its value as background against which to appraise the theater of our own day. The program of study, however, should concentrate less on the surface history of drama, more on the causes for the emergence of particular dramatic forms and theaters during different historical periods. For example, students better perceive the intentions of tragedy once they realize that it has been the product not of disillusioned, depressed cultures, but of societies, such as those during the times of Sophocles and Shakespeare, that most prized individual resourcefulness, personal freedom, and human happiness. As William Van O'Connor suggests: "The Greeks' joyful consciousness of life sharpened their awareness of death. . . . When life lost its zest for the Greeks the tragic muse departed." [6] Similarly, the comedy of manners or satirical drama should be seen in the context of the Restoration Period, broken loose from a decade of Puritan austerity, or of the eighteenth century, with its surface proprieties, material concerns, and inflexible class distinctions inviting the playwright's mocking or witty scrutiny.

Students should also be led to analyze the ways in which audience expectation and the actual shape of the theater building have affected the form and content of drama. Recent developments in the American theater arc illustrative: The present movement away from realism is being accompanied by a parallel movement away from formal staging, confining sets, explicit stage directions. We would not be exaggerating to suggest that probably the most significant—and precedent-setting —dramatic event of our century was the erection of the Stratford, Ontario, theater building, which discards the proscenium arch and the box seat, with their rigid frame around life, and brings the audience back again into more immediate contact with the play.

[6] William Van O'Connor, *Climates of Tragedy* (Baton Rouge: Louisiana State University Press, 1943), pp. 21–22.

Develop critical standards and taste in drama, film, and television.
In a memorable and still pertinent editorial in the *Saturday Review*
for Nov. 21, 1959, Norman Cousins accused television of perpetrating
a massive fraud—not that publicized by quiz show scandals, but the
incessant exploitation of crime and the glamorizing of violence. He
condemned, in particular, the excessive brutality on many programs,
their obvious indifference to the fragility and value of human life.
These objections have even more basis when applied to the majority
of present-day film and stage offerings, whose "adult entertainment"
formula or "subterranean nihilism" (so characterized by drama critic
Robert Brustin)[7] makes them increasingly questionable for immature audiences. As Mr. Cousins originally suggested, what is really
most disturbing is not the candid treatment of sex, crime, and abnor-
mal behavior nor, indeed, the total moral revolution reflected in our
mass media, but rather the possibility that young people may gradually be losing the capacity to be shocked, moved, or delighted by
what they experience. Like their parents, today's generation is discovering only too quickly that unprecedented affluence, personal freedom, and uninhibited opportunities for leisure are no guarantee of joy
in art or in living.

Good taste and genuine pleasure in the arts can never be forcefully
imposed but they *can* be nurtured in classrooms which maintain lively
exposure to and dialogue about the dramatic arts. One of the first
tasks the teacher should undertake is to help students become more
articulate about the films and plays they see, less ready to make mon-
osyllabic or cliché responses. Students also need to discover publications with provocative discussions and evaluations of the mass media
and should be asked to apply their own critical standards to current
television productions, films, and plays. They must also be taught to
evaluate drama both as art and as craft, as a medium demanding integrity, self-control, significance of theme and language, discipline of
body and voice, fusion of spectacle, technique, and idea. Through
such experiences, they should gradually learn to distinguish the artistic
and original production from the tawdry or imitative, to be able to
enjoy such phenomena as "multimedia happenings," yet be able to
place them in a larger cultural context than the transitory present.

[7] Robert Brustein, *Seasons of Discontent* (New York: Simon and Schuster,
1965), p. 310.

Encourage interest in playgoing and the support of community ventures in drama. Playwright Marc Connelly once commented that the United States is the only country that seems not to recognize the importance of theater to "national health." [8] He was, of course, implying a need for subsidies to the arts, especially in these times when production costs have become so prohibitive. His remarks remind us, however, that unless the school stimulates interest in playgoing, both through planned theater trips and regular publicizing of worthwhile community productions, the majority of our students will probably never shift from exclusive patronage of motion pictures and television, the less expensive and more accessible media. In addition, we must do more to encourage young people to support not only the tested and established drama, but the new—and on faith. Professor Ronald Mitchell advises:

> Let us be theatregoers, but not just "fashionable" theatregoers, seeing only those plays "everyone sees." This type of person is proud to wait for his tickets, pay double, and lord it over the person who is still waiting. Everyone then having seen the same thing—there is nothing to talk about! [9]

We need to educate students to determine hits for themselves and to resist the blinding power of the critic, whose judgment is surely fallible.

Increase students' understanding of the importance of drama as a source of insight into personal and social problems. As their tastes refine, young people should also grow in understanding of others and of themselves through the study of drama. George Jean Nathan said that great drama speaks to man "in solitude and in crowds"—and we know what he meant. We have all been lonely; and thus we can understand Frankie when she says in *Member of the Wedding,* "All people belong to a 'we' except me." And we know that feeling of inadequacy that Biff in *Death of a Salesman* suggests when he exclaims, "I'm a dime a dozen!" Or reading such plays as Elmer Rice's *Adding Machine,* or Capek's *R.U.R.,* or seeing such films as *La Dolce Vita* and *Judgment at Nuremberg,* we can recognize the forces in our own

[8] Marc Connelly, lecture at the University of Wisconsin, Milwaukee, July 23, 1962.
[9] Ronald Mitchell, "Learn by Theatregoing," lecture at the Winter Workshop of the English Association of Greater Milwaukee, Feb. 10, 1962.

society that threaten to destroy individuality, thwart creativity, induce disaster. Clearly, the experience of drama compels us to penetrating self-examination, to enlargement of sympathy and tolerance, to awareness of what it is to be a human being.

A SEQUENTIAL FOUR-YEAR PLAN
FOR THE TEACHING OF DRAMA

If these objectives are to be realized, drama must find its place in the total curriculum and be planned for and structured so that skills can be developed in sequence and constant overlapping avoided. One common shortcoming of our present procedures is that we often end up doing practically the same things with a dramatic work on every level and ignoring what the student has done before. There is surely room in our curriculum for handling drama by several methods—as a type or within thematic or chronological units—but surely it should not be handled as a type on all four levels, nor should the history of drama or the Shakespearean theater be discussed in detail every time students start a drama unit. By whatever method of organization, drama should be taught both as literature and as theater, not exclusively as one or the other. A play is language, rhythm, spectacle; and we do it injustice to act as though it were either permanently entombed on its pages or just as ephemeral as the life of a single production.

The study of drama, of course, must directly contribute to the development of the basic communication skills with which the English program is most concerned. The following outline of a four-year program attempts to take into account the kinds of skills needed to read and evaluate drama and to suggest kinds of assignments that simultaneously meet the objectives of the drama program as well as those of the over-all course. Starred (*) activities are recommended for able groups primarily or as optional assignments.

    I. English 9 and 10—Introduction to the Play as a Literary Type and as a Work for the Stage
        A. English 9
            1. Type: One-act plays primarily; three-act with capable groups

2. Skills to be developed
   a. Visualizing setting, character
   b. Interpreting characters from dialogue, action
   c. Detecting foreshadowing, plot unfolding, climax
   d. Identifying theme
   e. Supplying missing segments
   f. Recognizing stage directions
   g. Demonstrating clear, meaningful oral reading
   h. Distinguishing differences in techniques of TV, film, theatrical presentations
   i. Applying criteria for evaluating effective TV programs
3. Concepts
   a. Understanding why the author chose the dramatic form
   b. Being aware that plays reflect human life and experience
   c. Recognizing that a play can provide reading pleasure
   d. Being aware that playgoing is both enjoyable and worthwhile
4. Suggested activities
   a. Discussion
      (1) Give out a sheet of selected dialogue passages and have students make references about character traits, personal problems, social class, and so on. Such an exercise well illustrates what dialogue is used to reveal in a play.
      (2) Take a short story and discuss what changes would have to be made to transform it into a play. Emphasize the importance of dialogue to convey characterization and conflict. Identify ways of creating mood by means other than author description.
      (3) Inductively arrive at criteria for evaluating TV programs by starting with the question, "What is there to say about a TV program besides 'I liked it' or 'It bored me' "? Try to lead students to an awareness of the three "I's" with which to view and evaluate:
          Determine: Intention—purpose, theme (if any)
                     Invention—originality of plot treatment, quality of dialogue, use of setting, special effects
                     Impact—power to move, convince, apply to our own lives

(4) Plan varied experiences to develop skills in oral reading by having students undertake such activities as these:
   (a) Select passages to read that introduce a major character and reveal his dominant traits.
   (b) Pick out and read only the climax scene and state why you consider it the turning point of the play.
   (c) Pick out the *funniest* passage of a play and justify your choice by getting the class to laugh.
   (d) Choose passages that appeal to a specific emotion —grief, terror, hate, jealousy, and so forth—try to convey that emotion through skillful reading.

b. Composition
   (1) Assign various topics for expository writing, 1 to 3 paragraphs in length:
      (a) Why I *didn't* like a specific TV program
      (b) Reaction to a school play or dramatic assembly
      (c) The purpose for a minor character
      *(d) Proving why a specific judgment of a character is or is not false (In advance, distribute a sheet of quotations appraising a dramatic character. Have students find proof in the play to support the particular stand they are defending.)
      (e) Tracing clues that give away the ending (requires recognition of foreshadowing)
   (2) Encourage occasional narrative/descriptive writing:
      *(a) Dramatize a short ballad or one scene from a longer narrative poem.
      (b) Describe the most memorable movie "minute" in your film-viewing experience.
      (c) Describe an episode in your life that could well provide the basis for a dramatization.

*c. Individual/Small-group projects
   (1) Do a collage that suggests the different moods of a play you have read or seen.
   (2) Read additional one-act plays to discuss individually with the teacher. Possibly prepare an interesting report on one you would like to persuade others in the class to read.
   (3) Report on a community play you have seen and that you considered particularly effective.

       (4) Actually dramatize a short episode out of your own life or that of a person you have known closely.

B. English 10
1. Type: Three-act plays primarily; introduction to Shakespeare
2. Skills to be developed
   a. Review of skills from English 9
   b. Identifying mood and tone
   c. Reading a Shakespearean play
      (1) Reading blank verse
      (2) Adjusting to Elizabethan theater conventions: soliloquies, asides, absence of stage directions, archaic expressions, allusions, metaphor
   d. Discussing criteria for evaluating effective films
   e. Evaluating view of life in some current TV or movie productions (especially view of family)
3. Concepts
   a. Review of concepts from English 9
   b. Awareness of historical development of drama from Age of Sophocles to Age of Elizabeth
   c. Discovering universality of Shakespeare, pertinence of ideas to our own lives
4. Suggested activities
   a. Discussion
      (1) Provide and discuss a list of vocabulary words that suggest character traits, e.g., diabolical, furtive, pert, impudent, and so on. Then apply to various characters, having students justify their judgments with textual proofs. A list of verbs could be used similarly and applied to character actions.
      (2) Do occasional paraphrasing to check on meaning of selected passages—and not only from Shakespearean plays.
      (3) Discuss popular "family," western, or nature programs on TV. Identify common characteristics in these programs and evaluate to what extent they represent realistic life situations.[10]
      (4) Present Shakespeare within the context of his times. Find out what students already know and work from there. Discuss ways in which the stage and audience

---

[10] *See* Neil Postman, *Television and the Teaching of English* (New York: Appleton, 1961), pp. 105–107.

144 DRAMA IN THE LITERATURE PROGRAM

would affect the kind of play that could be presented. Identify some major differences in English language usage in Shakespeare's time and ours and different theatrical conventions. Discuss the term "Renaissance" and how Shakespeare fits into the movement.

(5) Drawing particularly from *Julius Caesar,* identify ideas that continue to have pertinence for our time, such as the difficulty of balancing personal and public loyalties, feeling and reason, practical goals with ideals.[11]

b. Composition
(1) Have students describe an idea for a TV show that they think would attract a large audience, but that, to their knowledge, has never been tried.
(2) Analyze:
  (a) Nature of conflict in a play—inward, outward
  (b) What the play has to say to us today
  *(c) Effect of a particular theater building and audience expectation on dramatic structure and content
(3) Compare two characters within the same play, emphasizing a dominant trait they share in common. Use proofs from the text to support your comparison.
*(4) Creative writing:
  (a) Write dialogues revealing character traits or attitudes (for example, arrogance, uncertainty, jealousy). Punctuate and paragraph conversation accurately and work for creating convincing and natural dialogue.
  (b) Rewrite the ending of a play to fit another logical interpretation.
  (c) Dramatize an episode that will arouse our indignation.
  (d) Write stage directions for a play that lacks them (especially Shakespearean).
*c. Individual/Small-group projects
(1) Prepare bulletin boards on such subjects as these: drama of different periods; worthwhile current movies and TV productions; ideas suggested by *Scholastic*

---

[11] *See* Mack, pp. 320–336, and Robert Ornstein, *Shakespeare in the Classroom* (Urbana, Ill.: Educational Illustrators, 1960).

or *Literary Cavalcade* material on personalities that have dominated the stage, and so on.

(2) Prepare tape recordings of significant episodes from plays studied.

(3) Design a model set or prepare a series of set sketches for a play studied in class or read individually. Adhere closely to directions given in the play and try to capture the essential mood and period.

(4) Present original oral-topics on aspects of dramatic history such as, A Visit to the Annual Festival of Dionysus, The Revival of Drama in the Middle Ages, The Debate over Shakespeare's Identity. Avoid the flat encyclopedia recital!

II. English 11 and 12—Evaluation and extended reading of drama
   A. English 11
      1. Type: Three-act plays primarily: American drama, Shakespeare
      2. Skills to be developed
         a. Understanding irony, symbolism, and implication
         b. Justification of outcomes
         c. Independent interpretation of plays
         d. Relating drama to larger themes, Puritanism, individualism, and so forth
         e. Applying criteria to the evaluation of a play, movie, or TV production
         f. Revealing drama as an exposition of significant ideas
      3. Concepts
         a. Insight about the place of drama in American life and literature
         b. Familiarity with major American playwrights and significant developments in American drama
         c. Introduction to idea of tragedy
         d. Evaluation of the view of American life commonly represented on TV and in films
         e. Developing empathy with characters
      4. Suggested activities
         a. Discussion
            (1) Acquaint students with major American dramatists, both by studying them individually and by using reading lists. Have students as a class compile their own annotated list of recommended plays.

(2) Discuss the impression that American films and TV convey to others, especially people abroad. To what extent is this view of American life convincing, real, precise? Identify productions that have given a valid or a deceptive view.

(3) Try role playing, in which students assume the roles of characters in a play and speak in justification of some action or conduct in the play.

(4) Have students select a TV program, film, or play and discuss how creative thinking could give it more richness, meaning, significance.

(5) Discuss how ideas in drama apply to contemporary situations. Explore such issues, for example, as what *Inherit the Wind* has to say about freedom of thought in a democracy, how *The Crucible* reflects on twentieth-century "witch-hunting," what *Point of No Return* suggests about the role of the individual in big business, and so on.

(6) Debate the responsibility of the protagonist for his actions: Is Macbeth a free agent or merely a pawn of fate? Is Captain de Vere justified in applying the death penalty to Billy Budd? Is Joe Keller of *All My Sons* to be condemned for thinking first of his family's well-being?

(7) Do oral paraphrases of difficult or especially significant passages.

b. Composition
  (1) Analysis:
    (a) Consistency and logic of ending, fate of protagonist
    (b) Characters as types, representations
    (c) Playwright's method of developing his theme
    (d) Some aspect of style: symbolism, irony, and so forth
    (e) Critical analysis of play read independently
  (2) Evaluate a movie, play, or TV production according to given criteria.
  (3) Compare handling of theme, character, or conflict in two different plays.
  *(4) Creative writing:

(a) Dramatize a short story or scene from a novel or biography.

(b) Attempt a parody of a selected scene. Study the style of the original carefully.

(c) Attempt an original scene suggested by a play and in the style of the original.

*c. Individual/Small-group activities

(1) Present a well-planned floor talk on a major American play.

(2) Organize a panel discussion on a significant TV production, such as a Hallmark Theater special.

(3) Attend special after-school sessions to hear special play recordings or tapes which cannot be fitted into the regular class program.

B. English 12

1. Type: Three-act plays primarily: Greek, Shakespearean, modern

2. Skills to be developed

a. Review of techniques for evaluating plays, movies, TV productions

b. Evaluating reviews of mass media in periodicals; distinguishing responsible and irresponsible reviewing

*c. Recognizing specific dramatic genres—comedy of manners, tragedy, melodrama, satire.

*d. Comparing drama of different historical periods, for example, Greek, Shakespearean, modern tragedy.

3. Concepts

a. Acquaintance with some key theatrical personalities of past and present times

b. Awareness of major English and world dramatists to explore for future reading

c. Enlightenment on recent developments in drama in the local community

*d. Insight into the place of drama, TV, film in contemporary life and recent developments in each media

*e. Deepened insight into the concepts of tragedy, its origins and development to modern times

*f. Knowledge of key periodicals dealing with evaluation, discussion of mass media, theater

4. Suggested activities

a. Discussion

(1) Hold roundtable talks on plays that students have read individually. These could be structured around a theme, for example, "Facing Reality"—or else each student could be asked to discuss a play he has most enjoyed, pointedly commenting on (a) the play's central conflict, (b) theme(s) the author has directly expressed or suggested, (c) key characters and the change in them throughout the play, (d) a key scene, in which the central character most reveals himself, (e) an estimate of whether the play provides a significant dramatic experience.

(2) Have occasional preplanned ten- to fifteen-minute discussions on "What's New on Broadway." Encourage students to bring in newspaper and magazine articles on dramatic personalities and writers. Also use "What's New in TV, in Films."

(3) Discuss characteristics of effective reviews as well as of irresponsible, destructive reviewing. Encourage comparison of reviews from several sources as well as confidence in one's own judgment.

(4) Discuss imaginative and unimaginative TV productions. Encourage a discussion about whether TV, movies, or theater is living up to its public responsibility. Stimulate thinking about the problems of the script writer today and the sponsor's potentially stifling power.

(5) Use various essays and articles that discuss modern drama and mass media. Identify some of the problems faced by drama today—the plight of Broadway, the subsidiary position of drama in American culture.

(6) Have panel presentations on important books on theatrical personalities or historical developments, *Act One, Prince of Players, Gertude Lawrence as Mrs. A,* and so on.

b. Composition

(1) Analyze:

(a) Use of minor characters as foils, contrast, "lenses"

(b) Moral dilemmas or themes, integrity, love, social protest, illusion/reality

        (c) Play's significance for revealing the values and norms of an age

        (d) The contributions of an individual to the theater —or price of success as revealed in a significant biography

        (e) The role of drama in our own community, in American life

      (2) Compare/contrast:

        (a) Author's handling of the same theme in two different plays

        (b) Dramatic techniques and conventions of different periods

      *(c) Play "Twins," for example, *Electra, Mourning Becomes Electra; Hamlet, Winterset*

      *(d) Play with its film or TV counterpart

      *(e) Various reviews of the same play

      (3) Evaluate:

        (a) A play's unity, integrity, effectiveness

        (b) A play as dramatic experience: staging, impact, actors' response to challenge of the role

      *(c) Extent to which a particular play fulfills intentions of its type: satire, tragedy, comedy, and so on

    *(4) Creative writing

        (a) Write an original scene suggested by a play, Ophelia's soliloquy, Saint Joan in prison, and so forth, in style of original.

        (b) Write a dramatic sketch suggested by a news story, choosing one with definite conflict.

  c. Individual/Small-group projects

    (1) Keep journals of individual play-reading, especially noting theme and resolution of conflict.

    (2) Report on major theatrical personalities, books revealing them.

    *(3) Explore some developments in the avant-garde or European theater, the theater of the "absurd," Bertolt Brecht Company in East Germany.

III. Activities for all levels

  A. Encourage attendance at and follow-up discussion of school plays.

  B. Plan occasional field trips to community plays. Publicize and discuss plays that students could get to; take advantage of the many opportunities for student rates.

C. Expand filmstrip library, such as those on the Shakespearean theater. Allocate important films to various levels and keep a department file on worthwhile films, records, filmstrips, tapes.

D. Use recorded scenes of plays not directly studied, but which illustrate emphasized concepts.

E. Try to have at least one drama-oriented bulletin board display during the year.

SPECIAL PROBLEMS IN DRAMA TEACHING

Unless a teacher plans wisely, drama study can easily become overextended and tedious. Nothing can be more depressing for both teacher and students than belaboring a play week after week until it has lost all vitality or appeal. Avoidance of both superficiality and surfeit thus requires a skillful varying of approaches and emphases.

Method of Discussion

Should a play be discussed in its entirety or piece by piece? Perhaps the best answer is a compromise: suit the method to the play. A Shakespearean drama, by virtue of length and complexity, usually requires a section-by-section approach. Students first starting to read three-act plays probably also need to be assigned individual scenes or acts one at a time. Yet in both instances the sections must ultimately be put together more meaningfully to illuminate the whole. When studying modern plays, students in the junior and senior years should generally be required to have read the entire work prior to initial discussion, then to go back for a second and, it is hoped, a third rereading and careful analysis of selected sections. This method has the advantage of putting greater responsibility on the student for drawing his own conclusions and seeing the play as an artistic unit; and it avoids the problem of holding all students to specific page limits. Rather than straining to make a single play yield all of its riches, the high school teacher will wisely distribute emphasis, letting one play reveal the possibilities of dialogue, another the force of ideas, yet another the use of irony, contrast, or symbolism. Ultimately the skills emphasized in one should transfer to and illuminate the reading of other plays. Above all, students must be encouraged to read widely, even at the expense of some detail, if teachers are to expect them to acquire an interest and skill in an area in which they usually have far too few experiences.

Oral Reading or Dramatizing of Play Scenes

We all know what happens when parts are assigned and deadpan Jane runs monotone through every passage, despite pre-preparation. We also know how tedious it is to hear a scene that students have carefully read first on their own massacred by poor classroom readers, then played on record, and finally dissected endlessly in class until it has lost all appeal. Here again a compromise must be made so that students have opportunities to cultivate skills in oral reading without killing all pleasure for the others in the class. The best solution is to make specific assignments in oral reading: students could be asked to select and read key scenes, passages revealing character, or moments of climax—all of which require careful selection, yet which are brief enough to retain classroom interest. Also, rather than stressing the same scenes again and again, teachers should use recordings for plays beyond the capacity of student readers but not duplicate what has already been sufficiently stressed in class.

The Best Use of Audio-Visual Aids

Audio-visual aids should fulfill the promise of their name—to serve as aids and enrichment rather than replacements for the original work. Too often records, films, and filmstrips totally supplant rather than supplement the dramatic experience or else constitute nothing more than time-fillers or incidental recreation. These media should be used instead to motivate study, to suggest an approach for reading, possibly to present a different interpretation. In addition, teachers need to make better classroom use of records of plays that have not been directly studied, thus enabling students to transfer skills acquired in the study of one work to the interpretation of another. More time should also be given to class evaluation of film and record interpretations—to appraising characterization, ensemble work, total effectiveness. And within the coming decade, no self-respecting school is likely to be without a well-equipped Materials Center, stocked with extensive film, record, and filmstrip resources for use by individuals and small groups. The multimedia revolution should really mean that the coming generation will have more opportunities to read, see, and hear drama than ever before.

Special Techniques in Teaching a Shakespearean Play

Enobarbus' words in praise of Cleopatra—"Age cannot wither her, nor custom stale her infinite variety"—apply to Shakespeare's works as well. W. H. Auden has noted that every one of Shakespeare's works is unique so that the reader must experience them all to get a proper idea of the Shakespearean world. However, he also comments that "no one is less a writer for the young, for persons, that is, under the age of thirty." [12] Difficult, mature, demanding—Shakespearean drama calls upon the full resources of a teacher's creativity, persuasiveness, and careful planning. In particular, the classroom teacher must overcome the problems of attention, of verse, of emphasis.

The problem of attention. While Shakespeare fills his plays with considerable attractions for the "groundlings"—murders, quarrels, suicides, duelings, insanity, slapstick comedy, patriotic fervor, and spectacle—his essential appeal is to the ear, to the mind, to refined perception. The problem of attention, then, is basically that of luring students to come to grips with a literature requiring mature thought, concentration, and insight. "Well digested in the scenes, set down with as much modesty as cunning," his plays call for an ear attuned to subtlety, paradox, ambiguity. In the first place, students must learn that a play can be enjoyable even when the plot is known in advance. Like more sophisticated members of the Greek or Elizabethan audience, they must learn to anticipate and enjoy the unique treatment of a previously worked subject and to let language more than spectacle and action work upon their imaginations and emotions. Robert Ornstein has well observed that "the relatively bare Elizabethan stage was perfectly suited to the drama of great personalities which Shakespeare created," for his heroic characters dwarfed their background and

---

[12] W. H. Auden, "Three Memoranda on the New Arden Shakespeare," *The Mid-Century*, No. 21 (January 1961), 3.

shaped their worlds and their own destinies.[13] The focus of attention must thus be upon the inner conflicts with which his characters struggle and the consequences of their actions—and especially upon the language they use to define these conflicts. Thus viewed, Shakespeare's characters take on universal significance, for they wrestle with and clarify problems men of all periods have struggled to resolve.

The problem of verse. Besides demonstrating maturity and sensitivity, students reading Shakespeare must develop specific skills for handling poetic drama. T. S. Eliot, in "The Three Voices of Poetry," reminds us that the poetic line in drama bears the weight of three responsibilities: conveying plot and character while retaining its poetic form.[14] Students must thus acquire a series of reading skills that work together. First they must learn to read blank verse without halting at the end of each line or being trapped by occasional archaic expressions or extended figures of speech. Then they must learn to see how specific passages reflect the character traits of the speaker. For example, they should come to detect how Polonius' mishandling of language reflects his mismanagement of human affairs, or how Laertes betrays a strain of superficiality by indulging in florid bombast. They should also become skilled enough to discern how Hamlet's shifts from introspection and depression to passionate anger with himself and the world are precisely reflected by the variety of his speech, the flavor of his rhetoric. Unless they see language as mirroring essential character traits, they will miss much of the impact of the Shakespearean line.

Students must also discover how richly Shakespeare uses imagery to enforce mood and idea. For example, how repeatedly throughout the history plays he apostrophizes sleep and thereby emphasizes the wearying responsibility of a king upon whose head "uneasy" lies the crown. Using the images of disease, plague, disruption, insanity, and revolt in *Julius Caesar, Hamlet,* and *Lear,* Shakespeare succeeds in conveying the very atmosphere of states whose social organization has suffered violent change and upheaval. John Ciardi also reminds us that Shakespeare's verse needs to be studied for its own sake as poe-

---

[13] Ornstein, *Shakespeare in the Classroom,* pp. 5–6.
[14] T. S. Eliot, *On Poetry and Poets* (New York: Farrar, Straus, 1957), pp. 96–112.

try, particularly for its precise word choice, skillfully suggestive overtones, and unified construction.[15] Rather than wearying every line
with exhausting interpretation, however, we need to vary discussion
procedures, letting one passage, for example, serve as a reflection of
an inner state of mind, another as revealing specific character traits,
yet another to show contrast and irony. Often it may be necessary to
concentrate on plot events alone, for verse analysis must never become so laborious that students feel they are making no headway in
the play.

The problem of emphasis. Those who have taught Shakespeare
over a period of years recognize how rewarding recurrent experiences
have proven to be, for each rereading with different classes brings new
insights and values. On the other hand, how dangerous it is to assume
that every student will gain as much from a first contact! The solution,
then, is to suggest, not exhaust, the possibilities of a Shakespearean
play, to make it rewarding enough that a student will want of his own
accord to return to it for rereading or to go out of his way to attend
an actual performance. Most teachers spend perhaps too much time
on a single play and do too much for the students, who thus fail to acquire the skills necessary for independent exploration in other Shakespearean works. Three to four weeks is ample time for most works
used in high school and is actually all that can be reasonably afforded
in the already overcrowded English program. However, since the major themes of Shakespeare's plays recur in literature of all periods, the
teacher has the opportunity frequently to refer back to the works studied earlier and thus revive their significance and applicability. Not
without warrant has it been said Shakespeare's plays were "for all
time."

THE DRAMA OF SOCIAL DISSENT

In an era in which protest has become almost a way of life and dissen-
sion a gospel, English teachers will make little headway by serving up

---

[15] John Ciardi, *How Does a Poem Mean?* (Boston: Houghton Mifflin, 1959),
p. 785.

pleasant plays with tidy conflicts and prudent themes. But today's adolescent can be strongly "turned on" by the drama of social dissent—the experience of plays in which outstanding individuals of different historical periods demonstrate that the actions of one person can still make a difference in reversing the course of injustice, civic complacency, and mass hysteria. A unit on the drama of social dissent invariably turns the secondary classroom into an arena of truly significant dialogue and demonstrates that the genuine heroes of history are also "men for all seasons," as relevant today as in their own times.

Selection of appropriate works for a unit on social dissent should not be difficult. Though technically not a drama, Plato's *Phaedo,* through its use of dramatic dialogue, actually provides an archetypal "drama of dissent," starring the most admirable protestor of all time —Socrates. One might profitably begin with the *Phaedo* and portions of the *Apology,* then move to Anderson's *Barefoot in Athens,* a most readable and discussable contemporary treatment of Socrates, which humanizes the man while combining humor and dignity in the re-creation of his unavoidable martyrdom. Immortal Joan is also available in several worthwhile works, most notably the plays of Anouilh and Shaw. Becket, the worldly saint, can be approached through Eliot's stylized treatment of the Archbishop rejecting his temptors in *Murder in the Cathedral* or through Anouilh's *Becket,* a portrait of the profligate playboy, compelled ultimately to defend the "honor of God," even at the expense of his long friendship with King Henry II and the price of his life. Sophocles' *Antigone;* Sir Thomas More, a true "man of all seasons"; tactless but admirable Thomas Stockmann of *An Enemy of the People* and John Proctor of *The Crucible* are obvious nominees to the select rank of dissentors whose actions can be said to have affected the course of human events, if only to stir the consciences of reasonable and moral men.

The three study guides which follow are intended to serve as aids in the development of a meaningful unit on the theme of social dissent. Under no circumstances should they be considered a definitive selection. But each has literary and dramatic merit; and each demonstrates, in action, an individual who dared act as a "majority of one," despite personal sacrifice, family pressures, and political considerations. Each is also highly discussible and likely to stimulate keen interest, lively discussion, and meaningful composition.

THE CRUCIBLE
Arthur Miller

I. Introductory Activities

A. As with all plays in this unit, try to get the students directly into the first act of the play, then through a complete first reading. Important scenes can later be re-created by means of class dramatizations and recordings. (Arthur Miller has recorded a very moving reading of Act II.)

B. Possibly precede introduction of this play by reading and discussing selections which reveal Puritan attitudes and values. Portions of Perry Miller's *The American Puritans,* selected short stories of Hawthorne (especially "The Maypole of Merry Mount," "The Minister's Black Veil," and "My Kinsman Major Molineaux"), and even Shirley Jackson's "The Lottery" would give students insight into the Puritan preoccupation with sin, the concept of a theocracy, and the concern with the dual nature of man which Puritans so fully dramatized.

II. Analyzing the Play

A. As history

1. Ask students to study the facts of the 1692 witch trials in Salem, then determine how faithfully Miller has reflected actual people and real happenings in the play. Two indispensable references for this purpose are Marion Starkey's *The Devil in Massachusetts* (New York: Dolphin Paperbooks, n.d.) and David Levin's *What Happened in Salem?* (New York: Harcourt, Brace & World, 1960). Students should conclude that, except for the fabricated adultery theme and emphasis on marital conflict in the Proctor household, the play very precisely re-creates real characters and conflicts of the period.

2. Examine the basis for belief in witchcraft, especially in a Puritan community, raising such questions as: Who qualified as a witch? According to common belief, what supernatural powers did witches acquire and what kinds of evil were they known to inflict? How could their evil influence be exorcized? (Students would be fascinated by the information in a delightful pamphlet on "Witchcraft in Olde Salem," available upon request from the Pilgrim Motel, 40 Bridge Street, Salem, Mass.)

3. Because *The Crucible* had its first public performance in 1953, shortly after Miller had been personally indicted for contempt of Congress because of his refusal to reveal information about the activities of some of his acquaintances, the play inevitably forces comparison with the guilt-by-association and smear tactics of the McCarthy hearings. It is clear that Miller intended his play to constitute a denunciation of witch-hunting not only in Salem, but in any era; and it is also clear that he was most bold and courageous in writing and presenting a work that could further enflame his critics. Students should be asked to ponder just why this play, which has been so enthusiastically acclaimed abroad and brilliantly revived in recent years, received such a relatively cool reception when it was first produced. Why did it suffer rather than become enhanced by comparison with this appalling episode in modern American history? Hopefully, students will recognize that a truly great play must have universal significance and must also do more than serve as a political pamphlet or dramatized polemic. Now that time has blurred its topical stand, *The Crucible* can be evaluated on its own merits. Some critics have now come to consider this play Miller's best achievement, his most successful fusion of historical drama and personal tragedy.

B. As a view of—and attack upon—Puritan values and practices.
   1. In several inserted prose segments in Act I, Miller comments at length on social, economic, and psychological causes of the Salem witch trials. Since these portions are highly sophisticated and abstract, they should really be read aloud and analyzed in class, with students listing both strengths and shortcomings in the Puritan way of life and system of values.
      a. Strengths: Students should note such admirable qualities as the Puritans' belief in self-denial and self-discipline; their insistence on purposefulness in daily occupations, avoidance of vanity and luxury, and the application of stern justice in cases requiring court judgment. They should also recognize how strongly Puritans were guided by the conviction that man is basically corrupt, that he could be saved only by "election," and that eternal happiness could be guaranteed only by visible demonstra-

tion of virtue and absence of hypocrisy, sensuality, self-preoccupation, and greed.

   b. Shortcomings: Students should easily identify such limiting aspects of Puritanism as: repression of children and youth activities; excessive self-denial and austerity; stultifying social insulation; open interference in the personal lives of individuals and minority groups; intolerance; hyperemphasis on surface appearances and public opinion; adherence to a single system of belief and conduct.

2. Ask students to determine which aspects of Puritanism are most under attack in the play (hypocrisy, emotional repression, inflexibility, and breakdown of communication, among others). But also point out that "tolerance" was a relatively new concept for Puritans, to many an "abomination," because it threatened the stability and permanence of the Puritan theocracy. Also stress Miller's idea, set forth in Act I, of the difficulty in any society of maintaining the balance between freedom and order. Ask students to analyze in what ways this balance was being threatened in the Salem community of 1692.

3. Discuss to what extent John Proctor actually qualifies as the best Christian of all the Salemites, even though he has committed adultery, failed to attend church regularly, and stumbled in his recitation of the commandments before Rev. Hale.

C. As an illumination of human problems and moral issues of universal significance.

1. Have students identify and discuss underlying sources of conflict in the play which have universal application, such as:

   a. The breakdown of communication, especially between husband and wife, priest and parishioner.

   b. The practice of determining "guilt by association," leading to unjust and brutal character defamation.

   c. Oppressive regimentation, disregarding individual rights and differences.

   d. The absence of sanctioned outlets for emotion or violence, contributing to periodic outbreaks of witch hunting and scapegoating.

   e. The power of fear, superstition, and irrationality to engender mass hysteria and injustice.

2. Examine the social and psychological conditions which Miller suggests are likely to lead to outbreaks of public hysteria and irrationality.
3. Determine the major themes and psychological truths which the play conveys, among them the following:
   a. Evil begets evil.
   b. Injustice and mass hysteria are common consequences of repression and bigotry.
   c. Breeches of the moral code can have far-reaching consequences.
   d. A man cannot live without self-respect. Preservation of one's honor and integrity are necessary if life is to have meaning.
   e. Any social system must maintain a balance between freedom and discipline, reason and emotion, in the conduct of human affairs.
   f. One honest man can turn the tide, can constitute a "majority of one."

D. As a psychological revelation of the hidden motives behind the actions of real people.
   1. For several characters in the play, a mask of virtue and Christian ardor conceals the true motives for vicious, destructive behavior. Have students examine, in particular, the personal history and character traits that might account for the destructive actions of each of the following: Abigail, Betty Parris, Mr. and Mrs. Putnam, Mary Warren, Rev. Parris, and Rev. Hathorne.
   2. The play is filled with moral dilemmas, forcing characters into decisions where neither alternative is really desirable. Examine closely what decisions each of the following characters is forced to make, determining why they decide as they do: Rev. Parris, Mary Warren, John and Elizabeth Proctor, Rev. Hale, Rev. Danforth, and Giles Corey.
   3. Several characters really change greatly throughout the play. Which are strengthened? Which deteriorate?

E. As a work of art, having both literary and theatrical merit.
   1. Is there any discernible organizing pattern, besides chronology, to unify the play?
      a. Students should discover on their own that the total action of the play is based on a series of *trials,* public and private. Each act portrays people undergoing rigorous in-

terrogation to explain or defend their actions and beliefs. In Act I, Parris cross-examines the hysterical children with ruthless persistence and is succeeded by an equally persevering Rev. Hale. In Act II, Elizabeth Proctor's frigid reproaches goad her husband to exclaim, "I cannot speak but I am doubted, every moment judged for lies, as though I come into a court when I come into this house!" Later in the same act John bears down upon the timorous Mary Warren, then is himself cornered by Rev. Hale and the delegation that come to take Elizabeth to jail. In Act III Proctor's efforts to impugn Abigail and terminate the trials end only in his public degradation, Elizabeth's public lie, and Mary Warren's failure to overcome her personal fears when she has the opportunity to tell the truth. Act IV is Proctor's Gethsemane, his night of agony, when he must weigh the cost of a lie against the loss of his life. Like Saint Joan, he signs the fraudulent confession, then rips it to pieces, recognizing that, for him, a life without honor is unthinkable. His death coincides with the rising of the sun, symbolic of his spiritual victory and the promise of a return to rationality and justice in Salem.

    b. Note the balanced organization of the play, the alternation of episodes of public frenzy with calmer views of private life. Acts I and III are high-pitched group scenes, each ending with the children in an active state of hysteria. Acts II and IV examine the effects of the trials on private life and focus on the tormenting decisions individuals are forced to make once their privacy is totally invaded.

2. Discuss various ways in which the title applies to the events and themes of the play. It suggests, of course, that Salem has become a "heated kettle" in which emotions have reached the boiling point. It further symbolizes the severe trials which take place and the many trials and testings which individuals and the entire town must endure.

3. Discuss the play as a work for the stage, raising such questions as:

    a. Some directors have emphasized the social themes, others the personal tragedies of individuals in the play. How,

dramatically, could these different emphases be conveyed?
  b. Can the characters emerge as credible human beings once the detailed commentary of the written version has been removed? It has also been charged that the characters are unconvincing, more symbolic than real. Is such a judgment warranted?
  c. In an early review of *The Crucible,* one critic charged that the play exercises only the mind, not the heart. Do the students agree?
  d. What are the key scenes and speeches? Dramatize a few, especially the final confrontation of John and Elizabeth Proctor in Act IV.
III. Possible Composition Topics
  A. Why has Miller named the play *The Crucible?* Analyze the various ways in which the title applies to events and themes of the play.
  B. Discuss: *The Crucible* is not so much a dramatization of "witch hunting" as it is an illumination of human weakness, hypocrisy, and vindictiveness.
  C. What could a psychologist learn about human behavior from a close analysis of *The Crucible?* For example, what insights could he gain about the effects of emotional repression, the bases of marital conflict, the sources of fear and irrationality, devices for avoiding reality, etc.?
  D. In what ways does *The Crucible* not only attack the weaknesses of Puritanism, yet also illuminate some of its finest strengths and values in the lives of individual characters?
  E. The play uses the "trial" situation as a dominant metaphor for the action of the entire play. Discuss various "trials" dramatized in the play, noting the appropriateness of this metaphor to the overall work.
  F. Just why are the children believed and the wise adults ignored? Reexamine the play to determine why irrationality and hysteria dominate the life of an entire community for more than half a year.
  G. Compare Abigail of *The Crucible* and Hester Prynne of *The Scarlet Letter,* both guilty of adultery, yet greatly differing in their response to public interference in their private lives and to their personal suffering.

A MAN FOR ALL SEASONS
Robert Bolt *

I. *Introduction and background*

A. Distribute a short summary of More's life, highlighting his many accomplishments in religion, literature, and public life. Stress his ambivalent relationship with Henry VIII—first as his religious spokesman, then as adversary—particularly as represented in the following events:

1518   More's first year in Henry's service

1521   "Ghost writer" of Henry's defense of the Pope and attack on Luther

1529   Wolsey's replacement as Chancellor—the first layman in English history to hold the office

1531   "Submission of Clergy"—religious officials accede to Henry's limitations of their power

1534   Act of Supremacy, acknowledging Henry VIII as supreme authority of the Church of England; occasion of More's first arrest

1535   July 7—the execution of Sir Thomas More on a charge of treason

B. Review the history of the Tudors and their accession to the throne, stressing the role of the Wars of the Roses in bringing Henry VIII to power.

C. Anticipate and clarify potentially difficult references:

1. "And . . . who recommended you to read Signor *Machiavelli?*"

2. "Since you seem to be violently opposed to *the Latin dispatch,* I thought you'd like to look it over."

3. "D'you think *two Tudors* is sufficient?"

4. "Do you remember *the Yorkist Wars?*"

5. "He sounds like *Moloch.*"

6. "May I not come simply, to pay my respects to *the English Socrates*—as I see your angelic friend *Erasmus* calls you."

7. Other terms: *farrier   advocate   pragmatist   bracken*

II. *Reading and analysis of the play itself*

A. With fast groups, assign pre-reading of the entire play. With

* From Gladys Veidemanis, "A Play for All Seasons," *English Journal,* LV (November 1966), 1006–1015. Used by permission of the author and the National Council of Teachers of English. Quotations from *A Man for All Seasons* used by permission of Random House, Inc., as publishers. (Robert Bolt, *A Man for All Seasons.* Copyright © 1962 by Robert Bolt.)

less able groups, take each act individually, perhaps reading the first scene aloud to clarify difficult references and introduce characters. Ask students to outline the sequence of events in each act, dating them according to the information given by the Common Man.

B. Discuss the extent to which the play parallels actual history, noting the individuals who played a comparable role in actual life. On this question Bolt, in program notes for a presentation of the play in Milwaukee in 1963, said:

"I will claim (diffidently) that all the events essential to the action of his life during the period covered are present in the play, and (confidently) that none of the events essential to the action of the play is entirely my own invention. That is, none of the events as they relate to More himself; the other characters have been combined and collapsed so as to keep the play to a tolerable length.

"He was a pivot of English life at a time when England was negotiating the sharpest corner in her spiritual history, and to have brought into the play even a fair sample of his acquaintances would have swamped it in a pageant of great names."

Students should, of course, recognize the historical accuracy of the following portraits:

Wolsey—a man of fantastic power and ignominious decline

Roper—More's son-in-law and later biographer

Henry VIII—a versatile, vibrant monarch, ruthless in securing his own will

Rich—a sycophant, willing to betray a friend to the highest bidder; a "lucky" traitor

Cromwell—a shrewd opportunist but ultimate victim of Henry's power politics

Norfolk—More's friend, who places personal safety above friendship and principles

C. Clarify any confusions about plot and action raised by students after a first reading of the play. (Some will surely be unclear about Roper's many philosophies, Wolsey's sudden disappearance, and Chapuys' strange behavior at the end of the play.) Other key questions:

At what point does More find it necessary to resign his office as Lord Chancellor?

On what charge is he placed in prison?

What major legal device does he use to avoid—temporarily —the death sentence?

How is More's death finally "engineered"?

Despite his death penalty, how does More really get the better of his accusers?

D. Explore possible reasons for the division of the play into two acts, leading to the awareness that Act I could be sub-titled "The Man, His Age, and His Dilemma," Act II, "The Hour of Testing and Decision."

E. Review with the class various techniques playwrights use to reveal character and identify the particular methods used in this play to illuminate More's many-faceted personality. Re-explore the text through such questions as these:

1. What personal qualities does More reveal through his conversation and actions with friends and family? (They should discern that he is witty, sophisticated, generous, practical, wordly [to the extent that he likes wine, good company, music], independent, resourceful, and intellectually brilliant.) How does he show himself throughout to be a man who truly understands human nature?

Does he fit the qualifications of a saint as defined by the Common Man early in Act I?

Does he change in any way throughout the course of the play?

2. What clues in Act I foreshadow More's coming resistance to Henry's divorce? (Students should note such passages as:

Wolsey: "If you could just see facts flat on, without that moral squint; with just a little common sense, you could have been a statesman."

Common Man as Steward: "My master Thomas More would give anything to anyone. Some say that's good and some say that's bad, but I say he can't help it—and that's bad . . . because some day someone's going to ask him for something he wants to keep and he'll be out of practice."

More: ". . . I believe, when statesmen forsake their own private consciences for the sake of their public duties . . . they lead their country by a short route to chaos."

"I neither could nor would rule my King. But there's a little . . . little area . . . where I must rule myself. It's very little—less to him than a tennis court.")

F. Have students define the central moral dilemma of the play (whether to obey conscience and God or the dictates of a temporal ruler) and explain why Henry forces More to take a public stand. Why *must* Henry insist upon More's support or his death? (Students should not miss More's conversation with Henry in Act I:

> More: "Then why does Your Grace need my poor support?" Henry: "Because you are honest. What's more to the purpose, you're known to be honest . . ."

Or Cromwell's comment to Rich in Act II:

> "The King's a man of conscience and he wants either Sir Thomas More to bless his marriage or Sir Thomas More destroyed. Either will do . . . If the King destroys a man, that's proof to the King that it must have been a bad man, the kind of man a man of conscience *ought* to destroy— and of course a bad man's blessing's not worth having. So either will do.")

G. King Henry, in his conversation with More, lists four major kinds of followers: "There are those like Norfolk who follow me because I wear the crown, and there are those like Master Cromwell who follow me because they are jackals with sharp teeth and I am their lion, and there is a mass that follows me because it follows anything that moves—and there is you." Explore these various character types, and others, in the play and various stands on Henry's divorce proceedings:

1. Henry himself

   a. What elements of Henry's personality are revealed directly and indirectly in the play? (Students should note his sensual zest for living, his impulsive behavior, his pride in his own achievements and artistic talents, his domineering, ruthless nature, his great skill in rationalization.)

   b. How does Henry try to justify his controversial divorce action? (Note that he cites the Bible (Leviticus) as long as it supports his case but rejects those portions in Deuteronomy on marriage to a brother's wife as "ambiguous." He considers his strongest argument the necessity of acquiring a male heir.)

2. Norfolk

   a. How does he demonstrate, throughout the entire play, that he always means well and yearns to remain More's friend, but doesn't dare to risk his status or security?

    b. What is the basis for the quarrel between More and Norfolk in Act II? Why does More initiate it in the first place? What is the purpose of More's references to water spaniels and his exhortation—"Is there no single sinew in the midst of this that serves no appetite of Norfolk's but is, just, Norfolk? There is! Give *that* some exercise, my lord!"?

3. The "Jackals"—Cromwell, Rich, Chapuys
    a. Cromwell
        (1) Does Cromwell have any admirable qualities? (Students should note that this son of a farrier has risen high by virtue of his legal ability and shrewdness. He is a hard-nosed realist who never masks his actions behind a layer of pretty words or rationalizations.) But where does he most fully reveal his ruthlessness, even a sadistic streak? (Note actions at end of Act I.)
        (2) What is Cromwell's doctrine of "political convenience" as defined in his conversation with Rich in the last scene of Act I? Is Cromwell correct in his assumption that "The situation rolls forward in any case," making the efforts of *"upright, steadfast* men" useless and ill-advised?
        (3) Why does Cromwell say, "And if I bring about More's death—I plant my own, I think"? (Note that he is realistic enough to know that Henry's tender conscience, which demands More's execution, will probably also require a scapegoat upon which later to transfer blame for More's death.)
    b. Rich
        (1) How does Rich demonstrate from his first line in the play—"But every man has his price!"—that he can be very easily bought? What are his major values? How does Cromwell manipulate him? How is he treated by the Common Man?
        (2) In how many ways does Rich betray More—and his own soul—and what is his "price" each time? Is Rich a true convert "to the doctrines of Machiavelli"?
    c. Chapuys
        (1) In what ways does Chapuys demonstrate that he functions for the King of Spain in the same capacity as Cromwell for the King of England? What

causes Chapuys to say of More, whom he earlier admired, "The man's utterly unreliable!"?

(2) Why are Cromwell and Chapuys, officials of opposing powers, shown leaving the stage together at the end of the play, arms linked, smiles conspiratorial? (Note that for these exponents of political convenience, More has become extremely *in*convenient and troublesome. As Chapuys learns in the letter episode, More's loyalty to England is unswerving. His conflict with Henry is essentially moral rather than political.)

4. The representative of the "mass that follows"—The Common Man
   a. Identify and discuss the three major functions of the Common Man in this play:
      (1) A one-man Greek chorus and stage manager to provide transition, background, commentary.
      (2) A means of introducing comic relief into a serious play.
      (3) A personality in his own right, involving the audience in the play by being its most direct representative and indicting by his own actions those people of any age who set self-interest above all other values.
   b. How far is the Comman Man willing to compromise himself? Where does he draw the line? How does he reveal himself to be a crafty opportunist, but a moral coward?

5. Other characters to note:
   a. Wolsey
      (1) What is the subject of the communication Wolsey shows More? Why does he ask him to read it? (Note that he is very much aware of More's "moral squint"!)
      (2) What reasons does Wolsey give for personally helping Henry secure a divorce? (Note especially his reference to the Yorkist wars.)
      (3) What are Wolsey's criticisms of More's character? What traits does he himself possess which he would like to find in More?
   b. Roper
      (1) Though courageous and outspoken, how does Roper reveal himself as immature and somewhat superficial? What qualities of More are lacking in Roper? (Roper is surely humorless and not a little obtuse!)
      (2) Why does More forbid Meg's marriage to Roper at

first, then later allow it? Altogether, what is Roper's major function in the play?

  c. Alice

    (1) In what ways does Alice make More's continued quarrel with Henry more painful? How do we know that family solidarity and well-being are her highest values? (Note her outburst when More removes his chain of office: ". . . Sun and moon, Master More, you're taken for a wise man! Is this wisdom—to betray your ability, abandon practice, forget your station and your duty to your kin and behave like a printed book!")

    (2) Why is Alice at first so cool and aloof when she visits More in prison? What causes More later in that scene to exclaim, "Why it's a lion I married! A lion! A lion!"?

  d. Meg

    (1) Meg is a remarkable young woman, almost *too* bright for a woman of her age. What exceptional abilities does she exhibit before King Henry during his surprise visit? What indications do we have that More dotes on his daughter? (Note that Alice is somewhat hurt when More speaks of "hiding" his daughter but makes no specific reference to shielding her.)

    (2) Why is Meg a most potent "Eve" to tempt her father after his year in prison? What four arguments does she present to try to persuade her father to swear to the Act of Succession? Are his responses convincing? How do her appeals compare with those of the four tempters in T. S. Eliot's *Murder in the Cathedral?*

6. More's personal stand and legal strategy

  a. How many different kinds of pressures must More resist to maintain his stand? (Note the hardships imposed on his family, Chapuys' letter from the King of Spain, the tempting offer of money from the bishops, the endless inquisitions, the miserable conditions in jail, the painful entreaties of his loved ones.)

  b. Why does More maintain his stand, even though he knows Henry will ultimately have his way anyhow? Note that his various comments indicate that his decision hinges on

      personal integrity: "Well, as a spaniel is to water, so

is a man to his own self. I will not give in because I oppose it— *I* do—not my pride, not my spleen, nor any other of my appetites but *I* do—*I!*"

religious conviction: "In matters of conscience, the loyal subject is more bounded to be loyal to his conscience than to any other thing."

concern for public morality: "Can I help my King by giving him lies when he asks for truth? Will you help England by populating her with liars?"

c. Study carefully the passage in which More declares to his family that he will utilize every possible means to escape martyrdom:

"God made the *angels* to show him splendor—as he made animals for innocence and plants for their simplicity. But Man he made to serve him wittily, in the tangle of his mind! If he suffers us to fall to such a case that there is no escaping, then we may stand to our tackle as best we can, and yes, Will, then we will clamor like champions . . . if we have the spittle for it. And no doubt it delights God to see splendor where he only looked for complexity. But it's God's part, not our own, to bring ourselves to that extremity! Our natural business lies in escaping—so let's get home and study this Bill."

Discuss ways in which More succeeds in living up to this philosophy.

H. Ask students whether they have noted any dominant pattern of imagery throughout the play. Hopefully they will have detected the many references to hunting, fishing, and snaring and to animals and animalistic behavior, such as these:

"But in the thickets of the law, oh there I'm a forester."

"Sir Thomas is going to be a slippery fish, Richard; we need a net with finer mesh."

"Better a live rat than a dead lion."

". . . they are jackals with sharp teeth and I am their lion. . . ."

More is hunted down and "mounted." Unfortunately, as the play implies, there are always too many "rats," too few "lions."

III. *Culminating activities*

A. Evaluate the appropriateness of the title. According to Bolt's program notes for the play: "The title of the play is taken from a passage which was composed by Robert Whittinton for Tudor schoolboys to put into Latin: "More is a man of angel's wit and singular learning; I know not his fellow. For where is the man of that gentleness, lowliness, and affability? And as time requireth, a man of marvelous mirth and pastimes; and sometimes of as sad a gravity; 'a man for all seasons.'"

B. Extract and discuss some of the moral issues in the play, such as those below, with which men of all ages have had to wrestle:
  1. How much can any one man affect the course of public events and remedy obvious evils? Should he even try?
  2. What comes first—loyalty to family, self, or principles?
  3. Do the ends justify the means?
  4. Can a man say one thing and believe another without betraying his principles?
  5. Is the Common Man right—"Better a live rat than a dead lion"?

C. Relate themes of the play to other important literary works and to life situations:
  1. Students could very profitably go on to read other works dealing with individuals facing comparable moral dilemmas, e.g.: Plato's *Apology*, Sophocles' *Antigone*, Shaw's *St. Joan*, Anouilh's *Becket*, Eliot's *Murder in the Cathedral*, Ibsen's *Enemy of the People*, Miller's *All My Sons*, and others.
  2. Ask students to write on one of the following topics:
    a. The Common Man states, "I'm a plain simple man and just want to keep out of trouble." To what extent has his philosophy of "no involvement" permeated modern life and in what ways has it proven—and can it prove—highly detrimental to public life?
    b. More has been called "the English Socrates." In what ways is the designation appropriate?
    c. Persuade us that More was or was not justified in his stand.
    d. How does the play present More as a figure deserving the designation "A Man for All Seasons"?
    e. Bolt wrote also that "The action of this play ends in 1535, but the play was written in 1960, and if in production one date must obscure the other, it is 1960 which I wish clearly to occupy the stage. The 'Life' of a man like Thomas More proffers a number of caps which in this or any other century we may try on for size." Analyze what makes the play relevant to our times and what "caps" we are offered to try on for size.

3. Dramatize key scenes, such as Henry's visit, More's quarrel with Norfolk, and More's last meeting with his family.

AN ENEMY OF THE PEOPLE
Henrik Ibsen

I. *Introducing the play*

   A. Assign complete reading of the play prior to discussion, but first present specific aspects of background information that have bearing on the play and its construction:

   Ibsen's role in developing the realistic theater; his concern with social problems and controversial issues.

   Ibsen's influence on other dramatists, especially men like Shaw and Miller, who shared his concern about social problems and moral issues.

   Ibsen's personal experiences, which classified him as a kind of Thomas Stockmann, ready to assume the role of a "majority of one" who must inevitably pay a severe price for standing up for the truth.

   B. Overcome student skepticism about the actual possibility of polluted baths by describing the happenings in Zermatt, Switzerland, in February, 1963, as described in *The Saturday Evening Post,* May 25, 1963. Elicit discussion about other situations in which the actual facts of a situation have been withheld from the public in order to assure community profits and continued stability.

   C. On what should major classroom emphasis be placed?

   1. Crucial moral issues raised in the play:

      What price integrity?

      What role should the individual seek to play in public affairs?

      What form of government is really best?

      What comes first—loyalty to family, to principles, to the larger community?

   2. Considerations of logic and persuasion in the action and rhetoric of the play:

      Where do we find instances of faulty reasoning? irrationality?

      What different tactics of persuasion are attempted in the play and for what reasons? How effective do these tactics ultimately prove to be?

      Are all of Dr. Stockmann's "discoveries" tenable, particularly those propounded in Acts IV and V?

3. Attention to structure, tone, characterization, and dominant symbols.

What does each act contribute to the total action of the play?

How does Ibsen want us to regard Dr. Stockmann and the plight into which he and his family are plunged?

What does Dr. S. learn as a result of this total experience that he did not know when he first exposed the pollution of the baths?

Is his learning complete?

How does Dr. S. contrast with his brother in character and motivation?

Are the other characters "round" or "flat"? For what purpose has each been introduced?

What elements in the play take on symbolic significance?

II. *Analyzing the play*

A. Clarify possible confusions about plot events by administering a factual quiz, covering such questions as these:

1. Short answers:

a. Why is Captain Horster dismissed from his ship command?

b. Following the town meeting, why does Marton Kiil buy up all the shares in the baths?

c. What reason does Hovstad give Petra for supporting her father?

d. What causes Dr. Stockmann to tell Aslaksen and Hovstad to jump out of the window?

e. What role has Dr. S. played originally in the development of the baths? What earlier advice that he had given was, unfortunately, ignored by the town officials?

f. Dr. S. is not perfect. Give one example that shows he also has personal faults.

g. If you had the opportunity, which character in the play would you nominate as *really* the worst "enemy of the people"? Why?

h. State one or two ideas which Dr. S. expresses at the town meeting which particularly frighten the townspeople and turn them against him.

2. Name the character who states each of the following convictions:

a. "There is so much falsehood both at home and at school.

At home one must not speak, and at school we have to stand and tell lies to the children."
b. "The whole town! Well, it wouldn't be a bad thing. It would just serve them right, and teach them a lesson. They think themselves so much cleverer than we old fellows. . . . Now they shall pay for it. You pull their legs, too, Thomas!"
c. "We shall proceed with the greatest moderation, Doctor. Moderation is always my aim; it is the greatest virtue in a citizen—at least, I think so."
d. ". . . and in my opinion a journalist incurs a heavy responsibility if he neglects a favorable opportunity of emancipating the masses—the humble and oppressed. I know well enough that in exalted circles I shall be called an agitator, and all that sort of thing; but they may call me what they like. If only my conscience doesn't reproach me, then."
e. "Oh yes, right—right. What is the use of having right on your side if you have not might? . . . good heavens, one has to put up with so much injustice in this world. . . . There are the boys. . . ."
f. "And then, when you have had six months to think things over, if, after mature consideration, you can persuade yourself to write a few words of regret, acknowledging your error . . ."
g. "I intend to be free to express my opinion on any subject under the sun."
B. Outline with the class ways in which each act contributes functionally to the overall development and effect of the play.
Act   I: Introduces all characters, provides inciting action (the letter), sets up *personal conflict* between the brothers, and presents Stockmann as idealistic, but highly naive about life and people.
Act II: *Rising action*
Hovstad, Aslaksen, and Billing agree to support Dr. S., but for purely selfish personal reasons.
Peter introduces the *political conflict* (power versus right) and arouses Dr. S. to passionate adherence to his original position, despite pressures from his wife.
Act III: *"Technical climax."*
Hovstad, Aslaksen, and Billing bandy brave words

and convictions until Peter apprises them of a few material facts.

Dr. S. appropriates the mayor's hat and stick a few minutes, until bluntly informed that the other three men have withdrawn their support.

The *reversal* begins, even though Dr. S. only partially recognizes what has happened.

Overcoming fears for her family, Mrs. S. nobly sides with her husband.

Act IV: The *reversal* is complete.

Stockmann forces the conflict to an *ethical* level and is branded an "enemy of the people" for his denunciatory and unconventional philosophy.

This act is essentially essential for Dr. S.'s personal enlightenment, but also reveals that he still has much to learn about "how to win friends and influence people."

Act V: Dr. S.'s convictions are put to the test and he is not found wanting. He vigorously resists three temptations to back down from his position and finally makes the decision to stay where he is and fight back.

Dr. S. is also further enlightened about the degree of corruption in other men and about the power of the independent man. His personal education and enlightenment are, however, far from complete.

C. Ask students to diagram the organization of the play, noting the inverse relationship of Dr. S.'s attempts to enlighten the community and his own personal growth in knowledge and insight.

Dr. S.'s path to enlightenment

Naiveté   Reversal

Hope of Success   External

Partial Enlightenment

Dr. S.'s practical efforts to clean the baths

Disillusionment   Failure

D. If one of the important patterns in the play is Dr. Stockmann's movement from ignorance and naiveté to greater enlightenment, students need to identify the idealistic beliefs he holds in the beginning of the play and which he is forced to abandon as the action unfolds:

1. He believes scientific facts carry weight and speak for themselves; he is unaware of the force of sociological/economic/political factors.

2. He believes individuals operate out of disinterested motives; only later does he realize that most men pay "lip service" to social ideals ("support stops where the pocketbook begins").

3. He assumes credit will go where credit is due and is unaware of the multiple interpretations that can be applied to human actions.

4. He believes that society ("the compact majority") honors reason and truth—and also honors the men who attempt to spread the truth—and has yet to realize the full extent of hypocrisy and rationalization in human life.

5. He believes that free men have the right to say anything they wish in public, regardless of who is offended or what is attacked; he has yet to learn that independent opinion can be strangled, censored, misinterpreted, ignored—*particularly* by the "liberal-minded independent press."

(Students must, of course, identify various experiences in the play which cause Dr. S. to alter these beliefs. They should also note elements of his background experience, such as his long isolation in a northern Norwegian rural community, that could account for his extreme naiveté. They should, in addition, note instances where Stockmann displays excessive pride and self-satisfaction, character traits that could limit his personal influence and effectiveness.)

E. Are all of Dr. S.'s new ideas ("discoveries") tenable? Which are half-truths? Students should critically examine such contentions as these:

1. Are leading men "like billy-goats in a young plantation; they do mischief everywhere. They stand in a free man's way whichever way he turns. . . ."?

2. "The majority *never* has right on its side. The minority is always in the right."

3. "These 'majority truths' are like last year's cured meat—

like rancid, tainted ham; and they are the origin of the moral scurvy that is rampant in our communities."

4. Can we agree with Stockmann that "isolated, intellectually superior personalities have a greater right "to pronounce judgment and to approve, to direct and to govern"?

5. Do we agree "that the strongest man in the world is he who stands most alone"?

In what ways is Dr. S.'s "learning" still incomplete? What does he need to learn about methods of changing the attitudes and behavior of others?

F. The entire play is really a series of discussions and debates, in which several characters display very faulty thinking or use ineffective tactics of persuasion. Have students point out some of these instances in the play and possibly read selected scenes as illustrations.

G. Even though Dr. S. has his faults, he is still a highly admirable man, especially when we compare him with the others in the play.

1. How does he contrast with his brother—in habits of living, family life, political beliefs, integrity? (It is hard to believe they have the same mother!)

2. What are Stockmann's motives for wanting to expose the pollution of the baths? Do the other men support him for the same reasons? (Students will quickly perceive that Dr. S.'s supposed supporters have only selfish motives:

Kiil—wants revenge for past slights, a chance to gloat over his critics.

Billing—is out for "kicks"; note his brave talk about dynamite and revolution.

Aslaksen—sees a means of dramatizing (inoffensively!) the unity and strength of the small tradesman.

Hovstad—sees an opportunity for self-important target practice on "authorities."

3. In what ways are Dr. S.'s former supporters revealed as moral cowards and true enemies of the people? Students should evaluate both their conduct and rhetoric:

Kiil guards his reputation at all costs; he is totally egocentric, unfeeling, blustery, and illogical, appropriately labeled "the Badger."

Billing is "a many-sided man" who talks big but risks nothing; he is an arm-chair hero and pseudo-non-conformist who runs from every real battle.

Aslaksen is a kind of Uriah Heep, always "moderate" and repulsively cautious, a total conformist and mealy-mouthed hypocrite.

Hovstad is really the vilest hypocrite of the group, as betrayed in his conversation with Petra about her translation, his belief that all men can be bought, and his glib declaration that "every animal must fight for its own livelihood" as justification for corrupt behavior.

4. What is the function of these minor characters: Mrs. Stockmann; Petra; Captain Horster; the drunkard at the meeting?

H. What is the *tone* of the play? How are we supposed to feel about the plight of Dr. S. and his family? (Proceed into a discussion of the mixture of humor, satire, and irony in the play; also note irony of the title.) Has Ibsen weakened the impact of the play by making the hero somewhat ridiculous and extreme?

I. What elements take on symbolic significance in the play? (Note especially the use of the baths to represent both physical and moral pollution; the mayor's hat and stick which Dr. S. briefly borrows in Act III just before the reversal occurs; the detailed use of animal imagery in Acts IV and V, especially the distinction between "cur men" and "poodle men.")

J. Identify some of the major themes of the play:

1. Society has far too few Stockmanns—men who dare translate ideals into action and act independent of groups or political parties.

2. Paradoxically, self-interest is ultimately best served by placing the welfare of the total community ahead of selfish personal and family concerns.

3. Social change is a gradual process, best achieved through education and skillful persuasion.

4. Democratic society moves forward only because of the courage, vision, and the example of an enlightened minority, ready to discard what is outmoded or corrupt. In contrast, the unrestrained majority is only too ready to limit individual liberty, free thought, and needed change.

K. Identify some of Dr. S.'s declarations that all men of integrity should support, for example:

"I mean to have the right to look my sons in the face when they are grown men."

"A matter of such great importance—the welfare of the town at stake—it is no time to shirk trouble."

"All the men in this town are old women—like you; they all

think of nothing but their families, and never of the community."

III. *Possible composition topics*

A. Trace the repetitive use of such key words as *truth, public opinion, majority, poison, self-government* throughout the play and then come to some conclusion on this question: Does Ibsen believe in democratic government?

B. Present your nomination of "Enemy of the People No. 1" in this play. Support your case adequately by reference to specific scenes and actions.

C. What does Dr. Stockmann learn about man and society that he did not comprehend before? In what ways is his education still far from complete?

D. Analyze the various devices used by characters in the play to justify inaction, unethical conduct, and hypocritical behavior.

E. One critic has stated: "A careful reading of Ibsen's play with the orientation of modern psychology may lead one to conclude that Stockmann suffers from an acute persecution complex, that he actually seeks his own destruction. At times he seems in a frenzy to develop hostility against himself, and we feel that all of his aims might have been accomplished if he had only been somewhat less hysterical." [16] To what extent do you agree or disagree with this interpretation?

The responsibility for developing a rich and meaningful drama program falls, of course, on already overburdened English teachers, who may also have to overcome the handicap of poor background preparation. Taking more courses in drama is surely only a partial solution, for the love of drama can be transmitted only by teachers who genuinely value reading plays, regularly attending theatrical productions, reading periodicals dealing with the dramatic arts, seeing effective TV and film productions, and following the development of drama in all its forms within our American culture and in other countries of the world. Only through such enthusiastic and dedicated persons can drama be withdrawn from the wings and restored to the center of the classroom stage, to share a leading role with the other dominant forms of our literary tradition.

[16] Edwin Sauer, *English in the Secondary School* (New York: Holt, Rinehart and Winston, 1961), pp. 192–193.

SELECTED BIBLIOGRAPHY (*Outstanding)

Bentley, Eric, *In Search of Theater* (New York: Vintage Books, 1954).
———, *The Playwright as Thinker* (New York: Meridian, 1955).
Bradley, A. C., *Shakespearean Tragedy* (New York: St. Martin's, 1904).
*Brustein, Robert, *Seasons of Discontent* (New York: Simon and Schuster, 1965).
———, *The Theatre of Revolt* (Boston: Little, Brown, 1964).
*Downer, Alan S. (Ed.), *American Drama and Its Critics* (Chicago: University of Chicago Press, 1967).
———, *Fifty Years of American Drama* (Chicago: Regnery, 1951).
*Esslin, Martin, *The Theatre of the Absurd* (New York: Doubleday, 1961).
Fergusson, Francis, *The Idea of a Theater* (New York: Doubleday, 1955).
Freedley, George, and John A. Reeves, *A History of the Theatre* (New York: Crown, 1943).
*Frenz, Horst, *American Playwrights on Drama* (New York: Hill & Wang, 1965).
*Gassner, John, *Directions in Modern Theatre and Drama* (New York: Holt, Rinehart and Winston, 1965).
———, *Producing the Play* (New York: Holt, Rinehart and Winston, 1942).
Goodman, Randolph, *Drama on Stage* (New York: Holt, Rinehart and Winston, 1961).
Gould, Jean, *Modern American Playwrights* (New York: Dodd, Mead, 1966).
*Granville-Barker, Harley, *Prefaces to Shakespeare* (2 vols.; Princeton, N.J.: Princeton University Press, 1926–1946).
Harbage, Alfred, *Shakespeare's Audience* (New York: Columbia University Press, 1941).
Harbrace Drama Sourcebooks (New York: Harcourt):
   Felheim, Marvin (Ed.), *Comedy: Plays, Theory, and Criticism,* 1961.
   Harrison, G. B., *Julius Caesar in Shakespeare, Shaw and the Ancients,* 1961.
   Kernan, Alvin B., *Modern Satire,* 1962.
   Levin, Richard (Ed.), *Tragedy: Plays, Theory, and Criticism,* 1961.
Knight, Arthur, *The Liveliest Art: A Panoramic History of the Movies* (New York: Crowell-Collier-Macmillan, 1956).
*Lerner, Max, "The Arts and Popular Culture" in *America as a Civilization* (New York: Simon and Schuster, 1957), Ch. 2.

*McCarthy, Mary, "Realism in the American Theater," *Harper's,* July 1961, pp. 45–62.

———, "General Macbeth," *Harper's,* June 1962, pp. 35–39.

*MacIver, R. M. (Ed.), *Great Moral Dilemmas in Literature: Past and Present* (New York: Harper & Row, 1956).

*McLuhan, Marshall, *Understanding Media* (New York: McGraw-Hill, 1964).

Roberts, Vera Mowry, *On Stage: A History of Theater* (New York: Harper & Row, 1962).

Rockefeller Brothers Fund, *The Performing Arts* (New York: McGraw-Hill, 1965).

Schramm, Wilbur and others, *Television in the Lives of Our Children* (Palo Alto, Calif.: Stanford University Press, 1961).

*Sewall, Richard B., *The Vision of Tragedy* (New Haven, Conn.: Yale University Press, 1959).

Sontag, Susan, *Against Interpretation* (New York: Farrar, Straus & Giroux, 1966).

Wilson, John Dover, *Life in Shakespeare's England* (Baltimore: Penguin, 1959).

SOURCES PERTAINING TO TEACHING OF DRAMA

*Benedict, Stewart H. (Ed.), *A Teacher's Guide to Modern Drama* (New York: Dell, 1967).

Boutwell, William D., *Using Mass Media in the Schools* (New York: Appleton, 1962).

Dunning, Stephen and Henry W. Sams (Eds.), *Scholarly Appraisals of Literary Works Taught in High Schools* (Champaign, Ill.: NCTE, 1965).

Evans, Bertrand, *Teaching Shakespeare in the High School* (New York: Crowell-Collier-Macmillan, 1966).

Lambert, Robert G., "An Enemy of the People: A Friend of the Teacher," *English Journal,* 54 (October 1965), pp. 626–628.

Loban, Walter, Margaret Ryan, and James R. Squire, "Literature: Drama and Poetry" in *Teaching Language and Literature* (New York: Harcourt, 1961), Ch. 7.

*Mack, Maynard, "Teaching Drama: *Julius Caesar*" in Edward J. Gordon and Edward S. Noyes (Eds.), *Essays on the Teaching of English* (New York: Appleton, 1960), Ch. 17.

NCTE Studies in the Mass Media, 508 South Sixth St., Champaign, Ill. Eight issues a year.

*Ornstein, Robert, *Shakespeare in the Classroom* (Urbana, Ill.: Educational Illustrators, 1960). NCTE publication.

Postman, Neil, *Television and the Teaching of English* (New York: Appleton, 1961). NCTE publication.

Rosenheim, Edward W., Jr., *What Happens in Literature* (Chicago: The University of Chicago Press, 1963).

*Sheridan, Marion C. and others, *The Motion Picture and the Teaching of English* (New York: Appleton, 1965).

The Teachers Guide to Media and Methods (Media and Methods Institute, Inc., 124 East 40th Street, New York 10016). Nine issues per year.

SELECTED MODERN PLAYS FOR CLASSROOM USE

Grade 9

One-act plays

The Valiant, Holworthy Hall and Robert Middlemas

A Shipment of Mute Fate, Les Crutchfield

Trifles, Susan Glaspell

The Devil and Daniel Webster, Stephen Vincent Benét

The Will, James M. Barrie

Two Crooks and a Lady, Eugene Pillot

Beauty and the Jacobin, Booth Tarkington

The Apollo of Bellac, Jean Giraudoux

A Night at an Inn, Lord Dunsany

The Mother, Paddy Chayevsky

TV and radio plays

The Weans, Robert Nathan

Invasion from Mars, H. G. Wells

Visit from a Small Planet, Gore Vidal

Out of Control, William Bruckner

Three-act plays

I Remember Mama, John Van Druten

The Barretts of Wimpole Street, Rudolf Besier

Life with Father, Howard Lindsay and Russell Crouse

The King and I, Richard Rodgers and Oscar Hammerstein II

West Side Story, Arthur Laurents, Leonard Bernstein, and Stephen Sondheim

The Hasty Heart, John Patrick

Abe Lincoln in Illinois, Robert Sherwood

The Late Christopher Bean, Sidney Howard

Antigone, Sophocles

Grade 10

The Miracle Worker, William Gibson

The Desperate Hours, Joseph Hayes

Sunrise at Campobello, Dore Schary

The Diary of Anne Frank, France Goodrich and Albert Hackett
Yellow Jack, Sidney Howard
The Admirable Crichton, James M. Barrie
Journey's End, R. C. Sherriff
The Winslow Boy, Terence Rattigan
Ah, Wilderness!, Eugene O'Neill
Teahouse of the August Moon, John Patrick and Vern Sneider

Ten Little Indians, Agatha Christie
A Majority of One, Leonard Spigelgass
Watch on the Rhine, Lillian Hellman
Romanov and Juliet, Peter Ustinov
Twelve Angry Men, Reginald Rose
Pygmalion; Arms and the Man, George Bernard Shaw
She Stoops to Conquer, Oliver Goldsmith

Grade 11

The Emperor Jones, Eugene O'Neill
The Adding Machine, Street Scene, Elmer Rice
Inherit the Wind, Lawrence and Lee
The Glass Menagerie, Tennessee Williams
The Green Pastures, Marc Connelly
The Little Foxes, Lillian Hellman
A Raisin in the Sun, Lorraine Hansberry
The Silver Cord, Sidney Howard
Death Takes a Holiday, Walter Ferris
A Bell for Adano, Paul Osborn
Our Town; Skin of our Teeth, Thornton Wilder

All My Sons; The Crucible, Arthur Miller
Of Mice and Men, John Steinbeck
The Time of Your Life, William Saroyan
What Price Glory?, Maxwell Anderson and Laurence Stallings
Billy Budd, Louis Coxe and Robert Chapman
The Andersonville Trial, Saul Levitt
The Caine Mutiny Court Martial, Herman Wouk
Member of the Wedding, Carson McCullers
Home of the Brave, Arthur Laurents
The Scarecrow, Percy MacKaye

Grade 12

Victoria Regina, Laurence Housman
Cyrano de Bergerac, Edmond Rostand
A Doll's House, The Wild Duck, An Enemy of the People, Henrik Ibsen

Caesar and Cleopatra, Saint Joan, Major Barbara, G. B. Shaw
The Cherry Orchard, Anton Chekhov
The Corn Is Green, Emlyn Williams

Death of a Salesman, Arthur Miller

Medea, Robinson Jeffers

Darkness at Noon, Sidney Kingsley

Winterset, Elizabeth the Queen, Mary of Scotland, Maxwell Anderson

A Man for All Seasons, Robert Bolt

The Mad Woman of Chaillot, Jean Giraudoux

The Importance of Being Earnest, Oscar Wilde

R. U. R., Karel Capek

Murder in the Cathedral, T. S. Eliot

Becket, Jean Anouilh

Blood Wedding, Frederico Garcia Lorca

Beyond the Horizon, The Hairy Ape, Mourning Becomes Electra, Eugene O'Neill

The Circle, Somerset Maugham

J.B., Archibald MacLeish

The Visit, Friedrich Duerrenmatt

Dear Brutus, J. M. Barrie

Rosencrantz and Guildenstern Are Dead, Tom Stoppard

The Bald Soprano, The Chairs, Eugene Ionesco

No Exit, Jean Paul Sartre

The Royal Hunt of the Sun, Peter Shaffer

The School for Scandal, The Rivals, Richard Sheridan

Oedipus the King, Sophocles

Tartuffe, Molière

The Zoo Story, Edward Albee

8
Biography and Essay
in the Literature Program

Biography, unlike fiction, is not an inherently popular form of literature. The general public *is* interested in people, but the popular taste in recent years has run to the personal narrative of adventure, which often has true literary merit, and to autobiographical confessions of the "I was a Communist" or "I was an alcoholic" variety, which have nothing of literary artistry about them. An occasional biography of high quality—such as Moss Hart's *Act One* or Catherine Drinker Bowen's *The Lion and The Throne*—catches the public fancy, but in general the reading of serious biography is limited to the intelligentsia and the specialists.

Compared with the novel, short story, poem, or play, biography is a minor form of literature, although school anthologies determinedly include selections from biographies, past and current, and teachers dutifully present the form in their classes. There is justice in this, for biography, which is actually more popular among adolescents than among adults, presents some important possibilities and advantages as well as some problems when it is used in the high school literature program.

BIOGRAPHY IN THE LITERATURE PROGRAM:
PROBLEMS AND OPPORTUNITIES

Foremost among the problems posed by teaching biography as a literary genre is the fact that between excellent mature biography and most junior biography there is a wide hiatus, much wider even than that between the better junior novels and mature novels of superior caliber. The best of adult biography, at least since World War II, is in the tradition of the scholar and the historian. The result is that it is often difficult reading—requiring analysis and reflection. By stating this face I do not argue for the exclusion of mature biography from the high school, but suggest that it often may not be feasible for the average and below-average readers.

The best biographies not only are often weighty in style and formidable in organization; they tend naturally to deal with mature phases of life and the conflicts and emotions that accompany these phases. Almost always the person of eminence, about whom a biography is likely to be written, has attained his eminence and made his greatest contributions in later life. Even in Bill Severn's *Adlai Stevenson: Citizen of the World,* for example, a biography for the teen-age audience, the mature phases of Stevenson's career have to be stressed, not his boyhood and youth. Biography often offers little inherent appeal to adolescents or chance for identification by them.

Then, too, the mature biography of the statesman, or scientist, or specialist in any area may demand a background of knowledge beyond that of the average adolescent. For that reason, biographies are especially difficult to use for reading in common. Also, for the adolescent reader, the adult biography, often organized in expository rather than narrative fashion, may be an unnatural kind of reading, far from the tradition of the well-constructed plot or the happy ending. Biography may well be a more valuable adjunct to the social studies or some other class than it is to the English class. Of course, the nature of adult biography points out clearly one responsibility of the senior high school English teacher: to teach students to read it as a distinct form of literature for purposes that may serve more than simple enjoyment.

Yet biography used in the high school program offers some advantages in widening reading horizons. For some adolescents, biography or autobiography has greater impact than fiction because the people and events are, presumably, real. The literal-minded student who has not yet developed a clear perception of why good fiction gets at the truth of human experience may be more impressed by the biography than by the novel. This is particularly true of adolescents who have a certain handicap, especially a physical one. To such students, the inspiration of a story like that of Helen Keller or of Glenn Cunningham, as told in David Boynick's *Champions by Setback,* or that of the girl who loses a limb in Louise Baker's *Out on a Limb* may be nothing short of phenomenal. The reality of the biography may make identification easier for some readers.

Biography, particularly that written for the juvenile audience, often features the kind of heroism, idealism, and martyrdom that the essentially romantic mind of the adolescent especially admires. The person who fights for what he believes in against great odds is a hero to many adolescents—probably to many adults, too, for that matter—and this theme frequently is present in biography such as John F. Kennedy's popular *Profiles in Courage.*

Certainly, biography offers an opportunity to meet students' differing individual interests in various fields. Madelene Goss for example, has written some excellent biographies of great musicians. There are many biographies of sports heroes. No matter what his interest, the adolescent can find it represented in biography. For this reason, biography is valuable in enriching study of science, social studies, and other subjects.

Reading and study of biography can also provide natural motivation for writing about personal experience. Both literature and writing contribute to the student's awareness of the significance of his own everyday experience, and the two come together naturally in connection with biography or autobiography. After reading autobiography students may be better prepared to write thoughtfully about aspects of their own personal experience, and writing an autobiography might be the culminating activity in a class unit on biography and autobiography.

APPROACHES IN TEACHING BIOGRAPHY

The problem of the transition from fiction to biography, in the junior high school, is one which best can be approached through biographies that are fictionalized or that use the techniques of fiction. Biography for the early junior high school should have the same qualities as fiction for that level—action and excitement, human daring and courage, humor and human interest. Fictionalized biographies such as those of Sitting Bull, Kit Carson, and Buffalo Bill by Doris Shannon

Garst are especially appropriate. Not only the content but the style must be considered in choosing "transition" biographies. Some relatively mature biographies utilize the techniques of fiction. For example, compare the passages below, which open biographies of Garibaldi and Leonardo da Vinci, respectively:

> A chill autumn rain was falling; the bitter wind swept it in gusts against his face as he turned into the quiet shabby street. He had left the noisy, lighted wineshops of the harbor quarter behind him. . . .
> The young sailor paused for a moment beneath a flickering gas light, examining the superscription of a letter.[1]

> When you go to Florence, Italy, and look at the city and the rocky, hilly country around it, you may think that all of this has changed very little since the great palaces and bridges were first built.[2]

There is little doubt that the first, which opens like a novel, is more effective in engaging the young reader's interest.

Though a sample unit on biography is outlined later in this chapter, the direct "biography" unit is not the only vehicle for teaching or introducing the genre. Often biographies and autobiographies can be included in thematic units that involve the various types of literature. Biographies of heroes in sports and other fields might be included in an eighth-grade unit on "Heroes Past and Present"; a tenth-grade unit on "To Dare Greatly" might be organized with autobiographical or biographical accounts of mountain climbing, undersea exploration, aviation, and so forth; and "Men of Destiny" in the twelfth grade might include drama and fiction as well as mature biography.

Reading Biography

No matter what the plan of organization for introducing and teaching biography, however, one responsibility is clear: students need to be taught how to read the form, just as they must be taught how to read the other genres of literature. Mature reading of biography demands two major skills: skill in following various patterns of organization, and skill in critical evaluation.

Biographies may be either narrative or expository in organization.

[1] Nina Brown Baker, *Garibaldi* (New York: Vanguard, 1944), p. 11.
[2] Emily Hahn, *Leonardo da Vinci* (New York: Random House, 1956), p. 1.

In the junior high school, of course, narrative biography will be the staple, forming the natural bridge from fiction. Senior high school students, though, should be introduced to biographies that are organized in a variety of expository patterns. For example, the biographer may choose to interpret the character and assess the stature of his subject through analysis of a number of key episodes in his life. This is true, for instance, of Benjamin Thomas' fine one-volume biography of Lincoln.[3] Or the biographer may analyze the various influences on the life and work of the subject. This is often done in biographies of literary figures. A familiarity with various expository forms of organization in biography is especially important for the able student in the senior high school.

Critical evaluation in reading biography, of course, as in reading other forms of literature, is vital. One useful method is for the teacher and the class to draw up a check list that can be used for critically judging biography, whether read individually or by the class in common. Such a check list might be based on two major points.

Authenticity.   It is often hard, without doing research on the subject, to make a judgment about the authenticity of a biography when the subject is relatively obscure or the events are remote. A first distinction that students need to make, with the help of the teacher, is that between biography and biographical fiction, such as the popular stories of Presidents' wives written by Irving Stone or the novels based on biography. Usually, simple examination of the book makes this clear, and permits one to expect that a writer assumed the responsibilities of either the biographer or the novelist.

Having determined that he is dealing with biography, how can the student arrive at some conclusions about authenticity? First, he can look to see whether any bibliography, or list of sources, is given. One or the other often appears even in the better junior biography. He can then consider the adequacy of those sources. Thus, he might be suspicious of one biography of the great Filipino, Carlos Romulo, that is based almost entirely on the speeches and writings of Romulo himself.

One difficulty in trying to assess authenticity is that even in the best of biography certain techniques of fiction might be used. Dialogue may be manufactured, events guessed at, and sequence occasionally

---

[3] Benjamin Thomas, *Abraham Lincoln* (New York: Knopf, 1952).

based on hypothesis. Lytton Strachey, who is represented frequently in high school anthologies, and who was the most influential biographer in the world during the early twentieth century, introduced the school of readable biography that "broke away from documentation and the rigid bonds of fact," [4] and paved the way for other biographers to exploit its innovations to the fullest. John Garraty writes:

> Some of them ventured daringly beyond the sources; they invented dialogue, described minute actions that *might* have occurred, and presumed to record the thoughts as well as the words and deeds of their subjects. Of course this practice was as old as biography itself—Xenophon could never have remembered Socrates' conversations in the detail with which he recorded them in the *Memorabilia*. Plutarch was a master of this technique as of most others, and even the conscientious Boswell was not above elaborating on his notes.[5]

However, even in the junior high school the pupils can begin to practice identifying obviously fictitious incidents and conversations in biography and those that might have been based on actual documentation. For example, in Garst's *Sitting Bull* there are some things that could have been verified by United States government records, others that could have come from no source but the imagination of the author.

Biographer's relationship to the subject. The significance and worth of a biography may depend much on the relationship of the biographer to his subject, and appraisal of this relationship is important to discriminating reading of the work. Most good biographies grow out of a biographer's natural affinity for his subject—not true of the authors of the potboilers relatively prevalent among junior biographies. Many junior (and adult) biographies are produced to fill a gap in the market, and the adolescent, after some experience in reading the form, can usually tell when a book "is the product of a harmonious mixture of writer, subject, and surrounding circumstance" [6]—and when it is not.

Garraty complains that "too many biographers drift to their sub-

---

[4] John A. Garraty, *The Nature of Biography* (New York: Knopf, 1957), p. 122.
[5] Garraty, pp. 126–127.
[6] Garraty, p. 155.

jects haphazardly, depending upon chance alone for a happy combination. They have not weighed their interests and capabilities against the requirements of their selected tasks." Furthermore, Garraty points out that "Many biographies are the result of mutual interest. A specialist in some field, whose work has made him aware of the contribution of one of his predecessors, decides to expand his knowledge and ends in writing a biography." [7] The high school reader of biography, then, can ask, "What qualifications does this biographer have for writing this biography?"

An intimate knowledge of the subject does not necessarily ensure good biography, of course. Quite frequently, the biographer may be a member of the subject's family—a wife or husband, son or daughter. Usually, when that is true, the work is designed as a monument, and the reader needs to separate this from the more objective type of biography. On the other hand, the high school reader should become familiar, too, with the "debunking" tradition in biography. Again, the biographer's background almost always will furnish the clues to this information, and one may guess, for example, that the lifelong conservative is not likely to write anything but a debunking biography of Franklin Delano Roosevelt.

The biographer, then, will be criticized on the grounds of his use of and access to authentic information about his subject, his relationship to the subject and his qualifications for writing the biography, and his literary artistry. The perfect combination of these will result in the biography that presents with vividness a human being and the significance of his achievement.

OUTLINE OF SEQUENCE FOR A UNIT
ON BIOGRAPHY (NINTH GRADE)

PEOPLE IN PRINT [8]

    I. The teacher leads a discussion of well-known contemporary persons who, in the class members' opinions, are leading interesting lives. Then the discussion switches to which well-known, contemporary people are making the greatest contribution to the welfare of the country or civilization as a whole.

[7] Garraty, p. 155.
[8] This unit was taught by the author in classes at East High School, Superior, Wisconsin, and at University High School, Minneapolis, Minnesota.

II. A teacher-prepared quiz is given in which the students are asked to identify a number of famous people in various areas—sports and entertainment, military, general adventure, science, education, the arts, politics, and so on. (Invariably, the students are able to identify more people in the sports-entertainment area than in any other. The teacher may do a bit of good-natured baiting at this point!)

III. The teacher leads a discussion of biographies and autobiographies that class members have already read, jotting various titles on the board. Discussion includes which ones were liked or disliked and why; then proceeds to the purposes and values of reading biography and autobiography.

IV. The teacher distributes a list, appropriate to the range of ability and interest in the class, of biographies and autobiographies available in the school or public library or locally in paperback form. The assignment is that each student must read one book.

V. The teacher and class draw up a check list for judging and evaluating biographies. (The teacher has this reproduced, and distributes it to the class.)

VI. For two or three days, while the class members are choosing books and beginning reading, the class as a whole reads and discusses the several short selections of biography and autobiography included in the class anthology. Reference is made to the check list drawn up earlier.

VII. While the individual reading is progressing, the class studies a series of poems about people, character sketches in verse, which are included in the class anthology, or which the teacher reads aloud or has reproduced from other sources.

VIII. Several subgroups are formed within the class, according to the types of biographies being read. For example, there may be groups of students reading about scientists, sports figures, adventurers, political figures, and so forth. Assignments of group and individual reports are made:

A. Group report: Each group prepares a report of a type such as the following:

1. A panel discussion on the field (science, politics, or others), its opportunities and obstacles, as revealed in the books read in the group.

2. A "This Is Your Life" program based on the career of one of the people read about in the group.

3. A series of interviews in which group members play the roles of people read about.

     4. A "Guess Who" quiz in which a series of clues are given until someone in the class can guess each of the subjects of the biographies read.

  B. Individual reports: All students must write an evaluation of their books, using the check list drawn up earlier.

  C. As enrichment activities, individual students may:

     1. Read another biography of the same person and compare the two treatments.

     2. Do library research on the person, using factual sources, and discuss the biography in view of this research.

IX. While individual reading is being completed and group reports are being prepared, the class members write character sketches of people they admire in real life. Class time is given to criticism and correction of the papers, as with any set of themes.

X. Group and individual reports are made.

THE ESSAY

The essential difficulty today in dealing with the teaching of the essay lies in defining "essay." The student in the junior and senior high school assuredly should deal with a wide range of nonfictional prose, other than the biography. But how much of this can be labeled "essay"? For example, are magazine articles essays? And what about editorials or letters? These types of writing—articles, editorials, informative and argumentative prose generally—are the province of all teachers, not only English teachers, just as the development of general reading ability is an all-school rather than an English-class responsibility.

Examination of courses of study in literature and commonly used textbook-anthologies shows that although the essay is a vaguely defined literary genre it enjoys a secure place in the school program. One popular textbook-anthology for the ninth grade, for example, includes eight different essays and articles, ranging from a humorous sketch by James Thurber to a deductively organized discussion of the habits and characteristics of Britons. But experienced teachers are aware of the general unpopularity of essays of the formal type. The major reason for this unpopularity of course is the inherent difficulty of the formal essay. In his very early book on the teaching of high school English, Charles Swain Thomas recognized this difficulty:

Our taste for story is innate, melody and rhyme delight us in our juvenile years, we are early won by the concreteness of the drama; but a liking for the essay has, in most cases, to be carefully developed. This is particularly true if a writer deals primarily with abstract subjects.[9]

Reed Smith has pointed out that the formal essay, such as that written by Bacon, Emerson, Macaulay, Huxley, or Newman, "is the product of an adult mind, written for other adult, trained minds." [10] Of course, even the much anthologized informal or personal essays of Addison, Lamb, and Stevenson, for example, are adult and urbane reflections and meditations.

Many students enjoy such light, humorous essays as those by James Thurber, Stephen Leacock, Robert Benchley, and Art Buchwald. The skills required in reading such essays are essentially the same as the skills required in reading fiction. Indeed, it is difficult to draw the line, for instance, between a Thurber essay and a Thurber short story.

The skills necessary to read the formal essay are the same as those needed to read general formal or analytical discourse—textbooks, for example. Many of the essays commonly included in anthologies for the eleventh and twelfth grades are extremely difficult and abstract. Naturally, it is all to the good for the able student to tackle Bacon or Emerson or Huxley. But it is futile to expect students of less than average ability to read essays by these writers. Essentially, the reading problem, of course, is one of organization. Reed Smith suggested in his book many years ago that teachers furnish the students with outlines of difficult essays. Yet perhaps the process is too often reversed; the teacher asks students to outline essays they are not ready to read. Reading the formal essay requires logical thinking and recognition of patterns of organization in expository discourse. Improvement in these abilities is as gradual as it is in other aspects of literary education. Though essay reading should not be the vehicle for grueling exercises in outlining, it may be extremely valuable as a springboard for student writing. This is true especially of the personal essay that deals with the seeming trivialities, the small awarenesses of living. Currently, this form of writing is largely relegated to newspaper and magazine columns and "departments." It is the mark of the immature ado-

[9] Charles S. Thomas, *The Teaching of English in the Secondary School* (Boston: Houghton Mifflin, 1917).
[10] Reed Smith, *The Teaching of Literature in the High School* (New York: American Book, 1935).

lescent to think that he has nothing worth writing about unless he has undergone harrowing adventure. His reading of informal essays may cause him to reflect, and thus to be prepared to write, on the everyday details of his own existence. And in this lies one pathway to maturity.

The Case for the Essay

Jerome Carlin, former head of the English Department in the Fort Hamilton High School of Brooklyn, presents a lively case for the teaching of the modern essay. A portion of Dr. Carlin's article follows:

> The case against the essay includes these charges: (1) It's dull. There's no story line. Kids won't be interested. (2) It's difficult. Since nothing *happens* and since so much is on an abstract level, those lower-I.Q. boys and girls especially won't stay afloat in an essay unit. (3) It's archaic. Addison and Steele haven't much to say to the generation of Lerner and Loewe. (4) Its form is hard to analyze. Plot, setting, climax, blank verse, rhyme scheme—terms like those, which are such handy labels in lessons on other works, are not to readily available for the essay. Let's look at these charges.

Appeal of the Essay

> Dull is it? Young people do take interest in dating, automobiles, flying, sports, comics, money, parents, vacation, college, and even high school. These are the topics of essays in today's textbooks.
> "Malinda didn't look as though she knew I was alive after we arrived at the dance . . . She didn't speak to me except to talk about other boys. . . . I found out among other things that she liked 'muscle goons.' I am definitely not athletic. . . . I ended up by walking home alone on my first date." One would be ashamed to accept his monthly check if he failed to draw fire from a class with those lines in the story essay "My Last Date." Written by a fourteen-year-old high school freshman, Philip Thompson, and published originally in *Boy's Life,* the essay appears in a recently published textbook. There is no need to analyze its fascination.
> There is no need to puzzle, either, over the appeal of a story essay which appears at the beginning of another textbook collection, the essay "Father Opens My Mail" by Clarence Day. The rights and responsibili-

ties of children and parents give rise to fighting talk even in a drowsy nine o'clock class. A few staunch supporters of respect for parents are bound to speak for patience and filial submission to Father's foibles. Some others will argue, perhaps with careful impersonality, "Yes, many parents are like that—but shouldn't be." With that lead the man behind the desk has a chance to say, "When you become a parent, how will you avoid the failings that you find in Father in this essay?"

For shock effect bring a class face to face with Art Buchwald's statement in "Don't Be a Pal to Your Son": ". . . we should give American children something they desperately need and crave for—brutality. We must make them feel neglected, insecure, unwanted and unloved. . . . They'll be so eager to be wanted that they'll do everything in the world to please us." Come on in, kids. The water is cold—but bracing.

Another kind of interest is aroused by Ruth Sawyer's poignant essay "Crippled: An Appeal to Motorists." "John Paul," says Mrs. Sawyer, "is four years old. He will never get up again—that is, never as a whole, free, exultant little boy. He will never throw back the covers of his cot, shoot across his room and ours, and drop like a plummet, stomach down, on our bed, shouting, "Here I come—Daddy and Mum!" Farther along, the author describes the youth who had been driving a borrowed car without a license, who still doesn't know what he has done—the boy who is restless, nervous, shallow; the boy who says "straightforwardly to the police: 'I was going fifty—late for a date.'" When he visits the hospital and learns that the crippled child is out of danger, this boy is "relieved of all responsibility. 'Gee, I'm glad. If he'd died now—I'd felt awful.'" Even if a student has never sat behind the wheel of a moving car, he is a potential driver. Many a one is eagerly awaiting the day when Dad and the law will allow him to unhitch the Chevrolet and gallop gallantly down the road. Once when I asked a wholesome class of average juniors—no intellectuals—what makes drivers like the one described in the essay so dangerous, I heard wonderful talk of the reckless use of the motor car as a prop to the weak ego, as a display of powers that the driver relates to himself, and as a status symbol of maturity falsely assumed by the immature.

Once drawn in by the lure of essays with such direct appeal to youthful interests, boys and girls won't flinch at tackling subjects of greater depth. In no other type of literature are the opportunities so great to deal directly with values. By the time a student has reached sixteen, the beginning of the middle age of youth, he is ripe for a look at Big Questions. If the groundwork is properly laid, he will react seriously and searchingly to the excerpt from Thoreau's *Walden* "Where I Lived, and What I Lived For." He will read critically Fosdick's "Six Ways to Tell Right from Wrong," and he will single out those of the six which seem most useful in everyday moral decisions. He will come to grips with problems of human relationships and justice in Neuberger's "Their Brothers' Keepers"; of economic relationships in Johnston's "A Warning to Labor and Management"; of governmental and political relationships in Russell's "How to Beat Communism."

So much of the time, the English teacher is a poor Don Quixote leveling his spindly red pencil against errors. If there were a Hippocratic Oath for those entering the profession of English teaching, surely it would declare, "You will exercise your art for the spiritual enrichment of your charges, and you will not spend all of your powers in the cure or prevention of material ills alone." The splendor of literature teaching is its illumination of life. With the essay, particularly, teacher and student can probe at the ideas about life and society that thoughtful writers have deliberately exposed to view. Other literary forms may have other aims. There is no ambiguity about the serious essayist's intention to put ideas before the reader.

What Is the Essay?

Some of the titles already mentioned provide evidence that the essay is a flourishing part of contemporary literature. What has become almost archaic in commercial usage is only the word *essay* itself. The form is as up-to-date as this morning's newspaper or this week's magazine. The current issue (when this was written) of the *Saturday Evening Post* includes in its contents: an article on social attitudes toward the physically disabled, "They Think We Have the Evil Eye," by Bentz Plagemann; a discussion of "Why I Deprive My Children" by Katharine Britton Mishler; and an analysis of economic thinking, pro and con, in "The Great Tariff Battle" by Joe Alex Morris. The current *Harper's* parallels the *Post* with articles on subjects attuned to the interests of its own readers: attitudes of the public toward contemporary art, proposals for a better way to teach deaf children, and the pros and cons of foreign policy regarding Africa, Asia, and the Western Alliance. Examples from local newspapers of the past week include an analysis of the problem of twin children whose capacities are not equal, an exposé and a slashing attack on abuses of mental hospitals, and a dance critique concluding that, in Jacques d'Amboise, America has at last produced a great male ballet dancer. If any of these examples seem too elevated for average readers in or out of high school, a few glances through the pages of teen and movie magazines will reveal the equivalents on another level. There is something for every taste and interest in the modern essay, which in newspaper and magazine goes by the name of article, feature, department, or column.

By the same token every level of reading difficulty exists among essays in commericial publications and has its counterpart in high school textbooks. Where your students tend to take their stand on the normal curve of reading ability should determine your choice of essays for their study. Whether you depend on the essay section of a general anthology or whether you have at hand a textbook collection solely devoted to the essay, you can command materials with a level of reading difficulty ranging from that of *Boys' Life* to that of *Atlantic*.

Neither from the student's point of view nor from the teacher's, need the essay be the psychological hazard that it sometimes becomes. True, if our teaching approach stresses form more than substance, it will prove to be bad magic, drying up that sea of hands around us.

Matters of form need not, should not, be overlooked. Labels enough are ready for application: formal, informal, personal, familiar, descriptive, reflective, philosophic, critical, abstract, factual. But these are mechanical matters of classification—too much like cataloguing books in a library instead of taking them home to read and enjoy.

Keep that shiny enthusiasm undulled. Bring the reader to any essays with the promise that it will reveal something worth considering about a live topic. "What do you think of the practice followed by many colleges in giving valuable scholarships to inferior students who are good athletes?". . . "How do *you* decide whether a particular action is right or wrong?" By such questions arouse interest in the topic; then study the essay for what it has to say on that subject; and only afterwards turn to the matter of form. "Now that we've considered what the author has to say, let's see *how* he said it . . . How did he organize his ideas? . . . What are the characteristics of his style? . . . What examples can you find of statements that are especially appealing or forceful in style? . . . What does this author do that you can put into practice in your own writing?" For the student there is much more excitement, as well as much more to be gained, in first dealing with the substance and in then briefly studying the technical processes by which that content is conveyed.[11]

The brevity of this chapter as contrasted with the chapters on teaching fiction, poetry, and drama is indicative of the author's belief that biography and essay should have a comparatively minor place in

[11] Jerome Carlin, "This I Believe—about the Essay," *English Journal,* LI (September 1962), 403–411.

the literature program. But he hopes, however, that the chapter has given ample reasons why they should not be ignored.

SELECTED BIBLIOGRAPHY

Carlsen, G. Robert, "Biography—The Bridge between Fact and Fiction," *Books and the Teen-age Reader* (New York: Bantam, 1967). Ch. 11.
Commentary on a number of biographies, junior and adult.
Cook, Don L., "On Teaching Essays." In *On Teaching Literature* (Bloomington, Ind.: Indiana University Press, 1967), pp. 135–150.
Identifies benefits in studying essays and discusses teaching approaches with Emerson's "Self-Reliance" and Orwell's "Shooting an Elephant" as illustrations.
Curwen, Henry Darcy, *Teaching Biography in the Secondary School* (Princeton, N.J.: College Entrance Examination Board, Publications Office, 1965).
A kinescript which discusses teaching approaches to Moss Hart's *Act One,* Maugham's *The Summing Up,* and Catherine Drinker Bowen's *A Yankee from Olympus.*
Garraty, John A., *The Nature of Biography* (New York: Knopf, 1957).
Kendall, Paul Murray, *The Art of Biography* (New York: W. W. Norton, 1965).
Two illuminating discussions of the genre.
Peet, C. Donald, "On Teaching Biography." In *On Teaching Literature* (Bloomington, Ind.: Indiana University Press, 1967), pp. 151–182.
A useful discussion ending in a suggestion for a major writing activity growing out of study of biography.

9
Organizing and Planning the Program in Literature

PATTERNS OF ORGANIZATION

Organizing instruction in the secondary school literature program is a perennial problem. English-teaching conferences and workshops have resounded for years with arguments about whether to teach certain "classics"; about whether to organize the literature program by types, by themes or topics, or by chronological survey. There is no magic inherent in any plan of organization; none can offer a sixty-day guaranty of success. The important outcomes discussed in the first chapter of this book can be sought quite successfully through various plans of organization, and the most successful junior and senior high school literature programs probably are eclectic in their basis. Each of the major plans has advantages and disadvantages, some of which are discussed below.

Organization through a Set of Specified Selections

A plan of organization popular several decades ago was based on specific selections. In those days it was customary to see, in senior high school classes at least, sets of thin volumes of individual works—*The Courtship of Miles Standish, The House of the Seven Gables,* and *A Tale of Two Cities.* Certain selections were allocated to each grade level, and entire classes studied them in common. However, this neat and uniform, and rather deadly, method of organizing the year's literature program disappeared, largely because of the appearance of the "omnibus" anthology for each grade, and the majority of teachers used the anthology to teach their grade, whatever the plan of organization of the book.

The wide distribution of paperbound books has brought a revival of the use of sets of novels, biographies, plays, and books of nonfiction. Many junior high school teachers, especially, have taken advantage of the facilities of the Teen-Age Book Club,[1] which offers a convenient monthly plan for buying paperbound books. Some teachers in both junior and senior high school have used sets of paperbound books both for reading by entire classes and for reading in small groups. Paperbacks have been widely used, too, as the basis for classroom libraries. A number of publishers have made available inexpensive editions of full-length works with study guides and teaching aids.

The absence of an overall pattern for the literature program may indicate in some schools that literature study is haphazard and aimless, with no meaningful context, a series of assignments or lessons that add up to nothing in the mind of the student. Some teachers, on the other hand, maintain that an overall pattern of themes, topics, or chronology is unduly restricting and distorting; that each selection of literature should be approached as a thing in itself, an individual work of art. Organization by individual selections is probably most effective in advanced senior high school classes in which the students already have developed rich backgrounds and sophisticated insights and are ready to progress through a series of major works.

Organization by Genres

One of the oldest and best-known ways of organizing the literature program is through study of the genre of literature—novel, short story, poetry, drama, biography, and essay. This plan is especially prevalent at the ninth and tenth-grade levels, and most of the textbook-anthologies for use in those grades are organized by literary types.

There are important advantages in this method. It is neat, orderly, easy to plan and administer, and easily understood by the students. Furthermore, it provides an obvious context in which to teach the skills necessary for reading the various forms of literature.

[1] 50 West 44th Street, New York 10036, N.Y.

There are some serious drawbacks, however, in this plan of organization. First, it is easy for the teacher to become preoccupied with technique, with literary craftsmanship—with verse forms and meter, plot construction, dramatic structure, and so forth. Of course these things have importance, but they should not be stressed at the expense of interest and broader interpretation. Skillful teachers can avoid this pitfall in the genre plan of organization as they can in any other. Then, too, some of the literary genres do not lend themselves readily to the genre approach. This is true of the longer forms—novel, epic, drama, and biography. It is virtually impossible for a class to read more than one of these types during one unit of work. Therefore the comparing and contrasting essential in the genre approach cannot be done except over a long period of time. Teachers—and anthologies —often resort to excerpts from long works, although as material for genre study excerpts have obvious failings, since they do not represent artistic wholes. Another drawback is that poetry does not fit well into the genre approach. A diet of poetry, sustained over several weeks, is too concentrated for many high school students. Even the most mature readers rarely read poetry that way.

Organization by Chronology

The chronological approach to literature is ordinarily limited to courses in the eleventh and twelfth grades, but there it is widespread. Tradition has placed American literature in the eleventh grade, English literature in the twelfth. In recent years there has been a trend toward other patterns of organization at these grade levels, but probably the majority of eleventh- and twelfth-grade teachers, and certainly the great majority of anthologies for the two grades, still follow the chronological plan. The principal advantage of the chronological survey lies in the perspective it can give to the origin and development of forms of literature and to the growth of the literary tradition as it is related to the development of English and American culture in general. Again, this plan is orderly, logical, and satisfying to the teacher who thinks it important to teach adolescents the historical development of literature.

A trenchant summary of the disadvantages of the chronological approach was made by Robert C. Pooley, in an article published more than three decades ago:

The grave danger of chronology in literature is the tendency to teach the history of literature rather than the literature itself. Facts, dates, and details of biography are stressed. Often relatively unimportant literature is dragged in to complete the historical picture, or student interest is sacrificed to scholarly thoroughness. The early periods in English and American literature are difficult and rarely interesting to more than a few students, yet they come at the beginning of the course when interest is hard to arouse. Furthermore, the chronological plan is exceedingly difficult to tie up with the normal voluntary reading of students. Only exceptional students will read voluntarily literature prior to 1800 with genuine enjoyment and profit.[2]

What is done within the framework of chronology may differ greatly from teacher to teacher. There is no doubt that in terms of student experiences, the chronological survey in many classrooms is deadly. Many teachers are unable to avoid the "factual error" in teaching literature, as defined by Thomas Clark Pollock:

> . . . the history of a work of literature is not the work of literature. Facts about a poem are not the poem. They may help a student to understand the poem. To the degree that they do, they are important to the teacher; but it is the literary experience itself in which the teacher should be primarily interested. Our literary heritage lies in the *actual,* if in one sense vicarious, *experiences* which literature can communicate. It is still true that the letter killeth, while the spirit giveth life; and we cannot make our literary heritage real to the youth of America through the letter of factualism.[3]

Yet some teachers, even within the context of the chronological survey, are able to avoid this as well as other pitfalls. One description of an enlightened approach to the survey of English literature is given in an article by Dorothy Bratton.[4] Within recent years, many schools have experimented with modest modifications of the traditional surveys. For example, such American writers as Herman Melville, Mark Twain, Thomas Wolfe, Ernest Hemingway, and William Faulkner are

[2] Robert C. Pooley, "Varied Patterns of Approach in the Teaching of Literature," *English Journal,* XXVIII (May 1939), 345.
[3] Thomas Clark Pollock, "Transmitting Our Literary Heritage," *English Journal,* XXXI (March 1942), 204.
[4] Dorothy Bratton, "English Literature for the Non-College-Bound," *English Journal,* XLV (February 1956), 84–91.

often studied in the twelfth grade. Many senior courses have also introduced "world literature," involving mainly selections from European writers but occasionally from Oriental, Latin American, or other literature. A few twelfth-grade teachers are even experimenting with chronology in reverse—starting with the present and working backward, rather than vice versa. Certainly, there is merit in this if the aim is to make literature of the past relevant to the concerns of youth today.

Organization by Themes

Organization of the literature program by themes has been, since the late 1930s, a popular, though continually controversial, pattern. Definition of the thematic plan cannot be as clearcut as that of any of the patterns discussed so far, for thematic organization may suggest anything from reading of a group of selections having something to do with a broad topic to close tracing of an archetype through a series of works.

Simple classification of selections under a topic supposedly of interest to students—The World of Sports, The Animal Kingdom, Suspense, Danger and Daring—has been common in textbook-anthologies for the junior high school for a number of years. In such organization, the topic provides a convenient way of dividing up the selections to be read, and the main stress is on the individual selections with little real concern for the topic itself.

In some units of teaching, on the other hand, the major stress is on a theme of significance to adolescents as it is illuminated by a series of selections, although there is usually concern with genre and form. A junior high school group studied, for example, "The Many Faces of Courage," to discover how different kinds of courage were exhibited in a group of selections of prose and poetry. A class of seniors studied attitudes toward nature, as expressed in literature, in a unit entitled "Every Common Sight." A series of themes may provide the framework for the entire program in literature. In the Curriculum Study Center in English at the Florida State University, a junior high school literature program was built on six "thematic categories," with one unit in each category introduced in each grade, according to the following chart.

Thematic Category	Seventh Grade	Eighth Grade	Ninth Grade
The Unknown	Qualities of Folk Heroes	Deeds and Qualities of Men of Myth	Concern for the Unexplained
Frontiers and Horizons	Faraway Places	The Village	Frontiers in Space
Decisions	Courage	Responsibility	Justice
Teamwork	Team Leaders	The Family	The Team and the Individual
Man in Action	Man and Nature	Man among Enemies	Man Alone
Relationships	Images of Adolescents	Close Adolescent Relationships	Mirrors (relation with self)

One great advantage of the thematic unit, no matter which of the three varieties of those just discussed it may represent, is that it permits the teacher to start with aspects of experience that students themselves recognize as important. There is an inherently better chance of interesting students by introducing a theme or topic—sportsmanship, qualities of success, attitudes toward love—than by announcing a unit on poetry or one on the next forty pages in the anthology. Most students are interested in ideas, and a skillfully chosen idea, stated as a theme for study, may serve as a real spark to student motivation.

The appeal to students' vital interests of a well-developed thematic unit furnishes built-in motivation and preparation for oral and written composition. A related advantage is that thematic organization makes for a natural and profitable relating of literature to other arts such as painting and music and to other media such as motion picture and television.

Another major advantage is that thematic organization provides an excellent opportunity to adjust the necessarily group process of teaching to a room full of individuals often startlingly disparate in their potentialities for emotional and intellectual adventure. Unable to deal profitably with the same selection or series of authors, they still may deal on a feasible level with the same theme or problem.

There are pitfalls to be avoided in the thematic plan of organization as in any other. The first of these pitfalls may lie in the selection of the theme. Is the theme significant to the intellectual and esthetic development of the students at a given grade level? This is a key question. Many thematic units probably dwell on fulsome platitudes or on ideas that may be bewitching to the teacher but completely baffling to the students. Though the teacher may have proudly produced a term paper on "The *Carpe Diem* Theme in Elizabethan Lyrics" in one of his graduate courses, the subject may not be appropriate for high school classes. On the other hand, student interest is not a completely reliable criterion either. Motorcycles may seem a vital subject to many adolescents but they will not provide a sound basis for a teaching unit.

Another pitfall lies in the selection of material to be read in a certain unit. Once the theme is selected, the teacher's next step is to choose selections of literature that are relevant in developing the theme and appropriate both to the students and to important aims in teaching literature. All these conditions are important; it is not enough that the selections represent a useful kind of propaganda—that they merely "have something to say" about the theme. They must fit into the teacher's broader purposes in teaching literature to a particular group of students.

Attempts to find selections that "fit" a certain theme have sometimes involved teachers in the ludicrous. Teaching Shelley's "To a Skylark" in a unit on "Living in an Air Age" seems farfetched. The problem of finding material appropriate to the theme may sometimes lead teachers to settle for inferior selections that give no real chance to teach literature or to lead students to higher levels of awareness. Doggerel about going swimming, for example, may be relevant to a unit on sports, but may not be useful in achieving the purposes of teaching poetry to a group of junior high school students.

The thematic unit also is rather easily prey to aimlessness or lack of direction. The teacher has to work constantly to keep the program of reading directed somewhere. Younger students, especially, may quickly lose sight of the theme unless the teacher keeps it constantly before them. Discussion of literature in a unit in which not everyone has read the same selections may wander into a directionless, though possibly interesting, morass unless the teacher carefully prepares and structures the discussions. Some teachers have found it helpful to prepare for and assign a discussion a day before it is actually to be held, rather than launch into it impromptu. Some years ago Bertha Handlan wrote an article on guiding a discussion of reading in a class where students had read different selections, and it remains a helpful reference on the topic.[5]

The most common criticism of thematic organization is that student attention is diverted from literature to social issues and matters of ethics and morals. This is not necessarily a valid criticism for it may be all to the good that literature study sometimes leads to such concerns, and these broader concerns and concern with literary art need not be thought of as a dichotomy. Yet it is important that student attention be focused essentially on literary matters.

Combination of Approaches

As noted at the opening of this chapter, an eclectic approach to organization is evident in many literature programs, and patterns often merge in well-conceived units of teaching. The illustrative sequence outlined in chapter 2, for example, combines three patterns of organization—by theme, by literary mode, and by genre. A course in world literature offered at the Jackson High School, Miami, Florida, includes the following major units:

The Middle Ages (including common reading of the *Iliad* and of excerpts from several national epics)

The Literary Hero (including common reading of Ciardi's translation of the *Inferno* and of Chaucer's *Prologue*)

Satire and Man's Search for Utopia (including reading of sections of *Gulliver's Travels,* More's *Utopia,* Plato's *Republic,* Voltaire's *Candide*)

Man Looks at the Devil (including reading of Part I of *Faust* and all or parts of other works; the Faust legend in music)

The Development of the Novel (including reading of Joyce's *The Dead,* Gogol's *The Overcoat,* Faulkner's *The Bear*)

Youth: The Search for Understanding (including group reading of John Knowles' *A Separate Peace*)

[5] Bertha Handlan, "Group Discussion of Individual Reading," *English Journal,* XXXII (February 1943), 67–74.

One genre frequently may be studied in relation to a theme, as illustrated in the grouping of poems suggested in chapter 6. Sometimes individual "classics" may be studied in thematic units—one class studied *Macbeth* as the climax of a unit entitled "Trial by Conscience." It is also quite possible to utilize chronological organization at some points in a year's course without casting the entire program in that mold. A class might study the neoclassical and romantic periods and then examine the contemporary influences of those periods, and at other times study genre or thematic units.

The trend toward de-emphasis of grades and toward module scheduling opens new possibilities for organization of the literature program. Some senior high schools have moved away from "tenth-grade English," "eleventh-grade English," and so on in favor of one-semester, or shorter, specialized courses—modern literature, growth in literature, Negro literature, and so forth, in which students from more than one grade may be enrolled. One form of module scheduling, such as that followed at the Florida High School, Tallahassee, Florida, features units of several weeks length in literature (and other aspects of English) focused on themes, modes, genres, or elements of technique in which students from various grades may be enrolled.

The Extensive Phase of the Program

The literature program should include intensive experiences that come from class study and analysis of selections of literature and extensive experiences that come from individual reading. The in-class literature program that does not lead to voluntary out-of-class reading by many of the students may well be suspect. But the choice of whether to carry on individual reading cannot be left to the adolescent. All students, it is hoped, will have some time and inclination to read for pure recreation, no matter whether their choices of material are or are not related to school subjects. Individual reading, as distinct from purely recreational reading (though the twain should often meet!), should be an integral part of the literature program. Individual and extensive reading grows very naturally out of the topical or thematic pattern in which students first consider together selections related to the topic or theme and then go individually, or in small groups, to other selections suited to their tastes and abilities but still relevant to the topic or theme. But whatever the plan of organization individual reading is essential in promoting reading interests and in providing for individual tastes and capacities. The individual reading program cannot be something separate, something divorced from the in-class study of literature. The fairly widespread requirement of "outside" reading—usually involving a written or oral book report every six or eight weeks—profits little if the outside reading program is not planned and individualized. The Tuesday book report session and the mimeographed reporting forms are remembered with distaste by the majority of high school graduates.

The extensive individual reading phase should be as carefully planned as the in-class, intensive phase of the literature program. There are two main general ways in which a planned out-of-class program may be set up. First, the teacher may outline several alternatives for independent reading in each of the literature units during the year, alternatives appropriate, of course, to the range of interests and capacities in the class. The literature units distributed, for example, by the Scholastic Book Services are organized usually in three phases, proceeding from total class activities, in the first phase, through small-group activity in the second, to individual reading relating to the theme or topic of the unit in the third phase.

Second, the teacher may set up with each student an individual reading design that will appropriately supplement and enrich the in-class literature study for the term and will reflect each student's interests and abilities. Stephen Dunning outlines a five-step plan for individual reading designs:

1. The teacher talks individually with students about possible reading programs that will fit their interests. Suggestions appropriate to the different capacities of students are made.
2. The student writes out his plan and perhaps includes a tentative bibliography.
3. The teacher discusses the plans with each student, giving further suggestions.
4. The student then submits a final plan or "contract."
5. The teacher keeps informal contact with the students as the plans are carried out and probably provides some kind of feedback for the class from some or all of the projects, which may range from

something as broad as "Literature of Pre–Civil War America" to something as specific as "Wives of Three Presidents." [6]

Some feedback to the class from the individual reading, as just suggested, often may be beneficial to the individual student or the class. Certainly the stereotyped book report on the standardized form is outmoded, and certainly the student should not be required to report formally on everything he reads. At times a general, informal class discussion on a certain category of books—current novels, for example —will serve in lieu of individual reports. The teacher-student conference, when feasible, may cover a lot of ground. Yet the individual report will occasionally be needed. Jerome Carlin describes a number of possibilities for the book report:

Analysis by a man of the future. In a time capsule or in the ruins on the planet Earth some man of the future finds the book and writes a paper on what it reveals of life of the earlier time.

The diary of a major character. At least three crucial days in the life of the character are dealt with as if they were being summarized in that person's diary.

A letter written in the role of a book character.

Written analysis from a specific standpoint.

Formal book review. The superior student can clip a book review from a newspaper and use it as a model for a review of the book which he has read.

The scholarly critical paper. Honors classes may combine research on "what the critics and authorities think of the author" with critical opinion on "what I think about those of his books which I have read." A separate section on the latter is a wise requirement, to encourage original thinking.

Round-table discussion under a student chairman.

Conversation. Students are paired for conversation about a book.

Oral reading and discussion of brief excerpts.

Significant incident or anecdote. Each student is a speaker on a TV program about good books. He must interest the audience by telling only one incident or anecdote from his book—comic, tragic, suspenseful, or otherwise possessed of human interest.

[6] "Sequence and Literature: Some Teaching Facts," *High School Journal,* XLVII (October 1963), 2–12.

Dramatization. A committee prepares and presents a scene in radio-script fashion.

Reporter at the scene. While it's happening, a crucial scene from the book is described on the spot by a TV or radio reporter.

The trail of a major character. Defendant, prosecuting attorney, defense attorney, and witnesses may participate in the case. The charge should preferably be one of acting unethically, unfairly, or even unwisely, rather than one of breaking a law.

Interview. A character in the book is interviewed by a reporter or by a TV interviewer.

The author meets the critics. Three, four, or five students may form a group. Thus Charles Dickens may defend his *A Tale of Two Cities* against two critics, as they ask: "Why didn't you save Carton by some plot twist, giving the book a happy ending? . . ."

Monologue or dialogue. A pupil takes the role of the major character and in a process of "thinking out loud" talks about the critical situation or problem he is facing at the high point of the story. This may be varied by using two students in a dialogue.

Sales talk. The student represents himself as a salesman endeavoring to sell the book to the class by means of a talk on its good points.

Presentation to a publisher. The class is the selection committee for a publisher or for one of the publishing book clubs. The student presents his report on a book from the standpoint of whether it should be published or of whether it should be offered to the book club membership.

Discussion of proposed production conducted by a "playwright" and a "producer."

Outline of a TV or motion-picture version.

Art and other creative work. Book jackets, advertising blurbs, maps, scenes from the story, pictures of characters, posters, and the like are generally useful as supplements, but they do not always serve the purpose of requiring thoughtful consideration of the book. An accompanying analytical talk or paper is desirable if the creative work is intended to serve as a book report.[7]

The teacher scarcely can expect the students to read extensively and to share reading in various kinds of reports if he himself does not show an enthusiasm for reading and for sharing his reading experiences with his classes. The teacher's comments on the books he is

[7] Jerome Carlin, "Your Next Book Report . . . ," *English Journal,* L (January 1961), 16–22.

reading or has read are a rich source of motivation for students. Not only is the well-prepared teacher of literature thoroughly grounded in the literary tradition; he also makes an effort to keep abreast of the current scene through active reading of new books and of magazines such as the *Saturday Review,* which presents reviews and a coverage of the literary world.

THE DIMENSION OF STUDENT POTENTIAL

Teachers in most situations will meet roomfuls of students with varied, sometimes startlingly so, potentials for experiencing literature. Though "individual differences" was a common refrain in the prospective teacher's professional courses, the encounter with the problem in the flesh often is a shock and it remains with the teacher at every turn in planning and organizing the literature program.

The problem of heterogeneity in potential probably is more acute in English, at least in the senior high school, than in other subjects since in most schools all students are required to take English in each grade. Students do not ordinarily enter classes in physics or chemistry, or in advanced algebra, geometry, or trigonometry, for example, unless they have shown some proficiency in earlier courses in mathematics or science. The major approach to the problem in schools with the traditional grade levels is homogeneous grouping or "tracking," in which the students within each grade are grouped, according to certain criteria, at three or four levels of ability. Controversy surrounds the system of ability grouping and its effectiveness has never been fully established or refuted. Many teachers are uneasy with the obvious fact that ability grouping in English turns out to be, by and large, also grouping according to socioeconomic status. Teachers of high-ability groups are usually pleased with the plan; teachers of low-ability groups are much less enthusiastic and, in fact, are often in despair. Discipline problems tend to pile up in the low-ability groups, and such groups lack the inspiration or leavening influence which the brighter students can give. In general, success with ability grouping in English seems to depend upon two conditions:

1. *The grouping is actually effective in separating students according to their ability in literature or in other aspects of the English*

course. Sometimes, groups may be real only on paper. Problems of scheduling individual students, carelessness, or lack of guidance may result in many students being out of place. Potential and actual achievement have to be balanced in grouping students. For example, a student with a very high IQ may be basically uninterested and unmotivated in English and may therefore not belong in the highest ability group. A combination of past achievement in English, a high IQ, and reading ability seems to be the most effective basis on which to group students for work in English.

2. *Once the students are efficiently grouped, the program must be differentiated in each group.* It is futile to group students at three or four levels and then to offer the same English program at each level, or to differentiate only in quantity of work or in the pace with which ground is covered. Yet this is what is done in many schools, accounting for many of the problems, disciplinary and otherwise, in lower-ability sections.

Homogeneous grouping, or tracking, is not the only, or necessarily the best, answer to the problem of a range of capacities. In smaller schools, track systems may not be feasible administratively. The development of ungraded programs, team teaching, modular scheduling, the replacement of year-long, grade-level courses with shorter-term, specialized electives, and other innovations in bringing students and teachers together may already have made the traditional ability grouping passé. Difference in potential for experiencing literature will remain no matter what scheme is used to bring a group together, and no matter what the scheme, the teaching of literature can be adjusted effectively to the range in potential through a combination of three basic approaches:

1. *Differentiation in the discussion or in the activities based on a selection read in common.* Reading of the same selection by all the members of a class does not rule out possibilities of adjusting to different levels of ability. In setting up guide questions for the reading, or in phrasing questions for discussion following the reading, the teacher can keep in mind the various categories of students in his class. Some questions should be beamed to the lowest ability level, some to the highest, some in between. (This is a matter treated more fully in the next section of this chapter.) Other kinds of oral or written activities which may be based on a selection read in common may be planned, too, to make greater or lesser demands on the student.

2. *Grouping within the class.* For many years, teachers in the elementary school have grouped classes for work in reading and other phases of the program. Often, a high school English class, too, may be divided into several groups to read certain selections or sets of selections. This method is common to the Scholastic Literature Units, referred to earlier in this chapter, and the technique is described in detail in an article by James Squire.[8]

3. *Individualization of reading.* At times good programs in literature will feature complete individualization in selections assigned or read. It was pointed out earlier that the thematic or topical unit is especially helpful in providing a core of unity for widely differentiated individual reading. The extensive phase of the program which may feature individual reading designs, as discussed earlier, offers obvious possibilities for each student to perform at his level of potential.

Planning for Groups with Specific Characteristics

What has been said so far in this chapter is directed to the inevitable problem of differing potential for approaching literature that any group of individuals represents, no matter what the basis for assembling the group. Plans for ability grouping and scheduling and sociological accidents which account for certain schools being located in certain areas, however, result in students of certain characteristics appearing in given classes and given schools. The last decade and a half has seen almost frenetic efforts to develop programs adapted to students with certain kinds of intellectual, cultural, and emotional characteristics. The remainder of this chapter attempts to identify and illustrate the characteristics of programs in literature for the superior, the untalented, and the disadvantaged student.

The Superior Student

Several years ago when the author was preparing the revised edition of this book there was a tremendous concern with English programs for gifted students. It seemed impossible to keep up with the publications on the subject. Now, at this writing, concern with the gifted

---

[8] James Squire, "Individualizing the Teaching of Literature," *English Journal,* XLV (September 1956), 314–319.

seems to have all but vanished if one is to judge by current publications. Today the major concern seems to be with English for the disadvantaged student. No criticism is implied in these remarks. Programs for the gifted are now probably well established whereas those for the disadvantaged are not, and the gifted student seldom is a teaching problem once his abilities are recognized and taken account of in planning. There has been a recognition possibly, too, that many of the best traditional curricula and materials in literature, offered to all students, actually are suitable only for the superior. In literature, the needs of superior students have been met by various applications of the basic procedures for differentiating instruction just discussed. A survey of actual practices of various schools throughout the country shows that the following are the principal ways of providing for superior students in literature:

Ability grouping. In English classes where only students of highest ability are enrolled, teachers can go far beyond the familiar boundaries of the high school course. Yet in these classes, the plans of organization and methodology tend to be similar to those in the heterogeneous classes. The most successful programs for high-ability students seem to be marked by wide reading of works too mature and difficult for the general run of students, by close analysis of individual works, and by exploration of themes or topics too advanced for average students. In the Portland, Oregon, public schools, superior students are allowed to enroll in "seminars" which carry the following kinds of projects:

> A sophomore project in one school presented the literature of certain high points in the development of Western civilization. The period of the Greeks, for example, students read *The Iliad,* Euripides' *Trojan Women,* Plato's *Apology,* and supplementary readings in Sophocles, Aeschylus, and Xenephon. . . . In a junior English seminar, students studied contrasts in the philosophies of American writers—for example, the pragmatic approach to life's problems as exemplified by Samuel Sewall and Benjamin Franklin in contrast with the theological approach of Jonathan Edwards; and the idealism of Whitman and Emerson in contrast with the critical realism of Sinclair Lewis. A senior seminar, aiming to deepen understanding of certain English masterpieces, made a comparative study of similar genres from other periods or countries: for example, in connection with study of *The Canterbury Tales,* stu-

dents also read *Tristram and Iseult* and *Aucassin and Nicolette,* and *Connecticut Yankee in King Arthur's Court,* and in comparison with *Macbeth,* certain Greek tragedies, and plays by Ibsen, Molière, and George Bernard Shaw.[9]

The Curriculum Study Center in English at the Carnegie-Mellon University developed a senior high school English curriculum for "able college-bound students." The outline of the literature program follows:

WORLD LITERATURE
UNIVERSAL CONCERNS OF MAN
Grade 10

Introductory Unit

"Old Milon," Guy de Maupassant
"The Stranger's Note," Lin Yutang
"The Stream of Days," Tāhā Hussein
"The Bet," Anton Chekhov

Unit One:
Social Concerns

A Tale of Two Cities, Charles Dickens
"Biryuk," Ivan Turgenev
"Rashōmon," Ryūnosuke Akutagawa
"Chastity," Lin Yutang
"Golden Bells," Po Chü-i
"Remembering Golden Bells," Po Chü-i
"My Lord, the Baby," Rabindranath Tagore
"Return: Two Poems," Abioseh Nicol

"Tell Freedom," Peter Abrahams
An Enemy of the People, Henrik Ibsen
"The Prisoner," Po Chü-i
"The Dwarf Trees," Seami Motokiyo
All Quiet on the Western Front, Erich Maria Remarque
A Child's Christmas in Wales, Dylan Thomas

Unit Two:
Love

The Cradle Song, G. and M. Martínez Sierra
"Love: Three Pages from a Sportsman's Book," Guy de Maupassant
"Chienniang," Lin Yutang
"Half a Sheet of Paper," August Strindberg

[9] Reported by Marian Zollinger, Supervisor of Language Arts, Portland Public Schools, in a talk at the convention of the NCTE, Minneapolis, Minn., Nov. 29, 1957.

"Our Lady's Juggler," Anatole France

The Book of Ruth, Psalms (selected)

"Hymn of Love to God," Rabindranath Tagore

"Song of Praise to the Creator," G. H. Franz

I Corinthians, Chapter 13

"Tāj Mahal," Rabindranath Tagore

Carmen, Prosper Mérimée

Cyrano de Bergerac, Edmond Rostand

Unit Three:
Reality and Illusion

"War," Luigi Pirandello

"A Character is Distress," Luigi Pirandello

"Maya," Vera Inber

"In a Grove," Ryunosuke Akutagawa

The General's Ring, Selma Lagerlöf

Unit Four:
Heroism

The Iliad of Homer, I. A. Richards (Trans.)

Exodus, Deuteronomy, The Story of Moses

Beowulf from The Medieval Myths, N. L. Goodrich (Ed.)

The Song of Roland from The Medieval Myths, N. L. Goodrich (Ed.)

The Cid from The Medieval Myths, N. L. Goodrich (Ed.)

Julius Ceasar, William Shakespeare

Plutarch's Lives (Caesar; Brutus)

"Mateo Falcone," Prosper Mérimée

Master and Man, Leo Tolstoy

Unit Five:
Human Weakness

"Christ in Flanders," Honoré de Balzac

"The Queen of Spades," Alexander Pushkin

"A Coup d'État," Guy de Maupassant

"My Uncle Jules," Guy de Maupassant

"A Piece of String," Guy de Maupassant

The Miser, Molière

"How Much Land Does a Man Need?" Leo Tolstoy

"The Father," Björnstjerne Bjornson

"As the Night, the Day," Abioseh Nicol

Unit Six:
The Search for Wisdom

"The Story of a Story," Selma Lagerlöf

"Sotho Boyhood," A. S. Legodi

"Rammone Returns to the Kalahari," M. O. M Seboni

Memoirs of Childhood and Youth, Albert Schweitzer

Wind, Sand and Stars, Antoine de Saint-Exupéry

The Plague, Albert Camus

"Chu-ch'ēn Village," Po Chü-i

"Watching the Reapers," Po Chü-i

"Passing T'ien-mēn Street," Po Chü-i

Haiku poetry (selected)

"Flute Players," Jean-Joseph Ra-
béarivelo
Ecclesiastes (selections)
"On This Tiny Raft," Rabindranath
Tagore

The Parables of Jesus (selected)
"What Men Live By," Leo Tolstoy
The Apology of Socrates, Plato
The Death of Socrates (from *Phae-
do*), Plato

AMERICAN LITERATURE
MODIFICATION BY CULTURE PATTERN
Grade 11

Unit One:
The American Puritan Attitude
The Crucible, Arthur Miller
The Scarlet Letter, Nathaniel Haw-
thorne
"Observations of the Bewitched
Child," Cotton Mather
"An Arrow Against Profane and
Promiscuous Dancing," Increase
Mather
"The Simple Cobbler of Agga-
wam," Nathaniel Ward
"Thomas Shepard's Autobiogra-
phy" (selections)
"A Narrative of the Captivity,"
Mary Rowlandson
"The Day of Doom," Michael Wig-
glesworth
"Young Goodman Brown," Na-
thaniel Hawthorne
Ethan Fromme, Edith Wharton
"New England," Edward Arlington
Robinson

Unit Two:
The American Desire for Success
The Autobiography (selections),
Benjamin Franklin
The Rise of Silas Lapham, William
Dean Howells

All My Sons, Arthur Miller
The Great Gatsby, F. Scott Fitzgerald

Unit Three:
The American Idealism
"The American Scholar," Ralph
Waldo Emerson
"Self-Reliance," Ralph Waldo Em-
erson
Walden, Henry David Thoreau
"To a Waterfowl," William Cullen
Bryant
"Thanatopsis," William Cullen
Bryant
"The Chambered Nautilus," Oliver
Wendell Holmes
"Days," Ralph Waldo Emerson
"Nature," Henry Wadsworth Long-
fellow
"Gettysburg Address," Abraham
Lincoln
"Second Inaugural Address," Abra-
ham Lincoln
"Song of Myself," Walt Whitman
O Pioneers!, Willa Cather
Selected Poems, Emily Dickinson
"Love Is Not All," Edna St. Vin-
cent Millay
"Renascence," Edna St. Vincent
Millay

"Chicago," Carl Sandburg
"The People Will Live On," Carl Sandburg
"Skyscraper," Carl Sandburg
"Mending Wall," Robert Frost
"Two Tramps in Mud Time," Robert Frost
"Stopping by Woods on a Snowy Evening," Robert Frost
"The Tuft of Flowers," Robert Frost
"all ignorance tobaggans into know," e. e. cummings
"what if a much of a which of a wind," e. e. cummings
Our Town, Thornton Wilder

Unit Four:
The American Darker Spirit
"The Fall of the House of Usher," Edgar Allan Poe
"The Masque of the Red Death," Edgar Allan Poe
"The Cask of Amontillado," Edgar Allan Poe
"The Boarded Window," Ambrose Bierce
"The Lottery," Shirley Jackson
"Wash," William Faulkner
"Flight," John Steinbeck
The Emperor Jones, Eugene O'Neill
Moby Dick, Herman Melville
"The Raven," Edgar Allan Poe
"Annabel Lee," Edgar Allan Poe
"To Helen," Edgar Allan Poe
"Ulalume," Edgar Allan Poe
"Margrave," Robinson Jeffers
The Glass Menagerie, Tennessee Williams

Unit Five:
The American Social Conscience
The Jungle, Upton Sinclair
The Adventures of Huckleberry Finn, Mark Twain
Winterset, Maxwell Anderson
"The Man with the Hoe," Edwin Markham
"The End of the World," Archibald MacLeish
"Factory Windows," Vachel Lindsay
"next to of course god america i," e. e. cummings
"pity this busy monster, manunkind," e. e. cummings
Babbitt, Sinclair Lewis

Unit Six:
The Modern American Quest for Identity
The Hairy Ape, Eugene O'Neill
The Red Badge of Courage, Stephen Crane
"The Day of the Last Rock Fight," Joseph Whitehill
"In Greenwich There are Many Gravelled Walks," Hortense Calisher
"Cyclists' Raid," Frank Rooney
"The Four Lost Men," Thomas Wolfe
"The Rich Boy," F. Scott Fitzgerald
"Birches," Robert Frost
"The Road Not Taken," Robert Frost
"To Earthward," Robert Frost
The Unvanquished, William Faulkner

ENGLISH LITERATURE
LITERARY ART FORMS, GENRES, TECHNIQUES
Grade 12

Unit One:
The Tale

The Decameron (selected tales), Boccaccio
Sir Gawain and the Green Knight, Brian Stone (Trans.)
The Canterbury Tales (selected tales), Geoffrey Chaucer
"The Prisoner of Chillon," George Gordon, Lord Byron
The Secret Sharer, Joseph Conrad
Introduction to *Tellers of Tales*, W. Somerset Maugham (Ed.)

Unit Two:
Tragedy

King Oedipus, Sophocles
Macbeth, William Shakespeare
Wuthering Heights, Emily Brontë
"The Substance of Shakespearean Tragedy" from *Shakespearean Tragedy*, A. C. Bradley

Unit Three:
Lyric Poetry I

"Out Upon It!", Sir John Suckling
"Let Me Not to the Marriage . . ." William Shakespeare
"Gather Ye Rosebuds," Robert Herrick
"On His Blindness," John Milton
"Edward," Anon.
"Since There's No Help . . . ," Michael Drayton
"That Time of Year Thou Mayst in me Behold," William Shakespeare

"To His Coy Mistress," Andrew Marvell
"Fear No More," William Shakespeare
"A Valediction: Forbidding Mourning," John Donne
"Song to Celia," Ben Jonson
"My Mistress' Eyes . . . ," William Shakespeare
"When in Disgrace . . . ," William Shakespeare
"Death, Be not Proud," John Donne

Unit Four:
The Epic

Beowulf, Edwin Morgan (trans.)
Paradise Lost, John Milton
from *A Preface to Paradise Lost*, C. S. Lewis

Unit Five:
Satire

Arms and the Man, George Bernard Shaw
Gulliver's Travels, Jonathan Swift
Don Juan, Canto I, George Gordon, Lord Byron
"The Nature of Satire" from *English Satire*, James Sutherland

Unit Six:
Lyric Poetry II

"Ah, Are You Digging on My Grave?", Thomas Hardy

"La Belle Dame sans Merci," John Keats

"My Last Duchess," Robert Browning

"Ulysses," Alfred, Lord Tennyson

"Journey of the Magi," T. S. Eliot

"The Lamb," William Blake

"The Tiger," William Blake

"Lines Composed a Few Miles Above Tintern Abbey," William Wordsworth

"Dover Beach," Matthew Arnold

"Ode on a Grecian Urn," John Keats

"Ode to the West Wind," Percy Shelley

"Neutral Tones," Thomas Hardy

"I Wake and Feel the Fell of Dark," Gerard Hopkins

"The World Is Too Much with Us," William Wordsworth

"Ozymandias," Percy Shelley

Unit Seven:
The Novel

Great Expectations, Charles Dickens

Far From the Madding Crowd, Thomas Hardy

"As They Look to the Reader" from *Early Victorian Novelists,* Lord David Cecil

The Horse's Mouth, Joyce Cary

The Heart of the Matter, Graham Greene

Unit Eight:
Social Drama

The Admirable Crichton, James M. Barrie

The Cocktail Party, T. S. Eliot

Man and Superman, George Bernard Shaw

from *A Treasury of the Theatre,* John Gassner (Ed.)

Elective courses.   In those schools in which the English curriculum is organized in short-term, specialized courses, particular courses such as Shakespeare, modern poetry and world masterpieces can be organized for the most able students. Some schools which generally follow the traditional pattern of year-long, grade-level courses, provide specialized courses which superior students can substitute for the general courses.

Special group or individual projects within regular classes.   Some teachers require special advanced work of superior students, either as a substitute for or in addition to the regular class work. Socrates Lagios describes a project in which four superior students in his senior class at the Concord, Massachusetts, High School read eighteen novels, one a week, starting with *Moll Flanders* and ending with *The Old Man and the Sea.*[10] These students were excused from some of the

[10] Socrates Lagios, "Challenging the Gifted," *English Journal,* XLVI (November 1957), 501–503.

regular class work. Phyllis Peacock reported that in her senior classes able students carried on independent projects which culminated in "lecturettes" or productions in which other interested students and parents were invited to attend.[11]

"Honors" work. A few high schools have experimented with plans in which superior students are exempt from a part of the curriculum in order to work independently. The English teacher, of course, directs projects in literature.

Literary clubs and special seminars. Well-guided clubs, functioning as extracurricular activities, have provided rich experiences for able and interested students in some schools. Some teachers have arranged special voluntary seminars in the evening or on Saturdays in which students discuss works of their choice or hear guest lecturers.

Literature study for gifted students needs to be carefully planned to avoid two common pitfalls. Superior students should certainly be concerned with structure and form, and they are able to deal with technique in a way impossible in the regular class. Yet they are not a breed apart so far as interests and rewards sought in reading are concerned. It is quite possible for bright students to present glib technical analyses of selections without necessarily developing any expanded interests or any really mature understanding of literature as reconstruction of experience.

There is another closely related danger. In some high-ability classes a number of classics may be "covered"—given a surface reading, without any real understanding or appreciation resulting. Depth rather than coverage should be the goal in classes for superior students.

The Untalented Student

"Untalented student" is a weasel term to an extent. At least the untalented student is harder to characterize than the superior student, especially when one plans to discuss the "disadvantaged student" in a separate section. As used here, the term "untalented" refers to the student who has marked intellectual and linguistic handicaps short of the mental retardation which would prevent participation in the regu-

[11] "Highlights of Senior English for the Superior Students," *High School Journal,* XLIII (November 1959), 71–74.

lar program of the public schools. Such students frequently come from disadvantaged cultural and social backgrounds, but the two sets of criteria—linguistic-intellectual on the one hand and social-cultural on the other—should be kept separate. This is the reason for differentiating in this chapter between the "untalented" and the "disadvantaged." Students often may legitimately fit both categories but, in many instances, culturally deprived students may not be linguistically or intellectually handicapped and students from the higher social-cultural mileus may be.

Students who are not necessarily culturally deprived but who are intellectually and linguistically handicapped (short of mental retardation) tend to fall into two major groups: (1) the student who has a specific disability in reading—the "retarded reader"—whose problem may be solved if he obtains remedial help. It is not, however, within the scope of this text (nor is it necessary, because a large amount of professional information exists on the subject) to deal with the problems of the retarded reader; (2) the "slow learner" who has low intellectual and linguistic potential. His reading level will be low, too, but within a range expected in view of his potential.

In planning literature study for slow learners, teachers will have to ignore traditional patterns. Much of the difficulty teachers have with low-ability groups comes from attempting to impose literature programs designed for average and above-average students. The problem of appropriate materials is a pressing one. Certainly the standard textbook-anthologies are hardly useful with low-ability groups. Realizing this, some teachers have, in desperation, virtually given up the teaching of literature to slow groups, and instead, stress exercises in reading manuals and workbooks. This type of activity is important, but literature study need not be abandoned in low-ability groups. The teacher should realize however that traditional literature patterns—chronological survey, reading of "classics," and analysis of types—will be of little avail. Short and very simple topical units—such as "Adventure at Sea" and "Brave People"—may be the most fruitful approach. In such units, junior novels and biographies can be used as well as such special series as the Landmark Books of Random House and the Teen-Age Tales of D. C. Heath and Company.

A ninth-grade program in literature for less able students might be organized around the following units:

Stories People Talk About—retelling of famous myths, legends, American folk tales. Much use of recordings, films, pictures, and oral reading by the teacher and invited guests.

People Who Were Different—short, simple biography and nonfiction featuring individualism, idiosyncrasy, people who have overcome handicaps.

Strange Things Happen—the weird and the grotesque in poetry, short stories, and nonfiction.

Western Days—reading of short selections and common reading of Jack Schaefer's *Shane*.

Slow learners will always find the printed page an obstacle. Obviously, rich experiences in literature should be provided through the nonprint media—recordings, screen, photography, and oral experiences should be stressed in any program in literature for slow learners. Short selections will be used most of the time, of course. One-act plays and TV plays are especially valuable in classes of slow learners. Though a certain amount of daily routine may give security in such classes, variety of activities is essential, and flexibility and improvization should be the teacher's slogans.

The Disadvantaged Student

The disadvantaged student—the child with a background of economic poverty and squalor and cultural deprivation and alienation—has become, at long last, a major concern of education in recent years. As noted earlier, the disadvantaged student often may be deficient in linguistic skill—at least from the traditional middle-class view—and handicapped intellectually; but his over-riding problem is one of morale, motivation, and self-image. He stands alienated from the cultural values underlying the school program, and his slogan often is "What's the use?"

The teacher of literature faces a formidable, but vital and often greatly rewarding, task with the disadvantaged student. Important with all students, the problems of relating life to literature and of providing immediate rewards in experiences with literature become the vitally important objectives with disadvantaged students. But development of skills and literary insights, though definitely secondary in importance, need not be lost sight of altogether with the disadvantaged. One of the most important projects on English for disadvantaged students is that carried out in the Hunter College Curriculum Study Center resulting in the Gateway English Program for grades seven, eight, and nine.[12] The following excerpts from an essay by the director of the Hunter project, Marjorie B. Smiley, points up the philosophy and principles generally basic in most work in English for the disadvantaged:

> Certainly students whose score on standardized reading tests are substantially below grade, who do not respond to traditional English curricula, who reject and are rejected by their schools and many of their teachers, require a different kind of English curriculum. But the differences introduced to meet retarded reading skills, to arouse latent interests, and to exploit particular experiences, and to build self-regard and self-confidence need not and should not subvert the special contributions which literature and the language arts can make in the education of all children. If it is true, as Muriel Rukeyser declared, that poverty "makes thin the imagination and the bone," poor children need all the riches literature can supply . . . To begin with, the curriculum is thematically organized. In each grade, three of the four units are developed around themes selected for their relevance to the personal and social concerns of adolescents; the literature core in each of these units consists of short works or excerpts from longer works in fiction, biography, other nonfiction, drama, and poetry. A fourth unit in each grade explores comparable themes but in this instance entirely through poetry.
> The seventh-grade units have these titles: *A Family Is a Way of Feeling, Stories in Song and Verse, Who Am I?,* and *Coping.* Eighth grade units are *Striving, A Westerner Sampler, Creatures in Verse,* and *Two Roads to Greatness.* Ninth grade units are *Rebels and Regulars, People in Poetry, Something Strange,* and a still untitled unit on *justice.* As their titles suggest, the themes for the seventh grade relate closely to the student himself; the literature presents familiar, personal, and relatively concrete situations in which mostly youthful protagonists cope with human relations in family, school, and peer group. In the eighth grade the themes are explored in literature in which the milieu is larger in scope and less immediately related to the students' own experience. In two of the eighth grade units the literature centers on life and historic figures in the American past. *A Westerner Sampler* introduces, through

---

[12] Published by Crowell-Collier-Macmillan, New York, N.Y.

literature about the American Indian the concepts of cultural identity and culture conflict; it also examines, through the American Western as a print and film genre, stereotyped versus more realistic presentations of character and solutions to social dilemmas. *Two Roads to Greatness,* an anthology of biography, drama, verse, and fiction, presents as parallel models of struggle, despair, and achievement the lives of Abraham Lincoln and Frederick Douglass. In the ninth grade, *People in Poetry* explores the relatively sophisticated concept of individuality in its inward and outward manifestations. *Rebels and Regulars* deals with the personally and socially important issue of conformity and nonconformity; *Something Strange,* through fantasy and science fiction, is concerned with such questions as what is man? what is human society? what is real? what is illusory?

Within this context students learn such reading skills as these: to follow a variety of narrative sequences—chronological, flashback, the story within a story; to locate details used in characterization; to read for explicit and for extended meanings; and to recognize clues to mood, tone, and foreshadowing to derive word meanings from context. These relatively sophisticated critical reading skills are achieved by previously slow and reluctant readers partly because the literature has extremely high interest for them, but also, we believe, because of the teaching approach employed in the program.

We have taken seriously characterizations of lower class children as more responsive to physically active than to merely verbal learning. Stories and poems are read aloud to and by the children. Role-playing of comparable situations is frequently used to introduce a selection. Incidents in stories are dramatized; choral readings of poems are planned and taped by students. Indeed, Louise Rosenblatt's description of good reading as a "performing art" even when silent, is particularly suggestive to those of us concerned with improving the reading of underprivileged and underachieving students. These children especially, though all children ideally, need to *live themselves* into what they read.

We have found students welcome opportunities to tape their reading —as well as their dramatic improvisations, and we have found, too, that such experiences lead to spontaneous self and peer "corrections" in reading. Since all the verse "read" in the Gateway English is on tapes or records, students hear a good oral reading of each poem before or as they read it themselves. Students' oral reading of these poems often reveals a very close approximation to the professional reader's intonations, stress, and rhyme emphases.

Students respond actively to the literature they read in the Gateway program by drawing scenes and characters. In the ninth-grade unit on *People in Poetry* students draw or construct masks to reflect the inner and outer qualities of characters in poems like Richard Cory. Here it is, of course, not the quality of the art product but the students' engagement with visualizing the author's intent which lays the graphic base for the student's eventual verbal formulation of the meaning of the poem. Photographs and reproductions of art works presented to students with the challenge that they associate them individually with individual stories, poems, and characters enable them to demonstrate understanding of mood and tone. Such active, involving, graphic experiences are steps on the road toward perceptive reading.[13]

Two other reports of English projects for the disadvantaged student amplify the points made by Professor Smiley. In *Hooked on Books,*[14] Daniel N. Fader and Morton H. Shaevitz report on the English program developed at the W. J. Maxey Training School, Whitmore Lake, Michigan, a penal institution for adolescent boys. Teachers in the school were successful in getting the boys to read a great variety of books through making them easily available and through permissiveness in what could be read, with an avoidance of traditional taboos on what adolescents should encounter in print. The report stresses the psychological advantage of paperbound books with disadvantaged students. Hardbacks, especially textbooks, of course, are symbols of defeat to such students. A report of an institute on urban education conducted by Princeton University and the Trenton, New Jersey, public schools emphasizes the importance of nonprint media with disadvantaged students. In the volume, David A. Sohn describes a film-based course and proves again that viewing of film stimulates reading of the works on which the films are based. The reports agree that in classes of disadvantaged students literature and social studies can be profitably integrated.[15]

Teaching materials oriented to the disadvantaged student are becoming increasingly available. In addition to the Gateway English pro-

[13] "Gateway English—A Literature Program for Educationally Disadvantaged Students," *Ivory, Apes, and Peacocks: The Literature Point of View* (International Reading Association, 1968), pp. 86, 88–92.

[14] New York: Berkley Medallion Books, 1966.

[15] Kontos, Peter G. and James J. Murphy (Eds.), *Teaching Urban Youth: A Source Book for Urban Education* (New York: John Wiley, 1967).

gram cited above, several others seem valuable to the author: *The Way It Is* program published by Xerox; the *Impact* program published by Holt, Rinehart and Winston; and the *What's the Name of the Game* program published by New Dimensions in Education. These programs, of the package type, are basically similar and feature paperback reading materials and related audio-visual materials of various types.

Some Summary Principles

Experienced teachers reading through the preceding pages in this section will become aware probably that certain perennial principles, stated or implied, underlie the planning of literature programs whether for superior, average, untalented, or disadvantaged students. It may serve some purpose to summarize some of these.

1. *Books should be made easily available.* Physical availability is an important factor in developing a reading habit. Classroom libraries help, and a good stock of paperbound books is important. Teachers of other subjects should be enlisted in the effort to promote reading.

2. *Literature study should bring immediate rewards, not just deferred ones.* Students need to become actively involved in the literature class and not merely watch the teacher perform with a selection. Varied types of oral and dramatic activities in connection with the literature are enjoyable to most students. Nonprint media—recordings, films, and so on—and other art forms—painting, music, photography—should be featured.

3. *Selections appropriate to the students' actual concerns and needs should be chosen.* A great degree of permissiveness in individual reading should be allowed.

4. *The extent to which the orientation of the program will be literary rather than personal and social will depend on the characteristics of given classes.* Matters literary may be the major focus for superior students but the orientation for untalented and disadvantaged students will be largely personal-social.

5. *The literature program should challenge students but not always.* It is possible to challenge able students to the point of encouraging superficiality and untalented and disadvantaged students to the

point of developing frustration. Many of the experiences of the litera-
tre class should be comfortable in terms of linguistic and intellectual
demand.

6. *The student's potential for literary experience should be re-
spected, whatever it may be.* His interests and values should be taken
into account and his viewpoints and reactions considered seriously
and respectfully.

DISCUSSING THE INDIVIDUAL WORK

Perhaps the most frequent type of planning, and among the most crucial, which the teacher of literature carries on, is preparation for discussion of a selection read by the class in common. This is the point
in the literature program at which the actual teaching process is most
acutely brought to bear. So often teachers just "have discussion" of
selections with no real planning, no real objectives for the discussion.
Much of the editorial paraphernalia that commonly follows selections
in the standard textbook-anthologies is unconnected, often trivial,
leading nowhere. Unstructured give-and-take about books occasionally may be enjoyable and profitable in a class, but group discussion
of a work, in which teacher questioning is vital, should have two general objectives: (1) to illuminate the student's reading of the work
and to increase his involvement with it; and (2) to increase his ability
to deal with the particular genre which the work represents.

Teacher questioning about a selection read in common is not meant
necessarily to lead to particular conclusions (though no teacher
should feel hesitant at expressing his own conclusions in the course of
discussion) but rather is aimed at helping the student with a process
appropriate to examining the given work. Individual responses, however far out to the teacher, should be considered with respect, but, of
course, students should become aware that some responses to given
questions are more defensible than others. Questioning, too, as indicated earlier in this chapter, can be an important way of taking into
account differences in student potential. Careful choice of questions
which make varying demands on the students can be a means for involving all students with the work at appropriate levels of sophistication.

In a useful essay, Royal A. Gettman suggests that the teacher has a choice of three possible areas in which questions can be asked about a selection of literature: (1) Author—how did the work come into existence? (2) Reader—what does the work do to the reader? (3) Work—what is the work? How is it to be described? Gettman suggests that the *first* question always concern the work, that it should not lead away from the work and should not provoke argument.[16]

Attention to a hierarchy of types of questions, as suggested by Edward J. Gordon, may be very helpful to teachers not only in planning effective discussions but also in involving students of different levels of ability.[17] Gordon's hierarchy of five levels of questions is based on the degree of abstraction demanded by each level, as follows (material in parentheses is the author's, not Gordon's):

1. Questions requiring the student to remember a fact in a selection
   (What objects did the poet refer to?
   What happened in the story immediately after the storm?)
2. Questions that require the student to prove or disprove a generalization someone else has made
   (One critic has said that _____. Can you cite any examples from the novel to substantiate this?)
   (Or the teacher may pose an hypothesis for the students to prove or disprove:
   This story is an attack upon_____.)
3. Questions that require the student to derive his own generalizations
   (What relationship do the coffee drinking scenes in the novel have to the central theme?
   How does the poet make use of flower symbols?
   If there is little or no response to the question, the teacher needs to go back to simpler levels and build up to this level again: Where is a red rose referred to in the poem? Can you find any support for this interpretation: The rose symbolizes _____. Now what other flower symbols do you find?)
4. Questions that require the student to generalize about the relation of the total work to human experience
   (What is the universal human problem dramatized in _____?)

---

[16] "Asking the First Question," *College English,* XXVIII (May 1967), 591–595.

[17] "Levels of Teaching and Testing," *English Journal,* XLIV (September 1955), 330–334.

5. Questions that require the student to carry generalizations derived from the work into his own life
(Is the kind of experience which this poem glorifies one that your friends value?)

Discussion of given selections does not always require that questions be asked at each of these levels, but it is true that teachers do not make sufficient use of questions at the lower levels of abstraction. Often when the question is answered after discussion begins at level 4 in the Gordon hiearchy, many students file the "school solution" away in their minds and are kept from learning how to examine a selection which discussion of it would afford.

Daniel A. Lindley, Jr., of Yale University, has developed a hierarchy of questioning in literature based on the kinds of thinking identified by J. P. Guilford. The following is an excerpt from an unpublished paper read by Mr. Lindley at the 1965 convention of the National Council of Teachers of English:

Let us start by considering some questions which might be asked in an English class discussing Shakespeare's *Julius Caesar*. Suppose that the class has reached Act III, scene 1—the scene in which Antony gets Brutus' permission to "speak in Caesar's funeral." This permission is, of course, crucial to the events which follow, and considerable attention to what happens is certainly justified. Here is the sequence of questions which the teacher uses to lead the discussion:

1. Where has Antony come from as he approaches Brutus?
(Answer: from his house; he left the scene of the assassination and then returned.)
2. Why might this be important for what will happen next?
(Antony has had time to think, alone, about what he might do.)
3. We know what Antony does do. What are some other ways in which he might have accomplished his goals?
(Kill Brutus. Organize a counter-conspiracy. Get the army on his side.)
4. Antony says, after the conspirators have left him:
"Woe to the hand that shed this costly blood.
Over these wounds now do I prophesy . . .
A curse shall light upon the limbs of men;
Domestic fury and fierce civil strife
Shall cumber all the parts of Italy;
Blood and destruction shall be so in use

> And dreadful objects so familiar
> That mothers shall but smile when they behold
> Their infants quartered with the hands of war . . ."

Is it right for Antony to start the very fury and strife which he seems to know will follow his speech to the "mob?"

The problem now is to go back over each question and analyze the kind of thinking involved for the student. In the first question, what must the student know? He must at least have *read the play*. Not only this, but he must have read with some care. In III, 1, we have this insignificant interchange:

Cassius: Where is Antony?
Trebonius: Fled to his house amazed.

Not much of a conversation, but there it is, and it is the answer to the question. Of course the student may not *remember* this; he may, when he hears the question, thumb back over his text and find it. In either event, however, familiarity with the text is the sole requirement for answering the question. It matters little how that familiarity was gained. This is, in other words, a *memory* task, and the mental activity involved is an operation called *cognitive memory* (adapted from Guilford).

The second question begins with the word *why*. This alone is usually sufficient evidence for the assertion that more than memory will be involved as the student gets down to work on the question. In the first place, the student must begin to put some elements together in his head before he can even speak. He must consider the answer which has been given to the previous question. Then he must consider what will in fact happen in the rest of the play. So far these are cognitive memory activities. But, having put these two pieces of his knowledge side by side in his head, so to speak, he must then *make a connection* between these two sets of data. It is this making of connections which is forced on the student by the word *why*. The student must fill in a missing piece; he must imagine Antony leaving and coming back, and he must infer that Antony has been using this time to sort things out and decide on a course of action. The more the student knows of Antony, the more logical this inference becomes; that is, the more the student sees Antony as a carefully calculating politician, the more he will infer careful calculation. In any case, all this inferring must take place within the framework supplied by the play. This is important. Guilford calls this kind of thinking *convergent*. To quote Guilford:

The second large group of thinking factors has to do with the production of some end result. After one has comprehended the situation, or the significant aspects of it at the moment, usually something needs to be done to it or about it . . . In convergent thinking, there is usually one conclusion or answer that is regarded as unique, and thinking is channeled or controlled in the direction of that answer. . . .[18]

It is particularly important to note that the 'channeling' or 'controlling' of the thinking is being done by the structure of the play under discussion. The thinking must "converge" on the play. If the student gratuitously leaves the play for some easier or more attractive (to him!) area, then the teacher may quite rightly chastize him for "not answering the question." For example, if the student begins his answer by saying, "Well, if *I* were Antony . . ." the teacher is surely within her rights to interrupt and point out that the question is about the *play*, not about the student.

The third question involves still another, and extremely important, kind of thinking. The key part of the question is "some other way"— ways, in other words, that the student must *make up*, or *imagine*. These ways will have some relationship to the play, of course, but the best answers will reflect much more about the students who provide them than about the play. For example, Antony might have killed Brutus then and there. Or he might have attempted to work for political power through the Senate. Or—as a student once suggested to me—he might have gotten so scared at the idea of running the country that he might have travelled north to join the Gauls. Guilford calls this sort of thinking "divergent." It is thinking that does 'diverge' from the subject at hand, but this is not to say that it therefore has no value. The suggestion of alternatives for the play helps to make clear why the play is in fact put together the way it is. But far more important is the idea that divergent thinking *involves the student with himself. His* inventions are being solicited and, ideally, rewarded by the teacher.

The problems of what the teacher rewards, and how much reward she hands out, in class, are better handled by the Flanders system. But in connection with divergent thinking, it is important to find out what the teacher intends to reward as an answer to a divergent question. Theoretically, I suppose, if the teacher knows she has asked such a question she should accept and praise *any* answer, however bizarre it may be—and she should be intolerant only of commonplace or obvious ideas. I suspect that whether a teacher actually will reward *any* answer is dependent on the amount of tolerance she has for different ideas. Once a teacher is made aware of the potential for student creativity in

[18] J. P. Guilford, "The Structure of Intellect," *Psychological Bulletin,* LIII, 1956, 267–293.

such questions, her tolerance of wild answers can, in my experience, be easily increased. The final question asks for a *moral* judgment. We, as adults, are sophisticated enough to wonder what "right" means. "Right" for a Machiavelli? In the case of an adolescent, I imagine that his answer is more likely to be based on some intuition about his own value system, along with an educated guess about what he thinks the teacher wants to hear. In any event, the problem is to make a moral judgment. This sort of thinking Guilford terms "evaluative." Aesthetic judgments are also included here—thus the question, "Is this a good play?" will also produce evaluative thinking.

Thus we have four kinds of questions, and four kinds of thinking: memory, convergent, divergent, evaluative. The first step for teachers is to recognize the four kinds of questions involved as they come up in normal class discussion. I have already mentioned the depressing conclusion of one piece of research—that given teachers tend to use only certain kinds of questions, and thus make no allowances for the ability levels of the classes they teach and few allowances for different kinds of thinking.

SELECTED BIBLIOGRAPHY

Albright, Daniel, "An Organic Curriculum for English," *English Journal,* LII (January 1963), 16–21.
  Applies the "techniques of literary criticism" to curriculum construction and proposes the elimination of in-class literature teaching in favor of a "free-reading program" and a series of short "courses" which students may elect.
Barosko, Sam, "Teaching the Novel to Slow Learners," *Wisconsin Journal of Education,* LXXXXIX (December 1966), 20–22.
  Presents a plan for helping slow learners sense achievement in reading the novel.
Burke, Etta M., "Project for Slow Learners," *English Journal,* LV (September 1966), 784–85.
  Describes a project in newspaper and novel reading carried on in twelfth-grade classes.
Carlin, Jerome, "A Pattern for Teaching Literature," *English Journal,* LV (March 1966), 291–297.
  Discusses various responsibilities of the classroom teacher in planning the literature program.

College Entrance Examination Board, *Freedom and Discipline in English* (New York: 1965), pp. 42–79.

A very influential report suggesting a works-centered curriculum for the college-bound student.

Damon, Grace E., "Teaching the Slow Learner, Up the West Staircase, With Apologies to B. K.," *English Journal,* LV (September 1966), 777–783.

Suggests various activities and methods in literature successful with slow learners in the junior high school.

Evans, William H., and Jerry L. Walker, "Literature and the New Method," in *New Trends in the Teaching of English in Secondary Schools* (Chicago: Rand McNally, 1966), pp. 37–50.

A lucid discussion of current trends in literature programs as influenced by the structure and subject emphasis of the "new method."

Frye, Northrop, "Elementary Teaching and Elemental Scholarship," *PMLA,* LXXIX (May 1964), 11–18.

Argues for a new theoretical conception of literature which places poetry at the center of the literature program.

Henry, George H., "The Idea of Coverage in the Teaching of Literature," *English Journal,* LIV (September 1965), 475–482.

A well-conceived argument that the development of concepts and not an attempt at "coverage" should and can guide the development of the literature program.

Herbert, Phil, ". . . That's the Question," *English Journal,* LVI (November 1967), 1195–1196.

Another insightful discussion of the art of questioning about a work of literature.

Hillocks, George, Jr., "Literature and Composition for Average Students in Grades Seven to Nine," *NASSP Bulletin,* XLVIII (February 1964), 62–75.

Discusses the program developed at a Project English Demonstration Center which integrates the "content" and "skills points of view into a viable literature program for junior high school.

Johnson, Frances, "A Unifying Theme for the Year," *English Journal,* LII (February 1963), 97–101.

Describes a program unified by the pursuit of one major theme throughout the year's work.

Keller, Charles R., "Humanities in the High School," *English Journal,* LIV (March 1965), 171–190.

Several articles discussing the possibilities of teaching literature within the framework of humanities courses and programs.

Largmann, Malcolm G., "The Novel and Bright Students: An Answer to Cynicism," *High Points* XLIX (May 1966), 25–32.

Noting that most of our brighter students are unprepared emotionally and by experience to deal with the cynicism of such authors as Joyce, Dostoevsky, and Lawrence, Largmann suggests that works stressing positive values are more effective and, surprisingly, are better received by bright students.

Lin, San-Su C., "Disadvantaged Student? or Disadvantaged Teacher?," *English Journal,* LVI (May 1967), 751–756.

A discussion of the functions of literature for disadvantaged students.

Mersand, Joseph, "Teaching the Slow Learner in English," *High Points,* XLVIII (May 1966), 38–52.

A specific discussion of ways to adapt the English program for slow learners.

Norvell, George W., "Watchman, What of Literature in Our Schools?," *English Journal,* LII (September 1963), 434–437.

Restates his earlier thesis that student interest is the crucial concern in selecting literature for study in high school English classes.

Sauer, Edwin H., "The High School Literature Program Reconsidered," *English in the Secondary School* (New York: Holt, Rinehart and Winston, 1961), pp. 141–158.

A provocative discussion of considerations in choosing literature for the secondary school program.

Simpson, Ray H., and Anthony Soares, "Best- and Least-Liked Short Stories in Junior High School," *English Journal,* LIV (February 1965), 108–111.

Report of a study assessing the reading preferences of junior high school students; presents several guide lines for selecting stories to teach.

Tincher, Ethel, "Helping Slow Learners Achieve Success," *English Journal,* LIV (April 1965), 289–294.

Specific discussion of the content of a literature program for slow learners.

Wertenbaker, Thomas J., Jr., "A Surfeit of Surveys: Thoughts on Chronology and Theme in American Literature," *English Journal,* LII (January 1963), 9–15.

Argues that unity of ideas and critical thinking are central considerations in construction of a literature course.

part three
THE FUNCTION
AND NATURE OF LITERATURE
FOR ADOLESCENTS

The term "literature for adolescents" may be a rather amorphous one for many people, even teachers. Unlike "children's books," a term which evokes a relatively standard image of appearance and content, "literature for adolescents" may suggest anything from the subliterary series book to the "classics" most often offered in secondary school English classes. This sweeping definition is a proper one if by the term one means anything that adolescents like to read—provided one also includes comic books and a number of other kinds of reading material. As used in this section, "literature for adolescents" refers, first, to the rather substantial and highly important body of literature produced by predominantly serious writers specifically for the audience aged from about twelve to about seventeen, in other words principally junior and senior high school students. Second, it refers to that adult literature which has particular relevance to the adolescent and particular significance to the aims of literature teaching in the secondary school.

The purpose of Part Three therefore is to discuss the function and nature of this body of literature. The discussions of the literature written expressly for adolescents or for adults and the suggested bibliographies are delimited by the author's convictions about what literature in either category is of concern to the teacher in the junior and senior high school. A number of varieties of nonfiction, both for the adolescent and the adult, that may be of interest to teachers of other subjects are not discussed. Neither is poetry nor drama discussed, since the earlier chapters on these genres incorporate concern with works written for or of special significance to adolescents.

10
The Function of Literature
Written for Adolescents

Literature for adolescents is written with an eye to the interests and concerns of teenagers which have remained relatively stable despite the great cultural changes of the past several decades. Satisfaction of interests, though important, is not the major aim of the literature program. The major function of literature written expressly for adolescents is to provide a vital transition in the literary education.

The point has been made earlier that the literary education represents the same kind of continuum as education in mathematics, science, or any other field of knowledge. The junior high school student cannot jump instantly from the experiences of children's literature to the adult masterpiece. Books for adolescents serve the transition function in two ways. First, in a broad sense, they prepare the young reader to comprehend mature works in later years, induct him into the processes of becoming involved with a work of literature. The student who can read the junior novel well, for example, probably will develop the ability to read the serious adult novel well. If in the junior high school the pupil is able to discern the simple symbolic treatment of the theme of good versus evil in something like Annixter's *Swiftwater*—in one exciting scene a boy fights with a wolverine—he is making important preparation for reading later, say, the novels of Thomas Hardy, or Nathaniel Hawthorne. Second, books for adolescents provide satisfying experiences in themselves at the stage of development represented by early and middle adolescence when many adult works do not provide such experiences.

"Start where they are," though an educational cliché, is still a viable motto for the teacher of literature. But where *is* the pupil in his potential for experience with literature when he enters the junior high school and encounters, in many cases, his first real study of literature? The answer will vary greatly from one individual to another, but some pertinent generalizations can be drawn about these young human beings who flock into seventh- and eighth-grade classrooms.

Most important, young students are not averse, in general, to reading and are eager for vicarious experience. In fact, voluntary reading may be more important to the seventh-grader than it ever was before or ever will be again. But much of this reading may be of the kind that chills the blood of the English teacher—comic books, for example. Although circulation of comic books has declined somewhat in the last few years, partly because of attempts to suppress objectionable ones and partly because of the influence of television, the comic book still remains near the top of the reading interest list for junior high school students and bulks fairly large even in the reading of senior high school students. A survey conducted by the author in several schools while this revision was being written showed that 75 percent of students in grades seven to nine and 53 percent in grades ten to twelve read comic books.

Today, though, the student's principal source of vicarious experience and entertainment, as well as the adult's, is the television screen. Junior high students spend nearly as many hours watching television each week as they spend in school (approximately the same number as their parents!) and senior high students spend about half as much time televiewing as they do in attending classes. (Both groups also spend a substantial amount of time listening to recorded music.)

BASIC APPEALS OF POPULAR SCREEN AND PAGE

The vicarious experiences most popular with the junior high school pupil—whether of television or the comic book—have certain common patterns of appeal. Examination of these patterns is important for the teacher of literature. One obvious appeal of the comic book and the television program is that they require little effort, much less effort than is required by the ordinary book. Although the vocabulary in many comic books is not particularly easy, the actual text need not be read at all. Looking at the pictures and reading a few words here and there are enough. Capable readers may read as many comic books as poor readers, but the less able reader may be especially attracted to the comics if the required reading in class is continually beyond him. Little imaginative effort is needed in looking at a TV show or in reading a comic book. There is no need to conjure up images in the mind's eye. The situations and characters, complete with bulging biceps, golden tresses, or evil visages, are there already. Because of these facts, there is a danger that these media may be a deterrent to real play of the imagination. It should be clear, of course, that the author is not implying that television is necessarily inferior to print. Some television programs do indeed stimulate and demand a real play of the imagination and may represent a valuable adjunct to the literature program.

The characteristics of the most popular comic books and of many popular television programs among early adolescents are very similar. Among girls, in the survey conducted by the author, the favorite comic-book subject matter was love, romance, and humor, while the content of the favorite television programs was love, romance, humor, and space adventure. Among boys, the favorite comic books feature superheroes, space adventure, humor, and the fantastic, while the favorite TV programs were in the same categories with the addition of westerns and violent adventure of the "Mannix" variety.

The content of such popular comic books and television programs is highly compatible with the nature of early adolescents. Common to them are the ingredients of adventure, violence, romantic love, humor, and the fantastic. The characters in the chosen programs are either superheroes—physically attractive and socially adept people who represent a kind of ideal fulfillment—or buffoons to whom the reader can feel superior. The adolescent, sensitive about his own finesse and acceptability, delights in the antics of Archie and his girl friends.

The appeal of the comic-book, popular-television level of experience is rooted, too, in the fact that its picture of life and the assumptions underlying it are naturally acceptable to the immature mind of the reader or viewer. Life is an exciting physical adventure or should be; heroism and courage are measured in physical daring—this is one assumption. Another assumption is that people are either good or bad. Often one can tell the difference by physical appearance alone. It is obvious that clean-cut Marshal Dillon is a "good guy," while his un-shaven adversary is a crook. The villains in various comic strips usually have revolting physical characteristics and mannerisms.

Another assumption underlining this type of representation of ex-perience is that romantic love and money lie at the heart of life's problems; a familiar twist ranges the affluent on the side of evil. Ro-mantic campaigning is waged pretty much on the "cave-man" level. Another assumption is that the end justifies the means. Though triumph of good over evil is a common theme, it matters not that the hero kills a few people and destroys countless dollars' worth of prop-erty so long as ostensibly he is on the side of righteousness.

A familiar assumption, too, is that people in authority—statesmen, teachers, civic leaders, and often parents—are misguided in their deci-sions and values, and their humiliation is appealing to the early ado-lescent who is under the thumb of adult authority and beginning to chafe from it. The rebellion against established authority, whether of the melodramatic or humorous variety, furnishes a very real lure. Sheer availability is an obvious advantage of the television and com-ic-book experience. Most American families now own television sets, and comic books and other popular magazines are on sale at any drugstore or supermarket.

GENERAL CHARACTERISTICS
OF TRANSITION LITERATURE

Generalizations such as those just made about dominant patterns in the comic-book reading and televiewing of early adolescents always need qualification. Though these patterns fit a great number of young people, it is true that individuals exhibit widely varying tastes. Some pupils, for example, enter the seventh grade already well beyond the road block of superheroes and the romantic writings of the comics. (Perhaps they never stopped there in the first place.) There are also young people who never develop the interests of the majority. For many pupils, however, the early junior high school may be a crucial period of transition from enthusiasm for comic books and certain tele-vision programs to liking for reading and viewing fare in which human experience is reconstructed in more mature modes. It is important for the literature program in the seventh and eighth grades to make available selections that can facilitate this transition. The nature of the basic appeals of popular reading and viewing fare furnishes the key to characteristics of such transition selections, which have similar basic appeals but which provide them in more artful form.

Transition literature will be easy to read.   Much work-reading must be done at any level of school, and a rigorous concern with reading skills is necessary in the junior or senior high school. However, a student's difficulty in recognizing more than one word in a hundred will quickly kill his pleasure in reading, and pleasure is basic to appreciation. Mature readers may enjoy the struggle with a profound and difficult selection, but the junior high school student, just embarking on his literary education, is often far from this point. Although the difficulty level is low, a selection may be artful and esthetically satisfying, as writers such as Eleanor Estes, Doris Gates, and Stephen Meader have demonstrated.

Transition literature will reflect experience compatible with the nature of the reader.   Identification with characters and situations in a selection is a keystone of appreciation. Many selections in the junior high school literature program should feature adolescent characters and exciting or familiar kinds of experiences with which the early adolescent wants to identify.

Transition literature will not grossly distort experience.   As teachers we may be willing that the experience represented be simplified, since life for most early adolescents is still relatively uncomplicated. Action still may occur mostly on the physical plane, but the plots will avoid the wild coincidence and improbability of the comic-book level of fiction. Often in these transition selections, it is true, the young protagonists may do surpassing things in a world curiously detached from adult control. Yet such "unreal" episodes may be acceptable at this stage of the pupil's literary education. Traumatic experiences involving macabre violence and the sordid should not be featured.

Transition literature will have action, suspense, danger, romance.   Pupils should not get the idea that the required or recommended selections are more likely to be dull than interesting.

Such selections will be easily available.   Classroom libraries, book exhibits and bazaars, and bulletin board displays of book jackets will help. PTA's and other groups that are disturbed by the nature of some popular television programs and with the comic-book "menace" should concern themselves with making other materials more plentiful and available.

LITERATURE FOR ADOLESCENTS AND PERSONAL CONCERNS

Books written expressly for adolescents are valuable not only in paving the way for perceptive reading of adult works in the future, but also provide immediately satisfying experiences at a certain stage, just as fairy tales, for example, provide satisfying experiences at an earlier stage.

Books for adolescents reflect various interests and concerns of young readers, but they have their greatest impact, probably, because of their connection with the personal problems of adolescents, and they afford the young reader a chance to stand off and view the seeming turmoil of his life in perspective, to reflect on things that are of the greatest moment to him, whether or not they may seem trivial to adults. Personal problems, inherent in the lifelong struggle toward self-realization and the search for identity, are not unique to adolescents. But the in-between period that is adolescence is a particular time of stress—a no man's land of questioning and doubting and fearing and aspiring. The happy vagueness of the "when I grow up" in the childhood period has given way to the sharp realization that the growing up is nearly complete and that, in the senior high school period at least, there must be a coming to terms with personal shortcomings and a facing of the question: How do I measure up to a role in the adult world? The high school period is frequently marked by a heightening of conflicts between adolescents and parents, as the teenager strives to advance toward independence and adult status faster than his parents think he should. And yet, despite his striving, the fact is—psychologically if not physiologically—that the adolescent is *not* adult. The adolescent culture has its own unique and rigid code, in which a type of conformity is at a premium, and the teenager who would have reasonably satisfactory status with his peers (and which one would not!) can only pretend to be adult within the boundaries of the peer culture and the rules enforced by adults. Around the stresses of the adolescent period a large body of literature has developed, particularly fiction, which has high popularity with adolescents. Most of the personal problems of adolescents cluster in the categories identified below with which much of the literature discussed in the following two chapters relates.

Coming to terms with self. Most adolescents are actively taking stock of themselves, even though for some the process may be carried on under a veneer of irresponsibility and devil may care. The student who has been struggling to maintain a "C" average realizes that MIT and a career in engineering are not for him. The plain girl with the unenticing figure faces the fact that the coming years probably will bring no increase in glamour. And the introverted, retiring boy decides, reluctantly or otherwise, that he will never be the center of "the gang." Though most adolescents tend to be realistic in their stocktaking, all need to establish a favorable personal image, though all do not succeed.

Problems of relations with peers. Popularity, which may be tempered ultimately to acceptance, is a major goal of adolescents. The pull to live up to peer-group or gang-set standards, to conform, may involve the teenager in conflicts with his parents, his teachers, and his convictions. For example, the intellectually gifted student may have to play down his ability in order to avoid being labeled "a brain." Of course, the whole web of boy-girl relations presents major issues of social know-how, of going steady, and of sexual morality. Senior high school students are much more serious about love than their parents or teachers frequently realize. A few students marry before completing high school, and many think seriously about marriage and their future roles as homemakers. The problem of dating is more serious to the girl, who is an outcast if she doesn't date, than to the boy, who may be merely labeled a "woman-hater."

Family problems. Although the adolescent tends to pull away from domination and control by his parents, he greatly needs their advice and guidance. Countless minor tensions are created by the adolescent in the household. Occasionally, his problems may be deep-seated. It is not unusual for the adolescent to feel ashamed of his home or of some member of his family.

Preparation for the future adult role.   His role as a marriage partner is not the only aspect of his future with which the adolescent is concerned. He also has the problem of deciding if he should or should not go to college, and of choosing a career or an occupation. Boys may be preoccupied with their military obligations.

Moral and philosophical problems and issues.   Few adolescents would admit openly to an interest in "philosophy of life." Yet teenagers are keenly concerned with values, with the things that people live for, and with the motives that impel men. The "Omar Khayyam" period has long been associated with the adolescent experience, and *weltschmerz,* sometimes serving as a defense mechanism, is a hallmark of the teen years. Often the adolescent has to carry on a lonely tussle with concepts of right and wrong. Typically, adolescence is a time of outward cynicism and inward idealism. Today there is much discussion of the generation gap as young people around the world are rebelling against the adult culture. The "hippie" and "beat" movements are part of this rebellion. Because of the cultural ferment, adolescents, in general, are interested in and concerned with social and political issues at earlier ages than they were until recently, and extremism, both of the left and the right, is more common today among teenagers.

Search for "kicks."   Partly related to the sharpened conflict between youth and adulthood is the fact that young people's search for "kicks" has intensified and taken more extreme forms such as experimentation with drugs.

The mere fact that the publication of books for adolescents increases each year is evidence that this body of literature has a secure place in the lives of teenagers. The school program can take good advantage of the appeal of these books directed to young people. It is the task of the school and of the teacher to identify the most significant and artistic in the outpouring of books for adolescents and make them serve the important purposes which they have the potential to serve.

11
Fiction for Adolescents

section I
THE JUNIOR NOVEL

THE ANATOMY OF THE JUNIOR NOVEL

The term "junior novel" apparently came into use in the 1930s at the outset of the great surge of books written expressly for adolescents. Some critics have attacked the quality of the junior novel, dismissing it as a "subliterary" genre, and it is quite true that the majority of these novels are slight, mediocre at best, and wanting greatly in literary quality. The same thing, though, can be said of fiction for the general audience: the majority of adult novels also are unworthy of serious attention. Good, mediocre, and wretched work is to be found both in literature for adolescents and in that for adults.

Though the great majority of junior novels are ephemeral, the genre cannot be dismissed lightly. Its value in the school program was cited in the preceding chapter and, as a literary form, the junior novel has established its respectability because of the achievement of some of its writers. The dividing line between the junior and adult novel sometimes may be tenuous. Some novelists have written for both audiences—Leonard Wibberley, James Ramsey Ullman, and Farley Mowatt among others. The junior novel is not merely "easier" or less mature than the adult novel, although in the main it is shorter and easier to read than its adult counterpart. Its general themes and categories of content are indicated by the divisions of this section. Its uniqueness, for better or worse, however, is born of some rather rigid conventions of form and content.

The taboos imposed upon writers of books for adolescents have called forth severe criticism of the overinnocuous quality of junior fiction. One scathing analysis concluded:

> The adolescent's world is fraught with change; its charms "are wound up," its horizons are pulsing with expectancies and actualities. His most heartfelt cry is, as Sherwood Anderson warned us long ago, "I want to know why!" The pastel, gum-drop fiction that has been wrought for him avoids both question and answer.[1]

The taboos of the junior novel are the same as those rigorously enforced as a rule by publishers of literature anthologies for the junior and senior high school. The "seamy" side of life is generally avoided; erotic drives are ignored; smoking and drinking are seldom alluded to (adolescents, of course, never drink in the books); swearing and bad grammar are avoided—these are some of the most obvious taboos. It can be argued, therefore, that in much junior fiction basic realism is avoided, and that a rounded view of life is not given. Insistence upon a too-narrow concept of "wholesomeness" may tend to cripple the junior novel as a true form of literature, but avoidance or violation of taboos such as those just cited has little to do with the quality of a work. Good taste as well as verisimilitude is important to adolescent and adult fiction alike. Criticism has centered mainly on the fact that in many junior novels there is slick superficiality, a failure to plunge below the surface into the deeper and more complex human emotions and motivations. In discussing junior novels in which the focus is on the problems of teen-agers, Richard S. Alm writes:

> . . . most novelists present a sugar-puff story of what adolescents should do and should believe rather than what adolescents may or will do and believe. Such stories reveal the novelists' lack of knowledge or insight into adolescent behavior as well as a lack of writing ability.

[1] Frank G. Jennings, "Literature for Adolescents—Pap or Protein?" *English Journal*, XLV (December 1956), 526–531.

These writers do not penetrate beneath the surface of the situation they create. Their stories are superficial, often distorted, sometimes completely false representations of adolescence.[2]

Superficiality obviously is not a unique shortcoming of fiction for teenagers. There is patterned, formula writing for both the adult and the adolescent markets, and there is the serious writing for both audiences. Even some talented writers for adolescents, however, apparently feel impelled to "write down," and their failure to probe deeply is intentional. With adolescents, as with adults, the superficial formula story may be popular, but it is important that teachers and librarians stock the fiction shelves and make up book lists from books that represent art rather than artifice.

Despite what has been said so far about the nature of the junior novel (substantially the same things said in the previous edition of this book), it is apparent that in the last few years there has been a relaxing of conventions and taboos and more significant substance in the better junior novels. There is less fluff of the beach party and prom date variety and a greater concern with the problems that can bring real unhappiness and emotional disaster to young people. While Henry Felsen's *Two and the Town,* the story of a forced teen-age marriage, brought a storm of controversy a few years ago, Jeanette Eyerly's *A Girl Like Me,* also about teen-age, out-of-wedlock pregnancy, raised few eyebrows in 1966. There is also increased concern with the non-middle class, less-fortunate levels of living, for example, S. E. Hinton's *The Outsiders,* dealing with the gang fights in New York City's East Side, and Louisa Shotwell's story of migrant Negro workers, *Roosevelt Grady.* Dialogue has become more real, and dialects more often are rendered with validity. Even some mild profanity appears, and we have occasional passages such as this from Carol Brink's fine *Snow in the River* which show a loosening of taboos:

> A thin girl with untidy hair and a pair of sailor's boots on her feet sat in a corner opposite and looked at him with calculating eyes. He avoided her gaze, and when she followed him into the street, he had no patience with her. He shook her plucking fingers off his sleeve.
> "Nay, lass, ye're too easy," he said, "I like to pick my own."

[2] Richard S. Alm, "The Glitter and the Gold," *English Journal,* XLIV (September 1955), 315–322.

The junior novel remains greatly didactic, frequently obtrusively so to the mature reader, partly because its sale depends largely on the favorable judgments of teachers and librarians who are much interested in the power of fiction to "teach" and to dramatize values. Though didactic, the junior novelist seldom attempts to be "inspirational" in the venerable success-story tradition; there is little of the Horatio Alger influence. Within the boundaries of its conventions, the junior novel is realistic, pointing toward adjustment and featuring the minor triumphs that are the best most people can hope for.

Accordingly, the adolescent reader finds himself mirrored, sometimes penetratingly, sometimes only in a vague blur with few of his own ideas or feelings. The young super-hero of a few decades ago is uncommon now. The adolescent finds it easy to identify with the characters of the junior novel, but only infrequently has he a desire to change places with them, to drop into the middle of the book, as one girl reading *Little Women* wished to do. He observes the people in the run-of-the-mill story with interest, but it is only in the extraordinary selection that he can identify with protagonists to the point of pain or exhilaration. The junior novel shares with contemporary adult fiction an oft-bewailed failing—memorable characters are hard to find.

In structure and technique, the junior novel tends to be quite rigidly patterned, though the past few years again have brought greater flexibility and maturity. The length of the junior novel is standardized at slightly more than half the length of the average adult novel. The time span of the action is usually short, almost never more than a year, often a summer or a school year. Generally, plots are straightforward and on a single plane, building to a climax near the end of the book and giving a very brief wrap-up, though variations such as the flashback are noticeable in recent junior novels. Style is plain and uncomplicated, an inevitability in works read mostly by twelve- to fifteen-year-olds. Traditionally, the junior novel has featured almost exclusively the omniscient point of view (with a few exceptions such as Maureen Daly's celebrated *Seventeenth Summer*) but there are interesting experiments with point of view in recent books. Hila Colman's *Classmates by Request,* for instance, alternates between the point of view of a Negro girl and a white girl in a school desegregation crisis.

VARIETIES OF THE JUNIOR NOVEL

Animal Stories

An analysis is not necessary here of the human psychology involving animals and pets to which the early adolescent's interest in animals is linked. The appeal of the vastly popular animal story probably lies partly in the flattering devotion of the dog or horse to the young master which is almost invariably stressed. Since adolescence is likely to be so much a time of doubts and fears and insecurities, the unswerving loyalty and faith and courage that the horse or dog often exhibits are qualities the young adolescent especially values. In the animal story that takes place in the wilds, from Jack London's *Call of the Wild* to the many basically similar contemporary selections, there is an added appeal. In such stories the animal survives and prospers according to his individual cunning and strength. This is the survival-of-the-fittest code that the young adolescent respects, as he demonstrates on the playground and in his neighborhood gathering places.

Learnings through class discussion. It is no problem, at any rate, to motivate most junior high pupils to read animal fiction. But where does such reading fit into the continuum of the literature program? By skillfully recommending books that will provide important comparisons and contrasts and by carefully planning discussions of them the teacher can lead a class to important learnings.

CREDIBILITY OF PLOT. The junior high school pupil should develop a healthy wariness of the fraud of undue coincidence and improbability in poor quality fiction. For example, the far-fetched plot of Farley's *The Black Stallion* can be contrasted with the down-to-earth, yet suspenseful sequence of events in Gipson's splendid *Old Yeller*. Foreshadowing is definitely evident in this book, and in, say, Street's *Goodbye, My Lady,* but is obviously lacking in the Farley story.

AWARENESS OF THEME. Even the juvenile animal story can say something significant about human experience, and the pupil must develop an awareness of theme at this level if he is to deal with it in more mature books. Most junior high school pupils will be able to recognize the theme, the boy's growing up, so sensitively handled in

Goodbye, My Lady. And they will be able to see by contrast that Lippincott's *The Wahoo Bobcat,* though it is excellent in some ways, has no recognizable theme to give the book unity.

A very common theme in animal fiction is that of faith justified; the faith, perhaps, of the young master that the animal will become a successful hunting dog or racing horse, despite the doubts of others. This theme can be handled skillfully, or clumsily and sentimentally. For example, James Kjelgaard develops this theme well in the popular *Big Red,* the story of a boy and his Irish setter. Oversentimentality is one of the most common faults of animal fiction, and junior high school pupils are sensitive to "mushiness" in anything. On this point alone, it is possible for them to recognize the adequacy of Thomas Hinkle's stories and the excellence of *Old Yeller* and *Goodbye, My Lady.*

CHARACTERIZATION.   The young people in animal fiction are monotonously similar from author to author. Often, there is no real attempt to bring them truly alive. As pupils discuss books they have read, describing and contrasting main characters, it may become apparent which authors have developed multidimensioned characters, such as those Eric Knight creates in *Lassie Come-Home.*

DIFFERENCES IN QUALITIES OF STYLE.   The best authors can communicate unobtrusively the wonder of wild places and the amazing rhythm of nature in locales where man does not usually penetrate— the deep swamps and thickets and high peaks. Joseph Lippincott, for example, suceeds in doing this in *The Wahoo Bobcat,* set in the Florida swamp land. Reading aloud by the students and teacher will be helpful in illustrating this point. Few pupils fail to respond to a passage like the following:

> Uncle Jesse slouched in his chair and puffed his pipe and took in the beauty of the words he did not understand, the words about marvels that only his fancy could picture; the prairies so different from the swamp and so far away. The hard dry gulches, the brave men, the brave land—the never-felt land of his own boyhood dreams.
>
> Out there the winds sang high and free. Thus the words said. Here in his world the winds hummed and sobbed, crying for something that had no answer—like something never seen but only felt and this something touching the strings to the heart of an unlettered old man who could not speak the things he felt and who felt them all the more because he could not speak them: the aching hurt of being old and the happy sor-

row of watching a boy grow up and knowing that he, too, must wear a symbol around his neck, that he, like all men, must carry some foul thing forever, some weakness—and also knowing that some day the swamp winds, the home sounds so long remembered, would feel for the strings to the boy's heart and bring forth only the echo of the melody of what used to be—the beauty of the sprouting years, the hope of longing, then the misery of loving something that must grow old; all this the mystery that the old man felt and could not say, this miracle of man's life on God's earth.[3]

"READING BETWEEN THE LINES." *Goodbye, My Lady,* again an example, is rich in symbolism. In this book, the obvious but satisfying symbolism of the coffee and its value in the theme of growing up is worth discussing. For this and other reasons already implied, Street's book is excellent for group reading in the seventh or eighth grade.

One of the well-known Scholastic Literature Units, entitled *Animals,*[4] represents a skillfully built unit for seventh-graders. The interest generated in reading from the unit anthology a series of short selections of fiction and nonfiction about animals leads into work in oral and written composition and small-group and individual reading of full-length books.

REPRESENTATIVE BOOKS *

Appell, David, *Comanche,* Harcourt.
    The horse which survived the Custer massacre tells the story. (E)
Balch, Glenn, *The Midnight Colt,* Crowell-Collier-Macmillan.
    Two young people and a spoiled, temperamental race horse.
Ball, Zachary, *Bristleface,* Holiday.
    The growing up a little of a boy and his dog some decades ago. (E)
Chipperfield, Joseph, *Storm of Dancerwood,* McKay.
    The theme of the part-wolf dog who returns to the world of man.
Corbin, William, *Golden Mare,* Coward-McCann.
    A ranch boy has to part with a wonderful horse. (E)

---

* In this and the other lists that follow, books discussed in the text are marked with an asterisk (*) and are not annotated. "E" means that the book is especially easy.

[3] James Street, *Goodbye, My Lady* (Philadelphia: J. B. Lippincott, 1954), pp. 137–138. By permission of the publishers.

[4] Stanley B. Kegler, *Animals,* a Scholastic Literature Unit (New York: Scholastic Book Services, 1962).

Gipson, Fred, *Old Yeller,* Harper & Row.
A boy and an incorrigible yellow dog in the Texas hill country of the 1860s. (Also *Savage Sam,* featuring the son of Old Yeller.)
Grew, David, *Beyond Rope and Fence,* Grosset & Dunlap.
The career of Queen, a buckskin horse.
Henry, Marguerite, *King of the Wind,* Rand McNally.
An Arabian boy and the ancestor of the great race horse, Man o'War. (E)
*Kjelgaard, James, *Big Red,* Cadmus Books. (E)
———, *Haunt Fox,* Holiday.
An unusual fox and the boy who hunted him. (E)
———, *Stormy,* Holiday.
Unusual story of a boy left alone with his dog in a lake cabin when his father is sent to prison. (E)
*Knight, Eric, *Lassie Come-Home,* Holt, Rinehart and Winston.
The moving story of the great collie and her long trek back to her real home.
*Lippincott, Joseph, *The Wahoo Bobcat,* Lippincott.
A boy and a magnificent bobcat in the Florida swamp country.
Lyons, Dorothy, *Dark Sunshine,* Harcourt.
A teen-aged polio victim finds new life in training her horse.
Montgomery, Rutherford, *The Golden Stallion and the Wolf Dog,* Little, Brown.
A mystery and a great white stallion that challenges the golden stallion —a series book. (Also, *Crazy Kill Range,* World. Another fine horse story.)
Powell, Miriam, *Jareb,* Crowell-Collier-Macmillan.
A Georgia pine country boy and his "no account" hound dog.
*Street, James, *Goodbye, My Lady,* Lippincott.

Sports Stories

The interest in sports fiction grows naturally out of the preoccupation with athletics in most junior and senior high schools. The thrill of the clash on gridiron or diamond or court is a part of the experience of almost every student, whether participant or spectator. Adolescents in the junior high school, especially boys, are likely to admire physical prowess more than almost anything else, and of course sports heroes are legion. A continuing spate of sports fiction is directed at this interest. These books, whether wretched or excellent, are guaranteed an audience. The minority of good books present credible, well-knit plots, solid characterization, authentic play-by-play action, and occasionally a theme of some significance.

Learnings through class discussion. Like animal stories, sports fiction has a place in the junior high school literature program, exciting the interest of some pupils who are likely to be classified as naturally "unliterary." From the soil of sports fiction can sprout some discriminating reactions to literature. In a seventh- or eighth-grade unit on "Sports and Sportsmanship" or "Heroes, Past and Present," for example, the class, or a group within the class, may consider sports fiction. The following questions discussed in class may lead the students in the direction of appreciating some of the elements of good writing.

DO THE ATHLETES AND THE COACHES IN YOUR BOOKS SEEM REAL? Does their conversation sound natural? The boys who are athletes themselves and who are working with coaches are in a good position to discuss these questions. Use of stereotypes or creation of real characters is a literary matter worth discussing here. In sports fiction, coaches, for instance, are likely to fall into two stock categories: dark villains who exploit their players or impossible bundles of omniscience who are concerned much more with building character than with winning games. In these books, dialogue is often badly handled. Scenes are common in which coaches deliver pompous orations in locker rooms between halves and thus send forth rejuvenated teams that sweep all opposition away before them. Pupils quickly catch the falseness of this. And they can recognize the ridiculousness in this statement by the gangling seventeen-year-old southpaw who has just been offered an athletic scholarship: "I appreciate the offer more than I can tell you, sir. But it isn't a real business proposition. I mean you are offering to lend us considerably more money than we can offer security for, are you not?" They can see the superiority of characterization in, say, John Tunis' *Keystone Kids,* in which the main characters chew tobacco and talk as many major league baseball players really do.

HOW DO THE SPORTS HEROES IN YOUR BOOKS GAIN SUCCESS, SOLVE THEIR PROBLEMS? What sorts of obstacles do they encounter? In the better sports fiction, success is not won easily; sacrifice and dedication, involving training and learning, are usually featured. The southpaw does not often move from the sandlot to the big league and strike out the "murderers' row" in his first appearance on the mound. And the junior high school boy, yearning for the athletic peak himself, is able to recognize the truth of experience. The most common theme in sports fiction is that of an individual coming to terms with himself, finding confidence or throwing off some immature pattern of reaction. Such themes are valid in sports stories—they can be mawkishly handled, featuring perhaps a sudden "coming to realize" twist; or well handled, in which the gridiron or the diamond becomes the proving ground that it can be for certain traits of character. Some writers have even injected social themes into sports fiction. One of John Tunis' books, for example, features a Jewish baseball player, another, a Negro football player. His two least popular books, *Yea! Wildcats!* and *A City for Lincoln,* are frankly political. Bill Carol's *Full-Court Pirate* is built around a sociological theme in that a high school basketball hopeful is convinced that his living in the "wrong" neighborhood jeopardizes his chance for success. Consideration of theme, then, is not out of place even in discussion of sports fiction.

HOW MUCH ACTUAL GAME ACTION DO YOUR BOOKS HAVE?　Does the author really reproduce the excitement of the game? Are there any lines in your books in which the action of a game is especially well described? Again, the junior high school pupil is in good position to judge these matters from his own experience. Although the adult reader might be appalled at the seemingly endless round of games and "tight spots," it is the amount and quality of game action that makes or breaks the book for the adolescent. Among the writers who usually can produce taut play-by-play are John Tunis, C. Paul Jackson, Dick Friendlich, and Curtis Bishop.

In the junior high school, sports fiction may open new avenues in reading and in thought. The nonbookish boy may be led from fiction to biographies of sports heroes or into other areas of fiction and nonfiction involving courage and prowess. Units such as "Sports and Sportsmanship" and "Heroes, Past and Present" may extend the conception of fair play and of heroism.

REPRESENTATIVE BOOKS

Bishop, Curtis, *Rebound,* Lippincott.
　Solid basketball action and a touch of romance.

Bowen, Robert, *The Big Inning,* Lothrop.
A big league baseball player overcomes an injury that forces him to give up baseball.
*Carol, Bill S., *Full-Court Pirate,* Steck-Vaughn.
Carse, Robert, *The Winner,* Scribner.
From high school competition to professional tennis.
Decker, Duane, *Long Ball to Left Field,* Morrow.
A hard-hitting young pitcher is reluctant to switch to the outfield.
Douglas, Gilbert, *Hard to Tackle,* Crowell.
An exciting football story with a racial theme. (Also, *The Bulldog Attitude,* basketball.)
Flood, Richard T., *Penalty Shot,* Houghton Mifflin.
Another Radford Academy story. Hockey action from page 1 to the end.
Friendlich, Dick, *Baron of the Bull Pen,* Westminster.
A relief pitcher and a feud between two young players—the self-confidence theme.
Jackson, C. Paul, *Rose Bowl All-American,* Crowell-Collier-Macmillan.
Exciting football with the "finding confidence" theme. (Also *All-Conference Tackle* and *Tournament Forward.*)
Jackson, C. Paul, and O. B. Jackson, *Puck Grabber,* Whittlesey.
Unattenuated hockey excitement—high school competition.
Meader, Stephen, *Sparkplug of the Hornets,* Harcourt.
A "shorty" makes the grade in high school basketball.
Tunis, John, *All-American,* Harcourt.
A high school football story with a well-handled racial theme.
*————, *Keystone Kids,* Harcourt.
A brother combination in major league baseball.
————, *Schoolboy Johnson,* Morrow.
A temperamental rookie pitcher becomes a winner and a man.
Waldman, Frank, *The Challenger,* Harcourt.
A hard-working athlete wins the heavyweight boxing title.

Stories of Physical Adventure and Ordeal

Though the literature of adventure belongs to no particular age group, it has special appeals to the adolescent, and a large body of adventure fiction has been written for young people. Whit Burnett describes adventure as "a climate of the mind." In the introduction to his anthology, *The Spirit of Adventure,* he says: "Adventure is an atmosphere and essence. . . . It is the man, plus the place and event; a man out of the ordinary in daring, endurance, and vision, and a place out of our common ken, even perhaps out of the world." [5]

Everyone likes to imagine that if circumstances demanded he would prove to be out of the ordinary in daring, endurance, and resourcefulness. During the pall of routine one keeps an inner vision of himself, and it is fascinating to hold this up to comparison with those who have met peril surpassingly. This is especially true of the adolescent, who feels a pressing need for private opportunities to test himself, vicariously as well as actually.

Hazardous undertakings, out-of-the-ordinary characters, and places "out of our common ken" have been the essentials of the traditional adventure story, and remain so in the junior novel of adventure. The popularity of science fiction, treated separately in this chapter, attests to the taste for the "out of this world." The more significant of the adventure novels retain these essentials but rise to a level at which the hero's understandings—and perhaps those of the reader—are enlarged and his attitudes modified as a result of his experiences.

Though the junior novel of adventure, like its adult counterpart, presents a broad spectrum of experiences, the major categories feature outdoor adventure and the sea and make their greatest appeal to boys. Adventure and peril may be at the heart, too, of other categories of novels treated in this chapter—such as stories of earlier times and of the adolescent culture. War is a prime interest of boys, but little has been done with the topic in the junior novel. Exceptions are John Tunis's *Silence Over Dunkerque,* featuring a peerless British sergeant in the great disaster of World War II, and Frank Bonham's *War Beneath the Sea,* which tells of a young sailor's experiences on the submarine *USS Mako.*

The theme of survival or man against nature is a most common one in the novels of outdoor adventure. Outstanding in this category is James Ramsey Ullman's *Banner in the Sky* (reprinted in paperback as *Third Man on the Mountain*), the story of a Swiss boy's battle to conquer the mountain on which his father had lost his life. The mountain is the obvious symbol of the boy's aspiration. This novel is a worthwhile one for group study in the early junior high school. Notable, too, is Armstrong Sperry's lyrically written little novel, *Call It Courage,* about a Polynesian boy's attempt to prove his courage through an

[5] New York: Holt, Rinehart and Winston, 1955, pp. 12–13.

ordeal on a deserted island. Other appropriate examples are Kerry Wood's *Wild Winter,* the account of a young writer's excruciating winter in a log cabin in northern Canada, and Kenneth Gilbert's story of the hazardous adventures of an Eskimo boy and an American boy in the far north, *Arctic Adventure.*

Another common theme in these books is the joy and therapy of wild places coupled with a strong didacticism concerning conservation of natural resources and wild life. James Kjelgaard and Montgomery Atwater are perhaps the major examples in this category. Both write highly masculine stories of adventure in the woods. Atwater is best known for his youthful forest ranger Hank Winton, and Hank's associates in the forest service. Kjelgaard's characters are generally inveterate hunters, and he usually injects some sort of mystery into his stories. Both authors are skillful in constructing credible, straightforward plots. Neither's style is distinguished and neither makes any attempt at real characterization.

The seas, covering a large proportion of the earth, have been a traditional setting for adventure fiction, from the blood and thunder tales of piracy to the profound allegory of *Moby Dick.* Byron's famous lines beginning, "Roll on, thou deep and dark blue ocean, roll!" express the eternal fascination with the power and vastness and inscrutability of the sea. The midwestern farm boy who has never seen an ocean is as interested in sea fiction as the boy who has spent his life on the seacoast.

Shipwreck, another variation of the survival theme, is prominent in adolescent fiction of the sea. Two suspenseful tales by Richard Armstrong are good examples. *Cold Hazard* recounts the perils of a small group of people set adrift when an iceberg collides with their ship. In *The Big Sea* a young sailor is left alone on board a sinking freighter, and the action is both physical and psychological. The traditional search-for-treasure theme, represented most prominently by *Treasure Island,* is a minor one in recent junior novels, though Frank Crisp and Harry Rieseberg have written appealing stories of modern treasure hunting. Perhaps the most talented writer of sea adventure for young readers is Ireland's Eilis Dillon. Into her thoroughly romantic stories —such as *The Lost Island,* in which a boy finds his long-shipwrecked father and a strange treasure on a lost island, and *The San Sebastian,* the mystery of an abandoned vessel on the Irish coast—she has injected an effect of mood and a sensitivity of style rare in the writer of junior novels. Though basically realistic, her stories are shot through with Irish legend, folklore, and superstition, and there is a fullness of characterization lacking in many writers of adventure tales.

Diving and underwater adventure is a common theme in recent adventure fiction for adolescents. A good example is Philip Harkins' *Where the Shark Waits,* the story of a sixteen-year-old boy's perilous adventures in diving.

These novels of adventure and ordeal usually feature characters of adolescent age, most often boys, who are placed more or less on their own in precarious situations. Although adults often play important parts, parents usually are conveniently absent for one reason or another. Almost never is there a love plot.

REPRESENTATIVE BOOKS

*Armstrong, Richard, *Cold Hazard,* Houghton Mifflin.
    (Also *The Big Sea,* McKay.)
*Atwater, Montgomery, *Hank Winton: Smokechaser,* Random House.
    A young forest ranger's adventures, underlain by a message on forest conservation.
*Bonham, Frank, *War Beneath the Sea,* Crowell-Collier-Macmillan. (E)
Crisp, Frank, *The Treasure of Barby Swin,* Coward-McCann. (E)
    Life in a whaler and a strange treasure story with a well-wrought villain.
Dietz, Lew, *Full Fathom Five,* Little, Brown.
    Three college boys become involved in a summer vacation mystery.
*Dillon, Eilis, *The Lost Island,* Funk & Wagnalls.
    (Also, *The San Sebastian.*)
Gates, Doris, *North Fork,* Viking.
    A summer in a logging camp toughens an aristocratic tenderfoot. (Also, *River Ranch.*)
*Gilbert, Kenneth, *Arctic Adventure,* Holt, Rinehart and Winston.
    (Also, *Triple-Threat Patrol.*)
    Adolescent boys solve a summer vacation mystery involving timber thieves in Puget Sound.)
Haig-Brown, Roderick, *Mounted Police Patrol,* Morrow.
    An exciting story of the Canadian Mounted Police.
*Harkins, Philip, *Where the Shark Waits,* Morrow.
Hoffman, Peggy, *Shift to High!* Westminster.
    Three boys take a trip in a rebuilt car—disaster in a humorous context all along the way.

Janes, Edward C., *Wilderness Warden,* McKay.

A young game warden's battle against poachers in northern Maine.

Kjelgaard, James, *Hidden Trail,* Holiday.

Outdoor winter fiction involving a young conservation department cameraman who solves the mystery of a lost elk herd. (Also *A Nose for Trouble.* Exciting forest adventure and mystery.)

Lathrop, West, *Northern Trail Adventure,* Random House.

More Canadian Mounted Police adventure in the far North.

Mays, Victor, *Fast Iron,* Houghton Mifflin. (E) (Also *Action Starboard.*)

Rieseberg, Harry, *My Compass Points to Treasure,* Holt, Rinehart and Winston. (E)

Searching for lost treasure ships in the Caribbean.

*Sperry, Armstrong, *Call It Courage,* Macmillan. (E)

Stanford, Don, *Crash Landing,* Funk & Wagnalls.

The son of a policeman is involved in a well-written adventure and mystery involving airplanes.

*Tunis, John R., *Silence over Dunkerque,* Morrow.

*Ullman, James R., *Banner in the Sky,* Lippincott.

Whitney, Phyllis, *A Mystery of the Angry Idol,* Westminster.

A girl's stay with her grandmother is taken up with a strange mystery.

*Wood, Kerry, *Wild Winter,* Houghton Mifflin.

Stories of Earlier Times

A quick survey of the shelves of any library or of publishers' lists is sufficient to illustrate the vogue for historical fiction, or at least for the historical romance in the adolescent as well as the adult novel. The reasons for the recurring popularity of historical fiction can be traced to the functions of literature, the rewards sought in reading, which are discussed in earlier chapters. There is, certainly, an inherent fascination in looking backward as well as in looking forward. Just as the science-fiction piece is an escape into the future, so the historical novel is an escape into the past. The past, in general, induces a special kind of nostalgia on the part of most readers, and "the good old days" are still very much revered. Since the past has been lived through, it always seems more orderly, and seems to present less complexity than "the fast pace of nowadays." And subconsciously, too, the reader may feel a certain satisfying superiority as he or the author compares the past with the present.

The kind of people and the events that tend to be emphasized in the typical historical romance are exactly of the type that appeals to the adolescent mind. The characters are people of action—the man of great physical prowess, the woman of surpassing courage. To the average adolescent, the exciting events of the past are physical, stressing action and daring, melodrama and spectacle. Frequently the role of the martyr or of the person who is willing to fight for his cause against great odds is accentuated. These are roles much admired by the adolescent.

So far as teachers and parents are concerned, historical fiction may seem to possess advantages that some other types of literature do not. Even in entertainment many teachers and parents are much concerned with what is "educational," and the supposed opportunities to learn history may make historical fiction seem more "worthwhile" than contemporary romance.

Perhaps, too, part of the appeal of historical fiction may be found in the fact that it stresses certain broad themes or ideas that find sympathetic response among most readers. Underlying the fiction of the American past, for instance, is the "American dream," its extension and implementation, and the triumph of individual liberty over tyranny is the basic theme in many a historical novel. The worth and dignity of the individual is at the heart of American historical fiction.

Then, too, the typical historical romance affords a comfortable type of excitement, akin to that of viewing the Friday night boxing match on television. Because the story is removed in time and because events already fully resolved are likely to receive more careful attention than are people, there is less likelihood of intense, and therefore possibly painful, identification than with some other genres. As John T. Frederick points out, " 'Spectacle' is the word that expresses the essence of traditional historical romance: spectacle as distinguished from drama." [6] The reader therefore is more likely to play the role of observer than of participant. As Frederick goes on to say, "In the best of historical romance the spectacle has meaning; in its totality it achieves grasp of an age, illustration of a general truth of human nature." [7]

If students are to approach historical fiction seriously, they must be made aware of a problem that lies at the heart of skillful reading, of

[6] "Costain and Company: The Historical Novel Today," *English Journal*, XLIII (April 1954), 173.
[7] Frederick, p. 80.

discrimination in the genre—the relationship between history, or historical facts, and fiction. Novelist John Hersey has commented cogently on this relationship:

> Palpable facts are mortal. Like certain moths and flying ants, they lay their eggs and die overnight. The important flashes and bulletins are already forgotten by the time yesterday morning's newspaper is used to line the trash can to receive today's coffee grounds. The things we remember for longer periods are emotions and impressions and illusions and images and characters: the elements of fiction.[8]

Hersey is implying that historical fiction *is* fiction, not history or journalism; its responsibilities are to fiction. Further, he implies that good historical fiction is timeless rather than timely, and its essential concern is not for events but for people, for the truth of human character, which is unchanging—the constant in human experience.

It is important to remember, too, that the function of historical fiction, as of any fiction, is not necessarily to set forth the literal truth, but rather only an impression of it. In good historical fiction, the major facts of a period must be adhered to, of course, but specific details and events may be secondary in the novel which, as James T. Farrell puts it, "re-creates the consciousness and the conscience of a period. It tells us what has happened to man, what could have happened to him, what man has imagined might happen to him." [9] Errors in minor historical details are unimportant. The difference might accurately be defined as that between fiction and journalism, a problem apparent in many war novels. Jessamyn West has explained the failure of many war novels—and of popular taste—in terms of this difference:

> . . . the reader's love of the "true story" is no help to the novelist. The wars produced more violence and cruelty, courage and devotion than the novelists of the world can equal. First-hand accounts satisfy the reader's hankering for facts and convince him that reality is what happened at a named place on a specific day. So the novels he reads in quantity tend to be either nostalgic retreat from "the facts," or them "the facts" are made even more irresistible by being attached to a narra-

---

[8] John Hersey, "The Novel of Contemporary History," *Atlantic Monthly*, CLXXXIV (November 1949), 80.

[9] James T. Farrell, "Literature and Ideology," *English Journal*, XXXL (April 1942), 269.

tive hook of a romantic-sexual nature which sinks deeply into frail flesh.[10]

The basic difference between the journalistic novel and that which rises above it lies probably in the complexity of characters and in the presence of an idea (or ideas) that gives unity to events. What a soldier did in a war is less important than why he did it, and in the great novel he becomes a symbol of humanity. The run-of-the-mill historical novel allows us to witness history; the truly good novel, to live it.

Another distinction is important in the relationship of historical facts and fiction: fiction, unlike history, may be highly selective, pretending to no rounded view. In a historical novel, some specific phase of history may be viewed through the eyes of an individual character, and the reader therefore sees and understands only what the character sees and understands. In fiction, the final impression of an actual historical personage may be quite at variance with the scholarly consensus. For example, Gertrude Finney's *Muskets along the Chickahominy,* a competent historical novel for adolescents, views Bacon's Rebellion, and the character of Nathaniel Bacon, through the eyes of a young indentured servant who much admires Bacon.

It goes almost without saying, too, that in historical fiction there still is need for the imaginative creation of comic and heroic and tragic events. The story woven through whatever facts of history is more important than the facts themselves.

Because of certain relationships it has to the school curriculum and to the reading development of adolescents, historical fiction can have considerable value in the high school program. Often in schools there is an attempt to correlate the content of social studies and English, and historical fiction, of course, is a particularly appropriate type of material for such programs.

In the field of social studies, especially in history, historical fiction can be a valuable means, not only of enriching the program generally, but of sharpening and deepening pupils' concepts of time, thus adding an important dimension to their study of the past. To many students, even after considerable exposure to American history, the American Revolution remains a rather remote and hazy mélange of tea in Bos-

[10] Jessamyn West, "Secret of the Masters," *Saturday Review* (September 21, 1957), 14.

ton Harbor, a midnight ride of Paul Revere, and patriots whose feet were frozen at Valley Forge. A novel like Esther Forbes's *Johnny Tremain* provides a moving close-up of that momentous time from the point of view of a realistic adolescent; understanding of the time and its issues as they entered the lives of people, which no history text can supply, is apparent in the imaginative work.

Through its stress on people and their reactions and emotions, thereby putting flesh on the skeleton of history, historical fiction, if it is good, can help develop an ability to see the past in perspective. Large movements and trends, momentous events, and great personages are, of necessity, the major stuff of history. It is for fiction to furnish the human element, the vision of the ordinary, historically insignificant individual. In Stephen Meader's well-written junior novel, *A Blow for Liberty,* the main character is a "bound" boy of Revolutionary times who longs for a life at sea. He is allowed to sign aboard a privateer and furnishes the reader with a personalized account of the perils and excitement of privateering as the issues of the war become real to him.

It is easy, however, to overstate the case for historical fiction, and mentioning certain limitations of the genre and cautions in using it is in order. One must remember that historical fiction *is* fiction. Though valuable as a supplement to the study of history, it can never be a substitute for history, though many teachers and laymen have been impressed by its apparent possibilities as a painless "backdoor" approach to the subject. Furthermore, many historical novels, even though set in the past, do not really have anything to do with the facts of history or with interpreting a period.

American backgrounds are predominant in the junior novel of earlier times, though non-American backgrounds have been featured more frequently in recent years. The settings and events of the American background stories most frequently feature the wars, the adventures and perils of frontier life, and the "Old West."

One authentic historical novel for adolescents stands alone in its conception and literary quality—*Johnny Tremain* by Esther Forbes. Out of her research on the pre-Revolutionary War years, the author, who won a Pulitzer Prize for her biography of Paul Revere, has wrought the authentic background for her story of a young Boston silversmith's apprentice who became involved in patriotic activities, including the Boston Tea Party, just prior to the outbreak of hostilities. Famous figures such as Paul Revere and Samuel Adams play important parts in the story.

Johnny Tremain, however, which is in rather wide use as common reading in grades eight to ten, is not a popularized history text. It is a genuine novel of exciting events and character. Tenn-age Johnny is one of the most interesting characters in junior fiction. At the outset of the story he is the completely vain and cocksure young bully. An injury to his hand ends his career as a silversmith's apprentice, completely changes his life, and involves him ultimately in the revolutionary movement. Johnny's personal tribulations are the major subject of the story, but the adolescent reader is able to live with Johnny through the stirring pre-Bunker Hill times in a manner that marks the best in historical fiction.

Several of Stephen Meader's long list of junior novels have historical settings. *A Blow for Liberty,* about a boy's experiences in privateering during the Revolution, was cited earlier. Meader also has written a sort of junior version of *The Red Badge of Courage* in *The Muddy Road to Glory,* in which a farm boy enlists in the Army of the Potomac which pursues and finally corners Lee at Gettysburg. The plots of both books are lusty and taut and there is some attempt at characterization in depth.

Two of the best of the recent stories of frontier life and pioneering are *Snow in the River* by Carol Brink and *The Far-Off Land* by Rebecca Caudill, both authors long established as writers for adolescents. *Snow in the River* is the story of two very different brothers who go to northwestern America from Scotland in the early nineteenth century. The story is narrated by the niece of one of the brothers who recounts memories from childhood—an unusual technique in the junior novel. There is tragedy and realism in the work along with touches of humor and a uniqueness of style. In *The Far-Off Land,* a seventeen-year-old Moravian girl travels with her brother and his family to a settlement in the Tennessee wilderness. A major theme is the protagonist's struggle to maintain her ideals in the face of the warring of Indians and whites.

The Old West of gunfighters and fearless marshals and women of beauty and courage, of stampedes and stage coach robberies seems invulnerable in appeal. The hour-long western romance is a staple of television fiction and accounts for some decline in the output of western novels.

Interestingly, the junior western, of which there are not many, seems of better quality, in general, than its adult counterpart. Perhaps the western best known among young readers is Jack Schaefer's *Shane.* Its plot is traditional horse opera: a lean, mysterious stranger appears at the Starrett farm, takes part in a war between the ranchers and the small farmers, and disappears, much to the chagrin of Bob Starrett, the young adolescent who tells the story. But the characterization of Shane comes through, even though that of the adolescent does not. Fortunately, the incipient love triangle involving Shane and Bob's mother and father never really develops, and there is no other love angle. A sense of values, unusual in western fiction, pervades the story.

A fifteen-year-old boy, son of an Army officer at Fort Dodge, is the principal character in Val Gendron's *Powder and Hides,* suitable for reading in the junior or senior high school. Accompanying two veterans, the boy goes on the last great buffalo hunt in 1873. Gendron's characterization is adequate and her style terse. A strong feeling for the passing of an epoch is threaded through the unmelodramatic story.

Much of the better western fiction has ignored the hackneyed cattle-rustling intrigues and sundown gun duels and has concentrated on the historically significant conflict with the Indians inherent in the westward movement. Elliott Arnold, for example, has been preoccupied with the relations between the Army and the Apaches. In writing a simplified version of his long *Blood Brother,* he has produced a worthy book for adolescents, *Broken Arrow,* dealing with the last stand of Cochise and his strange friendship with the white man, Tom Jeffords.

The Cheyenne Indians, whom she presents with insight, are the interest of Mari Sandoz. Though her style is in general undistinguished, she has a flair for detail in characterization and description and creates an admirable unity of plot. *The Horsecatcher* sensitively traces a Cheyenne boy's struggle for acceptance and prestige in his family and tribe. Younger adolescents may find much to discuss in the Indian boy's rejection of the role of warrior for the more pedestrian one of horsecatcher.

The theme of Eastern tenderfoot "making it" in the West is a familiar one in western fiction. An appropriate example of a reworking of the theme among recent junior novels is Lee McGiffin's *The Mustangers,* in which a New York boy goes to Texas and eventually becomes a first-rate mustanger, capturing his own special horse. The simple but picturesque story gives a real feeling for the Texas of the 1870's.

REPRESENTATIVE BOOKS

Allen, Merritt P., *The Wilderness Way,* McKay. (E)
A capture-by-Indians-torture-and-escape plot featuring an eighteen-year-old who accompanies LaSalle on his ill-fated attempt to reach the mouth of the Mississippi.
*Arnold, Elliott, *Broken Arrow,* Little, Brown.
Brink, Carol, *Snow in the River,* Macmillan.
(Also, *Caddie Woodlawn.* A girl and her family on a Wisconsin farm in Civil War days.)
Butters, Dorothy, *The Bells of Freedom,* Macrae.
A young adolescent boy is caught in a conflict between loyalty to a friend and his patriotism during the siege of Boston during the American Revolution.
Carr, Harriet H., *Gravel Gold,* Farrar, Straus. (E)
A sixteen-year-old prospects for gold in Colorado in the 1850s with moderate success and much adventure.
*Caudill, Rebecca, *The Far-Off Land,* Viking.
Cawley, Winifred, *Down the Long Stairs,* Holt, Rinehart and Winston.
An adolescent boy, his life complicated by his father's death in the Royalist cause in the English Civil War and his mother's decision to marry a Roundhead, runs away to join Royalist recruits.
Chute, Marchette, *The Innocent Wayfaring,* Dutton.
The adventures and romance of a boy and girl who run away from home and meet on the road to London—Chaucer's time. (Also *The Wonderful Winter.* A young man runs away to London and spends the winter acting in Shakespeare's company.)
*Finney, Gertrude, *Muskets along the Chickahominy,* McKay.
*Forbes, Esther, *Johnny Tremain,* Houghton Mifflin.
*Gendron, Val, *Powder and Hides,* McKay. (E)
Lane, Rose W., *Let the Hurricane Roar,* McKay. (E)
A young wife's excruciating winter on a Dakota homestead.
Maddock, Reginald, *The Last Horizon,* Nelson.
A talented South African writer of novels for adolescents tells the story of a young man who led his fellow Bushmen against the Boers.
Malvern, Gladys, *Behold Your Queen,* McKay.

Based on the life of Queen Esther of Persia. (Also *The Foreigner.* The biblical story of Ruth and Naomi.)

*McGiffin, Lee, *The Mustangers,* Dutton.

*Meader, Stephen, *A Blow for Liberty,* Harcourt. (Also *The Muddy Road to Glory.*)

Norton, Andre, *Stand to Horse,* Harcourt. (E) A young cavalry recruit fights the Apaches in 1859.

Patterson, Emma, *The World Turned Upside Down,* McKay. War and romance become real problems to a New York farm boy at the outbreak of the Revolution.

Richter, Conrad, *Light in the Forest,* Knopf. A white boy, reared among the Indians and returned to his parents, goes back to his Indian home and to divided loyalties.

*Sandoz, Mari, *The Horsecatcher,* Westminster. (E)

*Schaefer, Jack, *Shane,* Houghton Mifflin.

Sutcliff, Rosemary, *The Lantern Bearers,* Walck. A tale of Britain after the Roman withdrawal—battle and romance. More complicated and challenging than most novels for the adolescent.

Vocational Stories

Concern with his future role as an adult is a major preoccupation of the adolescent, especially when he reaches the senior high school. From this concern has come the "vocational story," which presents in fictional form information about professions and occupations. These books, though rather widely read, have little significance for the literature program. Most of them could quite fairly be called "subliterary," and many of them have doubtful value as sources of information. The senior high school student who is seriously considering a vocation is inclined—and should be urged—to consult authentic sources of information that lie outside the area of literature.

The vocational novel for adolescents probably had its beginning with the publication of Helen D. Boylston's first Sue Barton story in 1936. The subsequent series that takes Sue Barton through the various stages of her training to become a nurse and subsequent professional life has been extremely popular with girls in their mid-adolescence. For some reason—probably the romantic tradition surrounding the profession—stories of nursing have been a staple in this genre of writing for young people. Another popular series about nursing, somewhat better in quality than Boylston's, is that by Dorothy Deming. Mary Stolz, however, has contributed the best stories of nursing in her *Organdy Cupcakes* and *Hospital Zone.* Though these books lack the introspection and lyricism of other Stolz novels, and the "writing down" in them is evident, they are definitely a cut above most of the others in this genre.

Teaching is another of the professions most commonly treated in the vocational stories. All of them feature young women who encounter tribulations in teaching but who eventually win the devotion of their students. Often, of course, a romance is involved, and the profession is depicted as relatively attractive. One of the best of the more recent junior novels on teaching is Mary Dalim's *Miss Mac,* a supple, witty story of a young teacher's trying moments in the classroom and her romance with the assistant coach.

The better vocational novels, of course, are able to present authentic, unglamorized information in the context of a well-told story. Adele de Leeuw has accomplished this in some of her many vocational stories, the best known of which is probably *With a High Heart,* dealing with rural library work. Also unusually well done is Phyllis Whitney's *A Window for Julie,* in which the heroine starts as a salesgirl in a department store and finally becomes a window-display designer.

Another unusual book that fits loosely into the vocational category is Nancy Hartwell's *Dusty Cloak,* in which the tribulations of getting a start in the professional world of acting are delineated. The heroine experiences disappointment without disillusionment, and a deftly handled love plot is woven skillfully into the well-written story.

It is obvious from this discussion that most of the vocational stories are written for girls, though some of the boys' books, not principally vocational, include details about occupations and professions. The talented Nat Hentoff's fine story, *Jazz Country,* might conceivably be called a vocational novel. It is the story of a white boy's struggle to break into jazz music in Harlem.

Science Fiction

The teacher of adolescents is keenly aware of the modern vogue of science fiction, which is likely to envelop boys in about the ninth or tenth grade. Developing rapidly since the mid-1920's, science fiction was given tremendous impetus, as was science nonfiction, by the exploding of the atomic bomb—which ushered in a era possibly more fantastic than the science fiction writers had ever imagined. In his illuminating book, *Inquiry into Science Fiction,* Basil Davenport identifies the basic appeal of science fiction:

> . . . That man is a creature with awesome potentialities for achievement and for self-destruction, and that the inhabitants of Earth are not the only powers in the universe—these are truths that men have never been able to forget for more than a generation or two. It is science fiction which is telling them to us now." [11]

Science fiction reflects man's eternal curiosity about the unknown and his fascination with predicting the future. The fantastic imaginings of one day, the prophecies of science fiction, become the commonplace realities of another. The reader of science fiction asks himself, "How long before this will come true?" In March 1944, barely a year before the dropping of the first atomic bomb, *Astounding Science Fiction* magazine carried a story entitled "Deadline," about atomic weapons and how they were made. The story prompted an FBI investigation because the government was convinced there was a "leak" from the research laboratories!

Basil Davenport points out that science fiction, although in its present form dating from the founding of *Amazing Stories* in 1926, has forerunners that extend back across centuries. Francis Bacon's *The New Atlantis* in 1627, for example, predicted submarines, airplanes, refrigeration, and the conveying of sound over long distances. Of course, a specially important ancestor of science fiction is Jules Verne's *Twenty Thousand Leagues under the Sea,* still relatively popular with adolescents. In the early twentieth century H. G. Wells's fiction predicted atomic energy, rockets, and helicopters, among other things.

Like the western story and other popular forms of fiction, space adventure is widely associated with the comic book and the juvenile movie and television programs. Yet science fiction covers a broad range of subjects other than space travel, from radioactive mosquitoes

---

[11] Basil Davenport, *Inquiry into Science Fiction* (New York: McKay, 1955), p. 81.

to extrasensory perception, and some of its writers have risen to a rank of respectability in contemporary literature. Significantly, selections of science fiction have begun to appear in junior and senior high school literature anthologies.

Basil Davenport and other critics have identified several kinds of science fiction: the "space opera," the story based on scientific hypotheses, the gadget piece, the speculative story, and the fantasy. The space opera is that story in which the wild profusion of events just happens to occur in outer space instead of in the jungle, on the cattle range, or in the New York City underworld. It is the typical pulp-magazine adventure story in which the only requirement is action.

The gadget story, apparently in decline now, and the story based on scientific hypotheses both utilize scientific material. Based usually on some curious scientific fact, the gadget story is focused on a device. Some writers of science fiction, like Isaac Asimov who is a scientist himself, have utilized known information to develop and extend a hypothesis through a process of logical reasoning. Excellence or the lack of it in this type of story, dear to the original science fiction fan, who is at least an amateur scientist, may be lost on the ordinary reader— who may not be able to tell a ridiculous "scientific" hypothesis from a sound one. For example, as Davenport points out, many stories have included man fighting insects as large as man himself. The impossibility of this is not evident to the person who does not realize that because of the difference in circulation between mammal and insect, an insect cannot be much bigger than a tarantula or a mammal much smaller than a shrewmouse.

All science fiction is based essentially on the projection into the future of present trends or tendencies. The speculative story, however, is likely to be based on trends outside the natural sciences. From the nineteenth century, Edward Bellamy's *Looking Backward,* uncannily accurate at points, is still fascinating. It is interesting that contemporary authors of the speculative story usually foresee a grim future in which man, through his own distorted values, is again living in caves or in abject slavery.

Discussion of science fiction in class might lead into a writing assignment to which adolescents usually respond with interest—projecting into the future a trend they discern in the present. Or, conversely, the writing assignment may lead into discussion of science fiction. The main value of science fiction in the high school literature program lies not in any back door to scientific information that it might open nor in any light it might throw on eternal themes in human experience— though it may possibly have both these values. For some students, science fiction will provide another type of vicarious adventure, helping to satisfy the appetite for the unusual. Perhaps for even more students, science fiction is a respectable form of fantasy, the usual varieties of which are not popular in the adolescent culture, where the need for occasional fantasy is kept well camouflaged. "Fairy" tales, magic carpets, and jinns are not for the adolescent. But their counterparts, space ships and time machines and otherworld creatures, may be because they are tied, implausibly or not, to something called science. The main value of science fiction in the high school literature program lies in the fact that interest in the better-level science fiction may lead to a taste for other explorations of the unknown and unworldly in prose and poetry.

Science fiction is popular with adults as well as adolescents, and many of the science fiction novels popular with adolescent readers were written for the general reading public. The two principal writers who have concerned themselves with books specifically for adolescents are Robert Heinlein and Lester Del Rey. Heinlein's work is less unworldly than most science fiction. His concerns are family life and human problems, and experiences similar to those of today, in future settings. His books are also more lighthearted than most other science fiction novels. *Citizen of the Galaxy,* for example, is the story of a young businessman's problems with his family's interplanetary interests. *The Rolling Stones* recounts the interplanetary vacation of a family that buys a used rocket. In *Farmer in the Sky,* a group of colonists settle on one of Jupiter's moons and struggle to survive in an inhospitable climate. Lester Del Rey turns out well-plotted, absorbing stories with youthful protagonists. One of his better recent books is *The Runaway Robot,* in which a sixteen-year-old and his robot escape from a rocket ship and experience an assortment of adventures throughout the solar system.

In the list that follows some of the better adult science fiction novels are listed along with those written for adolescents.

REPRESENTATIVE BOOKS

Asimov, Isaac, *Caves of Steel,* Doubleday.
A robot teams with a human detective in solving a mystery in the New York City of the future.

Bonham, Frank, *The Loud, Resounding Sea,* Crowell-Collier-Macmillan.
An adolescent's adventures with a dolphin that talks.

Bradbury, Ray, *The Martian Chronicles,* Doubleday.
An earth group visits Mars in the twenty-first century.

Brown, Fredric, *Martians, Go Home,* Dutton.
The funniest science fiction episode results when the Martians—two and a half feet tall, green, and with very unpleasant personalities—invade Earth.

Del Rey, Lester, *Outpost of Jupiter,* Holt, Rinehart and Winston.
A plague threatens to wipe out the settlers on Ganymede until the Jupiter creatures assist them. (Also *The Runaway Robot,* Westminster.)

Heinlein, Robert, *Citizen of the Galaxy,* Scribner. (E)
(Also *Tunnel in the Sky, The Red Planet, Rocket Ship Galileo, Space Cadet, *The Rolling Stones, *Farmer in the Sky.*)

Leinster, Murray, *The Last Space Ship,* Frederick Fell.
A strong social theme underlies this prophecy of future despotism; "matter transmitters" are featured.

L'Engle, Madeleine, *A Wrinkle in Time,* Farrar, Straus.
A highly unusual story of three young people's search through a fifth-dimensional world for a missing physicist and their encounter with an evil being who threatens the freedom of the universe.

Norton, Andre, *Star Rangers,* Harcourt.
Adventures of a space patrol in A.D. 8054. "Mind control" plays a dominant part.

Shute, Nevil, *On the Beach,* Morrow.
The few survivors of a cobalt war find they are doomed from radiation.

NOVELS OF SOCIAL PROBLEMS

The tradition of social significance and of social protest has been a major one in the literature of the world. In 1956 the New American Library published a paperbound edition of the book by Robert B.

Downs entitled *Books That Changed the World.* On the cover is a reference to the fact that the books discussed "caused people to revolt against oppression, started wars, and revolutionized man's ideas about the universe and himself." Many of the books discussed in this particular volume do not belong in the sphere of imaginative literature; yet the novel has been a powerful shaper and inciter of public opinion on social issues and conditions. In the nineteenth century, Victor Hugo, with *Les Misérables,* and Charles Dickens, with books like *Oliver Twist,* centered attention on social injustice in France and England. One of the most incendiary books in American history is Harriet Beecher Stowe's *Uncle Tom's Cabin.* It is generally conceded that Upton Sinclair's powerful *The Jungle,* which revealed conditions in the Chicago stockyards at the turn of the century, was influential in bringing the passage of the pure food and drug laws. Sinclair Lewis' widely read novels savagely attacked America's small-town business culture. Later in the century John Steinbeck dramatized the plight of the migrant worker in *The Grapes of Wrath;* Richard Wright, in his *Native Son,* protested angrily against the condition of the Negro; Laura Hobson attacked anti-Semitism in *Gentlemen's Agreement;* Willard Motley pointed to the relationship between delinquency and living conditions in *Knock on Any Door;* Irwin Shaw etched the dilemma of the American liberal, caught between communism and extreme reaction, in *The Troubled Air.* The fundamental protest against conditions that diminish man and his spirit is reflected in the literature of all periods.

Teachers have realized for a long time, apparently, that literature which deals with social or group problems can aid in improving human relations and in developing a rational approach to social problems, an approach based upon an awareness of alternatives in our group life. First, literature can help to relieve group tensions by stressing the universals, the basic similarities in life as it is lived at many different levels and under many different conditions in our American society and in our world. Although we have in our society a number of economic levels, people in these varying groups are faced with the same basic need for finding some measure of success and happiness.

The basic problem of finding his or her place, of harmonizing the various forces playing upon him or her, is the same for the Seminole

Indian boy in Zachary Ball's *Swamp Chief,* the young Negro boy in Louisa Shotwell's *Roosevelt Grady,* and the older adolescent boy in S. E. Hinton's *The Outsiders,* although the three are of different nationalities and races, live in different parts of the country and are the products of vastly different cultures and environments. The dramatization of what different people have made of life under different conditions helps to make literature the integrating force it always has been in men's lives.

This integrating function can be applied, too, to literature dealing with the various minority groups. Books about Negro life and problems not only portray the unique problems of people of the Negro race, although these are important, but also serve the function of helping Negro children to find satisfaction in life, its beauty and humor as well as its squalor and pathos—as Langston Hughes suggests in *Not Without Laughter,* the story of a Negro boy's struggle to get an education.

The second of the dual purposes which literature serves in human relations is to develop a sensitivity to the problems of people living under conditions different from one's own and to reveal the stake each of us has in the plight of other groups. Most readers come away from Richard Wright's *Native Son,* for example, not only with a depressed feeling about the tragic and sordid net of circumstances in which Bigger Thomas is entrapped but also with an awareness of the importance for all of us of Bigger's experience. Wright's novel is meant to pose a problem, stir action. The same is true of Motley's *Knock on Any Door* or Steinbeck's *The Grapes of Wrath.*

Closely allied to the function of literature in improving human relations is that of aiding students to become aware of alternative approaches to group problems. Such awareness is the touchstone of the informed, individual conscience for which we can never substitute the censorship of constituted authority.

> The vicarious participation in different ways of life may have a . . . broadly social liberating influence. The image of past civilizations or of past periods within our western civilization, as well as images of life in other countries today, can help the youth to realize that our American society is only one of a great variety of possible social structures. When this insight has been attained, the individual is able to look at the society about him more rationally. He is better able to eval-

uate it, to judge what elements should be perpetuated and what elements should be modified or rejected.[12]

This "broadly social liberating influence" of which Dr. Rosenblatt speaks will not be manifest so much in terms of changed attitudes as in this awareness that alternative solutions to problems often exist. The whole matter of the relationship of a person's reading to his attitudes is a complex and controversial one, but research tends to indicate, for example, that the person who considers the Negro race anthropologically inferior to the white will not necessarily change his attitudes after reading Arna Bontemps' *We Have Tomorrow,* and may only deepen his prejudice by reading *Native Son,* although people with less entrenched predispositions may modify their attitudes considerably.

Intelligent reading in controversial literature makes for the informed conscience, the awareness of alternatives, which remains our best hope for finding solutions to group problems. One forte of literature is that it can translate the intangibles of experience—great abstractions such as equality, justice, freedom, and security—into the specific feelings and actions of human beings like ourselves.

Criteria for Judging Fiction Dealing with Group Problems

In judging and evaluating fiction that deals with a social problem, the reader has the formidable task of distinguishing his criticism of the selection as a piece of literature, a work of art, from his opinion of the importance of its theme or message. An ideology may favorably prejudice the reader's estimate of the literary worth of a selection, for when a book deals with values in which we believe deeply, which are interrelated with our security and by which we live, the matter of mere literary technique may become a minor one. On the other hand, a selection, wretched as an example of literary art, may receive serious attention because of the importance of the problem with which it deals. Most literary scholars agree that the importance of *Uncle Tom's Cabin* is historical rather than literary. *Gentleman's Agreement,* a well-known book in recent decades, can scarcely be defended as an

[12] Louise Rosenblatt, *Literature as Exploration* (New York: Appleton, 1938), p. 221.

example of mature technique in fiction, though the problem it emphasizes is vital.

It is important that teachers and librarians select fiction—and teach
students to judge it—as fiction rather than as sociology, economics,
political science, psychology, though fiction may have some elements
in common with all these disciplines. Steinbeck's *The Grapes of
Wrath,* or any other socially significant novel, must stand or fall on its
merits as a novel and not on its importance sociologically. This is
equally true of books written specifically for adolescents.

How do we distinguish between literary art and propaganda? What
are some criteria that will help students to tell when the socially significant selection is literary art and when it is propaganda, either of the
"good" or "bad" variety?

DOES THE SELECTION PLACE THE MAIN STRESS ON THE TIMELESS
RATHER THAN THE TIMELY?   Because we can say "Yes" to this question about *Anna Karenina,* for example, the novel stands as one of the
greatest of the world, though all the artifacts of life in nineteenth-cen-
tury tsarist Russia have changed. The human problem of Anna and
her decision remains timeless. Timeless elements are human emotions
and problems and characteristics, though timely events and problems
may have inspired many a timeless story. It is relatively unimportant
that Dickens' *A Tale of Two Cities* has as its background the French
Revolution; its memorable characters make the book live.

IS THE READER GIVEN ALTERNATIVES IN EMOTION OR ARE HIS FEEL-
INGS RIGIDLY CHANNELED?   This question, like any other that might
be posed in making a judgment of literature, brings different answers
from readers of the same selection. A principal characteristic of propaganda, whether in fiction or in some other form, is the attempt to direct the emotions into a narrow channel. Objectivity, in the sense of
impartiality, is not important. Little socially significant fiction is objective; much of it is impassioned. The essential difference again can be
defined in terms of characterization: Does the author make us feel
with the characters or only *about* them? When we feel *with* characters
we become concerned with the "why" rather than the "what" of
human acts; we are concerned with the basis of motivation. Thus, we
are offered alternatives in feeling.

Richard Wright's *Native Son* illustrates the point clearly. Though it
is an angry protest, the book offers the reader grounds for different

ways of feeling about the final result. Bigger Thomas, a teen-age Negro, is the semihoodlum product of the Negro district in a large northern city. He gets an unusual "break," a job as chauffeur for a wealthy family. One evening the daughter of the family, whose parents think she is attending a concert, persuades Bigger to drive her and the man with whom she is having an affair on a round of night clubs. When they arrive home, the daughter, who has gotten drunk, makes advances to Bigger, who is terrified that the whole matter may be discovered. He gets her to her room, but in a desperate attempt to keep her quiet, accidentally suffocates her. Then in panic he takes the body to the basement and puts it into the furnace, finding it necessary to sever the head from the body. The rest of the story concerns the flight and capture of Bigger, his trial and execution.

Most readers feel sympathy with Bigger, though few would excuse his crime, made purposely horrible, and few would deny the justice of his execution. On the surface, the reader has every right to believe that Bigger got what he deserved. The propagandist melodrama would probably have had Bigger "framed" by a white man. Considering the "why" of Bigger's act, the thoughtful reader is led to a condemnation of certain elements in the social system. And, of course, this was Richard Wright's purpose. In short, the novel has a message but it rises above the level of propaganda. The same thing could be said, for example, of *Oliver Twist* or *Les Misérables*. The reader tends to hate Fagin in *Oliver Twist* and Javert, the relentless pursuer of Jean Valjean in *Les Misérables,* but he understands why they are as they are, how they "got that way." Novelist Jessamyn West makes this point in a memorable article:

> Openness, persisted in, destroys hate. The novelist may begin his writing with every intention of destroying what he hates. And since a novelist writes of persons, this means the destruction (through revelation) of an evil person. But in openness the writer becomes the evil person, does what the evil person does for his reasons and with his justifications. As this takes place, as the novelist opens himself to evil, a self-righteous hatred of evil is no longer possible. The evil which now exists is within; and one is self-righteous in relation to others, not to oneself. When the writer has himself assumed the aspect of evil and does not magisterially condemn from the outside, he can bring to his readers understanding and elicit from them compassion. This is why we do not, as readers,

hate the great villains of literature. Milton does not hate Satan; nor Thackeray, Becky; nor Shakespeare, Macbeth. For a time Milton *was* Satan; Thackeray, Becky; Shakespeare, Macbeth. And the openness of the novelist (together with his talent and his skill) permits us, his readers, though we know that Satan must be cast down and that Macbeth must die, to respond to them without narrowness—with compassion instead of hatred.[13]

WHATEVER PROBLEM IS DEALT WITH, DOES THE STORY REPRESENT THE TRUE ART OF THE STORYTELLER?   The nature of the social problem on which the story centers, no matter how pressing it may be in contemporary society, has nothing to do with the worth of the selection as literature. The appeal of the original, well-constructed story must be there. Social significance cannot compensate for the absence of heroic or tragic or comic heroes and deeds, and of disciplined structure and artistic use of language.

These three are criteria that the high school student can learn to apply to all fiction, junior and adult.

RECENT JUNIOR NOVELS

In the revised edition of this book, the author noted the reluctance of junior novelists to treat social themes, a reluctance with certain obvious explanations: first, it is difficult to write a first-rate story of present-day social conflicts within the conventions, and especially the taboos, of the junior novel; second, adolescents, as a whole, for some years have not been greatly interested in social issues. The situation has changed somewhat, however, in very recent years. There has been a relaxing of taboos to some extent in the junior novel and a greater tendency on the part of writers to disregard traditional conventions. Too, young people of late have become much more concerned with social problems.

In the several years since the revised edition of this book was written, there has been a quickening of interest in certain social problems and a slackening of interest in others among writers of junior novels. The breakthrough in integration of the races in the schools and the

---

[13] Jessamyn West, "Secret of the Masters," *Saturday Review* (September 21, 1957), 13–14 and elsewhere.

heightened racial tension in the nation are reflected in the publication of junior fiction concerning Negro-white relations. Similarly, the increased recognition of the plight of the slum-dweller and disadvantaged generally has resulted in an increase of junior novels centered on young people in unfortunate social-economic situations. On the other hand, what was a flood of books a few years ago on the relations between ethnic and religious groups has abated greatly today.

Not only has the number of junior novels treating Negro-white relations increased, but the quality, in general, has improved in recent years. The mealy homilies which most of the earlier books represented have been replaced by at least a few junior novels which have reached a new depth of interest and feeling without obtrusive didacticism, though the taboos and happy endings are still there.

In her useful work, *Negro Literature for High School Students,* Barbara Dodd writes:

> In their dealing with race, junior novels tend to be optimistic. They usually relate specific incidents that high school students are likely to meet, like discrimination in athletics or student activities. Since they describe specific instances of discrimination rather than the cumulative psychological effects of prejudice, junior novels frequently have a happy ending. Those included here can be effective in helping white middle-class adolescents to understand Negro youths, for all show vividly the frustration and resentment of Negro youths when they are subjected to the common types of high school discrimination. Some of these novels may encourage white youths to stop discriminating; at least these books can help make white youths a little more sensitive to the feelings of their Negro classmates.
>
> Dealing as they do primarily with middle-class Negroes in integrated situations and often being written by white authors, junior novels do not reveal the explosive bitterness of the ghetto, the topic of many adult novels. Because junior novels generally hold to middle-class values and taboos—forbidding profane language, mention of sexual intercourse, or episodes of violence–they are unrealistic or too "nice," at times.[14]

Junior novels of Negro-white relationships continue to be set mostly outside of the South, despite the fact that problems of desegregation of the schools have been most severe in the South. Two earlier little novels by Jesse Jackson, a Negro writer, remain readable among

14 NCTE, Champaign, Ill., 1968, p. 69.

the better stories which incorporate the race relations theme while retaining a lively plot line. In *Call Me Charley,* Charley Moss, a thirteen-year-old Negro, moves into a formerly white neighborhood, where he has a paper route, and becomes the first Negro to attend the junior high school in the area. Charley is subjected to some hazing, and he encounters prejudice on the part of both age mates and adults, but he finds that the majority of his acquaintances come to judge him as a person. The story is lively and supple, free of sentimentalism, with a social thesis made clear—that the hope of the Negro lies in *some* white people, provided the Negro is willing to make the best of himself under the existing conditions. *Anchor Man,* the sequel, finds Charley a senior, a member of the track team, and still the only Negro in the school. When other Negro students are transferred to the school, Charley is caught in an emotional no man's land, becoming the pivotal figure in the tense situation that develops. Jackson's books have a fair depth of characterization and the scenes of adolescent boys together are most skillful.

One of the best school stories with the theme of Negro-white relations is Hila Colman's *Classmates by Request.* This is the story of two families, one Negro and one white, and their involvement in school desegregation and racial tension in a northern town. The focus of plot and point of view shift back and forth from one to the other of the protagonists, the teen-age daughters in each family, who become friends when a few white students integrate a formerly all-Negro high school to support the demands of the Negro community for integration. However, when the white girl's father, who is appointed chairman of a commission to resolve racial problems, refuses to appoint the Negro girl's father to a position he expected, the two girls become estranged. They are brought together again in a demonstration against racial inequity which ends the book. Even though the novel falters on characterization and occasionally in plot, the writer's interest in matters literary as well as social is evident, and the book affords an insight into the complex web of racial tension.

Another competent school story of race relations is Catherine Marshall's *Julie's Heritage,* in which a Negro girl encounters prejudice in a predominantly white high school. Her problem—and the theme of the story—is how to stand up for her heritage as a Negro and still develop cordial relations with both Negroes and whites. Through the main character and three Negro friends, the author illustrates four different reactions to prejudice. Of course, in neither the Colman or Marshall novel is the love element lost sight of, though it is minor in both.

Among nonschool stories of Negro-white relations with girls as main characters, the best one the author has read is Catherine Blanton's *Hold Fast to Your Dreams* in which Emmy Lou Jefferson, whose main interest is ballet dancing, goes to Arizona to live with an aunt and to avoid the handicap of race prejudice in her Alabama town. However, she encounters prejudice in Arizona, too: her dancing teacher is forced to take a lead part in the school ballet away from Emmy, and there is an attempt to keep her out of the civic ballet in the town. However, Emmy Lou wins recognition and the book ends on a note of hope. Although the style is terse and the story well paced, there is little introspection or depth of character portrayal.

Of the recent books with boys as main characters, three stand out in the author's reading: the versatile Frank Bonham's *Durango Street* and Lorenz Graham's *South Town* and *North Town. Durango Street,* the story of a Negro delinquent, is hard-hitting for a junior novel. It begins when Rufus returns from a reform camp to the gang culture of his ghetto neighborhood. The major conflict is that between Rufus' desire to "go straight" and improve himself and the entrapping nature of his environment which makes him need the gang. The ending, which leaves Rufus's future uncertain, is less pat than that of most junior novels of this type.

Lorenz Graham's two books rise above the field both in social insight and literary quality. *South Town,* one of few junior novels of race relations set in the South, is the story of teen-age David Williams and his family's resistance to discrimination which ultimately leads to violence and to the Williams's decision to leave the South. In the sequel, *North Town,* David enters an integrated school and finds that his problems are not over. He has difficulty with both white and Negro students, and through a combination of circumstances is dropped from the football team. In the end, he succeeds in school and in football. Neither of Graham's books is distinguished by quality of writing, but both probe sincerely into reality and into the emotions of characters.

Nothing of particular note has been done recently in the junior novel with intercultural relations other than those of Negro and white, but a few of the earlier works remain readable and deserve continuing mention. Two simple, brief stories by Zachary Ball, *Joe Panther* and *Swamp Chief,* feature, in the context of exciting stories, the problems of a young teen-age Seminole Indian boy in the Florida Everglades country who has one foot in the primitive culture of his people and another in the cosmopolitan life of Miami.

The problems of Spanish-Americans in the United States have been the focus for a number of junior novels. In this category, Florence Means has made a notable contribution, especially in *Alicia,* in which a Denver girl of Mexican heritage rids herself, while attending the University of Mexico, of her feelings of inferiority about her background. As usual, Mrs. Means does not let her message interfere with a good story. In this same area, Lucille Mulcahy captures the spirit and the idiom of the Spanish-American people in the Rio Grande Valley of New Mexico in her book, *Pita.* The plot of the story is slight, centering on teen-age Pita's problems at school and at home. Pita's father is the most interesting character in this book. Definitely in the protest vein is Phyllis Whitney's *A Long Time Coming.* After her mother's death, Christie Allard goes to live with her Aunt Amelia in the town in which her father, who had been divorced from her mother, owns a canning plant. The plant depends upon imported Mexican labor, and the story is mainly about the attempts of Christie and her friends to secure better living and working conditions for the Mexicans and to counter the prejudices of people like Aunt Amelia who consider the Mexican inferior. Although the various attitudes toward the Mexican laborers are skillfully identified, there is little characterization and some of the scenes are overdone. Christie's somewhat pallid romance with a young newspaperman is not too successful in injecting added interest.

Among the recent books centering on the problems of the disadvantaged and slum dwellers, one is outstanding—S. E. Hinton's *The Outsiders.* This is the hard-hitting, violent story of three brothers, ranging in age from fourteen to nineteen, who live alone and are part of the gang life of a tough New York City neighborhood whose inhabitants are known to those outside it as "greasers." The teen-age greasers are at war with the teen-age "socs," equally gang-minded boys from more fortunate neighborhoods. Ponyboy, the fourteen-year-old first-person narrator, and a friend are attacked one night by a gang of socs, and Ponyboy's friend kills one of them. The two boys flee and hide outside the city in an abandoned church which, while they are away on one occasion, catches fire, trapping some children who are picnicking in the vicinity. Ponyboy and the friend rescue the children, but the friend is fatally injured. The story is climaxed with a great "rumble" between the greasers and socs, after which understanding is established between the two groups. The story ends with the social welfare authorities looking into the plight of Ponyboy and his brothers, a relatively happy ending but not a pat, rainbow wrap-up. Though the "coming to understand" theme involving the socs and greasers seems unreal and contrived, *The Outsiders* is a moving story of teenage crime and gang life, with a true insight into the effects of environment on a sensitive, intellectually inclined boy. The book is a definite contribution to the art of the junior novel.

A few of the older stories, too, of young people in unfortunate economic situations deserve continuing interest. The talented junior novelist Mary Stolz, in *Ready or Not* and *Pray Love, Remember,* deals in sequence with a New York City semi-tenement family in which the mother is dead. Though neither story conceivably could be called a protest, Stolz, through skillful use of detail, makes the reader feel keenly the protagonists' feelings toward their environment—the moments of dull hopelessness in which the griminess seems to close in, the moments of elation, and the yearning for better things.

Always preoccupied with social themes but always the conscious storyteller, prolific Florence Means has produced a commendable story in *Knock at the Door, Emmy.* Emmy is the teen-age daughter in an itinerant family living in a pickup truck that carries them from one work area to another. Eager for education, Emmy yearns to "settle down" somewhere, and she detects the same longing in her mother. The settling down is achieved in a story marked with a great sympathy, but not sentimentality, toward the characters—even the shiftless father—and a vibrant style. Despite her concern with the social theme, Means recognizes the need for incident, and there are exciting ones worked into the texture of the story, not dragged in. The rather coy and naïve love plot is the poorest feature of an essentially fine story.

REPRESENTATIVE BOOKS

Ball, Dorothy, *Hurricane,* Bobbs-Merril. (E)
  Loosely-plotted, unpretentious but absorbing story of the friendship of
  a white and Negro boy in the Florida back country.
Ball, Zachary, **Joe Panther* and **Swamp Chief,* Holiday. (E)
Blanton, Catherine, **Hold Fast to Your Dreams,* Messner.
Bonham, Frank, **Durango Street,* Dutton.
Carson, John F., *The Twenty-third Street Crusaders,* Farrar, Straus.
  A gang of teen-aged hoodlums is reconstructed through participation
  in a church basketball league and the help of the coach who is recon-
  structing his own life.
Colman, Hila, **Classmates by Request,* Morrow.
DeLeeuw, Adele, *The Barred Road,* Macmillan.
  The story of a white high school girl's battle of conscience over belief
  in integration and interest in popularity.
Graham, Lorenz, **South Town,* Follett, and **North Town,* Crowell-Col-
  lier-Macmillan.
Hinton, S. E., **The Outsiders,* Viking.
Jackson, Jesse, **Call Me Charley* (E) and **Anchor Man* (E), Harper &
  Row.
Jacobs, Emma, *A Chance to Belong,* Holt, Rinehart and Winston.
  A teen-age Czech boy in New York City is caught between American
  teen-age mores and his European family culture.
Marshall, Catherine, **Julie's Heritage,* McKay.
Means, Florence, **Alicia* and **Knock at the Door Emmy,* Houghton Mif-
  flin.
  (Also *Tolliver,* Houghton Mifflin.) A Negro girl, graduate of Fisk
  University, regains faith and romance through experience as a teacher
  and freedom rider.
Mulcahy, Lucille, **Pita,* Coward-McCann.
Stolz, Mary, **Ready or Not* and **Pray Love, Remember,* Harper & Row.
Tunis, John R., *The Catcher from Triple A,* Harcourt.
  A Jewish catcher from the minors makes good on a major league base-
  ball team.

NOVELS OF THE ADOLESCENT CULTURE

Books about the adolescent culture, the stresses and preoccupations
and mores of the teen-age period, represent the bulk, as well as the

highest achievement, of work in the junior novel. Most of the books in this category deal with the personal problems of individual adolescents in their family and peer culture.

Personal Problems and Literature

What significance do the personal problems of adolescents have for the junior and senior high school literature program? Certainly, it is not the burden of the literature program alone to help students solve their personal problems. Reading of books can never be the sole means of solving problems at any stage of life, and to the high school student the entire school curriculum, along with varied out-of-school influences, should offer help. The study of literature has other objectives, among them to contribute to the esthetic life of the individual and to acquaint each person with his cultural heritage.

Yet there are highly important connections between the personal problems of students and their study of literature. For one, the problems that vex students can motivate reading and can provide an opportunity to convince students that literature really is a reconstruction of experience, that it is related to things that are important and vital to them, not just something vaguely cultural and worthwhile, in the eyes of adults, upon which to spend leisure time.

It is important for the teacher to keep in mind the key role of identification in the literary experience. When the adolescent locates in fiction a kindred spirit, a fellow sufferer, the identification is acute and moving, and an important step has been taken in esthetic development.

Does this identification, the vicarious attack upon one's problems through identification with a fictional character, help one to solve his real problems? Research can give no definite answer to this, though many readers have vouched for the personal therapy of literature. It is safe, at least, to assume that the literary experience gives the adolescent a chance to approach his problems from the objective role of observer, to gain greater insight because of the creative writer's power to order experience, to identify the vital components, and to clear away the irrelevancies and ambiguities.

It seems important, however, for the teacher to avoid certain pitfalls in dealing with fiction that takes as its theme the personal problems of adolescents. First, one of the major contributions of literature lies in the understanding it gives of human experience. Thus the major insights into specific problems, whether those of adolescent or adult, will inevitably come through the broader comprehension of human problems that the study of literature affords. It is important for teacher and student to realize that not only the contemporary piece of fiction reflects contemporary problems. Not only the contemporary selection can be vitally related to students' problems. The erosion of time is in itself a criterion of the older book, giving it the power to wash away the irrelevancies and provide a steady view of existence. It is always good in the literature class to link past and present, gaining the rewarding perspective that results. Chaucer's Canterbury pilgrims, for example, live today because their problems are not far different from those of people who ride home on the bus with us each night. And the motivations of Malory's knights are not essentially different from those of the carbugs in our classes. Finally, it is important that the teacher judge—and teach students to judge—the contemporary novel about the adolescent culture on the basis of literary rather than psychological or social criteria alone.

In selecting and recommending novels of the adolescent culture, and in conducting student discussions of them, the teacher might direct attention to three major criteria:

The treatment of the problem. Is the problem dealt with significantly? The nature of the problems that the book treats is unimportant. The run-of-the-mill book may deal with a serious problem, the estrangement of father and son, for example, and yet treat it superficially and patly with no real insight into its genesis or the motivations of the people involved. On the other hand, some junior novelists are prone to take a tongue-in-cheek attitude that assures the reader at the outset that the problem is really not important and that if he will be patient through 240 pages, all will be well.

By what means are problems solved or adjusted to? This is a key question by which the student often will be able to differentiate the valid from the formula piece. In the latter, solutions are often complete and phony, dependent upon external circumstance and coincidence rather than upon any development of the main character. For example, Jim's ambition is to make the football team, but he is woefully inept. His older brother takes him in hand for some private back-yard sessions, and Jimmy becomes a shifty tailback. Or Gretchen is, the wallflower, aspiring to be part of the round of dates and picnics with "the gang." This comes to pass when a worldly-wise aunt shows her certain tricks of dress and mannerism. The better books often avoid any complete and final solution of a problem, emphasizing rather the inner change of the character as he gains greater maturity and understanding.

The viewpoint of adolescence. The most competent novels about the adolescent period—and usually the ones most popular with adolescent readers—are fundamentally serious, presenting characters who are complex people with dignity. Many of the personal-problem novels are actually written from the adult's point of view and turn into faintly camouflaged homilies. The formula book usually plays to the adult grandstand. It is easy, of course, for the adolescent reader to recognize the book that consistently presents the adolescent's point of view, and the student's effort to do so is a good exercise in literary discrimination. A certain tradition in writing about the adolescent, dating probably from Booth Tarkington's *Seventeen,* is still evident in the junior novel. In this, adolescence is a kind of madness, a period about which one will laugh later, and adolescent protagonists are caricatured rather than characterized. The tradition has been particularly evident in motion-picture and television treatments of adolescence, about which the real teen-ager can become indignantly vocal.

The storyteller's art. The point has already been made that the novel centering on personal problems—or any other kind of novel—must be judged finally on the basis of literary rather than psychological (or some other) criteria. In the good junior novel, the art of the story-teller is evident—the author's sensitivity to language, his power to build a compelling, suspenseful story from tragic, comic, or heroic events, the aura of verisimilitude with which he is able to surround the narrative. The realistic story, true to human experience, need not be pedestrian in style or plot.

Three trends are distinguishable in the past few years in junior novels of the adolescent culture. First, as indicated earlier, the books tend to be harder hitting, less frothy, dealing fairly frequently with such themes as broken homes, pregnancy out of wedlock, and delinquency.

Second, though the paucity of good books about the personal problems of teen-age boys still exists, there have been more noteworthy novels of this kind in recent years than formerly. Third, a number of junior novels by non-American writers about adolescents in other lands have appeared in translation.

Representative Junior Novelists

Because of the importance of books about the adolescent culture in the field of the junior novel, it seems appropriate at this point to attempt to evaluate further the achievement in the form with fuller discussions of a few major writers.

Anne Emery

Prolific Anne Emery has enjoyed a huge following among adolescent girls. In content and in structure, Emery's books epitomize the average in the junior novel, though her competency in using language is better than average. Scrupulously observing all the standard taboos, Emery presents a world largely purged of unpleasantness, in which the problems of teen-agers are real but highly manageable. "Wholesome" has frequently been applied to Emery's works, but the wholesomeness is rather frequently overwhelming, and "innocuous" probably is more apt.

Her third-person, single-track narratives proceed rapidly with only mild suspense to a very predictable ending, which lays a satisfactory basis for the sequel. There is lavish use of dialogue and little introspection on the part of the teen-age girls who are the main characters. Along the way there is a satisfying—to the girl reader—amount of detail concerning dates and dress and parties.

Probably part of the appeal of Emery's books lies in the fact that they dramatize the upper-middle-class norm—the secure, the average, the comfortable. The fathers in the stories are professional men, and the Burnaby family, on which centers a major series of Emery's books, lives, for example, on Juniper Lane. Hickory Hill is the name of the farm—and of the book that is a sequel of the 4-H story, *County Fair*—and through the farm runs Lazy Creek. Departures from the norm are rare among Emery characters and are rather severely frowned upon. This is evident most clearly in *High Note, Low Note,* one of the books in the Burnaby family series. Jean Burnaby becomes friendly with Kim Ballard, a new girl in school whose family is bohemian. Jean's parents view the friendship, and the Ballard family, with a very troubled eye, exhibiting, in the eyes of an adult reader, a rather amazing lack of sympathy for Kim. Finally, as the elder Burnabys had feared, Kim leads Jean astray, albeit not too seriously.

Characterization in Emery, in general, is limited to categories rather than individuals. There are five categories: fathers, mothers, adolescent girls, adolescent boys, and less-than-adolescent girls and boys. Within each category, characters are very much alike. Fathers are usually rather vague and preoccupied with their work, coming into the story mainly when money becomes an issue. Mothers are youthful, attractive, calmly philosophical, and intelligent. This description from *Campus Melody* is typical: "Mrs. Burnaby looked cool and fresh as she sipped her second cup of coffee while she wrote out 'Thing to Be Done Today.' "

The theme of "Mother (and occasionally Father) is right" is the most prevalent one, sometimes irritatingly so, in Emery's books. Early in *Going Steady,* Sally decides: "How could her mother be so wise?" And in *High Note, Low Note:* "But deep down underneath, try as she would to ignore it, Jean could not help wondering if her mother were not right." Perhaps the most irritating play for adult favor occurs at another point in *High Note, Low Note.* The morning after a minor tiff with her father over going to a party with Kim Ballard and some other friends, Jean Burnaby comes down the stairs to find at the bottom a paper on which is written: "X marks the spot where the world came to an end last night." And shortly after, Jean decides: "Oh, well . . . it's just as comfortable not to stay mad—especially when you can't win."

The adolescent boys in Emery's books—with the exception of *Vagabond Summer,* in which there are some rather well-developed characters, and the cad in *Campus Melody*—are almost indistinguishable from each other. Scotty, who appears in several books and epitomizes "the boy who lives next door," is exactly like Jeff, for example, who at one point is described thus: ". . . Jeff returned at 7:30, shining with soap and water." And Jean and Sally Burnaby, who share the major roles in the Burnaby series, are identical.

Though not her most popular book, *Vagabond Summer* may be Anne Emery's best, because of its originality and sounder characterization. The story's teen-age heroine goes on a summer hosteling tour with a group of other young people and makes some tentative decisions about her future. In this book, unlike most of Emery's others, there is an interesting group of well-drawn personalities. Of course, there is a radiantly happy ending with the quite typical final lines: "The world lay before them. All their bright young world."

Despite her shortcomings from a literary point of view, Anne Emery has captured the interest of a large number of adolescent girls, and in so doing she has made a contribution. She presents characters who experience, after all, the mundane kind of problems that are true, although not the whole truth, of adolescence. Identification with her characters furnishes no moving experience nor any depth of insight. But her readers find in her books what they are seeking there—entertainment and, to some extent, wish fulfillment.

James L. Summers

The books that James Summers has so far written, though of mediocre literary value, have helped to fill a long-existing gap—competent stories about teen-age problems for boys. The dearth of such books is partly explained by the fact that boys are less interested in the story that centers on teen-age romance and family problems than are girls, and partly because most of the writers of teen-age problem stories are women who choose to write of girls' problems.

Essentially, Summers is a humorist. His books are amusing, at points hilarious, and his over-all approach is light, though he evidences good insight into the adolescent culture. His approach is perilously near caricature, however, when his attempts to amuse sometimes get out of hand. Several reviewers of his books have noted that fathers might enjoy some of the passages more than their sons for whom the books are written. *Wild Buggy Jordan,* for example, the problem-frought story of a high school junior, is a burlesque of the adolescent culture, ranging from the adolescent's philosophy of life to his eating habits.

Like Anne Emery's heroines, Summers' heroes are virtually identical from book to book. Rodney Budlong of *Prom Trouble,* Don Morley of *Girl Trouble,* and Roger Holman of *Trouble on the Run* are all slightly-less-than-average boys who aspire, above all else, to be average. These characters are fit subjects for light treatment and provide easy identification for most readers, who can be genuinely amused at the protagonists' foibles.

Summers' plots are very similar: they involve his heroes, who cannot do anything too well, in two types of problems—love and school. The love plot usually involves the hero's pining for the wrong (as the end of the book shows) girl and a failing (until the end) to appreciate the right girl who was there all the time. The school problem involves the hero's being saddled with a responsibility for which he is not quite qualified. In *Prom Trouble,* Rodney Budlong is elected junior class president as a "gag," and has the task of directing plans for the prom. In *Trouble on the Run,* Roger Holman is put in charge of preparing a float. Both muddle through with moderate success. A variation in *Girl Trouble* has Don Morley having to drop football in order to work so that he can pay a traffic fine.

Like Emery, Summers relies largely on categories of characters and general impressions rather than on detailed delineation. His mother and father categories are similar to Emery's except that Summers' fathers are small businessmen. The Morleys in *Girl Trouble* are typical: "Both the elder Morleys were slim and faintly youthful." Perhaps because of his experience as a high school teacher, Summers is at his best in characterizing school administrators and teachers, whom he treats with kind humor and gentle irony. The details of school life in his books are authentic and genuine.

Summers consistently overwrites, as this passage from *Trouble on the Run* reveals:

> Glenn Harlan, on the other hand, was little and thin and a pretty fair hurdler who would be a neat guy if he could ever lay off math. His brain was water-logarithmed on the stuff and anything he couldn't find the square root of in one minute he regarded with suspicion and disdain. When Harlan was quiet, a person could almost hear his brain whirring around like Univac, feeding itself data about people, distance, and time, squishing the information around in the right tubes, and coming up with the perfect answer. If he hadn't been so boring with

math, he could have been one interesting guy. The way it was, everybody expected him to be blasted off in a Navy rocket in the interests of national defense.[15]

And frequently Summers' dialogue, though usually amusing, is written in a jargon and in patterns of speech that border on the grotesque.

Most of the statements made so far about Summers do not apply to two of his books. One of his most unusual—though not necessarily his best—is *Operation ABC*. Apparently, the author had become interested in the problem of retarded reading ability and had read the work of Fernald or others who have used the "kinesthetic" approach to remedial reading. The book tells an engrossing story of a senior boy who is a retarded reader and very fearful that someone will find out. He faces his problem realistically in an ending that is hopeful but semi-tragic. Summers' most impressive novel, *The Limits of Love,* develops poignantly a theme highly unusual in teen-age fiction. The main characters, a boy and girl just out of high school, face the problem of controlling their passions. Deeply in love, they realize that immediate marriage is impossible, and they agree to separate. The love scenes are handled skillfully; in fact, in this novel Summers' style reaches a level not found in any of his other books. These last two books are proof that Summers can treat a serious theme competently.

Mary Stolz

Undoubtedly the most interesting and accomplished writer of junior novels is Mary Stolz. Though she has produced a surprising number of novels in a short time, the level of quality has remained consistently high. Several of her books are definitely within the conventions of the junior novel; several are iconoclastic.

Essentially, Stolz's books are love stories, though she injects minor social themes in several. Her treatment of love in late adolescence is far different from that of Emery, Summers, or even of Daly's *Seventeenth Summer*. Love, in the Stolz novels, is fraught with a tempestuousness and an anguish that is foreign to most other novels for the adolescent. This is true even of the books in the familiar junior novel

---

[15] From *Trouble on the Run* by James L. Summers. Copyright 1956, by James L. Summers, the Westminster Press, Philadelphia. Used by permission.

pattern—*To Tell Your Love* and *The Sea Gulls Woke Me,* for example. Serious, intense Anne Armacost, of *To Tell Your Love,* suffers a bitter summer of putting on appearances, hoping, waiting for the telephone to ring, and of final hurt when her intenseness "scares off" the boy she loves. The ending, highly characteristic of Stolz, features quiet resignation on Anne's part. Though the members of the Armacost family—father, mother, younger brother—are akin to those in Anne Emery, they come to life to a much greater degree, and the portrait of Anne is a real triumph. As with all the Stolz protagonists, there is a pain in the identification with Anne; the Stolz novels are designed for a more mature and sensitive audience than those of Emery and many other junior novelists. Not at all in the lighthearted manner, the Stolz stories are overhung with a sense of the sadness of life, the possibilities of emotional disaster, and the *weltschmerz* that is highly characteristic of late adolescence.

Stolz has explored the problems of family life as it is lived at several economic levels. In *Ready or Not* and *The Day and the Way We Met,* sequel books, the family lives in a semitenement district in New York City and the father is a subway token seller. The first book concerns the problems of an adolescent girl in managing the household after her mother dies. In the second, the younger sister takes over when the elder marries. *The Day and the Way We Met* is a tender story that shows the typical lack of concern for plot and structure in the late Stolz books. Essentially, it is a well-done character study, but many adolescent readers would find the slow-moving narrative boring. The wonderfully conceived ending finds the heroine answering the phone, wondering—with the reader—which of three men is calling!

Characterization is especially splendid in *Pray Love, Remember.* The theme of this hard-hitting novel is prominent in Stolz—the estrangement of the adolescent heroine from her family. The conflict is particularly marked between Dody Jenks, the heroine, and her older brother, who appears even more loutish in her eyes than he really is. The younger sister is the "ugly duckling" and the contrast between her and Dody is effective. Dody is a highly unusual and interesting character, enigmatic even to herself. She is a great social success in her senior year in high school and much envied, though she is almost without friends. Her essential coldness, making her anything but endearing, is in marked contrast to the heroines of most of the other Stolz books.

All the Emery-Summers patterns of the father and mother and of the family situation are smashed here. The dialogue in general and the dinner table conversations in particular are superb. Graduating from high school, Dody finally escapes her family and the town by taking a position as governess with a wealthy family. Dody's love affair with a Jewish boy seems a rather artificial and tangential addition, and ends with the boy's death in a car accident and Dody's near collapse. However, the end finds her returning to her job as governess with a new sense of her identity.

The originality of *Rosemary* comes as a mild shock. The book begins in a fashion highly standard in teen-age fiction. Rosemary, who is working in a store rather than attending the college in her town, meets the dashing college boy and a date is set. But the boy, quite understandably misinterpreting Rosemary's rather tawdry behavior at a dance, makes a pass at her. This provides the opening trauma in the development of Rosemary's love interests and her relations with several people, including her none-too-appealing father.

Departing completely from the mold of the junior novel is the moving *Two by Two,* the only Stolz story in which a boy is the main character. The plot involves the conflict between Harry Lynch and his father, a wealthy lawyer, and Harry's love affair with Nan Gunning. Sex and the erotic impulses are thoroughly probed in the love plot, which is a far cry from the round of dates, picnics, and cool-lipped kisses of the Emery stories. In fact, Harry and Nan are discovered in her bedroom by her father. And in a scene in which Harry and a friend visit a night club, a waitress "hovered over them, muskily perfumed, in a dress deeply cut at the bodice, confident in a society where mammary worship came second only to mammon worship."

An air of doom hangs over the story; the reader may suspect that Harry will commit suicide. Instead, he kills someone else, a drunkard, accidentally when he drives away from the night club. Actually, the swift ending is happy—the reconciliation of Harry with his own and Nan's father. Like several of the other Stolz books, *Two by Two* is slow moving, full of the introspection, sometimes bordering stream of consciousness, typical of Stolz. The action is mainly psychological and, as in several of her other books, there are rambling lyrical passages at times slightly reminiscent of Thomas Wolfe.

Mary Stolz is a talented and original writer with a deep regard for the dignity of the adolescent. Done in richly subtle shades, rather than in pastels, her work bodes well for the future of the junior novel.

Henry Gregor Felsen [16]

A prolific as well as an extremely versatile author of junior novels is Henry Gregor Felsen. Probably best known for his novels involving cars, his writings also include such diverse subjects as war, humor, and conflict with society.

In his earlier novels, such as *Navy Diver,* the style is masculine, the plot is exciting, and the characters emerge as real with only a slight "willing suspension of disbelief" on the part of the reader. The total effect is a kind of cross between Howard Pease and Ernest Hemingway. However, there are overtones of meaningful issues. In *Navy Diver,* Jeff's best friend on the farm had been a Japanese. Felsen tersely illustrates his hero's conflict during the World War II crisis.

Contrasted with the dramatic conflict portrayed in *Navy Diver* is the slapstick comedy saturating the Bertie novels. The roly-poly protagonist of the series is Bertie Poddle, an overfed junior edition of Walter Mitty. The difference is that Bertie naïvely attempts to make his dreams materialize. His efforts inevitably backfire in hilariously ludicrous situations.

The chapters in the Bertie novels are rather episodic, unified by Bertie himself and his rather motley assortment of type-cast friends— handsome, intelligent Ted Dale and his equally remarkable sister, Marcia; Wiggins Hackenlooper, Heeble High School's powerful full-back; Wilbur Frost, the caustic agnostic who is finally humanized by Bertie's intensely candid efforts; and the female antithesis of Bertie also providing humor, Hyacinth O'Houlihan. Hyacinth, a wild redhead and as skinny as Bertie is phlegmatic, falls in love with Wiggins only because he can beat her at Indian wrestling. These characters are introduced in the initial book of the series, *Bertie Comes Through.*

Bertie provides more than just entertainment, however. Pervading the comic situations are significant ideas. In *Bertie Takes Care,* the hero is rejected as a camp counselor because of his overweight. Making the best of his misfortunes, Bertie herds together the town rejects,

[16] Commentary by Helen O'Hara Rosenblum, formerly of Florida State University.

organizes his own camp, and finally triumphs when beating the snobbish and egotistical baseball team from Camp Ijoboko. The Bertie novels are entertaining stories of achievement and good sportsmanship that especially appeal to younger boys.

Felsen's car novels, however, interest boys (and girls) in a range of junior high school through the late teens. There is no absolute upper interest limit for these stories of life adjustment, especially for the very popular *Street Rod* and *Hot Rod*. Both novels deal with boys in their late teens whose interest in cars is portrayed as a means of adjustment, a kind of compensation or escape from an indifferent culture. Bud Crayne in *Hot Rod* is without parents. School and other societal institutions apparently offer little for Bud. In a defiant gesture reminiscent of Holden Caulfield and Huck Finn, Bud wears an old fedora hat with the brim turned up in front and fastened to the crown with a giant safety pin. He makes his own rules until the guidance of Ted O'Day, a patrolman, and Mr. Cole, a shop teacher, demonstrates the real tragedy of an accident in which all but one of Bud's companions are killed. These characters, like Bud, have all sought refuge from a society where adolescents don't "belong." Felsen vividly conveys the problem of the search for identity. The funeral is, perhaps, a dramatic précis of the theme:

> Avondale buried its dead and their dreams.
> Ralph Osler was buried with his dream of a college career in sports. La Verne Shuler was buried with her dream of escape to Hollywood. Walt Thomas was buried with his dream of getting away from the farm. Marge Anderson was buried with her dream of being popular. And the others were buried with their dreams. There was no buying Ralph out of this scrape, no smiling her way out for La Verne, no blustering his way out for Walt.
> The victims of a careless moment were laid to rest.[17]

The "careless moment" is likewise important in *Street Rod*. Sixteen-year-old Ricky Madison attempts to set up the Dellville Timing Association so that the hot rodders may race without breaking speed laws. When the village council refuses to cooperate, Ricky and his friends operate outside the law. With the help of his girl friend Sharon, Ricky enters and wins an auto-design competition. On his way back from the competition, his careless immaturity results in death.

[17] From Henry Gregor Felsen, *Hot Rod* (New York: Dutton, 1950).

Impulsiveness is dealt with in more profound terms in what may be Felsen's most controversial novel, *Two and the Town*. Buff Cody, the senior football star, has reached his moment of heroic glory only to find it sour in the defeat of the big game. Elaine Truro, overly protected, quiet, and scholarly, gives the rejected Buff genuine sympathy, warm and tender feeling. In this moment of intensity, abstract feelings lose their meaning. With deep psychological insight Felsen describes the situation:

> . . . She became as furiously unrestrained as Buff himself, made one last, frightened effort to break away, and, in a situation where Carol would have laughed and saved herself, Elaine wept and was lost.

The remainder of the novel deals with the manifest problems inherent in a "forced" marriage. Felsen realistically portrays the problem in a specific setting, but the implications of the theme are more universal in scope. Because he deals with very human problems, Henry Gregor Felsen writes novels for young people that capably meet their needs and interests. His themes are communicated in a professional style that may provide an important step in the development of literary appreciation.

Madeleine L'Engle [18]

Madeleine L'Engle's books for young teenagers express a sense of the depth and seriousness of life usually found only in works for older adolescents. With an impressive variety of settings, plots, and interesting characters, she adapts and expands conventional story patterns to accommodate a serious treatment of the adolescent's confrontation with the uncertainties of the adult world. Time and again her protagonists echo the sentiments of John Austin in *Meet the Austins:*

> Why do things have to change and be different! . . . Why do people have to die, and people grow up and get married, and everybody grow away from each other? I wish we could just go on being exactly the way we are!

Because L'Engle's protagonists tend to be young (twelve to fifteen), intelligent and sensitive, and because the seriousness of their problems requires the treatment of serious themes, there is an ambiva-

[18] Commentary by Bryant Fillion, University of Illinois.

lence in several of the novels. The themes and the characters' concerns often seem intended for a more mature audience than the stories or the ages of the adolescent characters are likely to attract. *A Wrinkle in Time,* for instance, which won the 1962 Newbery award, is an interesting and beautifully told children's fantasy, but its complex structure, literary allusions, and chilling portrayal of evil forces in the universe all imply an older reader.

This same ambivalence is found, to some extent, in *Camilla,* best-written of L'Engle's adolescent romances and reminiscent of Maureen Daly's classic, *Seventeenth Summer. Camilla* is the story of fifteen-year-old Camilla Dickinson's first romance and her attempt to cope with the realities of her parents' marital difficulties. Camilla's relationship with Frank Rowan, the sensitive and intense older brother of her best friend, Louisa, helps her to face and understand her mother's illicit love affair and attempted suicide. The picture of upper middle-class life in New York City is well-drawn, the characterization of Camilla, her parents, and the Rowans is excellent, and the first-person narrative is flawless. Camilla's typically early adolescent and increasingly unsatisfactory relationship with Louisa, her relationship with her parents and with Frank, and her growing sense of the sadness and complexity of adulthood are skillfully and believably developed. Yet such concerns may demand more maturity than young teen-agers bring to a novel, and the heroine's age may discourage slightly older adolescents from reading the book, though they could enjoy it more.

In *Camilla,* and in most L'Engle novels, the protagonists' confrontation with the inequities of the adult world—infidelity, death, the confusion of appearance with reality, and social evils—results in a crisis of identity for the adolescent and a desire to return to the securities of childhood. A resolution and deeper awareness are achieved through unselfish love, or a commitment to another person or a cause. This symbolic initiation into the realities of adulthood is handled sympathetically and believably; most of the adolescent dialogues about questions of love, death, personal identity, and God seem remarkably true to the sensitive adolescent's concerns and conversation. The intelligent and sensitive characters who make such awareness and concern plausible are problematic, however. At times, the cultural facility and encyclopedic knowledge of the L'Engle children and adolescents become somewhat overwhelming.

In *And Both Were Young,* most conventional of the L'Engle books, artistic and sensitive Philippa (Flip) Hunter manages to achieve popularity in an exclusive girls' boarding school in Switzerland. The most interesting character in the book is Flip's boy friend, Paul Laurens, a war orphan whose concentration camp experiences have blocked out all memory of his past.

Meet the Austins is an episodic first-person account by Vicky Austin of her family's reactions to a series of events following the death of a close friend of the family, and the arrival of an orphaned ten-year-old girl to stay with them. Dr. Austin, his cultured wife, the four children, and several pets constitute an amusing and interesting household. The children's attempts to reinterpret their secure lives in rural Connecticut and to face the realities of death and change are perceptively portrayed. The sequel, *The Moon by Night,* is more completely Vicky's book, telling of a trip with her family, and her growing difficulties with her parents as she experiences her first serious relationship with a boy, Zachary, of whom her parents disapprove, and his rival, Andy.

In *The Arm of the Starfish,* a novel of mystery and adventure, sixteen-year-old Adam Eddington becomes involved in international intrigue and murder during his summer's work with a famous scientist, Dr. O'Keefe, off the coast of Portugal. The tale is exciting and well told, and there is a serious undertone in Adam's adjustment to adults' deception. Canon Tallis, a mysterious sleuthing priest, and the precocious Polyhymnia O'Keefe are particularly interesting characters. Dr. O'Keefe's statement about his daughter summarizes the "ideal" love in L'Engle novels:

> Poly's greatest talent is for loving. She loves in an extraordinary way for a twelve-year-old, a simple, pure outpouring, with no looking for anything in return. What she is too young to have learned yet is that love is too mighty a gift for some people to accept.

A far-fetched story, but a more serious undertaking, is *The Young Unicorns.* The portrayal of nameless sinister forces, the intense sense of frustration, betrayal, and overwhelming evil, and the building of suspense are skillfully achieved. The protagonist, Josiah Davidson (Dave), a reformed street-gang leader in New York City, looks after Emily Gregory, a blind musical prodigy. Dave, Emily, the Austin family—now living in the city—and Canon Tallis all become involved in a strange plot to take over the cathedral church and New York City. Despite its improbabilities, the story is exciting and notable for its brooding sense of evil and impending catastrophe.

The Love Letters, Madeleine L'Engle's adult novel, interweaves the story of a distraught twentieth-century woman with the story of Sister Mariana, a seventeenth-century Portuguese Nun, who was seduced and abandoned by a French army officer. Although it is technically interesting, the novel will probably appeal to few adolescent readers.

Because her books are well written and true to serious adolescent experience, Madeleine L'Engle's work represents an important achievement in the junior novel.

Other Writers

Betty Cavanna, who is as prolific and nearly as popular as Anne Emery, especially with younger girls, has dealt more convincingly with the adult culture than has Emery, and is more sensitive to the pain as well as the enchantment of the teen-age period. She has a particular gift for handling the scenes in which adolescents are together. One of her most notable books is *Going On Sixteen,* in which shy Julie Ferguson, who grows more confident in the course of the story, is the main character. *The Boy Next Door,* a competently written story, represents the typical admixture of school, love, and family problems in her novels. Her two most interesting variations occur in *Almost Like Sisters* and *A Time for Tenderness.* The former is the most unusual of the author's several mother-daughter stories. In this one, an awkward seventeen-year-old finds her boarding school life complicated when her young, attractive mother comes to live nearby. In *A Time for Tenderness,* a non-happy ending story, teen-age Peggy Jamison's family moves to Brazil where her romance with a Brazilian boy founders on the rocks of social misunderstanding and prejudice. Though her books are uneven and, on the whole, undistinguished, Betty Cavanna maintains a consistently realistic point of view toward the adolescent period. Her humorous, plotless, and episodic books, written under the name Elizabeth Headley, feature Diane Graham, and have been very popular. Though shallow in characterization, these books present effectively the jealousies and rivalries of middle-adolescent girls, and a few of the episodes are memorable—for example, the one in *A Date for Diane,* in which Diane, cringingly sensitive about the new braces on her teeth, discovers that the boy of her dreams has worn braces for months.

Very much in the mold of Anne Emery, and equally popular, in writing of the problems of boy friends and the light side of middle-class family life, is Rosamond Du Jardin. In *Class Ring,* Tobey Heydon, who is the main character in *Practically Seventeen* also, struggles with the problem of going steady and decides, in good didactic fashion, that one should not become too serious too soon. Written competently in the first person, *Class Ring* is light, frequently humorous, and deals with the typical round of boys, dates, and school affairs and with minor family conflicts, such as a crisis involving the length of Tobey's fingernails.

More original than most books of this genre are those by Laura Rendina. Her best book is *My Love for One,* a moving story of a girl's efforts—and her family's—to adjust to a new way of life after the death of the mother. Debbie Jones' quest for fulfillment has an adult depth, and her final satisfaction in love is far from the usual girl-gets-boy pattern. A more recent book, *Lolly Touchberry,* though undistinguished in style, is a better-than-average story of a fifteen-year-old Florida girl, her school, family, and dating affairs. A minor social theme, which finds Lolly thinking faintly that racial segregation is not right, is gingerly presented.

Beverly Cleary's stories, though essentially humorous, are not fluff or burlesque. *Fifteen* handles with unusual skill the theme of the adolescent girl's emergence from the awkward stage, the transition period in which she is learning to suffer in a girdle and turning ankles in high heels. Characterization of the adolescent girls and portrayal of their relations with parents are realistically done, though the dialogue is somewhat unrealistic. The woes of baby-sitting, so much a part of the modern adolescent's culture, are cleverly and convincingly portrayed. *The Luckiest Girl,* though somewhat less successful because of a strained setting—a sixteen-year-old girl rather unbelievably visits friends for a year—has the aura of real modern high school experience, in which grades *are* important, and a feel for the modes of adolescent life. *Sister of the Bride,* a kind of junior counterpart of *Member of the Wedding,* features the involvement of a teen-age girl in the wedding plans of her older sister. The psychological problems the situation brings to both girls are well handled.

Among the better writers for older girls is Zoa Sherburne whose books, though occasionally marred by a pedestrian style, flash occasionally to the dark sides of life and possess unusual originality. *Almost April* is the story of a girl's adjustment to her stepmother, an attractive young woman, and her friendship with a boy figuratively from the "other side of the tracks." *The High White Wall* features an older girl's break with family ties and her romance with a young poet, who is the most interesting character in the story. The mother in this story is well drawn, too. It is unfortunate that the heroine remains a vague character. A mother's return to her family after nine years in a mental hospital is the theme of *Stranger in the House*. The story is supple and moving.

Like Zoa Sherburne, Jeannette Eyerly is one of the writers responsible for putting more substance into the novel of adolescent problems. *The World of Ellen March* traces to a happy conclusion the trauma of a girl whose parents are divorced. *A Girl Like Me* features the theme of teen-age, out-of-wedlock pregnancy. With an unusual and more complicated plot structure than that of most junior novels, the story is narrated by a high school girl who avoids giving way to her passions but whose friend does not. The protagonist's view of the whole situation is altered when she discovers that she is an adopted child, born to an unmarried girl. The scenes in which the narrator visits the friend in the home for unmarried mothers are devastating, but the story ends with the boy marrying the girl.

Catering to the interests of boys is the car or hot rod story of which there are dozens. Chief among their authors are Henry Felsen, Philip Harkins, William Gault, Gene Olson, and Don Stanford. The plot lines and themes are varied, but the appeal remains the same in all of the books—details of car lore and the thrill of the race. The really unusual car story is *Car-Crazy Girl* by Hila Colman who ranges widely in the adolescent culture for her subject matter. The novel has an impact beyond that of the usual junior novel, though it has the unfinished quality of Colman's other books. A seventeen-year-old girl is given a car for her birthday by her upper middle-class suburban parents, who live in an unreal world of comfort and philistinism. Mixed-up Dina causes the death of a boy and receives a short jail sentence which is a catalytic factor for both her and her parents.

Junior novels that treat perceptively the problems of adolescent boys are not numerous, as noted earlier. Some, such as S. E. Hinton's *The Outsiders,* were discussed under other headings earlier in this chapter. One of the best remains the poignant *Swiftwater,* by Paul Annixter, in which lonely fifteen-year-old Bucky Calloway strives to establish a refuge for wild geese. The excellence of the book lies in the fine characterization of Bucky and his family and in the author's unusual flair for conveying the atmosphere of wild places. Noteworthy among more recent books is Emily Neville's story of New York City middle-class life, *It's Like This, Cat,* which delineates a fourteen-year-old boy's year of relationships with his cat, his family, his girl friend, and his various other friends. The novel is loose in plot, strong in characterization and in the treatment of the boy's relations with his parents and peers. Similar to the Neville book in its introspection in treating a young adolescent protagonist and in the father-son conflict is Joseph Krumgold's *Henry 3,* the highly original story of a precocious eighth-grader, I.Q. 154, in a New York City suburban community. Henry's association with a school outcast and his trauma in trying to understand the values of his father's business world are the two major threads in this well-written novel. Worthy of mention, too, is *The Hollow* by Thomas Liggett in which a tough boy is sentenced to a work camp for car theft but is given a new view of life by the understanding manager of the camp.

Publication of junior novels in translation of the adolescent culture in other countries is, in the main, a recent development. Margot Benary-Isbert's excellent books of post-World War II Germany, *The Ark* and *Rowan Farm,* are now, of course, dated and may have lost some of their interest, but they remain sensitive portrayals of family life in that period of devastation. The themes and techniques of the non-American novels are similar to those of their American counterparts, though translation poses a problem in appraising the authors' use of language. Paule Daveluy's *Summer in Villemarie,* for example, is a teen-age romance in the Emery-Cavanna tradition with a French Canadian setting. In Anne Marie Falk's *Who Is Erika?,* a fifteen-year-old Swedish girl faces the problems incident to her mother's remarriage and the family's move to a new town. A French boy's school problems and relations with his parents are the concerns in Michel-Aime Baudouy's *More than Courage*. Outstanding is the Newbery award winner *Shadow of a Bull* by Maia Wojciechowska, in which the son of a great Spanish bullfighter feels impelled to follow his father's career for which he has no taste.

REPRESENTATIVE BOOKS

Annixter, Paul, *Swiftwater,* Wyn.

Baudoy, Michel-Aimé, *More Than Courage,* Harcourt.

Benary-Isbert, Margot, *The Ark,* Harcourt.
   A German family, minus the father who is a Russian prisoner, tries to rebuild life in post-World War II devastation as they move into an abandoned railroad car. (Also *Rowan Farm,* the sequel in which the father returns and Margret is able to plan a trip to the United States.)

Cavanna, Betty, *A Time for Tenderness,* Morrow.
   (Also *Almost Like Sisters,* *Going on Sixteen* (E).)

Cleary, Beverly, *Sister of the Bride,* Morrow.
   (Also *Fifteen* (E) and *The Luckiest Girl.*)

Colman, Hila, *Mrs. Darling's Daughter,* Morrow.
   A realistic treatment of mother-daughter conflicts. (Also *Car-Crazy Girl.*)

Daly, Maureen, *Seventeenth Summer,* Dodd, Mead.
   A classic, though now dated, junior novel of first serious love and a memorable seventeenth summer for Angie Morrow.

Daveluy, Paule, *Summer in Villemarie,* Holt.

DuJardin, Rosamond, *Class Ring,* Lippincott.
   (Also *Practically Seventeen.*)

Emery, Anne, *Going Steady,* Westminster.
   Two high school seniors plan to be married but change their minds after thinking it through. (Also *Campus Melody,* *High Note, Low Note,* *Vagabond Summer.*)

Eyerly, Jeannette, *A Girl Like Me,* Lippincott.
   (Also *The World of Ellen Marsh.*)

Falk, Anne Marie, *Who Is Erika?,* Harcourt.

Felsen, Henry Gregor, *Bertie Comes Through,* Dutton. (E)
   Bertie, the fat boy, tries everything in school activities, but never quite makes the grade in anything by the affections of his classmates. (Also *Bertie Takes Care* (E), *Hot Rod,* *Street Rod,* *Two and the Town.*)

Gault, William C., *Dirt Track Summer*, Dutton.
Two brothers take to dirt track racing against the wishes of their father, himself in the racing game.
Harkins, Philip, *Road Race*, Crowell-Collier-Macmillan.
A boy builds a jalopy into a hot rod club winner.
Hartwell, Nancy, *My Little Sister*, Holt, Rinehart and Winston.
Two teen-age sisters find serious conflicts between their parents' ideas and those of their social crowd.
Headley, Elizabeth, *A Date for Diane*, Macrae. (E)
Krumgold, Joseph, *Henry 3*, Atheneum.
L'Engle, Madeleine, *The Arm of the Starfish*, Farrar, Straus.
(Also *Camilla*, *The Love Letters*, *A Wrinkle in Time*, *The Moon By Night*, *Meet the Austins*, *And Both Were Young*, *The Young Unicorns*.)
Liggett, Thomas, *The Hollow*, Holiday.
Neville, Emily, *It's Like This, Cat*, Harper & Row.
Nielsen, Jean, *Green Eyes*, Funk & Wagnalls.
Senior Jan Morgan's problems as high school newspaper editor and with her family.
Ogan, Margaret and George, *Pancake Special*, Funk & Wagnalls.
Teen-age love and auto racing are the fate of a high school graduate who is forced to give up an Air Force Academy appointment because of a physical disability.
Olson, Gene, *The Roaring Road*, Dodd, Mead.
A car-lore filled story of sports car racing and romance involving the son of a great racing mechanic.
Rendina, Laura, *My Love for One*, Little, Brown.
(Also *Lolly Touchberry*.)
Sherburne, Zoa, *Too Bad about the Haines Girl*, Morrow.
A realistic, undidactic story of out-of-wedlock pregnancy. (Also *Almost April*, *The High White Wall*, *Stranger in the House*.)
Stanford, Don, *The Red Car*, Funk & Wagnalls.
A sixteen-year-old rebuilds a wrecked car and enters it in the big race.
Stolz, Mary, *To Tell Your Love*, Harper & Row.
(Also *Two by Two*, *Rosemary*.)
Summers, James L., *The Shelter Trap*, Westminster.
The rather zany story of a teacher and a group of high school students trapped in a bomb shelter. (Also *The Limits of Love*, *Prom Trouble*, *Girl Trouble*, *Trouble on the Run*, *Operation ABC*.)
Wojciechowska, Maia, *Shadow of a Bull*, Atheneum.

section II
ADULT FICTION OF SPECIAL SIGNIFICANCE TO ADOLESCENTS

Literature from the entire world tradition should be available to the secondary school student as earlier chapters have indicated. For study of the novel, *War and Peace* might be appropriate here, *Third Man on the Mountain* there in the same school. A considerable amount of space has been given to the junior novel because of its important functions in the literature program, discussed in Chapter 10, and because teachers and prospective teachers have available to them little organized information and criticism on the genre. The purpose of this brief section is to call attention to certain categories and selections of the adult novel which the author's experience and study have indicated may have special significance to adolescents. The discussion is highly selective. Comment on many novels long familiar in school programs or on those prominently mentioned in some previous chapter is omitted.

ADVENTURE AND PERIL

The types of adult adventure novels most prominent in the reading interests of adolescents are the same as those in the junior novel—the sea, war, the western. As in the junior novels of the sea, the man-against-nature theme is prevalent in the adult story. Symbolic is Nicholas Monsarrat's title—*The Cruel Sea*—for his long, well-written book about a British ship on convoy duty during World War II. Definitely the best of Monsarrat's books, it is excellent for senior high school boys, and a long excerpt from it appears in the twelfth-grade anthology of one publisher. Alistair McLean's *HMS Ulysses,* another story of British naval experience in World War II, is also an admirable treatment of the struggle against a formidable sea. Of course, Nordhoff and Hall's earlier *Men against the Sea* is memorable.

A recurring variation of the man-against-nature theme is found in the tales of shipwreck, beginning with Defoe's celebrated *Robinson Crusoe;* perhaps most prominent among them is Johann Wyss's *Swiss Family Robinson,* an extraordinary story of courage and ingenuity.

Among the best of the recent books is Kenneth Roberts' *Boon Island,* based on an actual shipwreck off the Maine coast.

Kipling's clumsy but well-known *Captains Courageous* epitomizes another use of the sea in fiction—as a leveler and tester of men. In the Kipling story a wealthy mollycoddle is rescued from drowning by a fishing boat crew, and its harsh and exacting routine "makes a man" of him. Jack London, like many other writers, views the sea as an escape from the falseness and artificiality of social position and privilege, against which he protested in most of his works. The plot of *The Sea Wolf,* perhaps London's best novel, resembles that of *Captains Courageous.* A wealthy and prominent young man is rescued by a seal-hunting ship under the command of the ruthless and barbaric Wolf Larsen. The young man survives the voyage in complete ignominy, thoroughly beaten and cowed by Larsen. The plot, featuring a "shanghaiing" and the subsequent experiences of the novice on the sea, is generally popular.

With the outbreak of World War II, the sea story turned to the theme of heroism and leadership in naval combat. Before this, however, C. S. Forester had written his exciting, satisfying stories of Horatio Hornblower, an officer in the British navy that kept England safe from Napoleon. Hornblower, a full-dimensioned character with his quota of faults, represents the British navy's proud traditions of courage and discipline. Though the Hornblower books were written for the general audience, they have been highly popular with high school boys. Forester also produced one of the more interesting books of World War II naval combat, *The Good Shepherd,* with another indefatigable captain as the main character. A less admirable but more complex captain is found in the best-known sea story of World War II, Herman Wouk's *The Caine Mutiny.* Though marred by a somewhat maudlin ending, emphasizing Wouk's defense of authority, the novel is a fascinating study in divergent character, and the gripping plot is beautifully wrought. Strong, too, in characterization are Monsarrat's *The Cruel Sea* and Kenneth Dodson's *Away All Boats,* which traces the career of an American transport in the Pacific war.

With the sea as background, a few books, treating man's moral condition and his relationship with his universe, rise far above those so far mentioned. Perhaps the greatest is Melville's *Moby Dick,* which some high school students may read with profit. Excerpts from the book, in some of the high school anthologies, may be useful. Splendid for reading in high school is Ernest Hemingway's Nobel Prize winner, *The Old Man and the Sea,* the moving and tragic struggle of an old Cuban fisherman and a magnificent fish. The novel, most appropriate of Hemingway's books for high school use, will appeal to some students as a tale of action; more able students will be able to discern the symbolic and allegorical value so ably discussed in an essay by Leo Gurko.[19]

The sea as background for the examination of man's personality is most readily associated with Joseph Conrad. Though many of his books are too subtle for the majority of adolescents, *The Secret Sharer,* classed by critics as both short story and novel, seems especially appropriate for reading in high school and is included in several anthologies for the twelfth grade. Though the story is slow in starting, it builds into a compelling narrative that, like *The Old Man and the Sea,* can be read with profit at both a literal and symbolic level of awareness. At the literal level, it is a suspenseful tale of a fugitive helped to escape by a young sea captain who ultimately finds self-confidence. At the symbolic level, it is an exploration of Conrad's theme of the bond of the great human family and of the good and evil mixed in the human personality. The technical perfection of *The Secret Sharer* adds to its importance for class study.

THE WESTERN STORY

Most of the adult westerns, so prominent on the racks of paperbacks, are of the formula type, in the tradition of Zane Grey and Harold Bell Wright, and have slight appeal to adolescent readers. A few writers, while relying on familiar plot patterns and situations, have invested their novels with depth characterization, authentic atmosphere, and distinctive style. Conrad Richter's short, lyrical *The Sea of Grass,* with its theme of the breakdown of the great cattle empires, is among the best in this category. So, too, is Ross Santee's *Rusty* and Hal Borland's *When the Legends Die. Rusty* is the story of buffalo hunting and herd riding in the earlier West. Borland's novel of the later West

[19] Leo Gurko, "The Heroic Impulse in *The Old Man and the Sea,*" *English Journal,* XLIV (October 1955), 377–382.

is about a Ute Indian boy's induction into manhood, his career as a bronc rider, and his embitterment at his treatment in the white man's world.

A few westerns may appeal especially to girls. Mari Sandoz's *Miss Morissa* features a woman doctor on the Nebraska frontier of the 1870's. General Custer, Calamity Jane, and Buffalo Bill all appear in the book. Rose Wilder Lane's *Let the Hurricane Roar,* about a young couple on a Dakota homestead and the young wife's excruciatingly difficult winter, is popular with older girls. Somewhat similar, though more involved, is Loula Grace Erdman's *The Edge of Time,* about a young couple homesteading in Texas in 1885.

Probably the most important writer to use a western background is Walter Van Tilburg Clark. Although in its surface events it is a rather traditional western, his best novel, *The Ox-Bow Incident,* is a moving tragedy involving the psychology of mob action. Three men are lynched for a murder and then are found to have been innocent; the leader of the lynching posse and his son commit suicide. Critics have lauded the technical perfection of this novel.[20] *The Ox-Bow Incident* and another excellent novel by Clark, *The Track of the Cat,* are appropriate for reading in upper high school years. *The Track of the Cat,* too, is a psychological novel, about a Nevada family in the early 1900's. The plot is simple: three brothers, all different in personality, track a mountain lion that has killed some of their cattle. Two of the brothers are killed, one by the cat and one by his own fear. The plot is exciting on the physical level, and on the allegorical level it is clearly the struggle between good and evil. The black mountain lion of course represents evil.

WAR NOVELS

The theme of man in battle runs through the legends and myths and epics—through all literature—of all countries. Unfortunately, the war experience has loomed large in the human drama, and each of the great wars has harvested its crop of fiction, much of it ephemeral.

Battle, of course, presents one of the great testing grounds of

[20] Frederic I. Carpenter, "The West of Walter Van Tilburg Clark," *English Journal,* XLI (February 1952), 64–69.

human courage and stamina, and exploring the depths of human courage is one of the major themes in all literature of adventure. It seems ironic, perhaps, to classify war fiction as "adventure." Yet action and peril, which furnish the lure of adventure fiction, are inherent in the war story, which makes it popular with high school boys.

The older tales of war tended to stress its romance rather than its tragedy. Sometimes war was the pathway to escape from a tragic or distasteful civilian life. The French Foreign Legion, about which so many popular tales centered, became the symbol of the soldier fleeing from his past. One notable foreign legion story, Percival Wren's *Beau Geste,* is still read occasionally. Recent war fiction emphasizes the nightmare qualities of terror and hardship, in inescapably hair-raising narrative—and it is this fast-paced narrative to which the adolescent is most responsive. Yet many modern war novels present the terrible hardship of war as they also portray the exalted heroism of men who rise to the near impossible. James Michener's excellent story of aerial warfare in the Korean War, *The Bridges at Toko-Ri,* with its smashing ending, is a kind of memorial to the heroism that combat exacts, whereas Alistair McLean's *The Guns of Navarone* recounts the near-impossible mission of a small patrol in World War II. Among the most suspenseful novels of World War II is Pierre Boulle's *The Bridge on the River Kwai,* a tale of British soldiers forced to construct a railroad bridge for their Japanese captors. This novel is notable, too, for the quality of its writing and for its irony.

If these books, despite the authenticity of the events, come near to romanticism, there are others that are rock-ribbed in their realism, although they present occasional flashes of humor and even of sentimentality. Perhaps most unrelenting is Elleston Trevor's *The Big Pick-Up,* which deals with a squad of British soldiers at Dunkirk. In fact, in Trevor's spare novels is some of the most distinguished writing about World War II. His *The Killing Ground,* based on the terrible Falaise campaign in Normandy, contains one of the most gripping passages in war fiction. Its hero, Corporal Pike, in his heroism of resourcefulness as well as of necessity, represents the best of soldiers who went to war unwillingly.

Of course, the love element is not absent from war fiction. The theme of warrior and the lover who waits and fears is eternal and has been no more neglected in modern than in ancient tales. A tender, mature, and basically wholesome love story, told against the background of the planning and launching of the great invasion of Normandy in World War II, is the basis of Lionel Shapiro's *The Sixth of June*. Nevil Shute's love stories of World War II, *The Legacy* and *Pastoral,* are appealing to older girls.

Naturally, many of the most mature war novels are essentially protests. Horrified at barbaric events involving civilized peoples, authors have sought causes for these events. Norman Mailer's long, angry *The Naked and the Dead* places the blame on the capitalistic system. Irwin Shaw probes some of the neuroses of society through individual characters in *The Young Lions.* Such books as these suggest one of the major problems of teaching war fiction to classes of adolescents—the language used and the type of experience frequently portrayed. In *The Naked and the Dead, From Here to Eternity,* and some other war novels the language is extremely profane and gross. Occasionally there are detailed scenes involving sex. Even in James Gould Cozzens' Pulitzer Prize winning *Guard of Honor,* lauded by many critics as structurally the finest novel of World War II, there is a hotel bedroom scene that would make many high school teachers and librarians loath to recommend it.

Such books must be recommended and included in literature units with care. As suggested earlier, teachers and librarians frequently have been overprotective. It is as easy to underestimate the background and sophistication of adolescents as to overestimate it, and teachers have sometimes predicted shock at elements that did not bring even a lifted eyebrow from their students. Two criteria may guide selection: (1) Is the work excellent as an example of the art of fiction? (2) Is the theme likely to be comprehensible to adolescents? Certainly meeting the first test are such hard-hitting novels as *The Naked and the Dead, The Young Lions,* Heggen's *Mister Roberts,* Hemingway's *A Farewell to Arms,* along with a number of others with little objectionable material, such as *The Bridges at Toko-Ri* and Hersey's *A Bell for Adano.* Using the second criterion, however, Mailer's book and perhaps Hemingway's might be eliminated. But the presence of "dirty" language or erotic scenes is not reason enough alone for eliminating a book.

Adolescents must learn to judge details, sordid or not, in terms of their relevance to theme and purpose. In the spate of war fiction, the truly unified novel stands out because it interrelates events and characters in a significant whole, in the manner of Tolstoi's masterpiece *War and Peace.* Many of the ephemeral novels of World War II merely recount amazing events as their authors experienced them; of these the better-written ones are skillful journalistic pieces. But the battle arena affords a canvas for fascinating character portraits. In Tom Heggen's *Mr. Roberts* the young naval officer is one. He represents the effects of a certain aspect of war on sensitive, intelligent men, brought up in an atmosphere of culture, and when the reader identifies this theme, he recognizes the Rabelaisian touches in the book not as spicy sidelights but as essential details.

It is well for adolescent readers to perceive that the real heroes of war fiction (or nonfiction), past and present, are not the swashbuckling killers, but men of compassion for whom it is a tragedy, which we all share, that they must do what they do. The nature of the hero is a good point of departure for discussion of war fiction.

ADULT NOVELS OF ADOLESCENCE

The problems of adolescence, of course, have appeared not only in junior fiction. In fact, one critic remarks that "a few American novels about adolescence have embodied some of the most adult wisdom that America has produced." [21] The classic example, naturally, is *Huckleberry Finn,* which represents universal adolescence through Huck's struggle to come to terms with adult ways and to fathom the complexities of motivation.

Of course, there is the tradition in which adolescence is viewed as a temporary kind of insanity, the problems of which will dissolve in the stability and serenity of adulthood. In this type of book the adolescent is caricatured. But as Frederic Carpenter points out, "at his best the modern American novelist of adolescence describes the problems of his protagonists so that they become also the problems of our adolescent civilization, with both its mixed-up confusion and its splendid potentiality." [22]

[21] Frederic I. Carpenter, "The Adolescent in American Fiction," *English Journal,* XLVI (September 1957), 314.
[22] Carpenter, p. 319.

Probably the clearest illustration of the truth of Carpenter's observation is Thomas Wolfe. Wolfe's long, fervid novels can be read with profit by a minority of senior high school students, but they arouse a tremendous response in some of these students who find in this impassioned writer an echo of their own inner shouts. Carpenter's statement applies also to two of the novels by the late Carson McCullers. Her finest work, in the author's opinion, is *The Heart Is a Lonely Hunter,* the haunting story of the intertwined lives of six characters among whom a deaf-mute is a central, Christlike figure. The most prominent character is Mick Kelly, an imaginative girl whose yearnings are thwarted by her environment. The maturing of Frankie Addams through the events surrounding the marriage of her older brother is the theme of *Member of the Wedding,* cast in the comic mold unlike most of the author's work. Both books are appropriate for reading and teaching in the high school.

The most celebrated treatment of adolescent character in recent fiction is J. D. Salinger's *The Catcher in the Rye,* which, with seeming artlessness, touches the most tender and sensitive spots in the adolescent make-up. In the story, mixed-up Holden Caulfield views his world as "phony" and "crummy," searches for values, and suffers a nervous breakdown. Because of the language in some of the scenes, the book has been controversial as a selection for use in high school. But a number of students should not—and will not—miss it, though it is difficult to discuss in some class situations.

Strikingly similar to *The Catcher in the Rye* in accomplishment, though notably more positive in effect, is John Knowles' splendid *A Separate Peace,* set in a boys' preparatory school in New England during the early years of World War II. Gene Forrester, the protagonist, misunderstands the friendship of his roommate, Phineas. Torn between love and hate, he pushes Phineas from a tree and causes an injury that ultimately leads to Phineas's death. Through his relationship with Phineas and the events of his last year at school, Gene makes his "separate peace," in existential fashion, before he ever gets into the war. *A Separate Peace* is commonly assigned—and deserves to be—in high school classes. It is, to this writer, the most artful treatment of the archetypal initiation theme, central to all the novels discussed here, in contemporary fiction.

The Negro counterpart of Holden Caulfield is Duke, the teen-age protagonist of Warren Miller's *The Cool World,* a novel about the sordid gang life of boys in the Harlem slums. Duke ends in a reform school, but there is hope for better days to come. Dialect is well rendered, and the subject matter is grimly realistic.

A very different type of book, but one full of insight, is *Cress Delahanty* by Jessamyn West. Cress's adolescence is "normal" and usually happy. The book has its hilarious scenes as well as its poignant ones. Though highly appropriate for reading by adolescents and a highly valid treatment of adolescence, the book may have its greatest appeal to the younger adult looking back on the tribulations of that period in his life.

SIGNIFICANT CONTEMPORARY AMERICAN FICTION

A paradox has existed for some time in the teaching of literature in the high schools: the most important contemporary American writers virtually have been ignored, despite the major stress on American literature in most schools. The giants of the American novel in this century and in the very near past, Faulkner and Hemingway, have been given short shrift in the high school. An occasional short story by one of the two is studied; *The Old Man and the Sea* was welcomed with a gasp of relief. But very rarely has a novel by Faulkner or Hemingway been the focus of study in the high school classroom. And, of course, even more rarely has there been consideration of the work of present practicing fiction writers of stature in this country.

The situation cries out for an explanation. The most common one is that teachers have had little training in contemporary literature. There is some validity in this rationalization as any one can tell from an examination of the major requirements in literature for prospective teachers. But even in schools in which the English teachers are relatively sophisticated in contemporary American literature, the paradox remains, and its roots may go deeper than teacher preparation. Either the fiction writers of significance today are producing work which can be experienced profitably by only a very small minority of their fellow citizens, or the teachers of literature in the high schools have a distorted view of the potential of many of their students, or crippling taboos have been fastened upon the literature program in the high schools. It is the view of this writer that all three of these explanations have validity. The first, though, is of the least validity. Fiction of today *is* more esoteric than fiction, in general, used to be. But the reasons for its being esoteric lie as much in the presuppositions and assumptions of its reader as in its subject matter and technique. More crucial are the other two explanations. The writer has stated earlier that teachers (and parents and librarians) have a diminished view of the potentiality of adolescents for strong and virile literary experience, and though they are loosening, the taboos born of protectiveness, hypocrisy, and ignorance fastened upon the high school literature program have robbed it of its impact. If the teaching of American literature is to be truly viable, it must make a place for the serious writers of today and the recent past—Hemingway, Faulkner, Bellow, Malamud, Salinger, McCullers, O'Connor, Updike, and others.

One can only be sympathetic with the high school teacher in his problems of planning contact with Faulkner and Hemingway. Faulkner's convoluted style, intricacy of technique, and mythic framework, and Hemingway's central thesis that life is a losing battle in which the only significance is the quality of the battle constitute a formidable barrier between the authors and adolescents. But with an optimistic view of the potential of adolescent readers and a relaxed stance on taboos, the teacher, himself knowledgeable in the fiction of the two writers, can make a substantial bridgehead through use of the novellas of Faulkner—*The Bear* and *An Old Man*—and such Hemingway novels as (in addition to *The Old Man and the Sea*) *A Farewell to Arms* and *The Sun Also Rises*.

Consideration of such works, as well as those by other lesser but significant contemporary American fiction writers, in class groups is facilitated by the new types of teacher-student contact discussed earlier—short-term electives and module units—and by small-group techniques in traditional grade-level classes.

The remainder of this section of Chapter 11 is an attempt to sketch a brief context for contemporary fiction, with the hope that teachers will find it helpful in planning their courses and in selecting works for class study or individual reading.

Fiction of today tends to be literature of idea and mood predominantly. Though there is active experimenting with technique among fiction writers, there has been, as Ihab Hassan has pointed out in *Radi-*

cal Innocence, a tapering off in the quest for new forms and a trend back from the search for the ultimate in form represented, for example, in Joyce's *Finnegan's Wake,* in which the subject matter disappeared into the form or method and became virtually unrecognizable as such.

Most readers find in the serious fiction of today a general mood of unhappiness and anxiety which reflects this basically unhappy era, this *age* of anxiety. Despite the material opulence of the age, at least in this country, there is the intercultural strife, war, and the knowledge that man has concocted the weapons to destroy himself totally in a few minutes. Among writers, this underlying dissatisfaction with our world takes many shadings—melancholy, resignation, nostalgia, defiant shout, savage cynicism, ironic laughter. Yet present-day fiction is not a literature of despair; rather, our major writers seem to be working generally toward new reasons for hope.

What follows is an attempt to identify some of the major concepts and characteristics of significant contemporary American fiction. Perhaps the greatest emotional and intellectual force influencing fiction writers is existentialism, the variety formulated, largely, in the Paris underground of World War II. Its primary tenet is that existence precedes essence; man is born nothing but a blob of matter; what he becomes is entirely up to him as an individual. Corollary tenets have been expressed by the dean of contemporary existentialists, Jean-Paul Sartre:

> Man is nothing but what he makes of himself
> Man is anguish
> Man is condemned to be free

Existentialism is more of a mood than a philosophy; probably it is really an anti-philosophy. But its impact on fiction has produced, among others, two underlying hypotheses that explain much about contemporary fiction and why it has unsettled many readers. These hypotheses are explored by Ihab Hassan: [23]

> Chance and absurdity rule human action. The hero recognizes this, and knows that reality is but another name for chaos. . . . The pattern of fiction is therefore one that recognizes disorder . . .

[23] *Radical Innocence* (Princeton, New Jersey: Princeton University Press, 1961), p. 116.

Therefore, anguish is the state of life, and the task of Sisyphus in attempting to roll the boulder uphill is the central metaphor for many existentialists.

> There are no accepted norms of feeling or conduct to which the hero may appeal. The eternal verities are either denied or affirmed in the spirit of irony.

A world without God, which is the existential world, creates an ethical vacuum. Holden Caulfield, for example, rejects the standards of the adult world as "phony" and "crummy," and only his fantasy of saving little children in the field of rye enables him to stave off madness. The individual is condemned to be "free" because there is no system or model which can chart his life.

The Beats in fiction clearly are offshoots of existentialism. *Big Sur* by Jack Kerouac, the king of the Beats in literature, provides a neat illustration of one facet of existential thinking. The existential philosopher Karl Jaspers found the embodiment of existential living in the meeting of "limit-situations," those high points of anguish or danger which life continually presents and in which the individual must assert his individuality or be lost. In *Big Sur,* the protagonist finds redemption in the survival of a limit-situation. After a typical Kerouac carnival of dissipation, the young man falls into an exhausted sleep fraught with terrible visions of death. He awakens to peace: "Just a golden wash of goodness has spread over all and my body and mind. . . . I will go back home across autumn America and it'll be like it was in the beginning—simple golden eternity blessing all."

Though the influence of existentialism is great in contemporary fiction, there are many works and writers that cannot be associated with it. There is still a considerable concern with values traditionally evolved in our culture. Bernard Malamud, certainly among the several most important figures in American fiction today, deals penetratingly, for example, with family values within the ironic mode of his work. Family unit and loyalty is a major theme of *The Assistant,* though disaster, emotional and material, is the fate of the little Jewish family featured in the book.

Middle-class and upper-class values and traditions, generally, have come in for some searching examination. John Steinbeck, in *Winter of Our Discontent,* takes a pained look at our excessive materialism.

John Cheever finds in suburbia a syndrome of boredom and philistinism, while corporation lawyer-novelist Louis Auchincloss nostalgically
celebrates the virtues of the private schools as the embodiment of upper-class tradition.

Some writers, while tacitly ruling out God and group norms, none-
theless fill in some sustaining force for existence. The best and most
cogent example is the late Carson McCullers. For her, love is the sustaining force, and her theory of love, consistently illustrated in her
novels, is stated succinctly in *The Ballad of the Sad Café* and explains
that strange novel as well as much of her other work:

> First of all, love is a joint experience between two persons—but the
> fact that it is a joint experience does not mean that it is a similar experi-
> ence to the two people involved. There are the lover and the beloved,
> but these two come from different countries. Often the beloved is only a
> stimulus for all the stored up love which has lain quiet within the lover
> for a long time hitherto. And somehow every lover knows this. He feels
> in his soul that his love is a solitary thing. He comes to know a new
> strange loneliness and it is this knowledge that makes him suffer. . . .
> Let it be added that this lover . . . can be man, woman, child, or
> indeed any human creature on this earth.
>
> Now, the beloved can also be of any description. The most outland-
> ish people can be the stimulus of love. . . . Therefore, the value and
> quality of any love is determined solely by the lover himself.
>
> It is for this reason that most of us would rather love than be
> loved. . . . And the curt truth is that, in a deep secret way, the state of
> being beloved is intolerable to many. The beloved fears and hates the
> lover. . . .

Another major characteristic of the contemporary American novel,
one related to the influence of existentialism, is the changed concept
and role of the hero. Frequently critics have bemoaned the lack of
heroes in recent fiction, ending with the familiar question, "Who cares
what happens to these people?" Just as Arthur Miller in drama has attempted to make the middle-class American a tragic figure, so have
the novelists attempted to build their narratives around the jetsam of
human existence, not the figures of stature. Hassan has pointed out
that in fiction the hero-protagonist is usually a victim or a rebel, perhaps both at the same time, and he has identified a number of "faces"

of the contemporary hero of fiction, of which the following examples seem to have especial affinity for the adolescent.[24]

"The lonely adolescent or youth, exposing the corrupt adult world . . ."
—Salinger's *The Catcher in the Rye* or Purdy's *Malcolm.*

"The Negro in search of the eternal, elusive identity which white men refuse to grant him . . ."—Ralph Ellison's *Invisible Man* or James Baldwin's *Go Tell It on the Mountain.*

"The Jew engaged with Gentiles in a harrowing dialogue of reciprocal guilt and ironic self-betrayals . . ."—Saul Bellow's *The Victim* or Malamud's *The Assistant.*

"The grotesque, sometimes hell-bent seeker of godliness . . ."—Flannery O'Connor's *Wise Blood* and *The Violent Bear It Away.*

"The comic picaro, traveling through a crowded life with verve, and sustained by a gift of hope, but never finding for himself a home, except in the mythical territory ahead."—Bellow's *The Adventures of Augie March* and Capote's *Breakfast at Tiffany's.*

"The hipster, the holy-goof, in search of kicks and revelation . . ."—Kerouac's *On the Road.*

The writer would add one more to this catalog, the ineffectual, the person who is not "making it," professionally, maritally, or otherwise, as illustrated by the main characters in John Updike's *Rabbitt, Run* and *Of the Farm.*

With the prominence of such heroes in recent fiction, one is bound to find compassion for the transgressors of conventional middle-class mores, and this element has bothered a number of people. Homosexuality is prominent; perhaps the most searing example of its treatment is found in Baldwin's *Giovanni's Room.* Marital infidelity is rife; John O'Hara, for example, keeps retelling the story of Madame Bovary. Dope addiction and alcoholism are common, as in Nelson Algren's *The Man with the Golden Arm* and Updike's *Rabbitt, Run.* Yet the perceptive reader is aware that the sordid is often used for highly moral purposes—to create awareness of evil and the reasons for transgression—and can be the subject matter of artful and moving fiction.

Recent fiction is characterized, too, by a concern with the personal, private experience of its protagonists and with their essential isolation and alienation, with the general theme of man and his inner self rather

[24] "The Character of Post-War Fiction in America," *English Journal,* LI (January 1962), 5–6.

than of man and other men—the concern of past major novelists such as Sinclair Lewis, John Dos Passos, Upton Sinclair, Jack London, and Frank Norris. Social protest is little evident in recent novels, except in some of the war novels and in those with a theme of race relations, and most of the latter are narrated from specific points of view and are basically psychological rather than social. The big panoramic novel interpreting the American experience, for which we continue to yearn—the American counterpart, perhaps, to Tolstoi's *War and Peace*—has not appeared, though something like MacKinlay Kantor's *Spirit Lake* makes the attempt.

Obviously there is a lack of humor in contemporary fiction. There is indeed laughter at times. There is a Milton Berle-like unknown-identity scene in a cab, for example, in Salinger's *Raise High the Roof-beams, Carpenter*. But when there is laughter it is usually sad or ironic laughter. Mention of that existential product, the novel of the absurd, may be appropriate at this point. Borrowing the absurd from the tragic situation, the grotesque from the comic, the appearance of the novel of the absurd is close to farce, but the effect is close to tragedy. Perhaps the best example of the juxtaposing of horror and hilarity is Joseph Heller's *Catch* 22.

Some critics have seen in the years since World War II a progression through a kind of romanticism to a developing concern with myth and archetype. The gothic elements in Southern fiction, the grotesquerie of incident and character, contribute one kind of romantic element; the taking of man away from organized society to play out his lonely ordeals, as Hemingway did in much of his fiction and as Bellow did in *Henderson, the Rain King,* contributes another. Now there is some tendency to confront man and society through myth and archetype. The quest and the initiation are particularly prevalent archetypal themes in recent writing. In John Updike's *The Centaur,* all the characters in a Pennsylvania town and its high school have counterparts in classical mythology.

It is particularly the emergence of myth and archetype in contemporary fiction that indicates that the major writers of today, far from despairing, are seeking an order which science and reason cannot provide, a new premise for security of emotion, new subject matter for lyric thinking, and new possibilities for self-realization through the imaginative life.

For these reasons, contemporary fiction, no matter how repellent some readers may find it and no matter how many taboos of the high school program it violates, should have a place in the secondary school literature program. One particular possibility for its inclusion is the individual reading program discussed in Chapter 9. Mature students should be encouraged to develop reading designs in contemporary fiction. In the regular classes, small-group reading of contemporary novels may be the best approach generally rather than total class consideration, although there are various novels that lend themselves to total class study. Some suggestions for particular novels that may be especially appropriate are given in the list of representative books that follows.

REPRESENTATIVE BOOKS

Adventure and Peril

Aldrich, Bess S., *A Lantern in Her Hand,* Grossett & Dunlap.
    The story of a young bride who goes to live in pioneer Nebraska.
Borland, Hal, *When the Legends Die,* Lippincott.
Boyd, James, *Drums,* Scribner.
    A young man fights under the command of John Paul Jones.
Cather, Willa, *My Antónia,* Houghton Mifflin.
    Antónia and her Bohemian peasant family in Nebraska's pioneer days.
Clark, Walter Van Tilburg, *The Ox-Bow Incident,* various publishers.
    (Also *The Track of the Cat,* Random House.)
Conrad, Joseph, *Typhoon,* various publishers.
    Captain McWhirr takes his ship through a furious storm. (Also *The Secret Sharer,* various publishers.)
Defoe, Daniel, *Robinson Crusoe,* various publishers.
Dodson, Kenneth, *Away All Boats,* Little, Brown.
Edmonds, Walter, *Drums along the Mohawk,* Little, Brown.
    Warfare and life in the Mohawk Valley during the Revolutionary War. (Also *Wilderness Clearing.*)
Erdman, Loula G., *The Edge of Time,* Dodd, Mead.
Forester, C. S., *The Good Shepherd,* Little, Brown.
Hartog, Jan de, *The Captain,* Atheneum.
    Story of a courageous Dutch tugboat captain in the North Atlantic during World War II.
Heggen, Tom, *Mister Roberts,* Houghton Mifflin.

Hemingway, Ernest, *The Old Man and the Sea, Scribner.
Hersey, John, A Bell for Adano, Modern Library.
  An American military government officer administers a small Italian town after the Italian surrender in World War II. (Also The War Lover, Knopf.)
Jones, James, Thin Red Line, Signet.
  One of the best novels of island warfare in the Pacific during World War II.
Kipling, Rudyard, *Captains Courageous, Doubleday, and Grosset, & Dunlap.
Kuznetsor, Anatolli, Babi Yar, Dial Press.
  A Ukrainian boy's involvement in the German occupation of Kiev in World War II and the Nazi atrocities against the Jews.
Lane, Rose W., *Let the Hurricane Roar, McKay.
London, Jack, *The Sea Wolf, various publishers.
McLean, Alistair, *HMS Ulysses, Doubleday.
  (Also *The Guns of Navarone, Doubleday.)
Melville, Herman, Moby Dick, various publishers.
Michener, James, *The Bridges at Toko-Ri, Random House.
Monsarrat, Nicholas, *The Cruel Sea, Knopf.
Richter, Conrad, *Sea of Grass, Knopf.
Roberts, Kenneth, *Boon Island, Doubleday.
Sandoz, Mari, *The Horsecatcher, Westminster.
  (Also *Miss Morissa, McGraw-Hill.)
Santee, Ross, *Rusty, Scribner.
Shapiro, Lionel, *The Sixth of June, Doubleday.
Shaw, Irwin, *The Young Lions, Random House.
  Three soldiers, two Americans and one German, in World War II.
Shute, Nevil, Pastoral, Morrow.
  A love story, in which the background is an RAF base in World War II. (Also The Legacy.)
Trevor, Elleston, *The Killing Ground, Macmillan.
  (Also *The Big Pick-Up.)
Uris, Leon, Battle Cry, Bantam.
  Marine combat action in World War II—one of the outstanding World War II novels.
White, Stewart E., The Long Rifle, Doubleday.
  A Pennsylvania farm boy runs away to become a mountain man; a saga about the fur trappers and the role of the Kentucky rifle.
Wouk, Herman, *The Caine Mutiny, Doubleday.

Significant Recent American Novels

Baldwin, James, *Go Tell It On The Mountain*, Dell.
Harlem Negroes attempt to find direction in life through religion.
Bellow, Saul, *The Adventures of Augie March*, Viking.
Long, picaresque novel of a big city boy's quest in life.
Ellison, Ralph, *The Invisible Man*, Signet.
Frank, haunting story of a young Negro's struggle for identity.
Faulkner, William, *The Bear*, various editions.
The most celebrated of the author's "hunting stories."
Heller, Joseph, *Catch 22*, Dell.
World War II Air Force story, a major example of the novel of the absurd.
Hemingway, Ernest, *A Farewell to Arms*, Scribner.
An American serves with the Italian Army in World War I and has a tragic love affair with an English nurse. (Also *The Sun Also Rises*.)
Kantor, MacKinlay, *Spirit Lake*, Random House.
Panoramic novel of pioneering and Indian fighting in the upper Midwest.
Kaufmann, Myron, *Remember Me to God*, Lippincott.
Powerful story of Jewish family life in Boston and the love and Harvard experiences of the adolescent son.
Knowles, John, *A Separate Peace*, Macmillan.
Lee, Harper, *To Kill a Mockingbird*, Lippincott.
A story of childhood in a Southern town and a Negro's unjustified conviction of rape.
Malamud, Bernard, *The Assistant*, New American Library.
A young outcast attaches himself to a struggling grocer and finds salvation through ordeal.
McCullers, Carson, *The Heart Is a Lonely Hunter*, Bantam.
(Also *Member of the Wedding*.)
Miller, Warren, *The Cool World*, Fawcett.
O'Connor, Flannery, *Wise Blood*, Noonday.
Powerful, grotesque story of twisted lives in a Southern town.
Salinger, J. D., *The Catcher in the Rye*, New American Library.
(Also *Raise High the Roofbeams, Carpenter*.)
Steinbeck, John, *Winter of Our Discontent*, Bantam.
The unscrupulous attempt of a young man to rebuild his financial status ends in tragedy.
Styron, William, *The Confessions of Nat Turner*, Random House.

The story of the famous slave revolt told in the form of recollections of Turner while awaiting execution.

Updike, John, *Rabbitt, Run,* Crest.

A former high school basketball star encounters defeat and tragedy in the adult world. (Also *The Centaur.*)

West, Jessamyn, *Cress Delahanty,* Harcourt.

Wolfe, Thomas, *Look Homeward, Angel,* Scribner.

Eugene Gant's boyhood and adolescence, based on Wolfe's experiences in North Carolina.

12
Nonfictional Prose for Adolescents

JUNIOR BIOGRAPHY

Paralleling the rise of the junior novel is that of the junior biography. Though the line of demarcation between the junior and adult forms in biography is less distinct than in the novel, the history of the two junior forms has been similar. Both became distinct genres in the 1930's and have since developed rapidly. Both are popular with the adolescent audience. Achievement in each genre ranges from the completely patterned potboiler to the truly and distinctively artistic work. Didacticism, the passion to teach, has hamstrung junior biography even more than it has the junior novel. Many of the juvenile biographies are sketches of the lives of the great, held up as examples ("Lives of great men all remind us . . ."). Hero worship is rife in the junior biography. Often, too, junior biography has been excessively preoccupied with "human interest," with the "color angle," to the detriment of character interpretation and evaluation of deeds. Despite such inherently crippling tendencies, however, there are some remarkable achievements in the field of junior biography.

Athletes and Adventurers

The themes of sports and adventure are as popular in biography as in fiction. Still popular is Doris Shannon Garst with her fictionalized biographies of frontier heroes, Indian and white—Sitting Bull, Crazy Horse, Buffalo Bill, Kit Carson, and others. Using the techniques of the adventure novel, Garst's books stress action and spectacle and the capacity of the superhero for surpassing deeds. Few early adolescent readers can distinguish between fiction and the biographies by Garst and there is little need that they should.

Biographies of sports figures are almost as plentiful as novels about sports; in each case, distinguished books are few. Gene Schoor has risen above the run of the mill with his biographies of Jim Thorpe, the great Indian athlete, and of Casey Stengel, the baseball manager. Frank Graham's biography, *Lou Gehrig, A Quiet Hero,* tells with extraordinary skill the thrilling and poignant story of a great baseball player, and makes a real attempt to re-create a personality. Highly successful, too, though more for its subject than for its technique, is Bill Roeder's *Jackie Robinson,* an account of the career of the first Negro to enter big-league baseball.

A truly masterful junior biography, which towers above most of the others in the field, is Geoffrey Trease's *Sir Walter Raleigh.* Of course, the colorful Raleigh furnishes a natural subject for an exciting biography, and Trease takes full advantage of the intrigue-surrounded, up-by-the-bootstraps career of this great Elizabethan. Raleigh's struggle for success despite humble origins and his historic rivalry with Essex are both themes with great appeal to the adolescent. The authentic background of Queen Elizabeth's court and the passing references to literary figures of the time are bonuses in this biography, which reads like a superior romantic novel.

Nina Brown Baker, one of the leaders and pioneers in junior biography, also usually chooses colorful political figures as her subjects. Her biographies, though relatively mature, employ techniques of fiction that make them highly readable, and many students have come to know such figures as Garibaldi and Juárez more vividly through her books than through their study of history. More than most junior biographers, Nina Baker stresses the significance of her subjects' endeavors.

Scientists and Nurses

There have always been adolescents, especially boys, who have found their major literary experiences in biographies of scientists. This age of science has swelled their ranks, and even the standard anthologies give increasing space to the lives of scientists. The junior biographies of scientists have suffered from the problem of having to explain difficult material and of interpreting the subject in an abstruse context. Yet courageous, and in some cases successful, attempts have been made. One of the most notable of these is Rachel Baker's *Sigmund Freud*. Most adolescents—as well as many adults—connect Freud vaguely with sex dreams; Baker boldly presents the famous psychiatrist in a thoroughly acceptable way. Though the book is eminently readable, explaining in elementary terms the basis of Freud's theories, a curiously poetic strain runs through the pages, exemplified in a line such as: "Now the green years of growing come upon the boy. . . ."

Outstanding, too, is the achievement of Elma E. Levinger in her biographies of Galileo and Leonardo da Vinci. The story of Galileo is cast in dramatic fictional form as it builds up to the trial scene in which the suspense is acute. Unlike many junior biographies, it does not ignore earthy aspects of the subject's life—Galileo's refusal to marry his mistress, for example. Levinger's dialogue, rather exaggerated in the Galileo biography, is patently unreal, even for a Renaissance life; it is markedly better in her book on Da Vinci. Levinger is one of the few writers who have conquered the problem of making intellectual and artistic adventure interesting reading for adolescents.

J. Alvin Kugelmass assumed a formidable task in his biography, *J. Robert Oppenheimer and the Atomic Story*. Though, like Rachel Baker, Kugelmass is able to put in elementary terms some difficult principles of science, he never really brings his subject—a genius—to life, and the final effect of the work is awe rather than understanding. Kugelmass is far more successful in his biographies of Louis Braille, Ralph Bunche, and Roald Amundsen, whose careers lend themselves more readily to junior biography. The great Albert Schweitzer inspires awe, too, and a number of junior biographies of him have been attempted. The most successful is Joseph Gollomb's readable *Genius of the Jungle*. The famous Negro scientist, George Washington Carver, has also inspired a number of junior, as well as adult, biographers. The best biography of Carver for the senior high school reader is undoubtedly that by Rackham Holt.

Nursing also has been as popular a theme in biography as in the junior novel and, from a literary point of view, several of the biographies of nurses are far superior to most of the junior novels about nursing. Of course, the two most world-famous nurses are Florence Nightingale and Clara Barton. Jeannette Nolan, a well-known name in juvenile biography, has written books on both. These books feature the technique of the novelist, particularly in the lavish use of dialogue. Though *Florence Nightingale* evidences a good sense of scene and handling of incident, it is less mature in organization and style than *The Story of Clara Barton.* Among the best of the many junior biographies of Florence Nightingale is that by Cecil Woodham-Smith, a rewritten version of his adult piece. Clara Barton receives her best treatment, perhaps, in the work by Mildred Pace.

An extremely moving biography of a nurse is that by Juliette Elkon, *Edith Cavell, Heroic Nurse,* the story of the English nurse who was put to death by the Germans for her underground activities in Belgium during World War I. Like most successful junior biographies, this one is cast solidly in the pattern of the novel, with skillful use of dialogue and detail. The tragic ending is dramatic without being melodramatic. As in other good junior biographies, a bibliography of sources is appended. Striking, too, is Rachel Baker's *Angel of Mercy,* the biography of "America's Florence Nightingale," Dorothea Lynde Dix. However, this book is not so well written as most of the others by Rachel Baker, and is not so popular as her earlier *The First Woman Doctor,* concerning Elizabeth Blackwell.

Literary and Artistic Figures

Biographies of people renowned in literature and the arts usually are not widely read, either in the adult or the adolescent field. However, in the senior high school, especially, such biographies can be helpful in enriching the study of literature and in meeting highly individual interests. For the latter purpose, the biographies of musicians by Madeleine Goss and those of figures in drama and dance by Gladys Malvern, for example, are especially appropriate. One of the most unusual biographies in the field of the arts is that of Louis Armstrong, the great jazz musician, by Jeannette Eaton—*Trumpeter's Tale.* Although the book gives little insight into the nature of jazz, it is an unforgettable story of a true rags-to-riches career of the Negro boy born in the New Orleans slums, who learned to play his horn in a reform school and later played before the crowned heads of Europe and in concert halls and entertainment centers all over the world.

Entreé into the life of a painter is perhaps best represented among recent biographies by Howard Greenfield's *Marc Chagall,* which relates not only the career and associations of the famous artist, but his life as a Russian Jew early in this century.

Of literary biographies, Cornelia Meigs's *Invincible Louisa* is easily the most popular. Its appeal lies mainly in its engaging picture of the family life of Louisa May Alcott rather than in the story of her writing career. None of the few other junior biographies of literary figures has found more than a handful of readers. May Lamberton Becker, in her *Presenting Miss Jane Austen,* has written the kind of biography that teachers wish adolescents would read! Actually, some of the more mature and literate girls do read it, and for them it is rewarding. It is more in the tradition of scholarly adult biography than in the typical novel pattern of junior biography. To the girl who reads it, it furnishes considerable insight into the major novels of Jane Austen. In the field of general literary biography, Marchette Chute, with her books on Shakespeare, Chaucer, and Ben Jonson, is a leader. These are useful reference works for senior high school classes studying English literature.

Varied Fields

One of the most publicized books in recent times is the *Diary of a Young Girl* by Anne Frank. This autobiography of the Jewish girl who hid from the Nazis with her family in an Amsterdam retreat during World War II, was ultimately captured, and died in a concentration camp, is dated in its setting and events, but its amazing insight into the personality of an adolescent girl and the traumatic impact of its story will undoubtedly make its popularity endure.

Prolific Jeannette Eaton, already mentioned as the author of a junior biography of Louis Armstrong, has contributed some excellent biographies of people famous in public life. Among her best is *Gandhi, Fighter without a Sword,* the story of the great Indian patriot and pacifist. Many girls will find her biography of Eleanor Roosevelt interesting also.

Political figures, difficult to treat in junior biography, have been a greater focus of interest among writers in recent years than formerly. Probably the leader in this field among junior biographers is Bill Severn with his *Adlai Stevenson: Citizen of the World,* which gives considerable attention to this unique statesman's high school and college days, and his *Mr. Chief Justice: Earl Warren,* which features an unabashed admiration of the man as well as discussion of the political issues which furnish the backdrop for his career. In *A Dawn in the Trees* the talented and versatile Leonard Wibberley has produced a well-balanced portrait of Thomas Jefferson in the crucial years, 1776–1789, by presenting the multitalented Revolutionary from the varied viewpoints of those who surrounded him personally and politically. John D. Weaver's *Tad Lincoln* does as much for Abraham Lincoln as for Tad Lincoln, and adds importantly to the lore of Lincolnia in the junior field. No one has yet accomplished as much for the junior audience in writing about Franklin Delano Roosevelt as has Frances Cavanah in *Triumphant Adventure,* the story of FDR's personal and political triumphs and failures.

Though not aimed specifically at the junior audience, Ruth Painter Randall's books about the wives of famous men have attracted a following among adolescent girls. *I, Mary, I, Varina,* and *I, Elizabeth* are about, respectively, the wives of Lincoln, Jefferson Davis, and George Custer.

Shirley Graham has taken biographies of outstanding Negroes as her field, and from this effort has come one of the best junior biographies of Booker T. Washington, as well as some of lesser-known Negroes. Elizabeth Yates's Newbery prize-winning book on a Negro slave who purchased his freedom, *Amos Fortune, Free Man,* is appealing to pupils in the early junior high school, and her biography, *Prudence Crandall, Woman of Courage,* of a teacher who fought for the right of all to be educated, is of interest to older girls. Though Clara Ingram Judson's fine biographies are more appropriate for elementary school children than for adolescents, some of her books, such as *City Neighbor,* the story of Jane Addams, also are appropriate for the junior high school.

REPRESENTATIVE BOOKS

(Biographies discussed in the preceding chapter are marked with an asterisk [*]. Titles are annotated only if the nature of the content was not made clear in the chapter. [A] indicates adult biographies.)

Baker, Louise, *Out on a Limb,* McGraw-Hill. (A)
A girl who loses a leg early in life learns to dance and swim and becomes a reporter.

Baker, Nina Brown, *Garibaldi,* Vanguard.
Well-written story of the great Italian patriot. (Also *Juárez, Hero of Mexico.*)

Baker, Rachel, *The First Woman Doctor,* Messner.
Elizabeth Blackwell overcame prejudice to enter the medical profession a century ago.
(Also *Sigmund Freud,* Messner, and *Angel of Mercy,* about Dorothea Lynde Dix.)

Becker, May Lamberton, *Presenting Miss Jane Austen,* Dodd, Mead. (A)

Cavanah, Frances, *Triumphant Adventure,* Rand, McNally.

Chevigny, Hector, *My Eyes Have a Cold Nose,* Yale University Press. (A)
Autobiographical account of conquering blindness with the help of a seeing-eye dog.

Curie, Eve, *Madame Curie,* Doubleday. (A)
The amazing story of the discoverer of radium told by her daughter.

Davis, Sammy, Jr. and Boyar, Jane and Burt, *Yes I Can,* Farrar, Straus. (A)
The struggles and beliefs of the Negro entertainer.

Eaton, Jeannette, *Trumpeter's Tale,* Morrow.
(Also *Gandhi, Fighter without a Sword.*)

Elkon, Juliette, *Edith Cavell, Heroic Nurse,* Messner.

Frank, Anne, *Diary of a Young Girl,* Doubleday.

Garst, Doris Shannon, *Sitting Bull,* Messner.
Exciting fictionalized story of the great Sioux chief. (Also *Buffalo Bill* and *Kit Carson.*)

Gollomb, Joseph, *Albert Schweitzer, Genius of the Jungle,* Vanguard.

Goss, Madeleine, *Beethoven, Master Musician,* Doubleday.
The strange childhood and life of the great composer.

Graham, Frank, *Lou Gehrig, A Quiet Hero,* Putnam.

Graham, Shirley, and George Lipscomb, *Dr. George Washington Carver, Scientist,* Messner.

Greenfeld, Howard, *Marc Chagall, Follett.

Holt, Rackham, *George Washington Carver, Doubleday. (A)

Inouye, Daniel Ken, Journey to Washington, with Lawrence Elliot, Prentice-Hall. (A)
Autobiography of the first Japanese-American to become a U.S. Senator.

Judson, Clara I., *City Neighbor, Scribner.

Keller, Helen, Story of My Life, Doubleday. (A)
Famous story of Helen Keller and her teacher, Anne Sullivan Macy.

Kugelmass, J. Alvin, *Roald Amundsen, Messner.
(Also *Ralph J. Bunche: Fighter for Peace and *Louis Braille.)

Levinger, Elma E., *Galileo, Messner.
(Also *Leonardo daVinci.)

Malvern, Gladys, Curtain Going Up! Messner.
The career of Katherine Cornell to 1943.

Meigs, Cornelia, *Invincible Louisa, Little, Brown.

Miller, Floyd, The Electrical Genius of Liberty Hall: Charles Steinmetz, McGraw-Hill.
A readable treatment of Steinmetz' human and intellectual qualities.

Olsen, Jack, Black Is Best, Putnam. (A)
Subtitled The Riddle of Cassius Clay, the book describes the career of the controversial boxer and tells why he thinks "black is best."

Pace, Mildred, *Clara Barton, Scribner.

Randall, Ruth Painter, *I, Elizabeth, Little, Brown.
(Also *I, Mary and *I Varina.)

Russell, Bill as told to William McSweeney, Go Up to Glory, Coward-McCann. (A)
The great basketball star recounts the highlights of his career and comments on a variety of subjects including civil rights.

Severn, Bill, *Adlai Stevenson: Citizen of the World, McKay.
(Also *Mr. Chief Justice: Earl Warren.)

Strachey, Lytton, Elizabeth and Essex: A Tragic History, Harcourt. (A)
The dramatic story of Elizabeth I and Essex.

Syme, Ronald, African Traveler: The Story of Mary Kingsley, Morrow.
Miss Kingsley's unusual adventures in exploring Africa.

Trease, Geoffrey, *Sir Walter Raleigh, Vanguard. (A)

Warner, Oliver, Nelson and the Age of Fighting Sail, American Heritage.
A well-documented and readable narrative of the great British sea captain.

Weaver, John D., *Tad Lincoln, Dodd, Mead.

Wibberley, Leonard, *A Dawn in the Trees, Farrar, Straus.

Woodham-Smith, Cecil, *Lonely Crusader (Florence Nightingale), Mc-Graw-Hill.

Yates, Elizabeth, *Prudence Crandall, Woman of Courage, Dutton.

Collective Biography

Boynick, David, Champions by Setback, Crowell. (A)
Inspiring short accounts of the careers of athletes who overcame serious physical handicaps to become champions.

Briggs, Peter, Men in the Sea, Simon and Schuster.
Biographies of nine pioneer workers in oceanography, with a chapter on the Alvin, the submarine that found the missing bomb in Spanish waters.

Gunther, John, Procession, Harper & Row. (A)
Biographies of fifty world leaders of the past three decades.

Hirsch, Phil, Fighting Aces, Pyramid Books. (A)
Twelve stories of famous combat airmen.

Porter, C. Fayne, Our Indian Heritage: Profiles of Twelve Great Leaders, Chilton. (A)

Rollins, Charlemae, They Showed the Way, Crowell.
Sketches of the careers of forty outstanding Negroes.

Schaefer, Jack, Heroes without Glory, Houghton Mifflin. (A)
The exploits of ten "good guys" of the Old West whose adventures are as exciting as the better known ones of the outlaws.

Shapiro, Milton, The Day They Made the Record Book, Messner.
The exploits and records of Babe Ruth, Lou Gehrig, Don Larsen, Roger Maris, Maury Wills, Joe Dimaggio, and Sandy Koufax.

OTHER NONFICTIONAL PROSE

As noted earlier, the range of nonfictional prose is wide and has relevance to all areas of the school curriculum, not just to English or the literature class. On a highly subjective basis the writer has decided to include here discussion of two general categories of nonfictional prose which he thinks especially appropriate for consideration in literature programs—that concerned with personalized treatment of major historical events and that concerned with true adventure.

Personalized Views of Historical Events

The contributions in this category, though still highly limited and largely aimed to the general audience of readers, promise to form ultimately one of the more exciting genres of nonfiction for both junior and adult readers. A form of history, these books are also a form of personal, probably partly fictional, narrative as they bring to life from personal viewpoints the crucial moments of history. Their audience is largely the male one, adolescent and adult. Probably leading the way in this genre are Cornelius Ryan and Walter Lord, both treating major turning points of World War II.

Ryan's *The Longest Day* is an engrossing narrative of the first twenty-four hours of D-Day in Europe, told from the viewpoints of various Allied and German officers and soldiers, while his *The Last Battle* is a day-by-day chronicle based on eye-witness accounts of the twenty-one days prior to the fall of Berlin in 1945. Lord's *Day of Infamy* and *Incredible Victory* are similar approaches to, respectively, the Japanese attack on Pearl Harbor and the Battle of Midway, featuring both American and Japanese points of view.

What Lord does with the attack on Pearl Harbor, Carroll Glines does with the first bombing raid over Japan in *Doolittle's Tokyo Raiders* and Norman Polmar with the mysterious sinking of the atomic submarine *Thresher* in 1963 in *Death of the Thresher.*

The human interest approach to historical events is the basis also of a Messner series entitled *Milestones in History* which includes such titles as *Survival: Jamestown, After the Alamo, The Cloud over Hiroshima,* and *Disaster 1906: The San Francisco Earthquake and Fire.*

True Adventure

The period following World War II may well be cited in future literary history for the flowering of nonfictional prose. Certainly, the personal narrative of adventure, firmly rooted in the age-old longing to live dangerously, represents some of the finest in contemporary writing. The books of true adventure furnish a rich resource for the high school program in literature.

The true adventure narrative finds its earlier origins not only in the many adventure tales involving man against nature, but in such works as those by Izaak Walton and especially in *Walden* by Thoreau, works that explore the role of nature in the good life and its effects upon the personality of man.

Conquest of the sea, of the mountains, of the sky, or of remote and inaccessible places in general is the subject of a group of important true adventure books, beginning with Thor Heyerdahl's *Kon-Tiki* in 1950. Heyerdahl, a Danish anthropologist, and his associates made an amazing ocean voyage in a primitive craft to test a theory, and their exploit caught the public fancy. It is the underwater world, however, that has most challenged men's imaginations and ingenuity in recent years, and a number of books on undersea exploration have appeared. Jacques-Yves Cousteau and Frédéric Dumas, the authors of one of the finest of these, *The Silent World,* point out that since ancient times men have tried to penetrate the mysterious depths of the sea; even Leonardo da Vinci designed diving lungs—albeit they were somewhat impractical. Other superb books of undersea adventure are Philippe Diole's *The Undersea Adventure* and Hans Hass's *Diving to Adventure.*

The towering mountain peaks, long inaccessible to man, have always posed a challenge. Within very recent years the highest have finally been conquered. Probably the finest story of mountain climbing is Maurice Herzog's *Annapurna,* which describes the scaling of the giant Himalayan alp—at the time the highest peak ever climbed—a feat that permanently disabled Herzog. The feat, though not the book, was surpassed by an expedition commanded by Sir John Hunt, whose *The Conquest of Everest* records the ultimate victory in mountain climbing.

Adventure in remote places also has produced a long series of books. Of particular stature is Heinrich Harrer's *Seven Years in Tibet,* years in which the adventurer-writer became a sort of right-hand man to the fabulous Dalai Lama. Comparable is the account of a year spent among the Eskimos, *Kabloona* by Gontran de Poncias.

Superior books of personal adventure have certain elements in common with good fiction—exciting events, suspense, revelation of character, quality of style. Yet, as Gorham Munson points out, the fact that they are based on true experience gives them a stronger impact in disclosing man's great reserves of courage and resourcefulness, affording a catharsis to the reader even though the narratives of true adventure—unlike those of war—are romantic rather than tragic.[1]

What gives the true adventure narrative significance and what distinguishes the superior from the run of the mill? Why, in the first place, would a mature person want to climb a mountain when there is nothing but ice at the top, or plunge to the bottom of the ocean? Perhaps Maurice Herzog gives one of the most effective answers:

> Rocked in my stretcher, I meditated on our adventure now drawing to a close, and on our unexpected victory. One always talks of the ideal as a goal towards which one strives but which one never reaches. For every one of us, Annapurna was an ideal that had been realized. In our youth we had not been misled by fantasies, nor by the bloody battles of modern warfare which feed the imagination of the young. For us the mountains had been a natural field of activity where, playing on the frontiers of life and death, we had found the freedom for which we were blindly groping and which was as necessary to us as bread. The mountains had bestowed on us their beauties, and we adored them with a child's simplicity and revered them with a monk's veneration of the divine.
>
> Annapurna, to which we had gone emptyhanded, was a treasure on which we should live the rest of our days. With this realization we turn the page: a new life begins.
>
> There are other Annapurnas in the lives of men.[2]

In the books by Herzog, Cousteau, and Diole, for example, there is a nobility of motive, a symbolic value to their physical feats that invests them with significance, not just the thrill to be found, for instance, in the big-game hunting tales of Robert Ruark or Jim Corbett. The superior narrative of adventure makes clear the point of the experiences recounted, leading the reader to realize, with Herzog, that "events that seem to make no sense may sometimes have a deep significance of their own."

A maturity and sensitivity of style also distinguish the excellent adventure narratives. Again, Herzog, Diole, and Cousteau may be cited along with others such as Antoine de Saint-Exupèry and William O. Douglas. The following passage is an example:

[1] "High Up and Deep Down," *English Journal,* XLIII (December 1954), 481–487.
[2] Maurice Herzog, *Annapurna* (New York: Dutton, 1952), p. 311.

Like the sea, [the desert] reveals the depths of being within us. Through it, there is every chance of our arriving at a certain secret door within ourselves. From this threshold other inner landscapes appear before our eyes. When consciousness makes its way beyond this wall, it achieves the greatest of all transitions: the transplanting of the inner man.

It is here that the sea and the desert have an equal value, are one in their human significance. It is here that the spell of the Sahara and the spell of the ocean depths bring a richness and satisfaction to certain spirits that the charm of cities, the smiles of women, the sweetness of home cannot bestow. Is this the arrogance of choosing a bleak and naked destiny? The vanity of the hermit? I am not so sure of that. In these retreats into sparseness and solitude, these voluntary divestments of all that is extraneous, the same psychological alchemy is at work. There is always the question of a spiritual gain. The stake is the appropriation of the world by irrational means: a stake à la Rimbaud.

I have found again in the desert—or rather, I have brought to perfection there—the magic process by which, in the water, a diver is able to loose the ordinary bonds of time and space and bring life into consonance with an obscure inner poem: to bypass habit, language, memory. . . .[3]

Recent events have brought concern with adventures on social as well as physical frontiers. The Peace Corps, involving a great number of idealistic young people in educational missions in far-flung places, has resulted in at least two memorable books of interest for teenagers. In Earle and Rhoda Brooks' *The Barrios of Manta,* a young engineer and his teacher-wife describe their adventures among the poverty-stricken people of Manta, Ecuador. Leonard Levitt, a real individualist in the Peace Corps, tells in *An African Season* of his reception among the villagers of Tanganyika.

Books of true adventure can figure importantly in the high school program. The increasing prominence of nonfiction in contemporary literature makes it especially desirable to teach students to recognize excellence in this genre as well as in fiction. Selections of true adventure may be used along with fiction in units on the nonfiction of adventure by requesting permission from publishers to duplicate excerpts from such books, listed at the end of this chapter. Another

[3] Reprinted by permission of Julian Messner, Inc., from *Sahara Adventure* by Philippe Diole. Copyright September 27, 1956, by Julian Messner, Inc.

possibility is for all the students to read one of the true adventures together, using a paperback edition, and to read others from the library individually.

REPRESENTATIVE BOOKS

(All titles are of adult books. * Indicates those discussed in the text.)

Belfrage, Sally, *Freedom Summer,* Viking.
   The disturbing experiences of the author during a summer in Greenwood, Miss., as a SNCC worker.

Brooks, Earle and Rhoda, *The Barrios of Manta,* New American Library.

Conot, Robert, *Rivers of Blood, Years of Darkness,* Bantam.
   On-the-scene account of the events before, during, and after the 1965 Watts riots in Los Angeles.

Corbett, Jim, *Man-eaters of Kumaon,* Oxford.
   Hunting man-eating tigers in India.

*Cousteau, Jacques-Yves, and Frédéric Dumas, *The Silent World,* Harper & Row.
   Undersea exploration and salvage in the Mediterranean.

*DePoncins, Gontran, *Kabloona,* Reynal.

*Diole, Philippe, *Sahara Adventure,* Messner.
   Exploration by camel in the Sahara Desert. Poetic style. (Also, *The Undersea Adventure,* a classic of skin-diving, and *World Without Sun,* Harper, adventure in man's first underwater colony.)

DuFresne, Frank, *My Way Was North,* Holt, Rinehart and Winston.
   The twenty years of experiences in Alaska of a U.S. Biological Survey agent.

Glines, Carroll V., *Doolittle's Tokyo Raiders,* Van Nostrand.

*Harrer, Heinrich, *Seven Years in Tibet,* Dutton.

*Hass, Hans, *Diving to Adventure,* Doubleday.

Hersey, John, *The Algiers Motel Incident,* Bantam.
   Searing account of the incident in Detroit in which two young Negroes were shot by policemen.

*Herzog, Maurice, *Annapurna,* Dutton.

*Heyerdahl, Thor, *Kon-Tiki,* Rand McNally.

*Hunt, John, *The Conquest of Everest,* Dutton.

Levitt, Leonard, *An African Season,* Simon and Schuster.

Lord, Walter, *Incredible Victory,* Harper & Row.
   (Also *Day of Infamy.*)

Polmar, Norman, *Death of the Thresher,* Chilton.

Ryan, Cornelius, *The Last Battle,* Simon and Schuster.
(Also *The Longest Day.*)
Saint-Exupéry, Antoine de, *Wind, Sand and Stars,* Harcourt.
Adventures of an aviator on three continents. Poetic and philosophical.
Scott, Robert, *Between the Elephant's Eyes,* Dodd, Mead.
A hunting story with a strange ending.
Tenzing, Norgay, and James Ramsey Ullman, *Tiger of the Snows,* Putnam.
The career of the Sherpa, Tenzing, who, with Edmund Hillary, reached the summit of Everest.
Wilkinson, Doug, *Land of the Long Day,* Holt, Rinehart and Winston.
Describes a year of living as an Eskimo.

INDEX

A

Abraham Lincoln, 188n
Act One, 184
Adams, Franklin P., 120
Adams, Jane, 9
Adding Machine, 139
Adlai Stevenson: Citizen of the World, 185, 332
Adolescent culture, novels of the, 286–307
Advise and Consent, 135
Aesthetics and Criticism, 33n
African Season, An, 339
Aldrich, Thomas Bailey, 6
Algren, Nelson, 321
Alm, Richard S., 248
Almost April, 304
Almost Like Sisters, 302
"Alterwise by Owl-light," 37
Amos Fortune, Free Man, 332
Anchor Man, 282
And Both Were Young, 301
Angel of Mercy, 330
Anglo-American Conference on Teaching of English, 5, 18n
Animal Farm, 22
Animal stories, 251–254

Anna Karenina, 278
Annapurna, 337
Annixter, Paul, 9, 305
Antigone, 22, 131
Apology, 155
Arctic Adventure, 259
Ark, The, 305
Armour, Richard, 120
Arm of the Starfish, The, 301
Arms and the Man, 131
Armstrong, Louis, 9
Armstrong, Richard, 259
Arnold, Elliot, 267
Assistant, The, 12, 319
Atlantic, 197
Atwater, Montgomery, 259
Auchincloss, Louis, 320
Auden, W. H., 152, 152n
Audio-visual aids, 151–152
Auto Wreck, 122
Away All Boats, 309

B

Babbitt, 24
Bacon, Francis, 271
Baker, Louise, 186

345

V

Vagabond Summer, 291–292
Verne, Jules, 271
Vidal, Gore, 22
Visit, The, 136
Visit to a Small Planet, 22

W

Wahoo Bobcat, The, 252
Walden, 337
Walker, Jerry L., 17n
Walton, Izaak, 337
War Beneath the Sea, 258
War novels, 311–314
War and Peace, 314
Weaver, John D., 332
We Have Tomorrow, 277
Wells, H. G., 271
West, Jessamyn, 263, 264n, 279, 280n, 316
West Side Story, 135
Western story, the, 310–311
When the Legends Die, 310
Where the Shark Waits, 260
White, T. H., 135
Whitehead, Frank, 18, 44
Whitney, Phyllis, 270, 284
Who Is Erika?, 305
Wibberley, Leonard, 22, 247, 332
Wild Buggy Jordan, 292
Wild Winter, 259

Wilder, Thornton, 22, 104
Wilkinson, Andrew, 41–42
Wind in the Willows, 8
Window for Julie, A, 270
Winter of Our Discontent, 319
Winton, Hank, 259
With a High Heart, 270
Wojciechowska, Maria, 306
Wolfe, Thomas, 11, 315
Wood, Kerry, 259
Woodham-Smith, Cecil, 330
World of Ellen March, The, 304
Wouk, Herman, 134, 309
Wren, Percival, 312
Wright, Richard, 275–276, 278–279
Wrinkle in Time, A, 300
Writing Themes about Literature, 48
Wuthering Heights, 75
Wyss, Johann, 308

Y

Yates, Elizabeth, 332
Yea! Wildcats!, 256
You Can't Go Home Again, 11n
Young Lions, The, 313
Young Unicorns, The, 301

Z

Zoo Story, The, 135